Monsanto®: une Enquête Photographique

Monsanto®: a Photographic Investigation

par / by Mathieu Asselin

ACTES SUD

Introduction par Mathieu Asselin

Monsanto® compte plus de 50 Superfund Sites (des zones contaminées ultra-prioritaires) au sein des seuls États-Unis. Ces sites affectent des centaines de communes et leurs environs, avec des conséquences sanitaires et écologiques désastreuses sur le territoire américain comme ailleurs. Pour autant, Monsanto®, s'appuyant sur ses relations au sein de l'administration américaine – la Food and Drug Administration en particulier – et d'autres centres de pouvoir dans le monde, continue d'opérer à sa guise : vastes campagnes de désinformation, acharnement sur les institutions et les individus qui osent révéler ses crimes. Survivant contre vents et marées, la firme n'hésite pas à répandre des technologies et des produits qui inquiètent les scientifiques et les organisations humanitaires et écologiques du monde entier quant à leur impact sur la santé, la sécurité alimentaire et l'environnement – des domaines intrinsèquement liés à la question de notre survie sur cette planète. Aujourd'hui, Monsanto® écrit un nouveau chapitre de l'histoire des échecs à succès, avec la création et la commercialisation des organismes génétiquement modifiés (OGM). Regard sur le passé et le présent de Monsanto®, ce projet vise à représenter ce que sera le futur proche de Monsanto®.

Introduction by Mathieu Asselin

Monsanto®'s dozens of Superfund sites (large contaminated sites of high priority for the US Environmental Protection Agency) across the United States alone are affecting hundreds of communities and their environment with terrifying health and ecological consequences. Monsanto® maintains strong ties with the US government, and especially with the FDA (United States Food and Drug Administration). It is a bedfellow with many other economic and political powerhouses around the world. The company engages in campaigns of misinformation, as well as the persecution of institutions and individuals, including scientists, farmers and activists who dare to disclose its crimes. Monsanto® is spreading new technologies and products, while scientists, ecological institutions and human rights organizations are putting out alerts about issues like public health, food safety and ecological sustainability — issues on which our future on this planet depends. This is all particularly troublesome since Monsanto® is entering a new chapter of disregard for our planet through the creation and commercialization of genetically modified organisms (GMOs). Looking at the company's past and present, this project aims to picture what Monsanto®'s near future will look like.

Avant-propos par Jim Gerritsen, agriculteur biologique

Wood Prairie Family Farm. Bridgewater, Maine, États-Unis

Doit-on encore s'étonner de voir la Monsanto® Corporation honnie avec la même ardeur partout dans le monde ? Sa course effrénée à la notoriété, au pouvoir et à la richesse se heurte partout à un public de mieux en mieux informé, écœuré par ses manœuvres déloyales et cupides. Ses cent dix ans de pratiques ignominieuses dans l'industrie chimique, au mépris de toute humanité, son existence sans cesse secouée par des obstacles dont elle est elle-même responsable, illustrent les bénéfices qu'offre son intégration dans le complexe militaro-industriel. Les machinations de Monsanto® et sa facilité à externaliser les coûts environnementaux et sociétaux lui confèrent une puissance et des richesses difficiles à imaginer.

C'est là que le travail photographique époustouflant de Mathieu Asselin nous est précieux et tombe à point nommé. Une œuvre incisive, aussi bouleversante que libératrice.

McDonald's®, Walmart® et British Petroleum® peuvent engendrer la colère citoyenne en tant que symboles de la dérive alarmante des grands groupes. Mais la défiance profonde et généralisée que suscite la multinationale Monsanto®, basée aux États-Unis, est sans équivalent ni précédent.

Il est à noter que certains agissements de la firme donnent toute leur légitimité aux critiques acerbes de la société. Par ses récentes tentatives pour se réinventer en récrivant l'histoire et en reniant son passé, Monsanto® montre inconsciemment qu'il partage le mépris de la société pour ses propres erreurs.

L'attitude artificielle, mesurée et rassurante des porte-parole de Monsanto® rompus à l'exercice indique *a contrario* à quel point la firme est consciente de l'hostilité que suscite son comportement destructeur. Il n'est pas surprenant que ce manque d'authenticité et ces contradictions devant le réel provoquent un juste retour de bâton.

Au cours des dernières décennies, le nouveau Monsanto® a fait de l'industrialisation de l'agriculture le territoire sur lequel asseoir son emprise par un contrôle monopolistique.

Ces propos de Henry Kissinger prononcés en 1970 résonnent aujourd'hui avec une justesse prémonitoire : « Contrôlez le pétrole et vous contrôlerez les nations ; contrôlez la nourriture et vous contrôlerez le peuple. » L'offensive de Monsanto® sur le brevetage des semences transgéniques a entraîné des conséquences désastreuses sur l'agriculture et l'environnement. Sa prétention à se vouloir « l'ami des fermiers » est remise en cause par les attaques qu'il subit de toutes parts. Quel « ami des fermiers » se montrerait aussi tyrannique sur le marché des brevets, avec une violence jamais vue dans l'histoire ? Les agriculteurs savent à quel point la stratégie de la peur de Monsanto® menace les exploitations familiales qui se trouvent sur son chemin.

Où sont la générosité et l'intégrité de cet « ami des fermiers » qui furent à la source de son entrée forcée sur le marché mondial des semences ? La prise de contrôle systématique de dizaines de sociétés autrefois indépendantes a conduit à un monopole ahurissant sur l'approvisionnement mondial en semences. Le résultat de cette pratique est-il un phénomène imprévu ? On peut sérieusement douter que l'extraordinaire augmentation des tarifs et le déclin subit de la diversité génétique des semences soient une pure coïncidence avec la prise de contrôle de Monsanto®. Les effets dévastateurs du Roundup, herbicide extrêmement rentable et monstrueusement nocif à base de glyphosate, se font sentir sur des millions d'hectares de terres agricoles partout dans le monde. N'est-ce pas là la preuve ultime du legs sinistre d'un monde tenu en otage par une obsession sans fin pour une culture de mort ?

Nous ne pouvons qu'être reconnaissants à Mathieu Asselin de nous offrir cette fenêtre unique sur l'avenir de Monsanto®.

Foreword by Jim Gerritsen, organic farmer

Wood Prairie Family Farm, Bridgewater, Maine, USA

Is it any small wonder that the Monsanto® Corporation is so infamously and universally reviled by the public worldwide? Monsanto®'s headlong frenzy for notoriety, power and riches has been met with criticism from a world that is increasingly savvy and irritated by its duplicitous and self-serving behavior.

Monsanto®'s sordid 110-year history as an inhuman chemical company — persistently and continually dogged by trouble of its own making — offers a case study in the benefits of close ties to the military-industrial complex. The corporation's machinations and success at externalizing environmental and societal costs have landed them power and wealth difficult for most people to imagine.

It is therefore with timeliness and sharp incisiveness that Mathieu Asselin's new breathtaking photographic work serves an important role. Asselin's book is at once both shocking and liberating.

McDonald's®, Walmart® and British Petroleum® may have earned citizens' ire as symbols of injurious corporate decadence. However, the deep-seated prevailing distrust of American-based multinational Monsanto® stands without parallel or precedent.

Remarkably enough, Monsanto®'s own actions reveal that they themselves accept the public's strongly negative assessment. Recent attempts to reinvent themselves by rewriting history and jettisoning their past lies are an unconscious admission that they share the public's disdain for their dark pathology.

The trained, strained, practiced, artificially calm demeanor of Monsanto® spokespersons unwittingly communicates acute awareness of the public's outrage for their destructive behavior. Unsurprisingly, such lack of authenticity triggers public backlash against the false contradictions to reality.

In recent decades, latter-day Monsanto® has targeted industrialization of agriculture as the new frontier it has decided to dominate through monopoly control. Henry Kissinger's 1970 comments were apt and prescient of Monsanto®'s soon-to-come full-fledged invasion of agriculture: "Control oil and you control nations; control food and you control the people." Monsanto®'s foray into patented and genetically engineered seeds has impacted agriculture and the environment in epic proportions.

Its self-congratulatory and far-fetched assertion that it is the "friend of farmers" has seen Monsanto® mercilessly assailed from all quarters. What "friend of farmers" would also be the most aggressive patent bully in the history of the world? It acts as a recalcitrant bully whose harvest-of-fear is widely known throughout farming circles to threaten and litigate against family farmers dragged into its crosshairs.

Was it the loftiness and integrity of this "friend of farmers" that was behind its forced entrance into the world seed trade? Monsanto®'s systematic takeover of many scores of once independent seed companies has resulted in rapid and stunning monopoly control of world seed supplies. Were the following events unplanned phenomena? It is doubtful whether the extraordinary seed price increases and rapid declines in genetic seed diversity were mere coincidences after Monsanto®'s seed industry takeover.

The soil-deadening effect of Monsanto®'s enormously profitable and monstrously destructive glyphosate-based herbicide Roundup has impacted hundreds of millions of acres of farmland worldwide. Is this fact not the ultimate testimony to Monsanto®'s dark and miserable bequest to the world?

We are thankful that Mathieu Asselin's book serves as a window into Monsanto®'s future.

Publicités pour Monsanto® dans les magazines, entre 1949 et 1980.

Monsanto® magazine ads from 1949 to 1980.

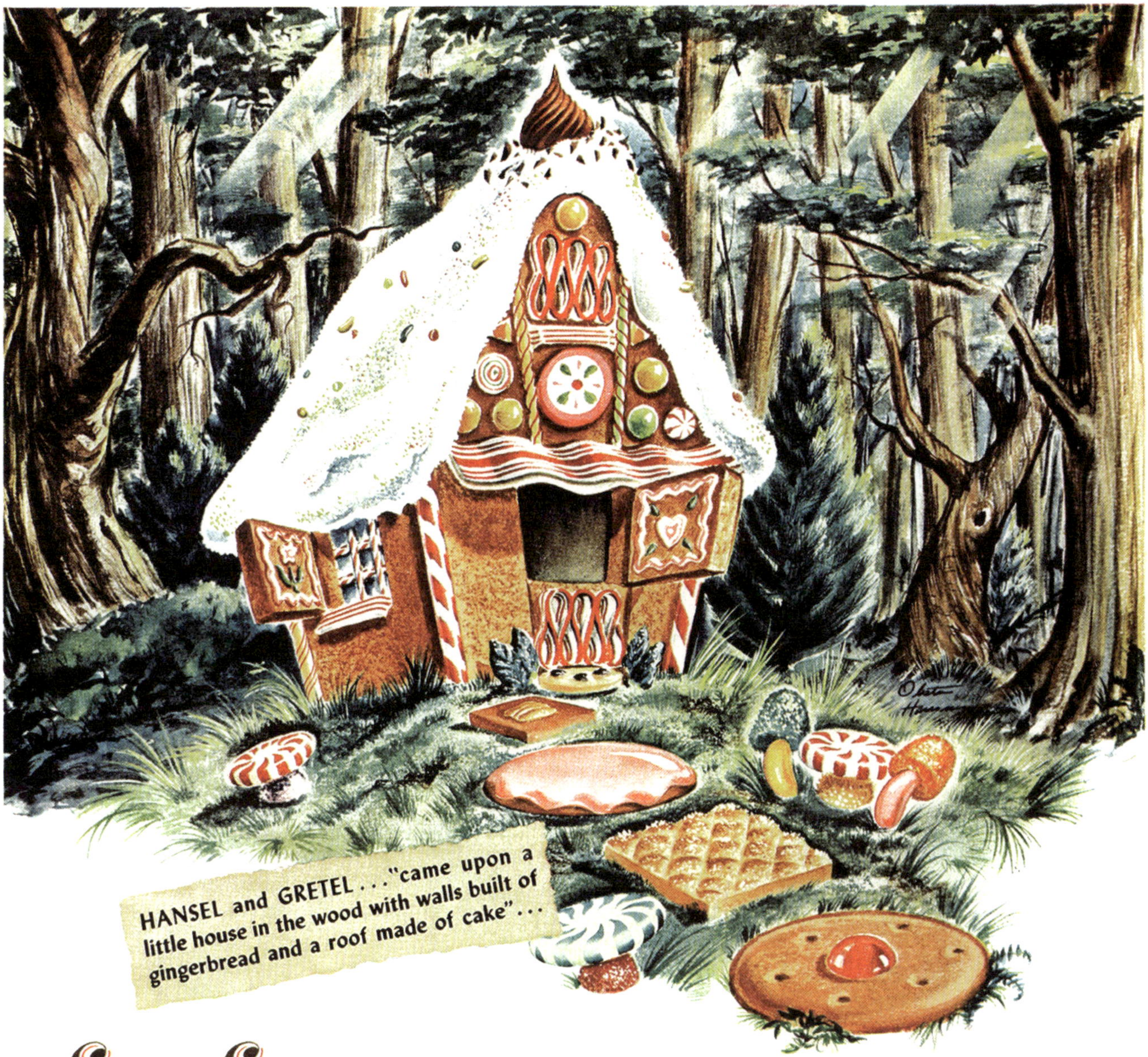

Sweet Story

Today, in almost every corner store, you'll find hundreds of sweet stories that don't come in books. Instead, they come in packages—sweets and confections that look good, smell good, taste good. They're better by far than the "gingerbread and cake" found by Hansel and Gretel—more tasty, more enjoyable—thanks, in many cases, to Ethavan. Ethavan is one of Monsanto's flavor principles. Its use gives an appealing taste boost to candies, ice cream, cakes, cookies, doughnuts and other sweets. It adds more than flavor—it has an intriguing aroma that makes taste an even more pronounced pleasure.

Ethavan is not sold in stores. It is used by manufacturers of flavors and confections to give their customers the utmost enjoyment in the things that are sweet to eat.

Sweet Story for Executives . . . Ethavan has several distinct advantages as a flavor principle. It is three times stronger than vanillin, another Monsanto product. It has great "staying" power—retains all its goodness, even when subjected to extremes in processing temperatures. . . . If you are interested in the manufacture or application of flavorings, you'll find a sweet story in Ethavan. Ask about it. Write—or return the coupon, if more convenient.

MONSANTO CHEMICAL COMPANY
St. Louis 4

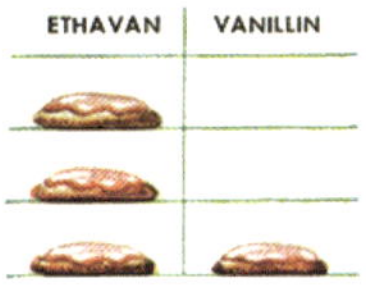

THREE TIMES STRONGER Manufacturers find Ethavan more economical than vanillin, since it is at least three times stronger.

Ethavan: Reg. U. S. Pat. Off.

MONSANTO
CHEMICALS AND PLASTICS

MONSANTO CHEMICAL COMPANY
1722 South Second Street
St. Louis 4, Missouri

Please send information on Ethavan for use in. . . . .
. . . .
Name. . . . . Title. . . . .
Company. . . . .
Address. . . . .
City. . . . . State. . . . .

SERVING INDUSTRY . . . WHICH SERVES MANKIND

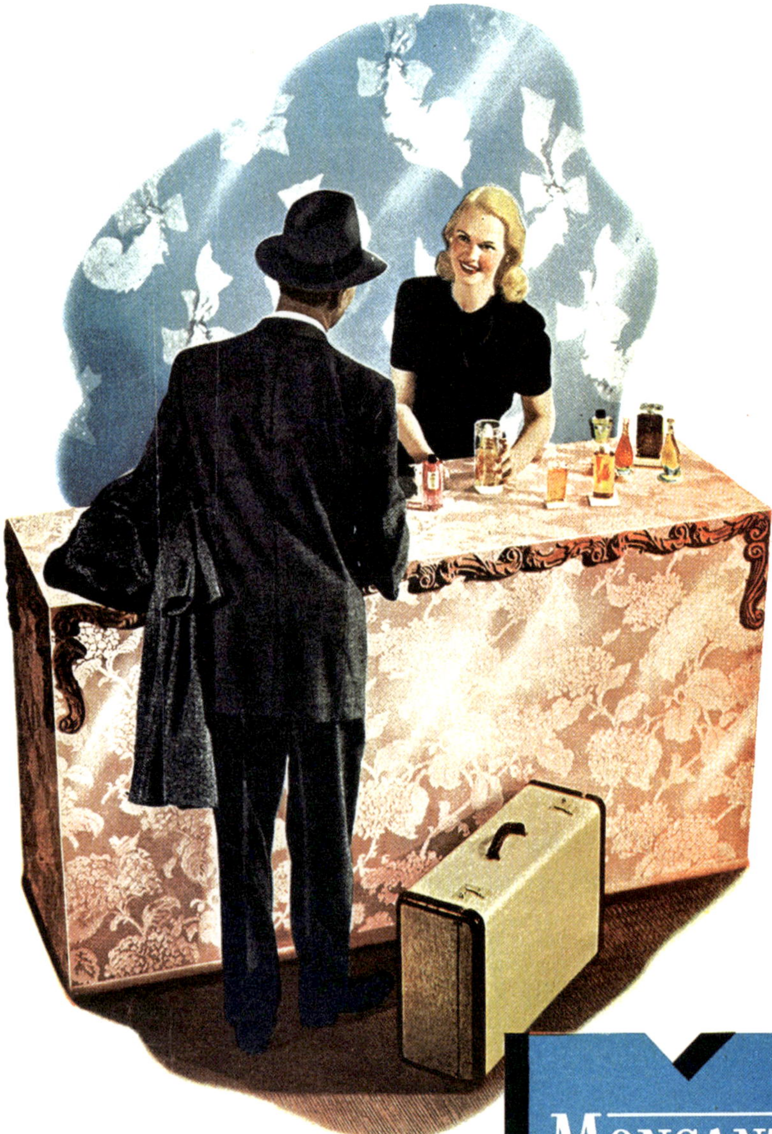

Baking Recipe for an Interior Decorator

Take 10 gallons Monsanto X500, a new plastic in liquid form. Add catalyst and stir well.

Take suitable molds to form furniture, wall and floor panels or what you will. Add layers of cloth, covering each layer well with X500.

Bake in moderate oven for five hours. Remove and use.

* * *

That's a simplified version of an industrial recipe that may become standard practice in manufacturing a variety of familiar objects now built laboriously, piece by piece, from wood and metal.

To this revolutionary technique Monsanto has made a significant contribution with development of the X500 series resins, third important new plastic announced by Monsanto this year.

Today these resins are going into vital military applications, most of them secret. Tomorrow they may make possible the brightly patterned store counter of fabric-and-plastics you see here —also the lightweight, sturdy suitcase. Even floor and wall surfaces might be amazingly strong composites of wood veneer, paper or cloth alloyed with X500 resin.

Other large objects of great strength, yet light in weight, which could be formed in one piece by the simple process of contact or low-pressure laminating range from boats to bathtubs, baby buggies to bobsleds.

In fact, this may well be one of the more important of the many war-stimulated advances that American industry will soon be able to turn to the *peaceful* service of mankind.

MONSANTO CHEMICAL COMPANY
St. Louis 4

MONSANTO
CHEMICALS AND PLASTICS

SERVING INDUSTRY... WHICH SERVES MANKIND

The best way to tame a wildfire is with chemicals.

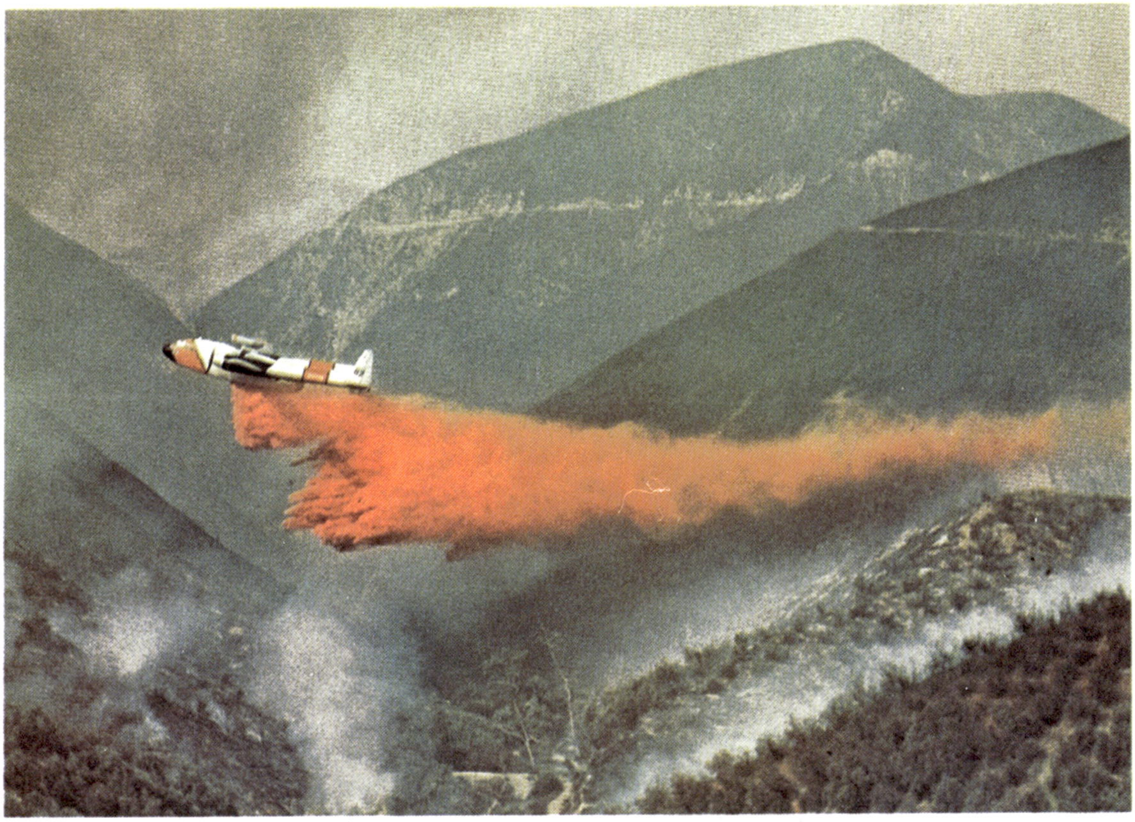

Di-hydrogen oxide, one of the world's most common chemicals, isn't enough. Because di-hydrogen oxide (water) evaporates too quickly.

Yet combine it with di-ammonium phosphate and you have a chemical called Phos-Chek® fire-retardant. Made by Monsanto, Phos-Chek fights fire by absorbing heat and depriving fire of its fuel. A plane can drop 3,000 gallons on a fire, reload and be back in action within 20 minutes.

The chemical's bright red color lets ground crews and pilots quickly locate areas that have been treated. And, when the fire's over, Phos-Chek helps fertilize the ground to promote new plant growth.

No chemical is totally safe, all the time, everywhere. But if we want to protect ourselves from the rampages of nature (such as fire, famine and disease) we'll have to use chemicals. And use them properly.

For a free booklet explaining the risks and benefits of chemicals, mail to:
Monsanto, 800 N. Lindbergh Blvd., St. Louis, Mo. 63166. Dept. A3NA-NG1

Name ______________________

Address ______________________

City & state ______________________ Zip ________

Monsanto

Without chemicals, life itself would be impossible.

IS YOURS ONE OF THESE

"BUSINESS BABIES"

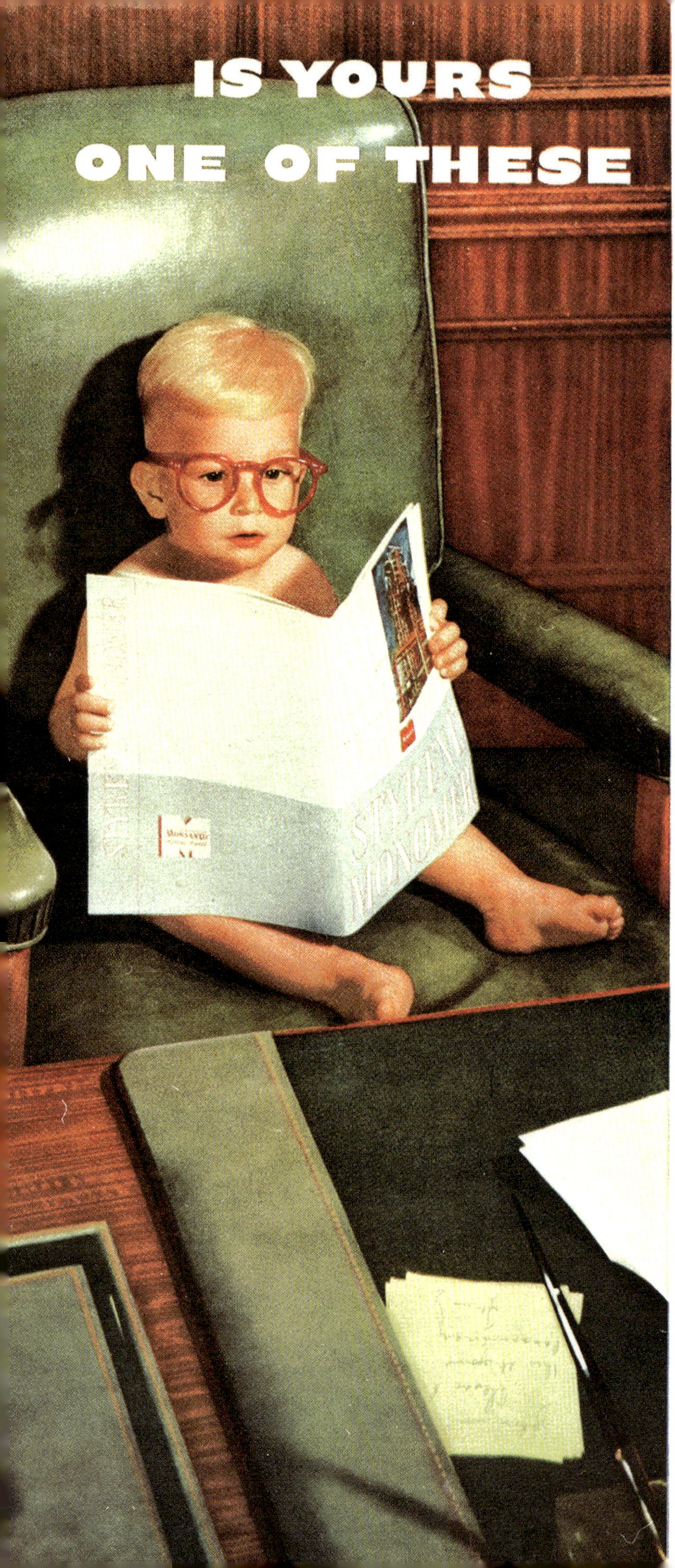

that will grow to GIANT SIZE on Styrene Monomer?

Who hasn't wished he'd been in on the ground floor when plastics or synthetic detergents or any of scores of other major chemical developments first came along? *Right now* a whole new ground floor is opening up for alert executives and research men in the use of styrene monomer and its end products. For the first time, large-tonnage supplies are *immediately* available.

What's *your* pet idea—waiting only for the *right* material to come over the horizon? Versatile styrene monomer is available now . . . in drum, tank-truck and tank-car lots from Monsanto's giant new plant at Texas City! Already in a top tonnage spot among the basic chemicals of industry! Today's foundation for hundreds of brand-new businesses tomorrow!

The list below scarcely scratches the surface. For the *full* story, wire or write on your company letterhead for your free copy of a big, new illustrated brochure just off the press. It's full of thought-starting nourishment for your "business baby." MONSANTO CHEMICAL COMPANY, Texas Division, Texas City, Texas.

APPLICATIONS OF STYRENE MONOMER AND ITS END PRODUCTS

In dispersions for new coating effects on textiles and papers; high-efficiency binders in water-based paints; better adhesives, liquid waxes and polishes. **In polyester resins** for a multitude of revolutionary new low-pressure laminations of glass fiber, glass cloth, paper and other materials . . . and for large contour molding where new markets await a material requiring inexpensive molds, little pressure and low heat to produce scores of products.

In elastomers for the new handsome, long-wearing shoe soles, heels and uppers that already are taking new markets by storm; for luggage, apparel accessories, transmission and conveyor belting, gaskets, grommets, floor tile . . . or what's *your* pet idea?

In modified alkyd resins for fast air-drying coatings on metals or wood; in baking enamels for metal furniture, electrical and office appliances, lockers, fixtures, metal outdoor signs; in anticorrosion spray coatings for heavy machinery, toys, farm and garden equipment. **In styrenated vegetable oils** for exceptionally fast-drying paints, enamels and varnishes with excellent gloss.

In dozens of new fields—rewettable and pressure-sensitive adhesives; heat-sealing coatings; cationic ion exchange resins for water purification, food-liquor processing, chemical manufacturing; a whole new family of organic chemicals yet to be thoroughly investigated; a wide range of new resins for film formers, molding compounds and casting and coating.

MONSANTO CHEMICALS AND PLASTICS ®

Serving Industry . . . Which Serves Mankind

Without chemicals, life itself would be impossible.

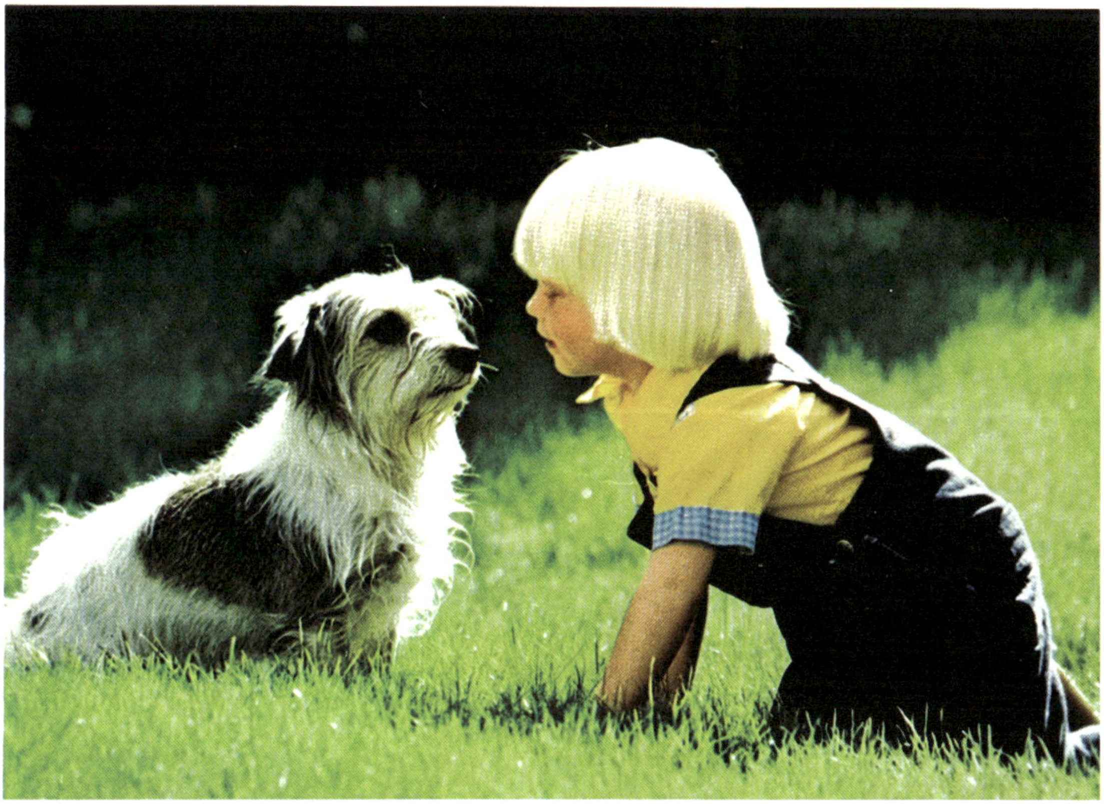

Some people think anything "chemical" is bad and anything "natural" is good. Yet nature is chemical.

Plant life generates the oxygen we need through a chemical process called photosynthesis. When you breathe, your body absorbs that oxygen through a chemical reaction with your blood.

Life is chemical. And with chemicals, companies like Monsanto are working to help improve the quality of life.

Chemicals help you live longer. Rickets was a common childhood disease until a chemical called Vitamin D was added to milk and other foods.

Chemicals help you eat better. Chemical weed-killers have dramatically increased the supply and availability of our food. But no chemical is totally safe, all the time, everywhere. In nature or the laboratory. The real challenge is to use chemicals properly. To help make life a lot more livable.

For a free booklet explaining the risks and benefits of chemicals, mail to:
Monsanto, 800 N. Lindbergh Blvd., St. Louis, Mo. 63166, Dept. A3NA-NG2.

Name ______________________

Address ______________________

City & state ______________________ Zip ________

Monsanto

Without chemicals,
life itself would be impossible.

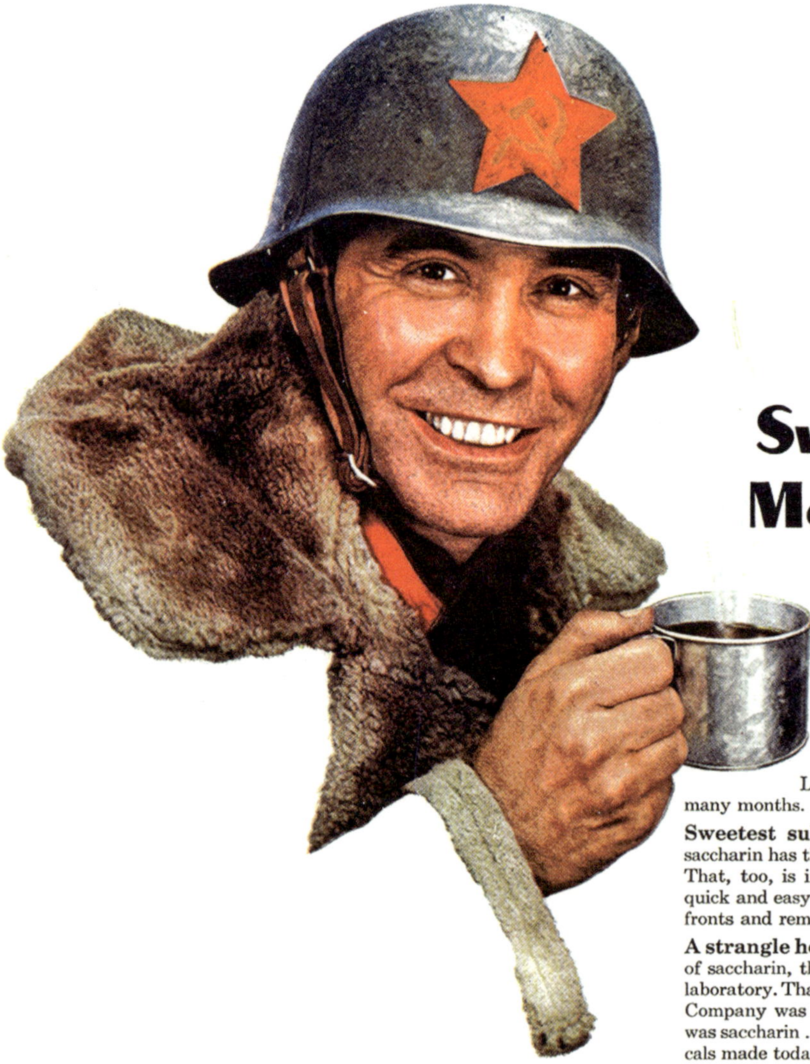

Ivan knows...
Sweetness is a Matériel of War

In the bitter cold of an Eastern winter front, tea is a vital matériel of war. But, to satisfy the Russian inner man, tea must be *sweet* as well as strong and hot. How could this need be met when the Nazis held or destroyed the high-tonnage beet sugar areas of the Ukraine?

Saccharin Monsanto has been the answer. Large quantities have been flowing to our ally these many months.

Sweetest substance known to man, a single pound of saccharin has the sweetening power of 400 to 550 pounds of sugar. That, too, is important in terms of vital convoy space and for quick and easy distribution from the docks to widespread fighting fronts and remote interior points.

A strangle hold once was held by Germany on world production of saccharin, though the product was discovered in an American laboratory. That hold was broken in 1901 when Monsanto Chemical Company was formed. The first product of the infant company was saccharin . . . forerunner of the hundreds of Monsanto Chemicals made today.

Just another instance where free American enterprise, producing something new through the initiative of everyday people and at the risk of private capital, is serving our allies today as it will serve the world of peace tomorrow. MONSANTO CHEMICAL COMPANY, St. Louis (4).

SACCHARIN MONSANTO is produced as white crystals or as a powder. It is derived from coal tar, salt, sulphur, air and water. It is widely used domestically for tobacco; for tooth pastes and powders, mouth washes and for drugs where the use of sugar is not desirable and the element of nutrition is not involved. Because it has no nutrient value, saccharin is often prescribed in tablet form for diabetics and for those who must avoid sugar for health or diet reasons. During the sugar shortage of World War I, saccharin was in daily use by millions of soldiers and civilians for several years.

MONSANTO CHEMICALS

SERVING INDUSTRY . . . WHICH SERVES MANKIND

"E" FOR EXCELLENCE—The Army-Navy "E" burgee with two stars, "representing recognition by the Army and the Navy of especially meritorious production of war materials" over a two-year period, flies over Monsanto's executive offices in St. Louis and over Monsanto plants at Anniston, Ala., and Monsanto, Tenn. The Army-Navy Production Award also has been won by five Monsanto plants at St. Louis, Mo., Monsanto, Ill., Karnack, Texas, and Springfield, Mass.

Without chemicals, many more millions would go hungry.

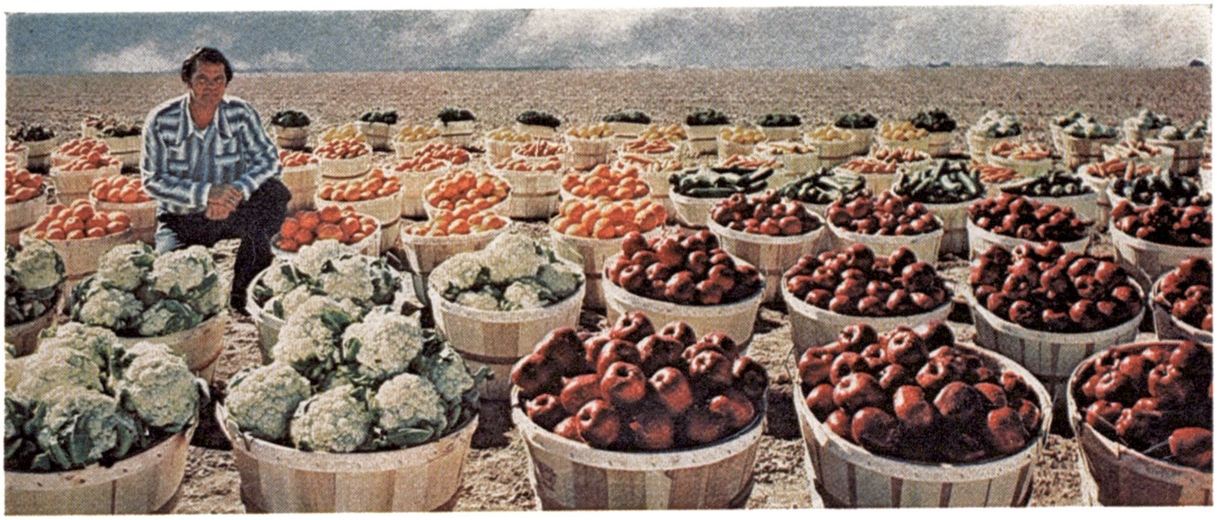

Millions of people around the world already don't get enough to eat. Without chemicals, the problem would be much worse.

We need chemical fertilizers to add nitrogen to the soil. Chemical weed-killers and insecticides to help save the 45 percent of the world's food production now being destroyed by weeds, insects and other pests.

Some people think that anything grown with chemicals is "bad." And anything grown naturally is "good." Yet nature itself is a chemical process. (Interestingly, your body cannot tell whether a chemical was made in the laboratory or was made by Mother Nature.)

So the real need is to differentiate between safe uses for chemicals and potentially dangerous ones.

No chemical is totally safe, all the time, everywhere. The challenge is to use them properly. To help make life a lot more livable.

For a free booklet explaining the risks and benefits of chemicals, mail to:
Monsanto, 800 N. Lindbergh Blvd., St. Louis, Mo. 63166. Dept. A3NA-U3

Name ______________________

Address ______________________

City & state ______________________ Zip ________

Monsanto

Without chemicals,
life itself would be impossible.

I.

Pendant des années, il y a eu une porte tournante entre Washington et Monsanto® – anciens fonctionnaires du gouvernement fédéral travaillant pour Monsanto® et *vice versa*. Cela a tendance à amener les gens à remettre en question l'équité et l'objectivité des personnes censées surveiller cette société agricole géante.

For years, there has been an open revolving door in Washington — sending workers from the federal government to Monsanto® and from Monsanto® back to the federal government. This has a tendency to make people question the fairness and objectivity of the folks who are supposed to be overseeing the giant agricultural corporation.

La Maison du Futur & La Rivière Rouge

The House of the Future & The Red River

Le 12 juin 1957, Disneyland® en Californie inaugure au Tomorrowland The House of the Future, sponsorisée par Monsanto®. Cette maison avant-gardiste supposée améliorer le quotidien des ménagères du monde moderne est entièrement mécanisée, au grand bonheur de tous. L'intégralité de son ossature est réalisée en matières plastiques – innovation technologique de l'époque – grâce au travail de trois cabinets d'architectes dont celui de Monsanto®. La nouvelle attraction est un immense succès et reçoit 20 millions de visiteurs jusqu'à sa fermeture en 1967.

Pendant ce temps, de l'autre côté du continent, en Alabama, Anniston meurt et étouffe sous la même main de Monsanto®. Cette petite commune, née à la fin du XIXe siècle, avait très vite su tirer parti de la richesse en fer de son sous-sol. Elle a développé des fonderies, réinvesti ses capitaux sur place en améliorant ses infrastructures et en modernisant sa vie quotidienne. Dès lors considérée comme *la* ville de la révolution industrielle en Alabama, Anniston attire de nombreux investisseurs et entrepreneurs. En 1917, pendant la Première Guerre mondiale en Europe, la Southern Manganese Corporation® implante son usine de fabrication d'obus pour l'artillerie. Puis, en 1925, devenue la Swann Chemical Company®, elle se lance dans la production de PCB, le « miracle chimique[1] ». Les PCB – polychlorobiphényles – sont des dérivés chlorés du biphényle, un hydrocarbure utilisé entre autres comme conservateur alimentaire. Selon leur teneur en chlore, les PCB sont plus ou moins visqueux ; ils sont insolubles dans l'eau, très stables à la chaleur et peu sensibles aux acides. Pendant cinquante ans, ils vont envahir la planète dans des domaines aussi divers que les liquides réfrigérants, les lubrifiants, les plastiques, les peintures, les encres ou les papiers.

En 1935, Monsanto® rachète la Swann Chemical Company® d'Anniston. La Monsanto Chemical Company®, alors installée à Saint Louis (Missouri), s'est déjà bien agrandie depuis sa création en 1901. Après avoir été le producteur exclusif de saccharine pour Coca-Cola®, elle s'est lancée dans la production d'aspirine (dont elle restera jusqu'aux années 1980 le principal fournisseur aux États-Unis) avant de réaliser sa première acquisition en 1918 : une fabrique d'acide sulfurique. En 1929, elle a déjà racheté plusieurs entreprises chimiques aux États-Unis puis en Australie, et elle résiste au krach boursier. Monsanto® s'impose peu à peu comme l'un des plus grands fabricants mondiaux de caoutchouc, de plastiques, de fibres synthétiques et de phosphates, mais surtout il affirme insidieusement son monopole sur les PCB avec son produit phare, l'Aroclor.

L'arrivée de Monsanto® à Anniston fera de cette petite cité modèle une cité fantôme.

Entre 1929 et 1971, 308 000 tonnes de PCB ont été fabriquées à Anniston, selon un rapport de l'EPA, l'Agence américaine de protection de l'environnement, en 2005[2]. 27 tonnes se sont répandues dans l'atmosphère, 810 tonnes ont été déversées dans le canal de Snow Creek *via* les canalisations et 32 000 tonnes de déchets ont été reléguées dans une décharge à ciel ouvert située sur le lieu de production, quasiment en pleine ville.

Pourtant, ce n'est qu'en 1995 que la population d'Anniston découvre les dangers et les risques encourus durant ces nombreuses années. L'avocat Donald Stewart, contacté par le pasteur et quelques fidèles d'Anniston, prend en charge l'affaire de l'église Mars Hill : Monsanto® propose de racheter l'église située face à l'usine, et les maisons alentour. Comprenant les implications sous-jacentes, Donald Stewart conseille à la « Community against pollution », un collectif d'habitants d'Anniston, d'effectuer une action judiciaire collective. Ainsi naît la plainte « Abernathy *vs* Monsanto® » : 3 516 plaignants s'attaquent au géant de l'industrie chimique.

Pendant le procès, le juge Laird demande à Monsanto® d'ouvrir ses archives internes[3]. Ce qu'il y découvre est particulièrement édifiant. Dès 1937, Monsanto® connaît la dangerosité des PCB. Au fil des années, il repère tous les effets toxiques des PCB sur la santé et sur l'environnement. Pourtant, il attend patiemment sans agir que les PCB soient interdits aux États-Unis en octobre 1977, avec comme leitmotiv : « Nous ne pouvons pas nous permettre de perdre un dollar de business[4]. » Pour Monsanto®, il est préférable, « face à une situation d'urgence qui met en danger un produit très rentable », de « dégager des moyens financiers et humains pour se protéger[5] ».

Le jugement de l'affaire « Abernathy *vs* Monsanto® » est rendu le 23 février 2002 : Monsanto® est reconnu coupable d'avoir pollué « le territoire d'Anniston et le sang de sa population avec les PCB » selon l'*Anniston Star*. Il doit verser 700 millions de dollars de dommages et intérêts à répartir entre les 3 516 plaignants d'Anniston, la décontamination du site et le financement d'une clinique spécialisée. Monsanto® se dédouane financièrement. Anniston est à l'agonie.

1 Marie-Monique Robin, *Le Monde selon Monsanto*, La Découverte/Arte Éditions, Paris, 2008.

2 « Technical report evaluation of Monsanto's polychlorinated biphenil (PCB). Process for PCB losses at the Anniston Plant », Agence américaine de protection de l'environnement, mars 2005.

3 www.chemicalindustryarchives.org.

4 Note interne de N.Y. Johnson intitulée « Pollution letter » du 16 février 1970.

5 Note interne du comité de direction de Monsanto® de 1969.

June 12, 1957: Disneyland in California inaugurates "The House of the Future," sponsored by Monsanto®, in Tomorrowland. The avant-garde home, conceived to improve the day-to-day lives of the households of the modern world, is entirely mechanized, to the great delight of all. The entirety of its framework is constructed from plastic materials — technological innovations of the time — owing to the work of three architectural firms, including Monsanto®'s own. The new attraction is an immense success, receiving 20 million visitors before its closure in 1967.
At the same time, on the other side of the continent, Anniston, Alabama is suffocating under Monsanto®. The small city was founded at the end of the 19th century and quickly learned to draw profit from the wealth of iron below its surface. It built foundries and reinvested the capital to improve infrastructure and modernize daily life. Recognized from then on as the model city of the Industrial Revolution in Alabama, Anniston attracts numerous investors and entrepreneurs. In 1917, during the First World War, the Southern Manganese Corporation sets up a factory for the manufacture of artillery shells. In 1925, having become the Swann Chemical Company, it begins production of PCBs, heralded as "chemical miracles."[1] PCBs, or polychlorinated biphenyls, are chlorine compounds derived from biphenyl, a hydrocarbon employed as a food preservative, among other uses. Depending on their chlorine content, PCBs are more or less viscous; they are water insoluble and highly heat resistant, and demonstrate little sensitivity to acids. Over the course of 50 years, they besiege the planet in diverse forms ranging from liquid coolants to lubricants, from paint to ink to paper.
In 1935, Monsanto® purchases the Swann Chemical Company of Anniston. The Monsanto® Chemicals Company, based in Saint Louis, Missouri, has already seen significant expansion since its creation in 1901. From its origins as the exclusive producer of saccharine for Coca-Cola®, it launches into the production of aspirin (of which it remains the United States' principal supplier until the 1980s) before making its first acquisition, a sulfuric acid factory, in 1918. In 1929, having purchased a number of chemical companies in the United States and Australia, it proves resistant to the stock market crash. Little by little, Monsanto® imposes itself as one of the world's leading producers of rubber, plastics, synthetic fibers and phosphates. Above all, it insidiously expands its monopoly on PCBs with its flagship product, Aroclor.
Monsanto®'s arrival in Anniston turns the small model city into a ghost town.
Between 1929 and 1971, 308,000 tonnes of PCB are produced in Anniston, according to a report by the Environmental Protection Agency (EPA) in 2005.[2] Twenty-seven tonnes are released into the atmosphere, 810 tonnes are flushed into the Snow Creek canal, and 32,000 tonnes are relegated to an open-air landfill site near the city center.
Yet it is not until 1995 that Anniston's population discovers the risks it has been exposed to over many years. When Monsanto® offers to purchase the church located across the road from the PCB factory, along with the surrounding homes, concerned parties understand the underlying implications.
Lawyer Donald Stewart, contacted by the Anniston pastor and several congregation members, takes charge of what will become known as the "Mars Hill Church affair." Stewart advises the "Community Against Pollution," a collective of Anniston residents, to launch a class action lawsuit. And so begins the Abernathy v. Monsanto® case: 3,516 plaintiffs versus the chemical industry giant.
While the complaint is being prepared, Judge Laird, who is handling the case, orders Monsanto® to open its internal archives.[3] The information discovered within is scandalous. Monsanto® had been aware of the dangers posed by PCBs since 1937. In the following years, it had come to recognize all the toxic effects of PCBs on human health and the environment. Yet the company waited patiently, taking no action until PCBs were outlawed in the United States in October 1977, on the grounds that "We can't afford to lose one dollar of business."[4] Monsanto® found it preferable, in light of an urgent situation that put a very profitable product at risk, to deploy financial and human resources to protect itself.[5]
The ruling in the Abernathy v. Monsanto® case is delivered on February 23, 2002. Monsanto® is judged responsible of having polluted the town and harmed its citizens, according to the *Anniston Star*. The $700 million settlement includes damages to be distributed among the 3,516 plaintiffs, along with decontamination of the site and financing of a specialized clinic. Monsanto® absolves itself financially. Anniston continues to suffer.

1 Marie-Monique Robin, *Le monde selon Monsanto* (*The World According to Monsanto*), Éditions La Découverte/Arte Éditions, 2008.
2 "Technical report evaluation of Monsanto's polychlorinated biphenyl (PCB). Process for PCB losses at the Anniston Plant," US Environmental Protection Agency, March 2005.
3 www.chemicalindustryarchives.org
4 Johnson, N.T. *Pollution letter* [Monsanto internal memo], February 16, 1970.
5 Monsanto® Board of Directors [Internal memo], 1969.

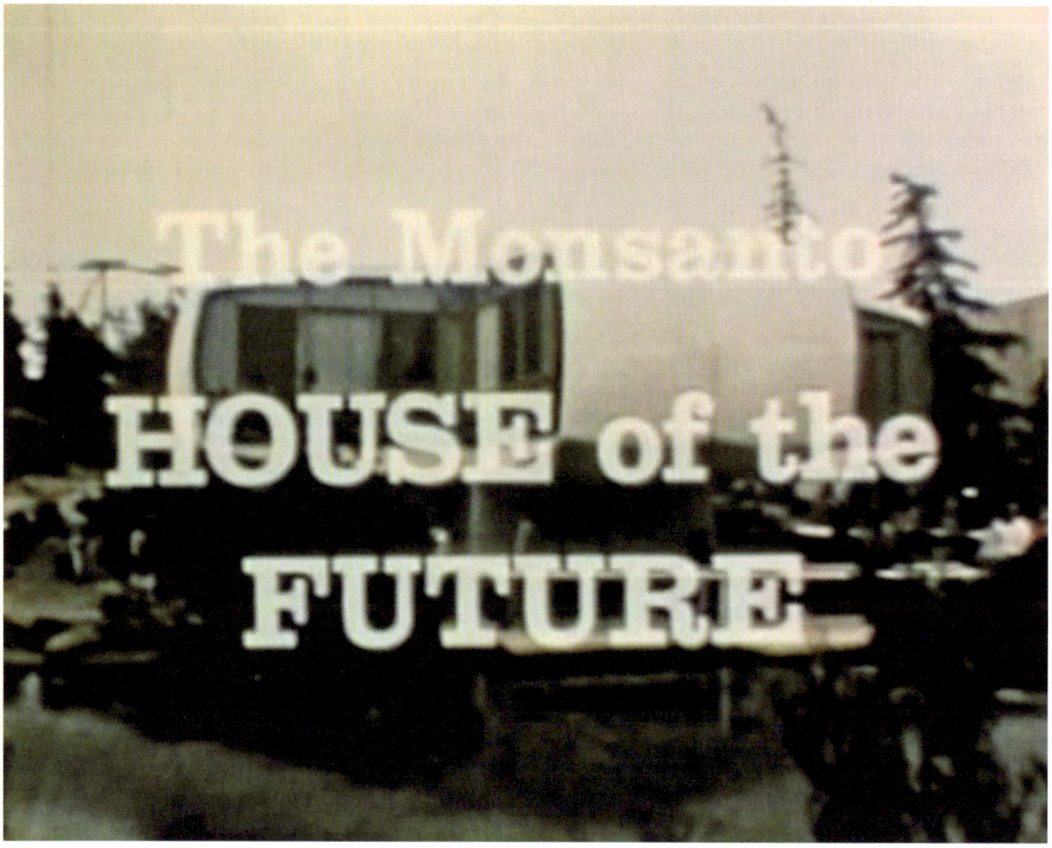
The Monsanto
HOUSE of the
FUTURE

Capture d'écran de la vidéo de Walt Disney®, *La Maison du futur*, sponsorisée par Monsanto®, 1957.

Screenshot from the Walt Disney® video *House of the Future*, sponsored by Monsanto® in 1957.

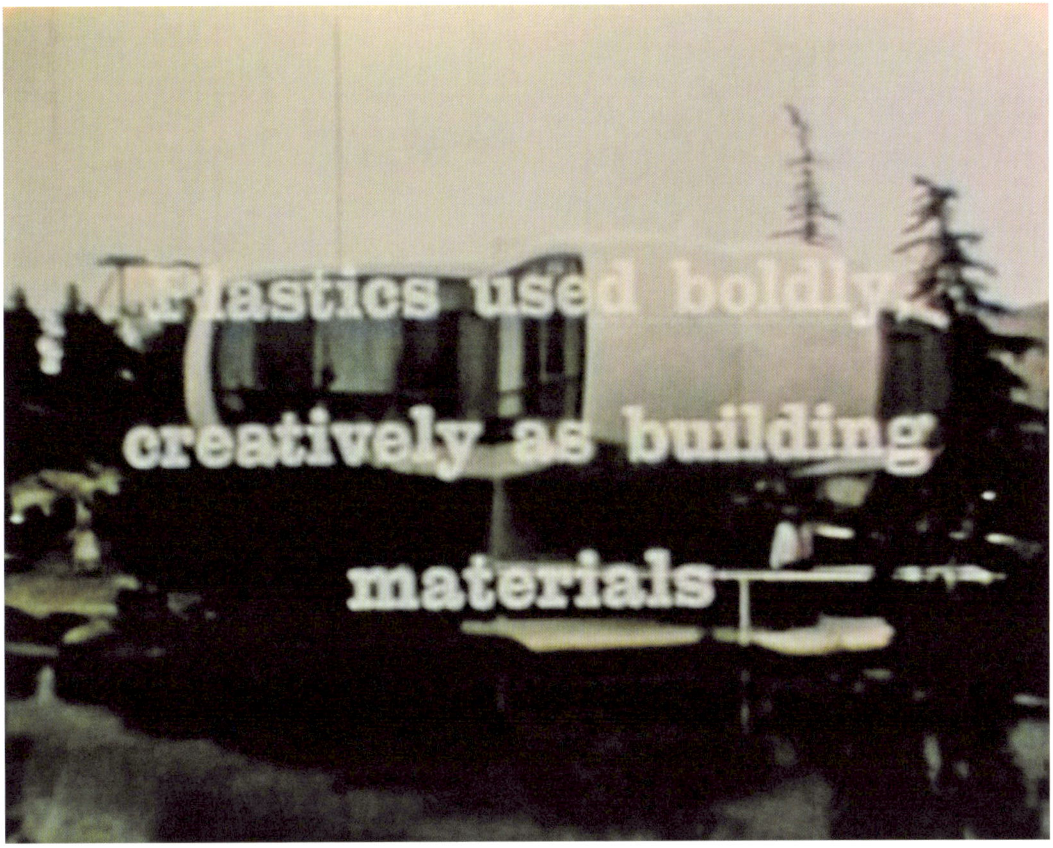

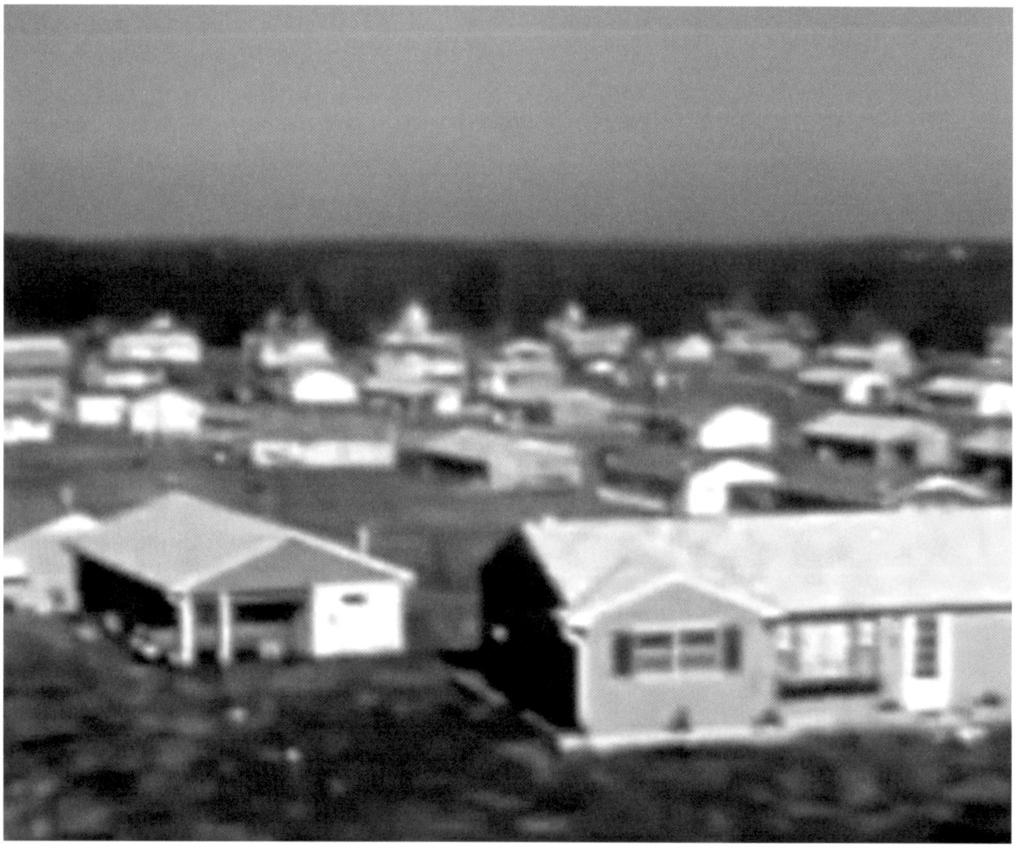

Capture d'écran de la vidéo de Walt Disney®, *La Maison du futur*, sponsorisée par Monsanto®, 1957.

Screenshot from the Walt Disney® video *House of the Future*, sponsored by Monsanto® in 1957.

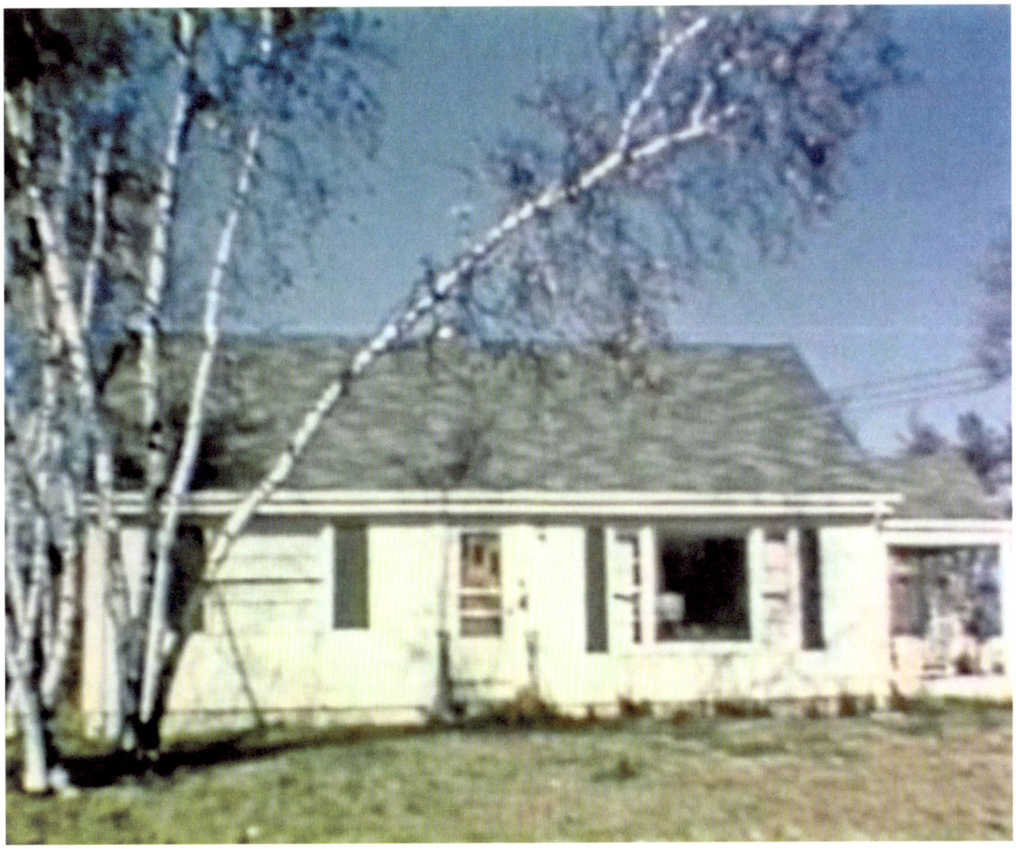

Maison abandonnée en raison de taux extrêmement élevés de PCB, dans les environs immédiats d'une ancienne usine Monsanto®, aujourd'hui exploitée par Solutia Inc®. Plus de 20 000 résidents de cette zone défavorisée ont été affectés par une unique contamination : il s'agit du cas le plus grave constaté sur une population. Au cours des dernières années, Monsanto® a racheté et démoli une centaine de maisons et entreprises contaminées par les PCB, transformant les environs en une quasi-ville fantôme.

A house abandoned due to high levels of PCBs in close proximity to the Solutia Plant, formerly a Monsanto® plant. With more than 20,000 residents affected in this low-income area, it represents the biggest impact on a single community by one contamination. In recent years, Monsanto® has bought and demolished around 100 PCB-contaminated houses and businesses in the area, turning the neighborhood into a virtual ghost town.

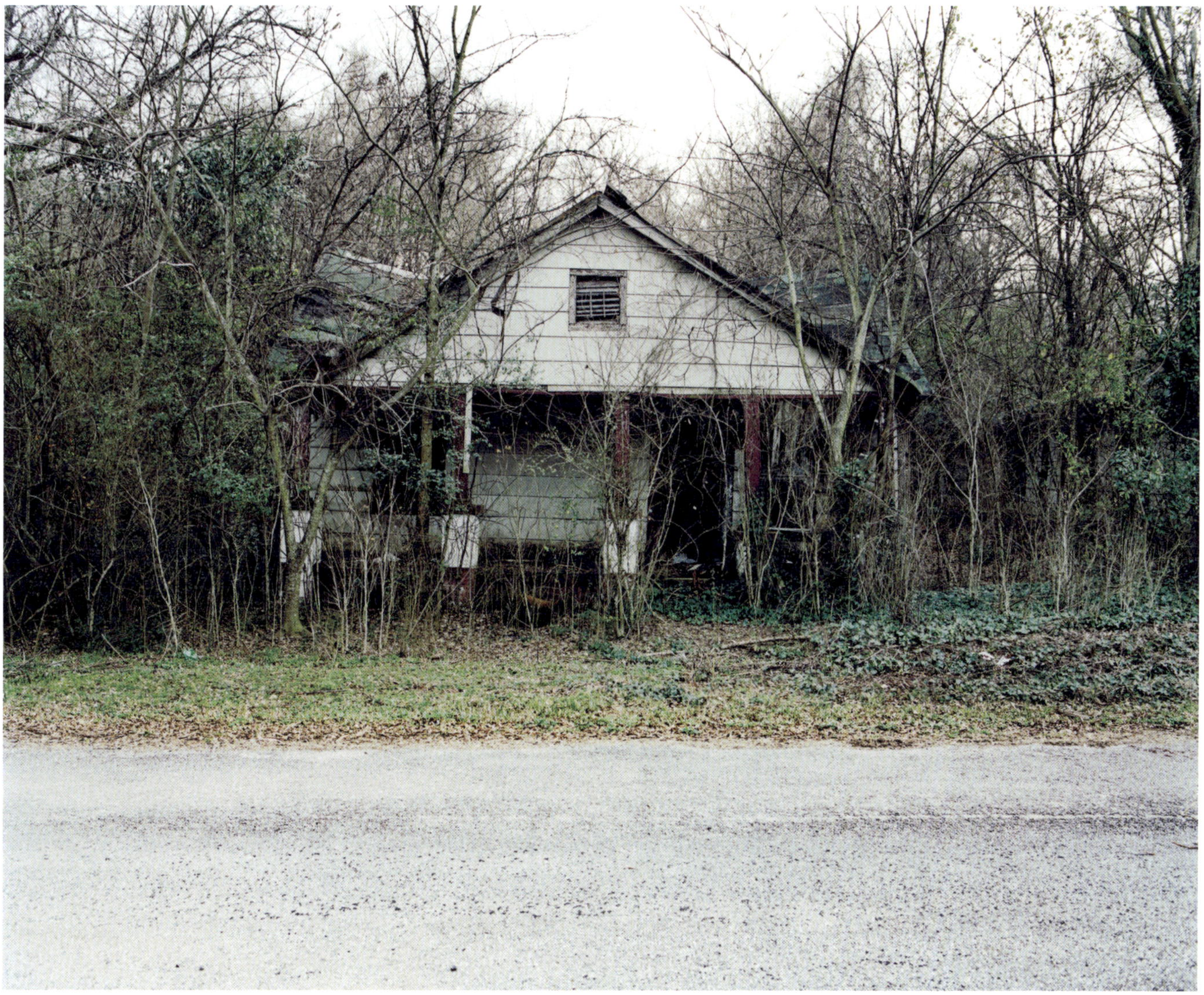

 WEST ANNISTON, ALABAMA, 2012

David Baker (65 ans) devant la tombe de son frère Terry. Terry Baker est mort à l'âge de 16 ans des suites d'une tumeur au cerveau et d'un cancer du poumon causés par l'exposition aux PCB. Le taux moyen de présence des PCB à Anniston est 27 fois supérieur à la moyenne nationale.

David Baker (65) at his brother Terry's grave. Terry Baker died at the age of 16 from a brain tumor and lung cancer, caused by PBC exposure. The average level of PBC in Anniston is 27 times higher than the national average.

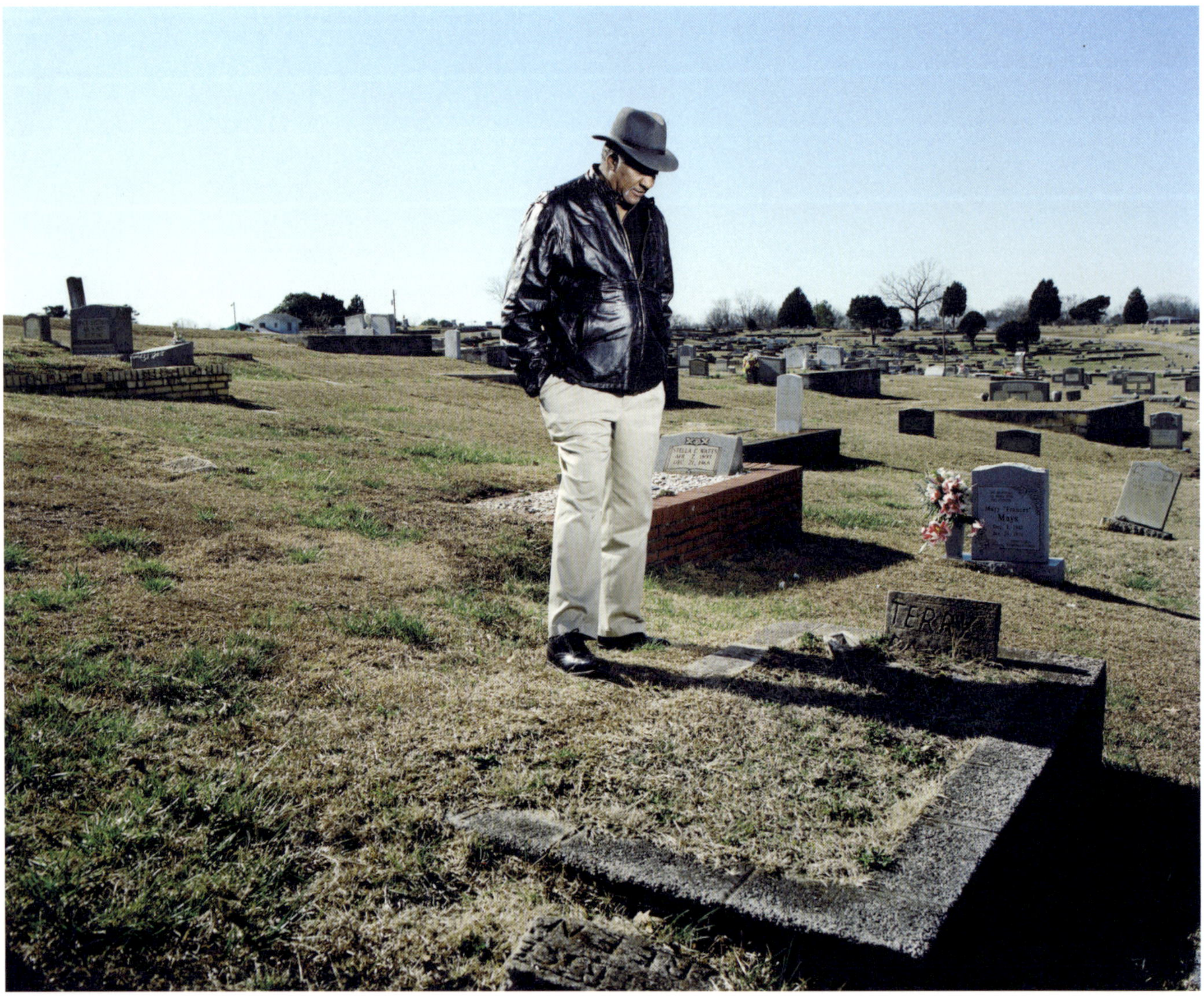

CIMETIÈRE D'EDGEMONT / EDGEMONT CEMETERY. WEST ANNISTON, ALABAMA. 2012

Parc abandonné.

Abandoned park.

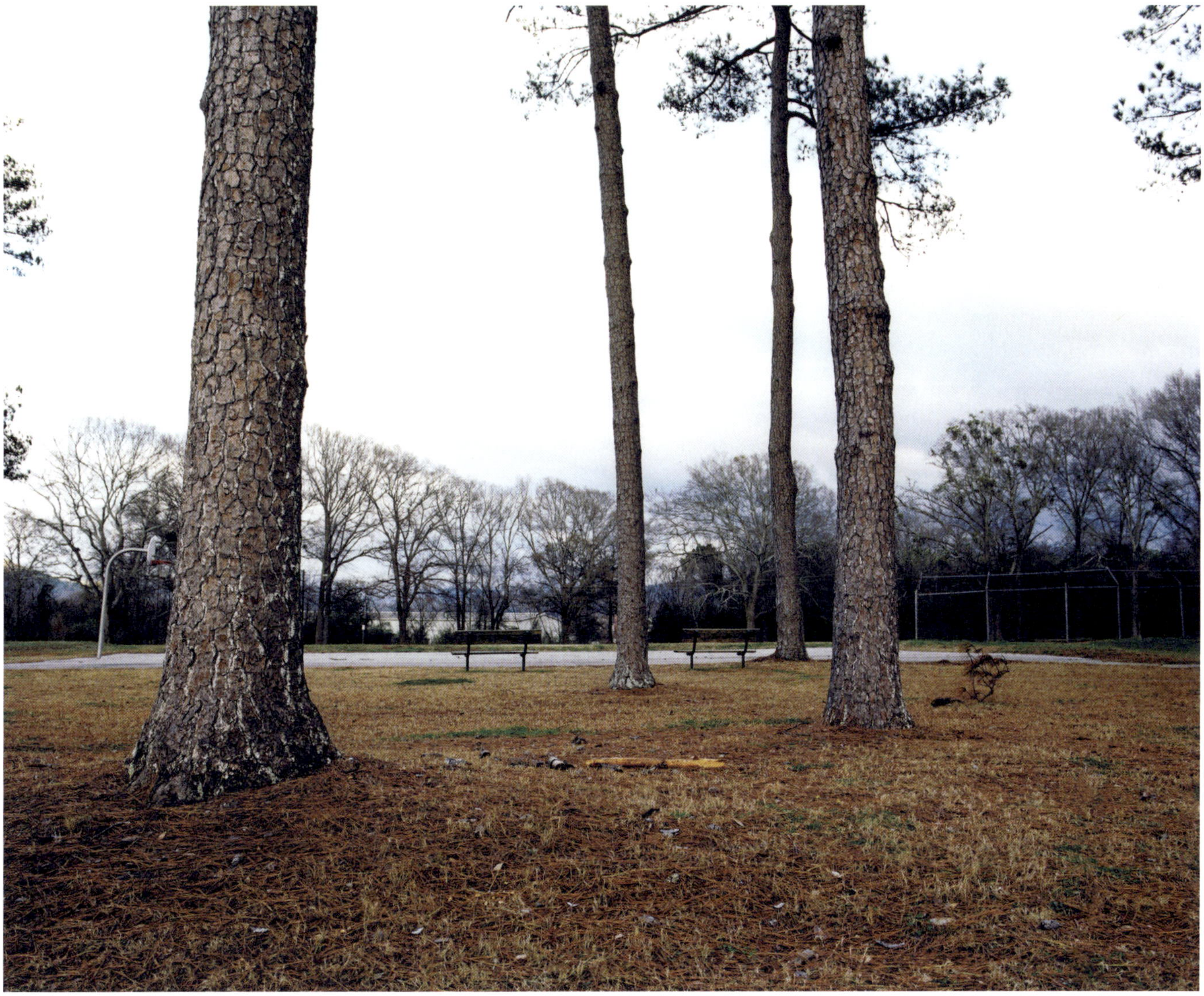

One of the largest chemical plants in Anniston, approximately 1,000 employees.

Hi! Maggie

Everything is all right here an hope it the same with you. The weather here now is nice an cool. We'll be ship out soon and hope I go north, so I can see you. Was in town an had a good time. Give my regard to the Daviaus an Sozanne an also to ~~the~~ your family. Will write soon.

Reggie

MADE IN U.S.A. BY E. C. KROPP CO., MILWAUKEE, WIS. (KJL)

4287N

Pvt. Reginald Ferland
... Battalion
... Mc Clellan Ala.
U.S. Army

FORT McCLELLAN, ALA. AUG 27 10:30 AM 1942

POST CARD

PLACE STAMP HERE

Free

Miss Marguette Taylor
15 Sanger Ave.
Waterville
Maine

Carte postale de l'ancienne usine Monsanto® d'Anniston, 1936.

Postcard of the former Monsanto® factory in Anniston from 1936.

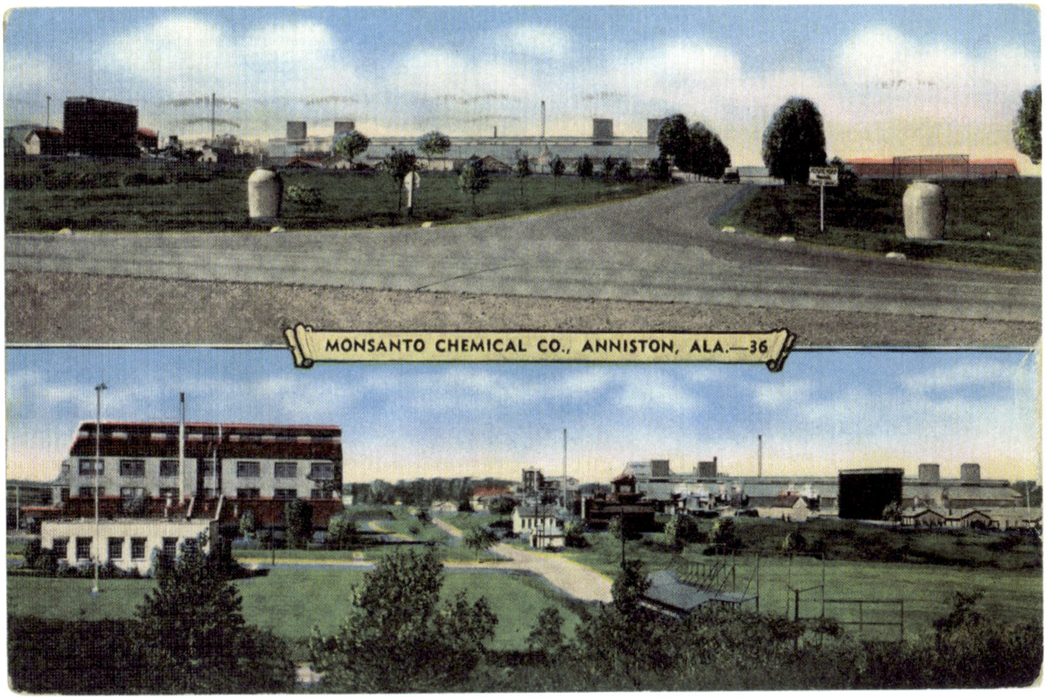

Station-service désaffectée.

Abandoned gas station.

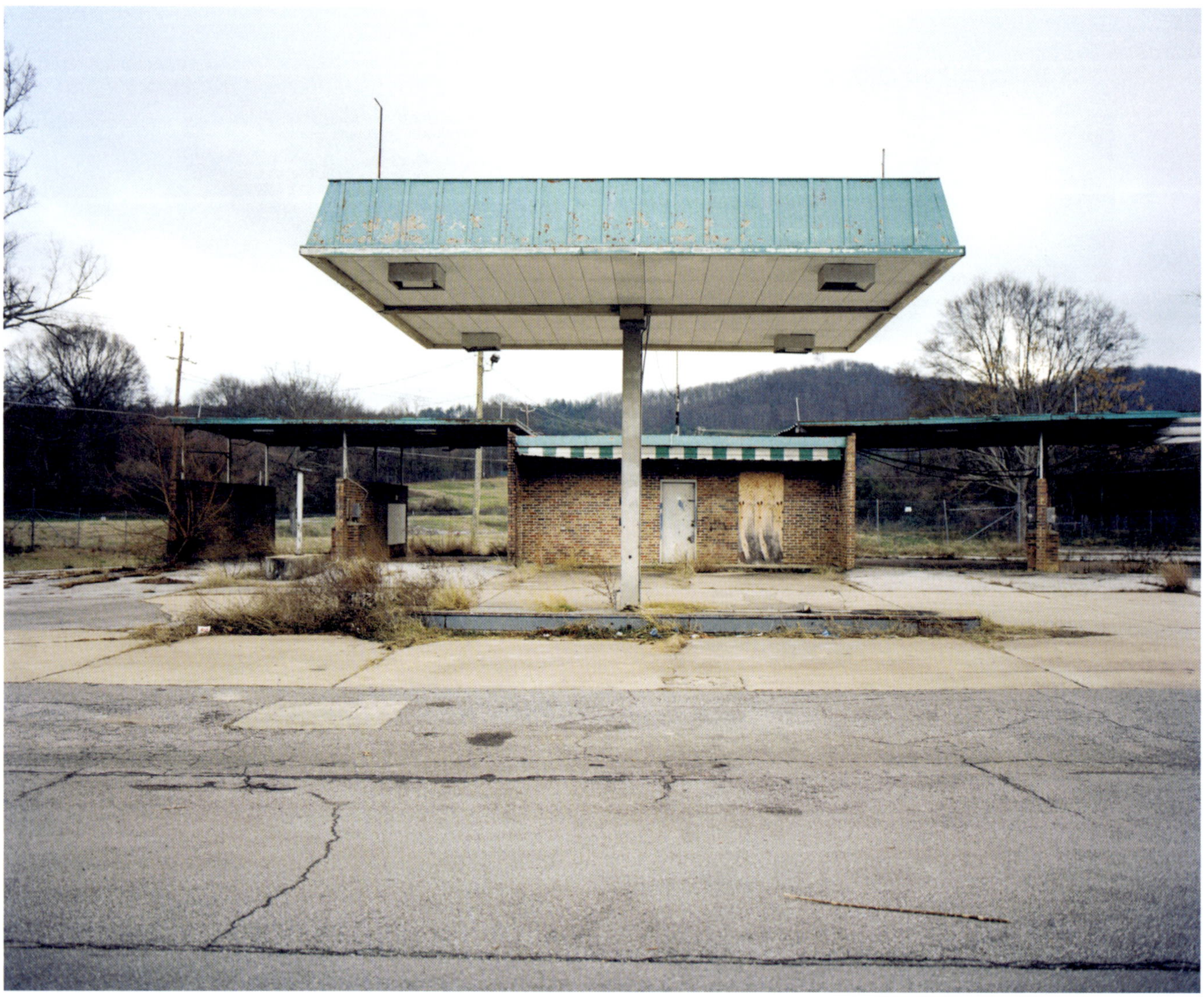

WEST ANNISTON, ALABAMA. 2012

Garage abandonné.

Abandoned garage.

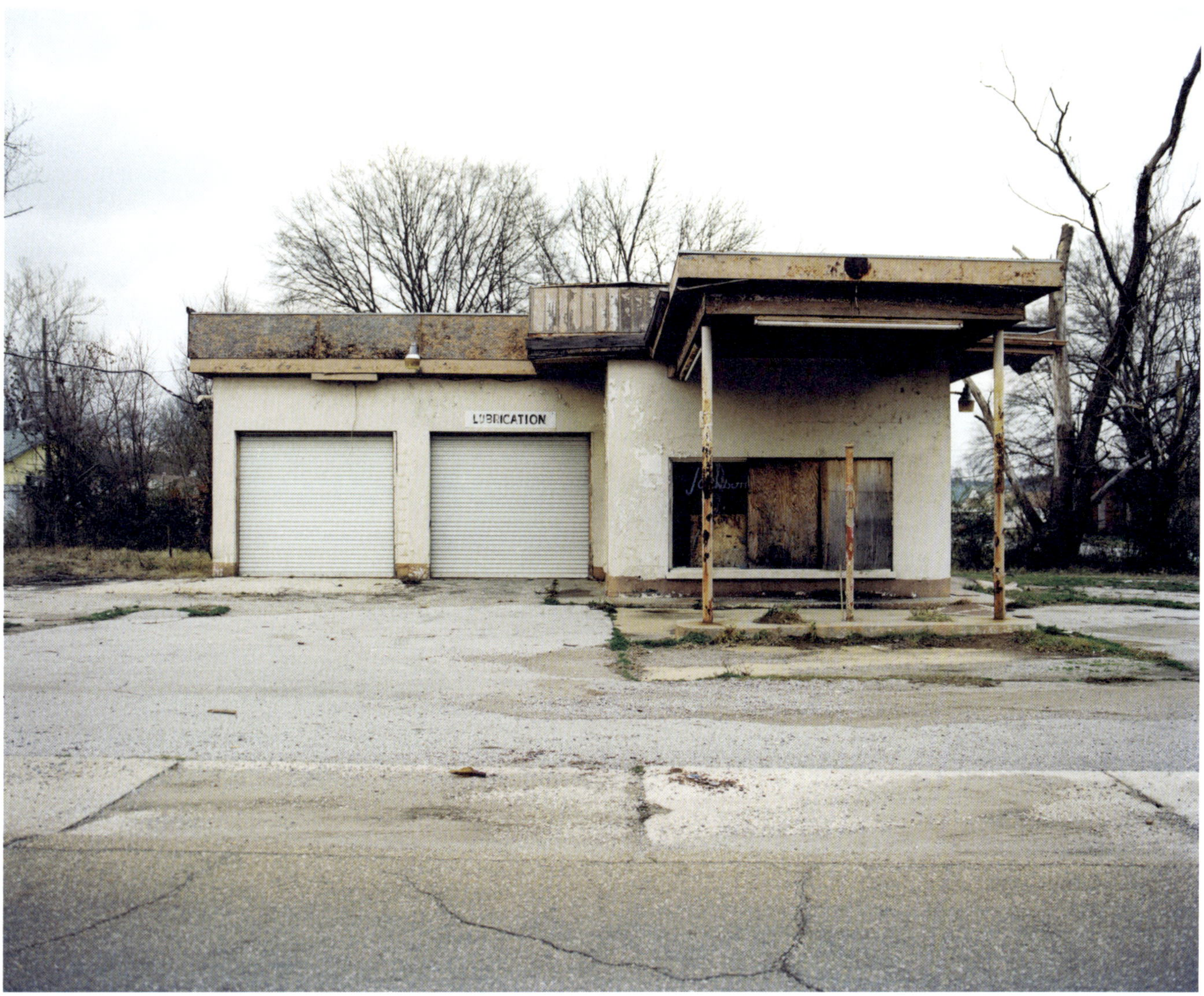

 WEST ANNISTON, ALABAMA. 2012

Maison démolie.

Demolished house.

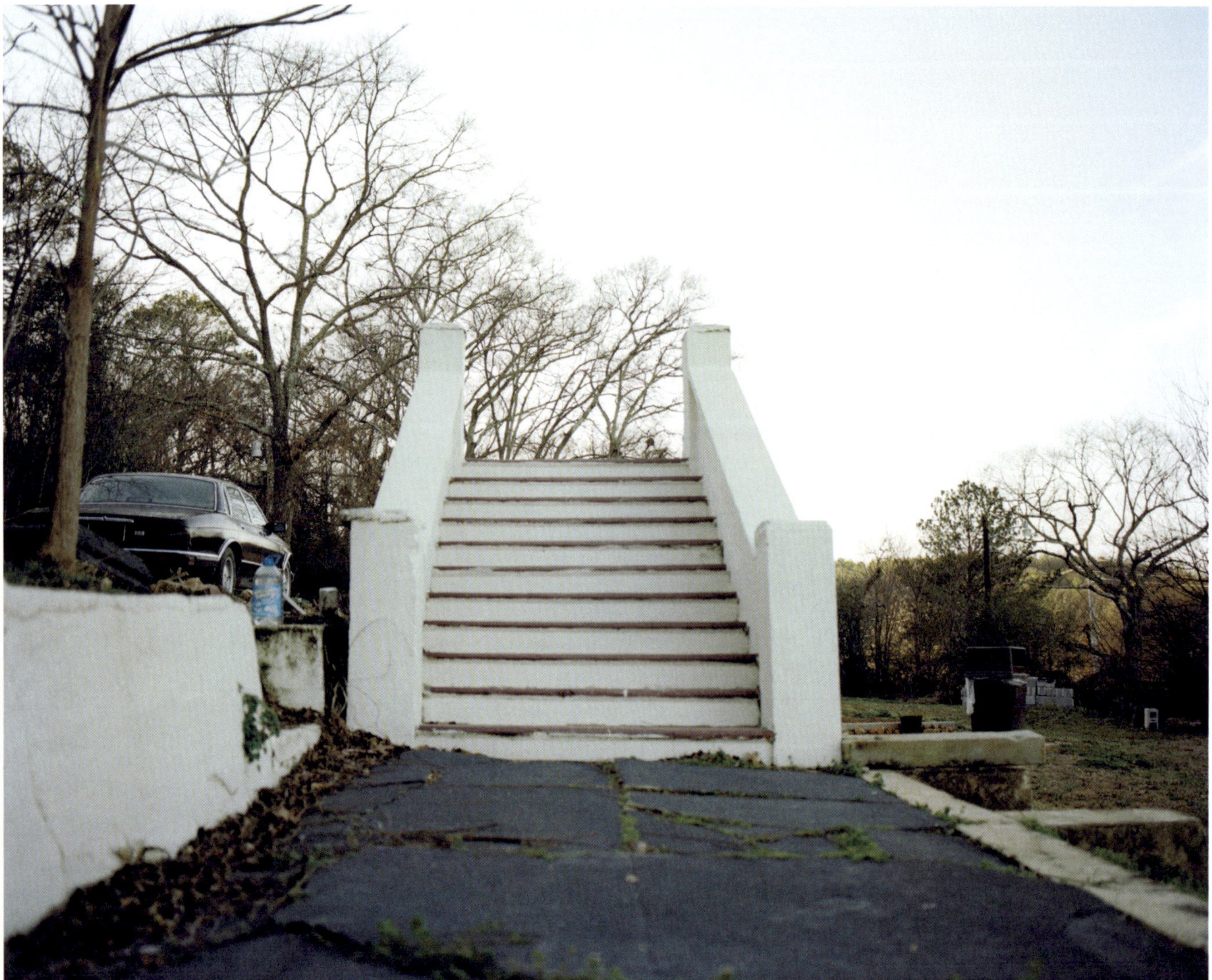

WEST ANNISTON, ALABAMA, 2012

Thomas Long souffre d'une longue liste de maladies dues à une exposition prolongée à des PCB. Parmi elles, diabète, immunodéficience et problèmes cardiaques.

Thomas Long suffers from a long list of illnesses due to high exposure to PCBs. Among his afflictions are diabetes, immune system deficiencies, respiratory problems and heart problems.

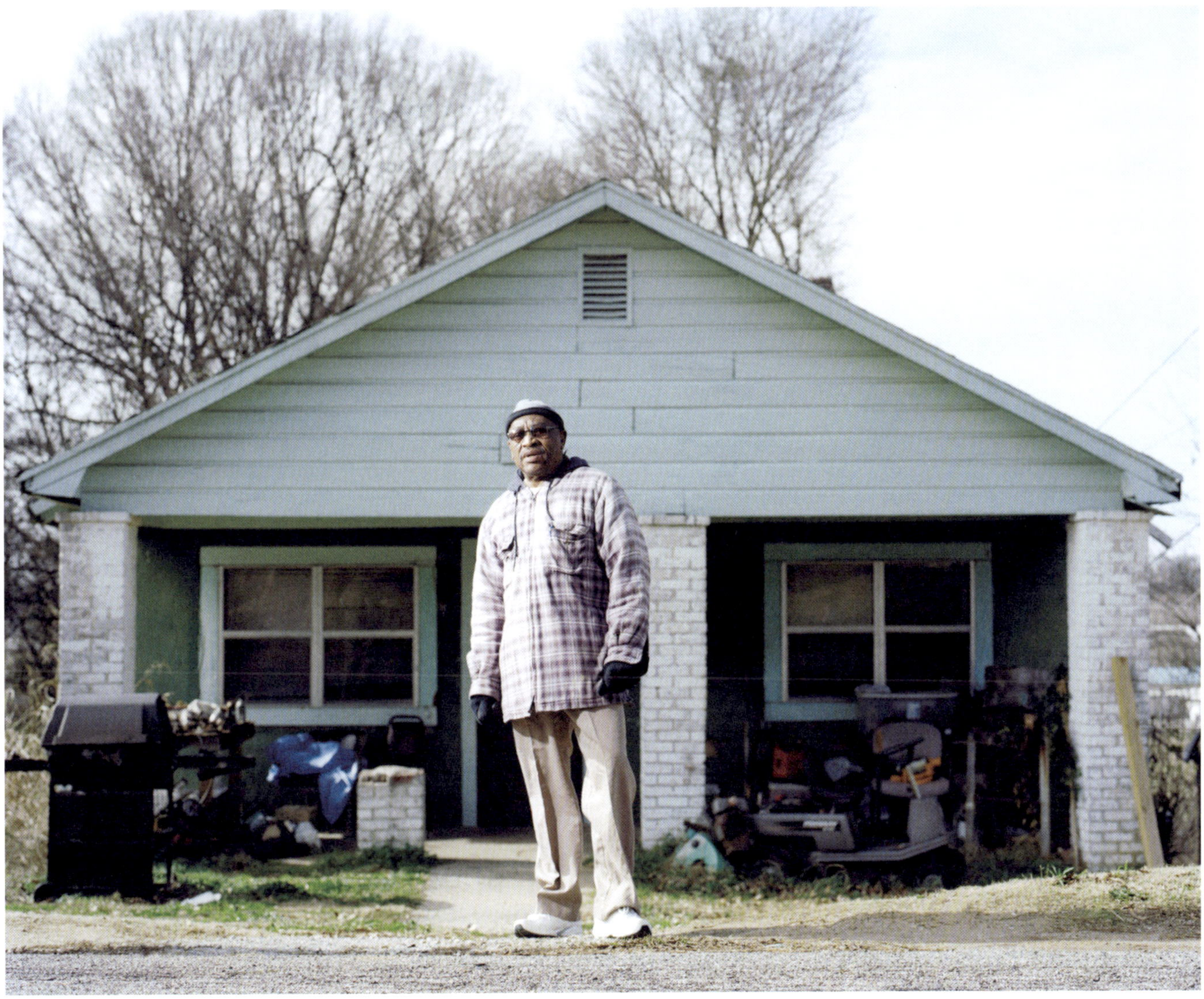

 WEST ANNISTON, ALABAMA, 2012

Monsanto

FROM (NAME & LOCATION) N. T. Johnson St. Louis

DATE February 16, 1970

SUBJECT

REFERENCE POLLUTION LETTER

TO

P. Craska - Wilmington
C. Clay - St. Louis
J.H. Davidson - Los Angeles
R.A. Damiani - Chicago
G.F. Fague - Detroit
R.A. Garcia - Akron
R. Garnsworthy - Melbourne
J. A. Heilala - Akron
R. Irwin - Houston
J.S. Pullman - New York
J.J. Roder - Chicago
R. Giles - Melbourne

cc:

P.J.A. Marsh - Brussels
R. Enrhardt - New York
T.W. Oneson - Montreal
J.N. Haggart - Brussels
V. Morse - St. Louis
J. Brydon - Montreal
R. Graham - New York
P.G. Benignus
J.G. Bryant
D.E. Roush
J.R. Fallon
D.A. Hall
D.R. Pogue
D.F. Smith
D.A. Olson

Attached is a list of questions and answers which may be asked of you by customers receiving our Aroclor-PCB letter. You can give verbal answers; no answers should be given in writing. If the customer asks a question you can't answer or if he wants an answer in writing, then send his questions to me and we will answer from here.

We want to avoid any situation where a customer wants to return fluid. The new reformulated products will be available within a month. We would prefer that the customer use up his current inventory and purchase Pydraul 625A, Pydraul ACA, Pydraul ACA Winter Grade and Pydraul 540A when available. He will then top off with the new fluid and eventually all Aroclor 1254 and Aroclor 1260 will be out of his system. We don't want to take fluid back. Sell him the replacement.

We must be very positive in our approach with each customer relative to our decision to eliminate the use of Aroclor 1254 and Aroclor 1260 in our Pydraul products. We (your customer and Monsanto) are not interested in using a product which may present a problem to our environment. We certainly have no reason to be defensive or apologetic about making this change. The decision to change makes good sense and our customers should commend us, not criticize our actions. No one has forced us to make this

Documents internes de 1970 témoignant de la volonté de Monsanto® de maintenir l'opinion dans le flou en ce qui concerne les effets des PCB. Ils révèlent par ailleurs la manipulation d'études scientifiques par Monsanto® en sa faveur. La stratégie de la compagnie durant la période de production des PCB fut loin d'être exemplaire. Le rétropédalage actuel sur ces prétendues preuves scientifiques et les tentatives de la compagnie pour se dédouaner de toute responsabilité quant à la saturation en PCB au niveau mondial sont aussi accablants pour Monsanto® que ses campagnes hors de prix déployées pour se donner une image plus « verte ».

Internal documents from 1970 show Monsanto®'s attempts to keep the public in the dark about PCBs. These documents further demonstrate Monsanto®'s efforts to manipulate scientific studies in Monsanto®'s favor. Monsanto®'s conduct throughout the period during which the company produced PCBs was less than commendable. Their attempts today to backpedal on what they represented as science and avoid responsibility for the global saturation of PCBs are equally discouraging, as are their repeated attempts to "green" their image with flashy, expensive PR campaigns.

2

change. We have done it to keep our customers out of possible trouble. They should appreciate our effort, and stay with us as a customer on the reformulated Pydrauls. To make this change has cost us research monies and time. Fortunately, we possess the technical skills to make a change in our formulations without affecting the performance of products. Be positive, Take the offense. Don't let a customer or competitor intimidate you. I doubt if our competitors know whether their product could present a problem to our environment. You might ask your customer, if he has ever asked Houghton or Stauffer, Carbine, etc. about the effects of their products.

We should also recognize (point this out to your customer) we must clean-up. The Chemical Week article gives him an idea of laws in effect in his state. Read this yourself. Be familiar with the data on each state in which your customers are located. Use this in your discussions.

We have no replacement products for Aroclor 1254 and Aroclor 1260. We will continue to make these products; however, customers will have to use their own judgement on continued use.

We can't afford to lose one dollar of business. Our attitude in discussing this subject with our customer will be the deciding factor in our success or failure in retaining all our present business. Good luck.

(We have also attached a copy of the letter sent to transformer customers.)

N. T. Johnson

lb

Panneau avertissant du danger de contamination aux PCB. En raison de leur présence importante dans le sol, des centaines de résidents ont quitté West Anniston, de nombreuses maisons ont été démolies et la commune a aujourd'hui des airs de ville fantôme.

PCB contamination warning sign. Due to the high level of PCBs in the ground, hundreds of residents have moved away from West Anniston, and many houses have been demolished in what looks like a ghost town today.

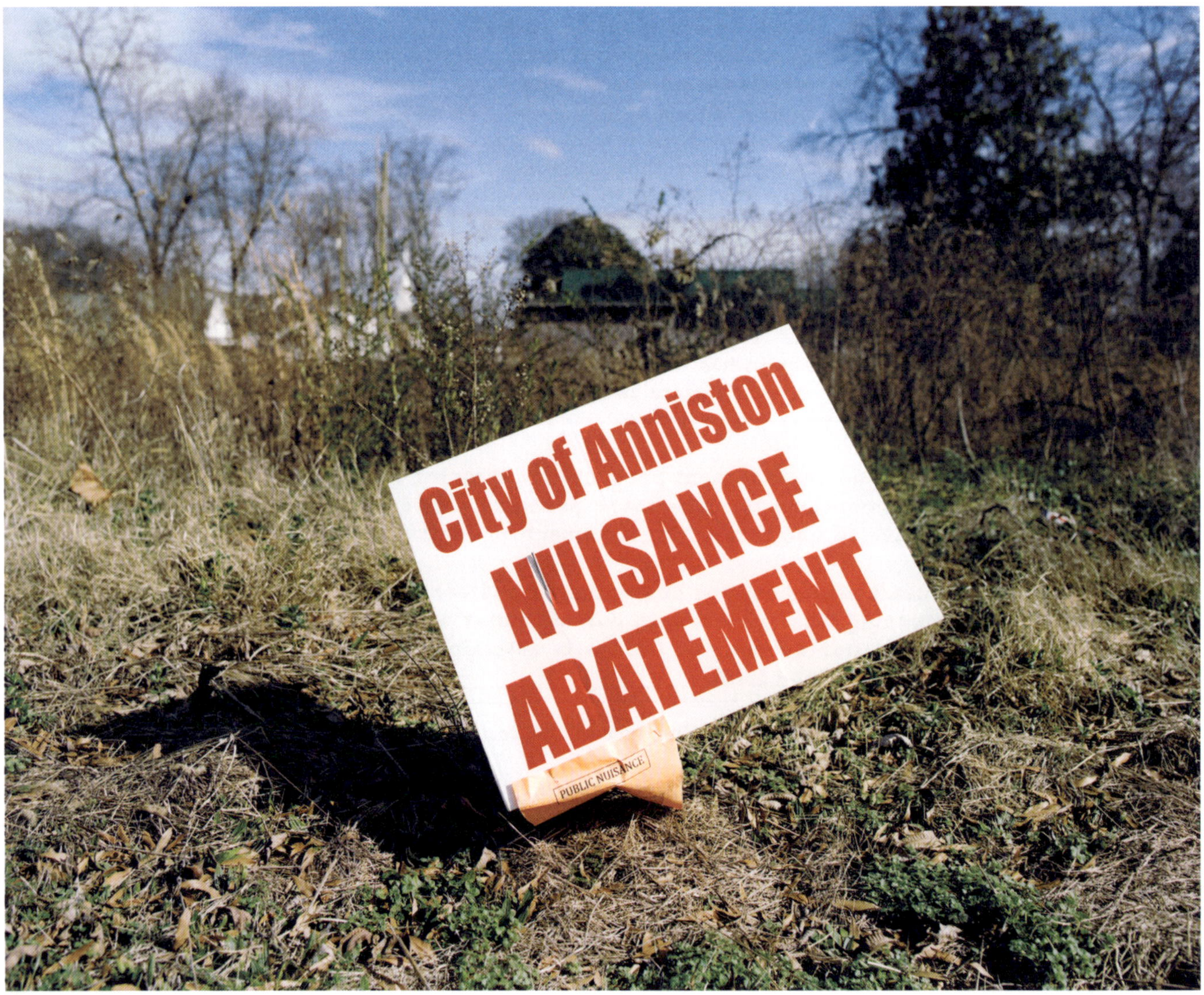

WEST ANNISTON, ALABAMA, 2012

David Roddick : « La plupart d'entre nous avons des PCB dans le sang. » Le taux moyen est de 2 parties par milliard. À l'instar de David Roddick, qui souffre, entre autres, de diabète et de difficultés respiratoires, plus d'un tiers de la population de West Anniston affiche un taux supérieur à 10 parties par milliard, d'après un test sanguin réalisé sur 3 000 résidents d'Anniston en vue du procès. Pour 41 des personnes testées, ce taux dépassait les 100 parties par milliard.

"Most of us have some PCBs in our blood — the average level is two parts per billion," says David Roddick, who suffers from multiple health problems such as diabetes and respiratory deficiency. According to a survey of 3,000 Anniston residents whose blood was tested for the lawsuit, more than a third of the population in West Anniston have levels greater than 10 parts per billion, and 41 tested greater than 100 parts per billion.

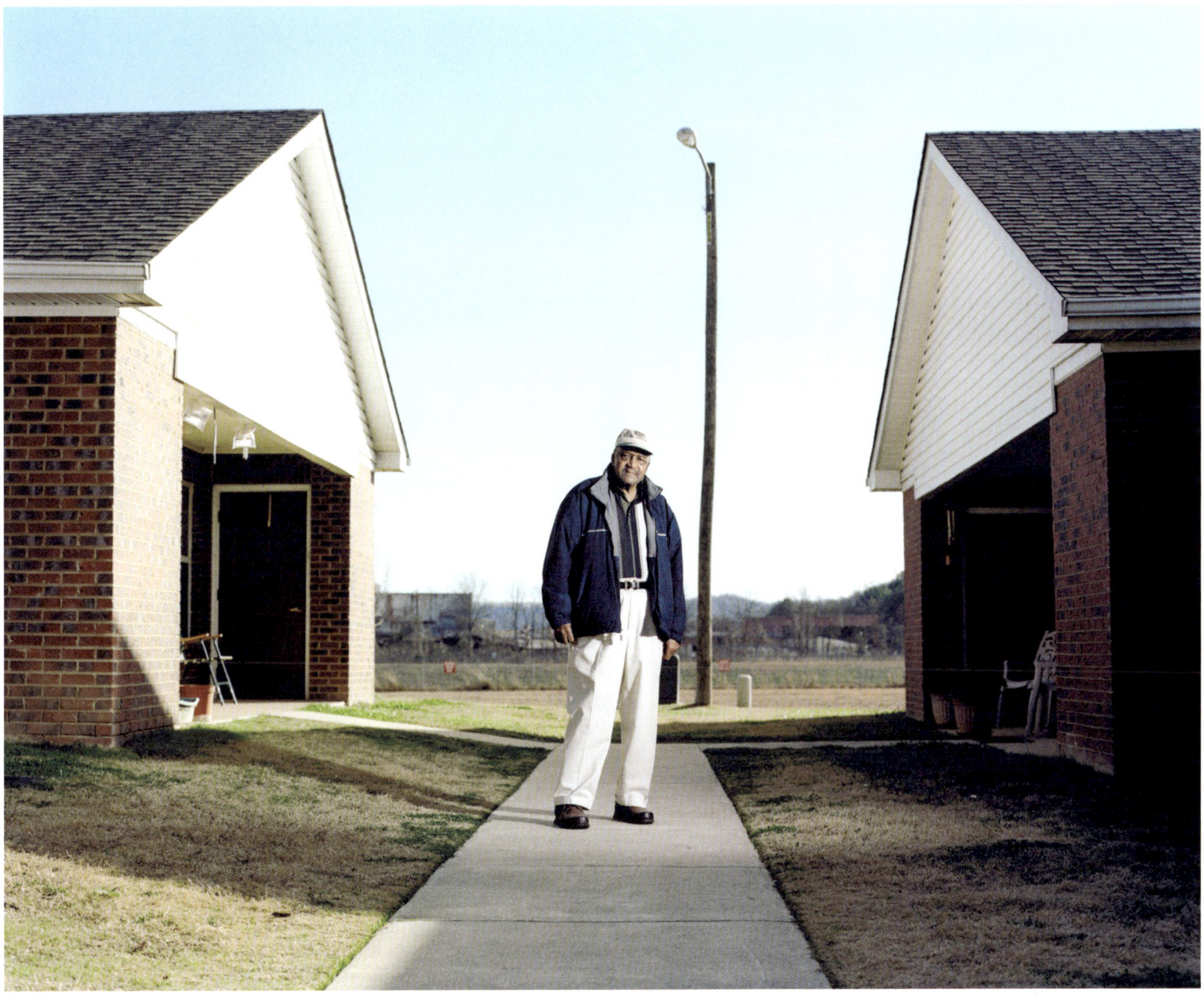

Pendant près de quarante ans, Monsanto® a produit dans une usine locale un liquide de refroidissement industriel à base de PCB, aujourd'hui interdit. Quarante ans au cours desquels la compagnie a rejeté des déchets toxiques dans un ruisseau de West Anniston et déversé des milliers de tonnes de PCB dans des décharges à ciel ouvert. Des milliers de pages de documents internes de Monsanto® — nombre d'entre elles parées d'un avertissement du type « confidentiel : à détruire après lecture » — indiquent que, depuis des dizaines d'années, la firme a dissimulé la nature des activités qu'elle faisait en toute connaissance de cause.

For nearly 40 years, while producing the now banned industrial coolants known as PCBs at a local factory, Monsanto® routinely discharged toxic waste into a West Anniston creek and dumped millions of pounds of PCBs into oozing open-pit landfills. Thousands of pages of Monsanto® documents — many emblazoned with warnings such as "Confidential: Read and Destroy" — show that for decades the corporate giant concealed what it did and what it knew.

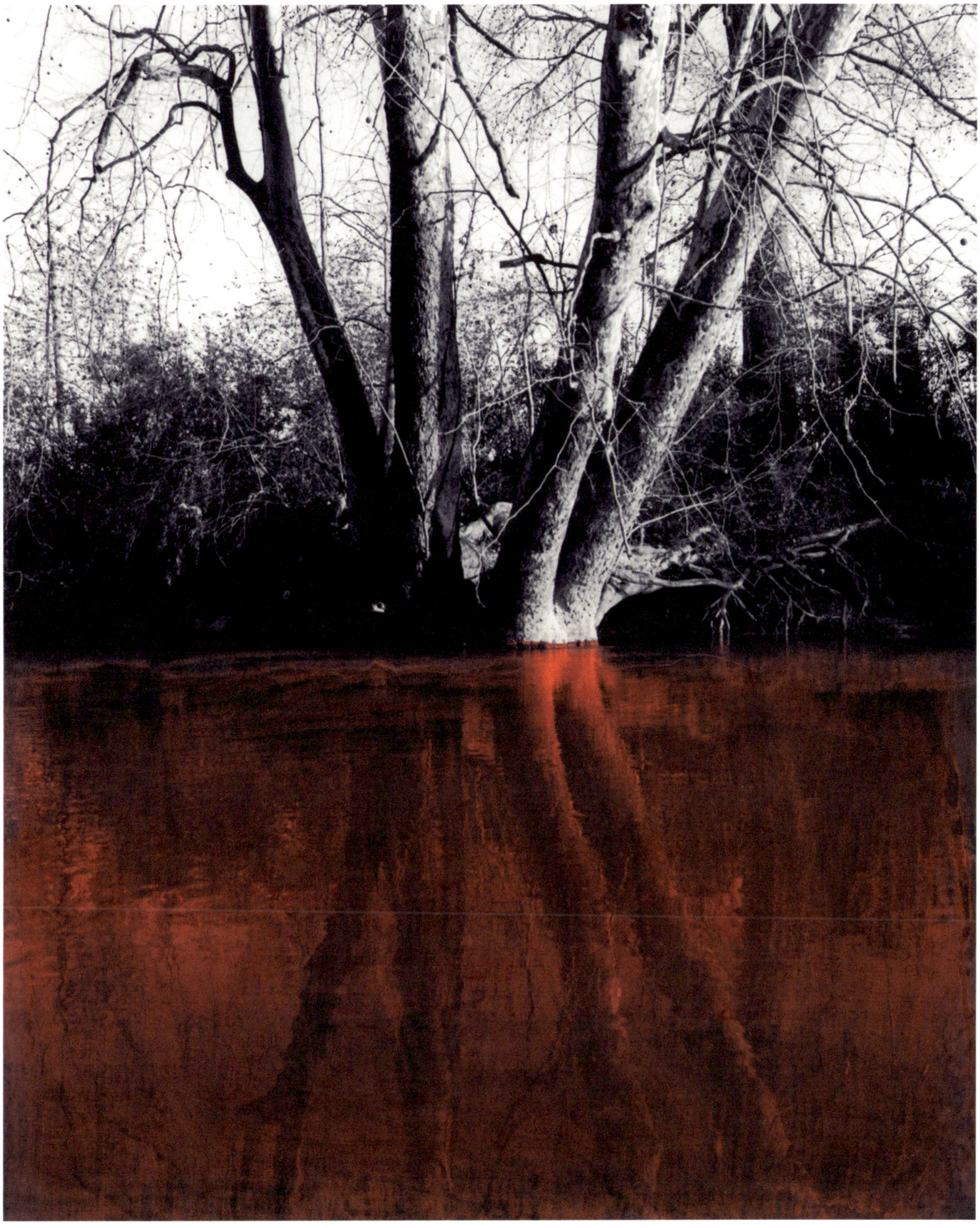

RUISSEAU CHOCCOLOCCO / CHOCCOLOCCO CREEK. WEST ANNISTON, ALABAMA. 2012

II.

L'Organisation mondiale de la santé et son Centre international de recherche sur le cancer (CIRC) ont reclassé le produit phare de Monsanto®, l'herbicide glyphosate, comme « probablement cancérigène pour l'homme ».

The World Health Organization and its International Agency for Research on Cancer (IARC) reclassifie Monsanto®'s flagship herbicide glyphosate as "probably carcinogenic to humans."

2,4,5—T
Agent Orange

Dès 1948, Monsanto® se lance dans la fabrication d'un herbicide à base d'acide : le 2,4,5-T. Puis, sans tenir compte ni de ses études ni des études publiées sur la toxicité des dioxines émises lors de la production de son herbicide, Monsanto® engendre un produit à la nocivité décuplée avec « l'Agent orange », un 2,4,5-T contaminé par la 2,3,7,8-tétrachlorodibenzo-para-dioxine (TCDD). Comparable à une arme chimique, l'Agent orange sera déversé pendant plus de dix ans par l'armée américaine sur les forêts du Sud du Viêtnam entre 1959 (premiers essais) et 1971, causant ainsi « une des plus grandes tragédies du siècle dernier[6] ».

Au début des années 1940, l'hormone de croissance des plantes est isolée par des chercheurs britanniques et américains qui la reproduisent de manière synthétique. À faible dose, cette hormone artificielle pulvérisée sur les plantes stimule leur développement, mais à forte dose, elle provoque leur croissance incontrôlée et leur mort. Or la synthèse de cette hormone libère des produits toxiques dérivés, dont la dioxine TCDD.

La dioxine est une substance générée lors de la fabrication de certains procédés chimiques chlorés (comme les PCB) ou de leur combustion à haute température. Elle recouvre une famille de 210 substances, dont la molécule TCDD, considérée comme la plus toxique pour l'homme et l'environnement. Cette molécule très stable et très résistante est dite « bioaccumulatrice », c'est-à-dire qu'elle ne se détruit pas au passage d'un organisme vivant à un autre. Elle peut donc se transmettre de l'animal à l'homme puisqu'elle s'accumule au cours de la chaîne alimentaire, et, tout comme les PCB, elle peut contaminer les enfants pendant la grossesse ou l'allaitement[7]. La TCDD est reconnue cancérigène pour l'homme[8], alors que d'autres types de dioxines provoquent des malformations de l'embryon (elles sont tératogènes), des baisses de fertilité ou des troubles endocriniens et hormonaux.

La découverte de l'hormone de croissance des plantes amène simultanément deux laboratoires britanniques et deux américains à l'invention des désherbants au cours de la Deuxième Guerre mondiale. Deux herbicides redoutables voient alors le jour : le 2,4-dichlorophénoxyacétique (2,4-D) et le 2,4,5-trichlorophénoxyacétique (2,4,5-T). Ces herbicides « sélectifs » permettent, selon un dosage précis, de détruire les mauvaises herbes (dicotes) sans abîmer les céréales (monocotes). L'ère de « la révolution agricole[9] » a sonné.

Dans un complet vide juridique, les laboratoires se disputant le brevet d'invention, de nombreuses entreprises chimiques se ruent sur le marché des désherbants. Et parmi elles, Monsanto®.

En 1948, Monsanto® ouvre une usine de production de 2,4,5-T à Nitro, en Virginie-Occidentale. Le nom Nitro est dérivé de nitroglycérine, constituant essentiel de la dynamite. Lieu de production d'explosifs pendant la Première Guerre mondiale, la région devient un centre d'usines chimiques au cours de la Deuxième Guerre mondiale. Nitro se situe dans la vallée de la rivière Kanawha, aujourd'hui surnommée la Chemical Valley où depuis plus d'un siècle se concentrent de nombreuses usines produisant des substances toxiques[10].

Le 8 mars 1949, une fuite dans le système de fabrication de l'usine de Monsanto® provoque une explosion qui libère un nuage de dioxine TCDD, le produit n'étant pas alors identifié. Quelques jours après, les ouvriers soumis à ces hautes doses de dioxine ressentent des nausées et de violents maux de tête, accompagnés d'éruptions cutanées purulentes (la chloracné, encore inconnue). Monsanto® demande un suivi médical interne de ses ouvriers à Raymond Suskind, médecin de l'Institut Kettering de Cincinnati, dans l'Ohio. Ce dernier lui remet un premier rapport daté du 5 décembre 1949, suivi en 1950 d'un second rapport[11]. Dès lors, la relation entre les symptômes que présentent les ouvriers et l'accident qui vient d'avoir lieu est établie. Les conclusions de cette étude ne sont pourtant dévoilées que trente-cinq ans plus tard, lors du procès « Kemner *vs* Monsanto® » en 1984[12].

Depuis 1949, les dirigeants de Monsanto® connaissent donc les risques de contamination à la dioxine auxquels les ouvriers et les populations voisines de l'usine sont exposés. Mais loin de divulguer ces informations, Monsanto® enferme ses fantômes dans un placard et continue sa production de 2,4,5-T à Nitro jusqu'en 1971 sans se soucier des effets sur les hommes et sur l'environnement. En 1969, l'étude de Diane Courtney[13] prouve la toxicité des dioxines et amène le Gouvernement américain à interdire l'utilisation de la 2,4,5-T aux États-Unis en avril 1970. En 2007, les habitants de Nitro portent plainte contre Monsanto®, accusé d'avoir diffusé « illégalement » de la dioxine dans les environs de l'usine[14]. En 2012, plus de soixante ans après l'accident de Nitro, Monsanto® accepte un accord de principe et verse 93 millions de dollars aux résidents de Nitro pour créer un fonds leur assurant des soins médicaux. Seuls 9 millions de cette somme sont alloués à la décontamination de la zone, les estimations de dépollution oscillant pourtant entre 945 millions et 3,8 milliards de dollars[15].

Une fois encore, Monsanto® se débarrasse financièrement du problème en laissant derrière lui une des zones les plus polluées des États-Unis.

6 William Bourdon, in André Bouny, *Agent Orange Apocalypse Viêt Nam*, Demi-Lune, Plogastel-Saint-Germain, 2010.

7 www.combat-monsanto.com.

8 Cancérigène de groupe 1 selon la classification du circ, Centre international de recherche sur le cancer (oms).

9 James Troyer, *Weed Science*, n° 49, mars-avril 2001.

10 Laura Parker, « A Century of Controversy, Accidentsin West Virginia's Chemical Valley in Lead-Up to Spill », *National Geographic*, 16 janvier 2014.

11 Raymond R. Suskind, « Progress Report. Patients from Monsanto Chemical Company, Nitro, West Virginia », *Unpublished Kettering Report*, 20 juillet 1950.

12 Procès lié à l'accident de Sturgeon (Illinois) en 1979 et à la plainte déposée contre Monsanto® (cf. chapitre iii).

13 Diane Courtney, « Tetratogenic evaluation of 2,4,5-T », *Science*, 15 mai 1969.

14 Soren Seelow,« Monsanto, un demi-siècle de scandales sanitaires », *Le Monde*, 16 février 2012.

15 Kate White, « Monsanto vows $93M to Nitro residents », *Charleston Gazette-Mail*, 24 février 2012.

In 1948, Monsanto® begins production of an acid-based herbicide: 2,4,5-T. Soon after, showing no regard for its own studies, nor for others that have been published concerning the harmfulness of dioxins emitted during the production of its herbicides, Monsanto® creates a new product of devastating toxicity: Agent Orange, a 2,4,5-T contaminated with the dioxin 2,3,7,8-tetrachlorodibenzop-dioxin (TCDD). Effectively a chemical weapon, Agent Orange is showered over the forests of South Viet Nam by the American army for over a decade between 1959 (preliminary trials) and 1971, in "one of the greatest tragedies of the last century." [6]

In the early 1940s, British and American researchers succeed in isolating the hormone that controls plant growth, and proceed to reproduce it artificially. When sprayed on plants in low doses, the hormone stimulates development. In high doses, it provokes uncontrolled growth that leads to plant death. The synthesis of the hormone releases toxic by-products, including the dioxin TCDD.

Dioxin is a substance produced during the manufacturing of certain chlorinated chemicals (including PCBs), or during their combustion at high temperature. It is a family of 210 substances of which the molecule TCDD is considered the most toxic to humans and the environment. This highly stable and resistant molecule is considered "bioaccumulative," meaning it does not break down as it passes from one living organism to another. It can therefore be transferred from animal to man, accumulating as it rises up the food chain, and, as with PCBs, it can pass from mother to child during pregnancy or through breastfeeding.[7] TCDD is known to be carcinogenic to man,[8] whereas other types of dioxins are teratogenic, meaning they can provoke malformations of the embryo, as well as decreased fertility, and endocrinal and hormonal problems.

The discovery of the plant growth hormone leads to the invention of herbicides, which are developed simultaneously by two British and two American laboratories during the Second World War. At this time, two formidable products are created: 2,4-dichlorophenoxyacetic acid (2,4-D) and 2,4,5-trichlorophenoxyacetic acid (2,4,5-T). These "selective" herbicides, applied in precise doses, destroy weeds (dicots) without causing harm to cereal crops (monocots). The "agricultural revolution"[9] has arrived.

Operating in a complete legislative void, the laboratories fight for patents while numerous chemical companies slip into the herbicide market. Among them, Monsanto®.

In 1948, Monsanto® opens a facility for the production of 2,4,5-T in Nitro, West Virginia. The name Nitro is derived from nitroglycerin, a fundamental component for the manufacture of dynamite. Exploited for the production of explosives during the First World War, the region becomes a center for chemical production during the Second. Nitro is situated in the Kanawha River Valley, now known as "Chemical Valley," where factories producing toxic substances have been implanted for over a century.[10]

On March 8, 1949, a leak at the Monsanto® plant produces an explosion, releasing a cloud of TCDD dioxin, a product yet to be identified. A few days later, the employees exposed to these high levels of dioxin begin to experience nausea and violent headaches, accompanied by purulent eruptions on the skin (a condition known as chloracne, then unknown). Monsanto® calls upon Raymond Suskind, a physician of the Kettering Institute of Cincinnati, Ohio, and requests internal medical monitoring of the employees. Suskind submits a primary report on December 5, 1949, followed by a second in 1950.[11] The relationship between the symptoms presented by the affected employees and the preceding accident at the plant is established. However, the results of these studies are not revealed until 35 years later, during the Kemner v. Monsanto® trial in 1984.[12] By this time, Monsanto® has been aware of the risks of dioxin contamination to its employees and the population surrounding its production sites for decades. But far from sounding the alarm, the company locks its skeletons in the closet and continues production of 2,4,5-T in Nitro until 1971, showing no concern for its effects on human health or the environment. In 1969, a study by Dr. Diane Courtney [13] demonstrates the toxicity of dioxins, leading the American government to prohibit the use of 2,4,5-T in the United States in April 1970.

In 2007, the residents of Nitro file a complaint against Monsanto®, accusing the company of having "illegally" diffused dioxin in the area surrounding the plant.[14] In 2012, more than 60 years after the Nitro incident, Monsanto® accepts an agreement in principle and pays $93 million to the residents of Nitro to create a fund to cover their medical costs. Of the settlement, just $9 million are allocated for the decontamination of the area. Estimates for the real cost of decontamination oscillate between $945 million and $3.8 billion.[15]

Once again, Monsanto® uses its financial resources to exonerate itself, leaving behind one of the most polluted regions in the United States.

6 William Bourdon, in André Bouny, *Agent Orange: Apocalypse Viêt Nam*, Éditions Demi-Lune, 2010.
7 www.combat-monsanto.com
8 Group 1 carcinogen according to the classification of the International Agency for Research on Cancer (WHO).
9 James Troyer, *Weed Science*, N°49, March-April 2001.
10 Laura Parker, "A Century of Controversy, Accidents in West Virginia's Chemical Valley in Lead-Up to Spill," *National Geographic*, January 16, 2014.
11 Raymond R. Suskind, "Progress Report. Patients from Monsanto Chemical Company, Nitro, West Virginia," *Unpublished Kettering Report*, July 20,1950.
12 Case related to the 1979 accident in Sturgeon (Illinois) and the complaint filed against Monsanto® (cf. Chapter III).
13 Diane Courtney, "Teratogenic evaluation of 2,4,5-T," *Science*, May 15,1969.
14 Soren Seelow, "Monsanto, un demi-siècle de scandales sanitaires" (Monsanto, a half-century of health scandals), *Le Monde*, February 16, 2012.
15 Kate White, "Monsanto vows $93M to Nitro residents," *Charleston Gazette-Mail*, February 24, 2012.

Pendant des années, les fuites des sites d'enfouissement ont contaminé la Poca River, un affluent de la Kanawha River, la plus grande voie navigable intérieure de Virginie-Occidentale.

For years, leaks from the dump sites have contaminated the Poca River, which flows into the Kanawha River, the largest inland waterway in West Virginia.

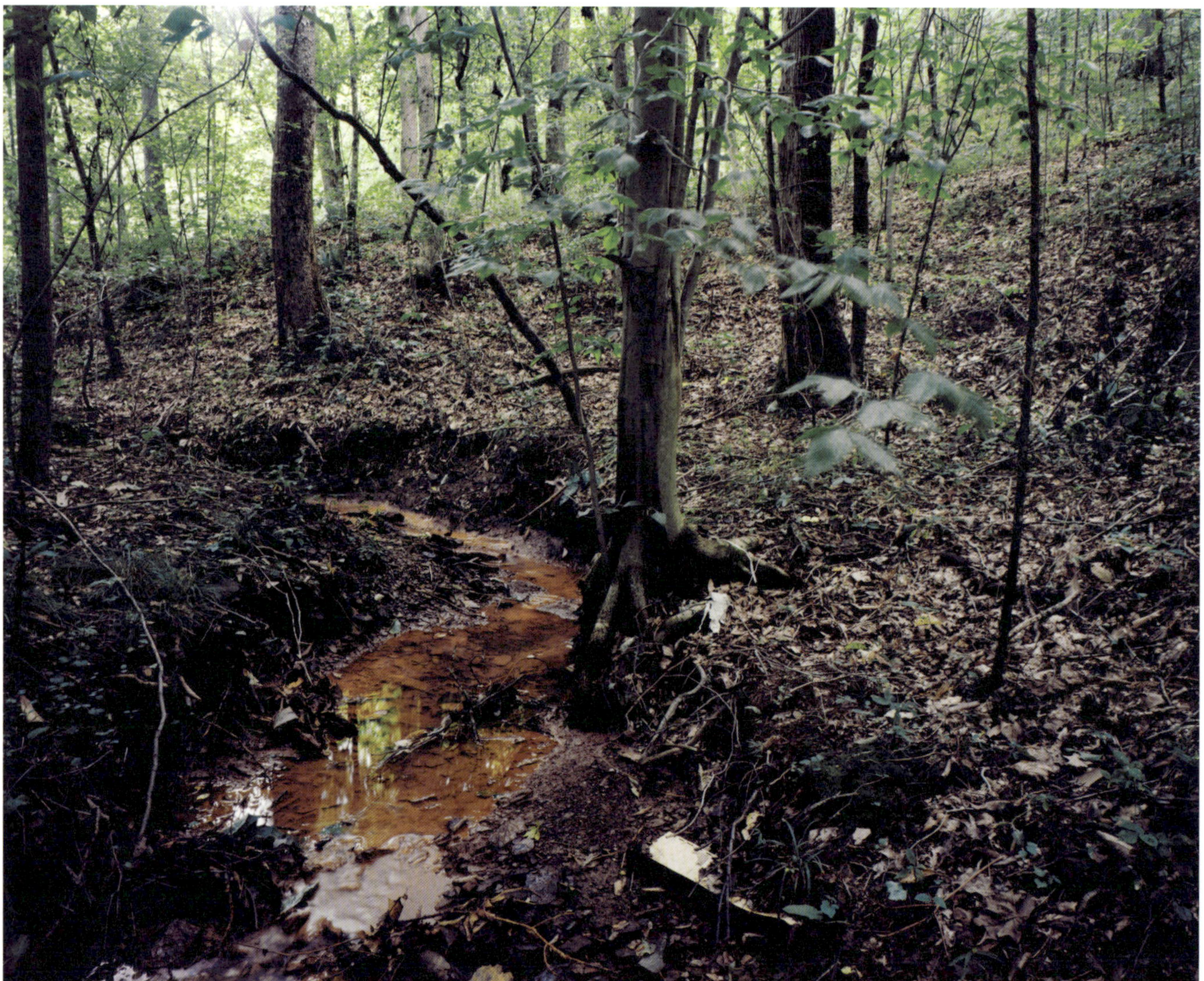

BASSIN DE LA POCA RIVER / POCA RIVER BASIN, VIRGINIE-OCCIDENTALE / WEST VIRGINIA. 2012

Le bassin de la Poca River fait partie d'une zone connue localement sous le nom de Chemical Valley. Dans les années 1950 et au début des années 1960, la région fut le premier producteur mondial de produits chimiques. L'usine Monsanto® située à proximité de la ville de Nitro fut le premier producteur de l'Agent orange. Les déchets étaient rejetés illégalement dans les alentours. Pendant des années, les fuites des sites d'enfouissement ont contaminé la Poca River.

The Poca River basin is part of an area locally known as the "Chemical Valley." During the 1950s and early 1960s, the area was the leading chemical producer in the world. Monsanto®'s plant near the town of Nitro was the primary manufacturer of Agent Orange.

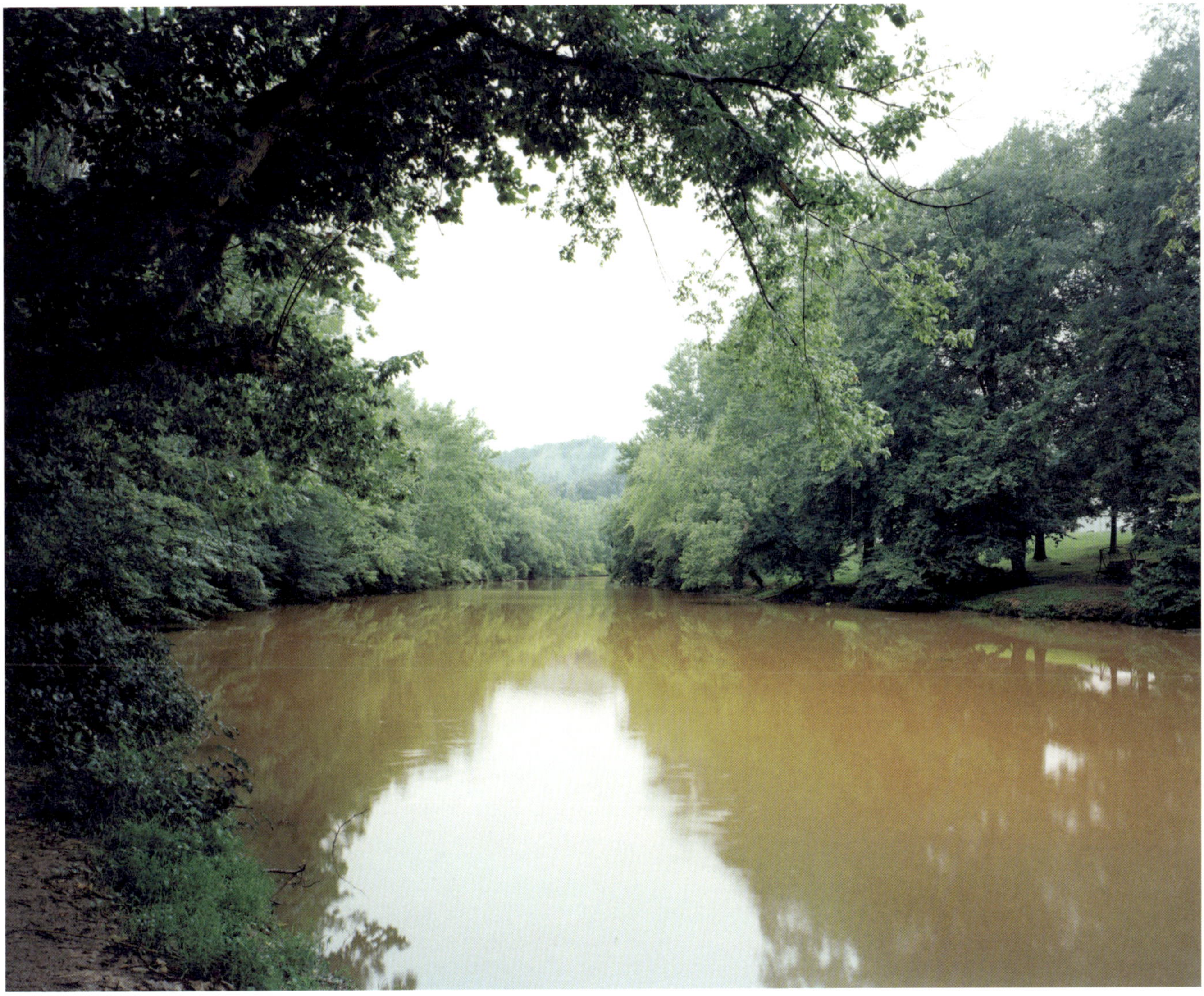

BASSIN DE LA POCA RIVER / POCA RIVER BASIN, VIRGINIE-OCCIDENTALE / WEST VIRGINIA. 2012

Les déchets étaient rejetés illégalement dans les alentours. Pendant des années, les fuites des sites d'enfouissement ont contaminé la Poca River, affluent de la Kanawha River, la plus grande voie navigable intérieure de Virginie-Occidentale.

The waste and residues from the Nitro plant were illegally dumped in the area.

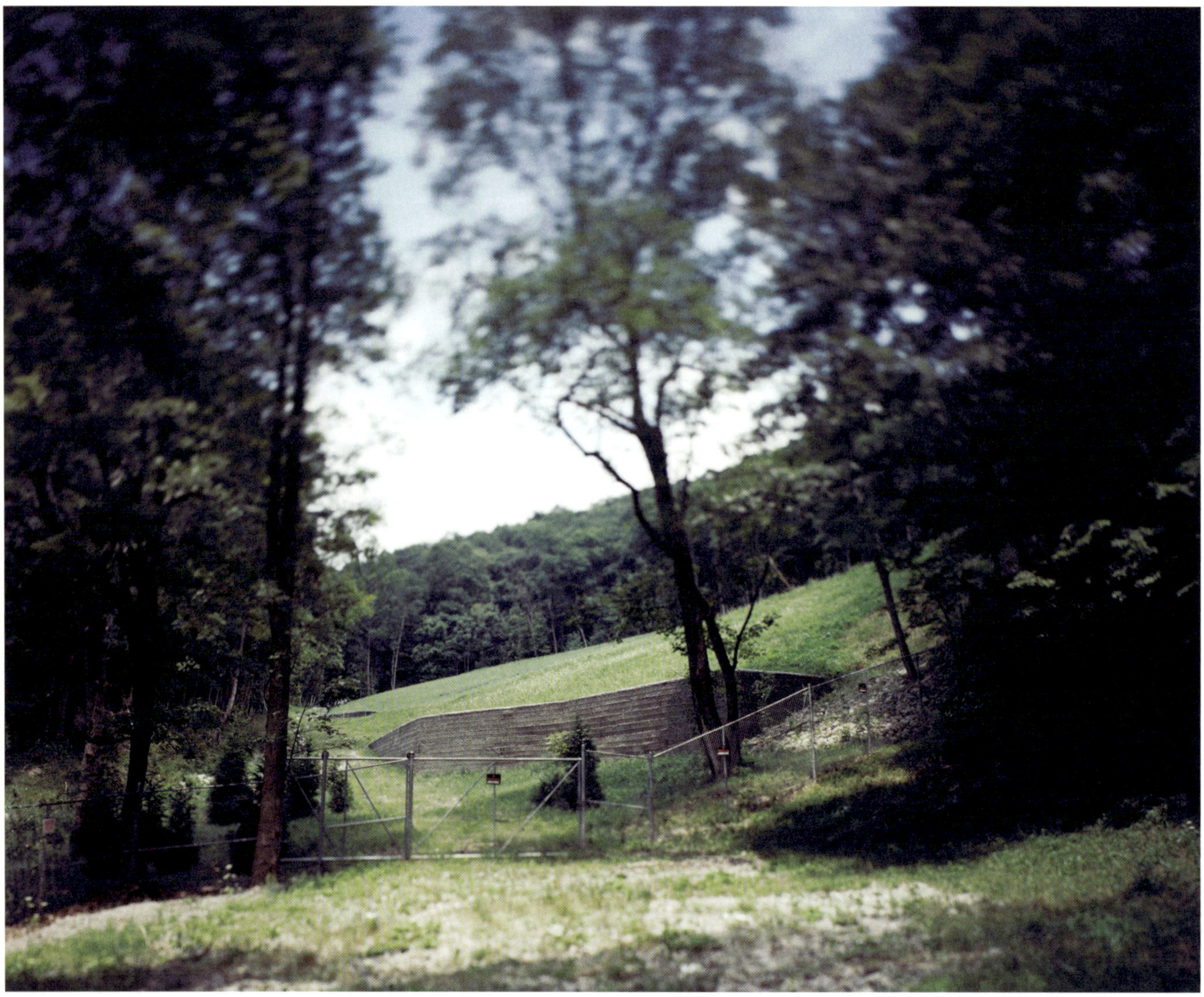

BASSIN DE LA POCA RIVER / POCA RIVER BASIN, VIRGINIE-OCCIDENTALE / WEST VIRGINIA. 2012

Serpent sans tête sur un site contaminé.

Headless snake in a contaminated site.

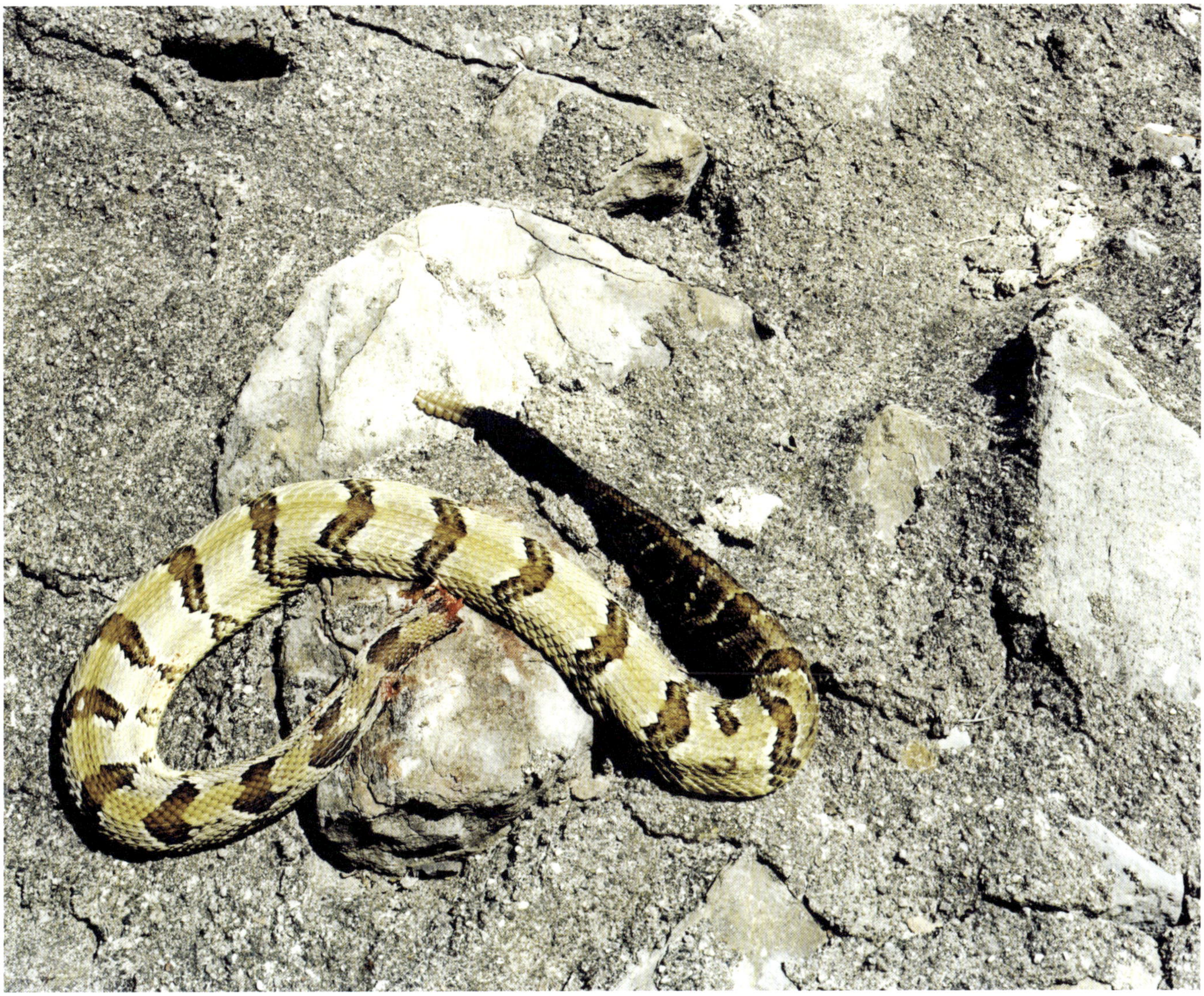

 BASSIN DE LA POCA RIVER / POCA RIVER BASIN, VIRGINIE-OCCIDENTALE / WEST VIRGINIA. 2012

Site d'enfouissement illégal.

Illegal dump site.

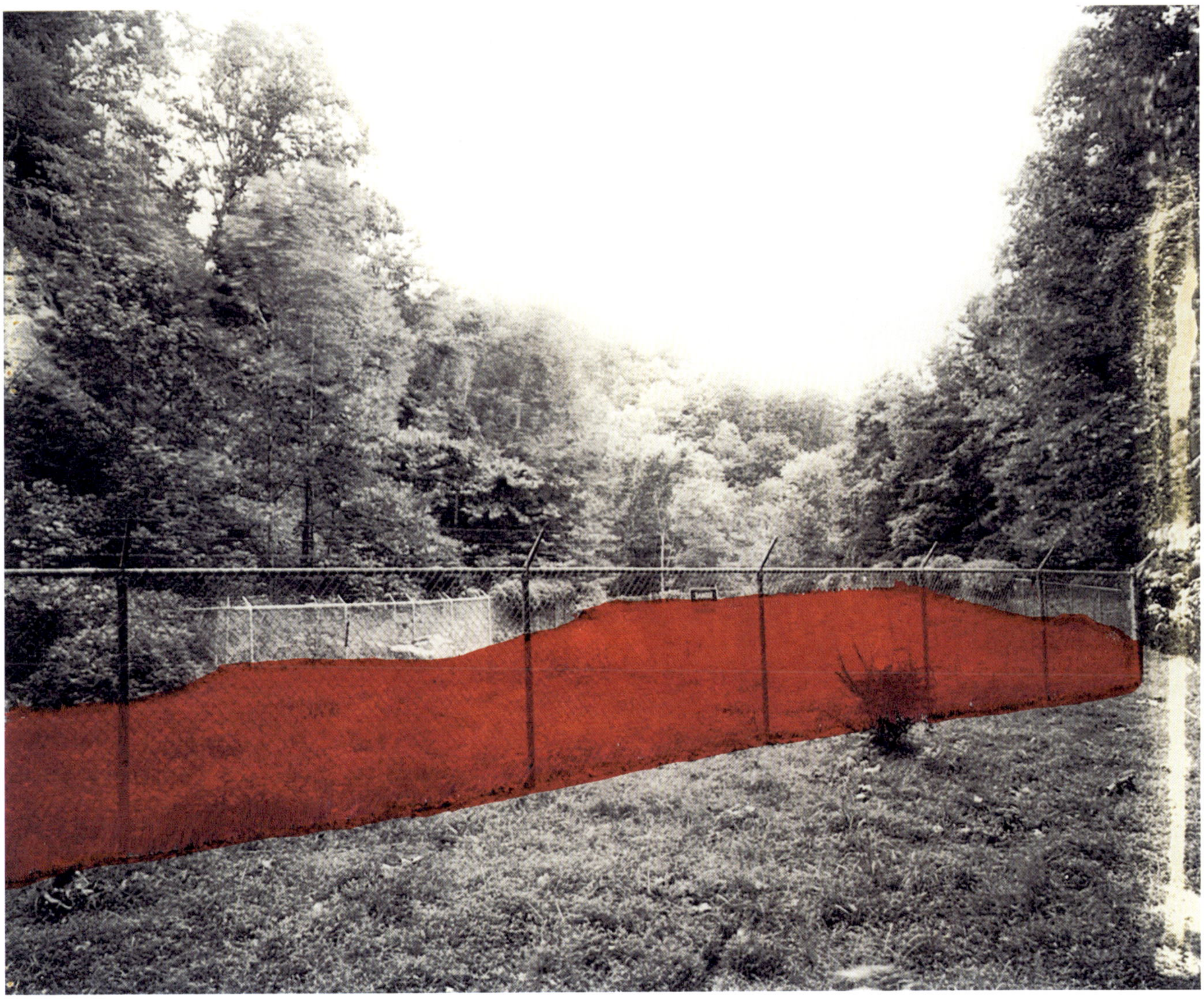

 BASSIN DE LA POCA RIVER / POCA RIVER BASIN, VIRGINIE-OCCIDENTALE / WEST VIRGINIA. 2012

Lee Roy Muck chez lui, dans le bassin de la Poca River, à proximité d'un des sites d'enfouissement illégaux de Monsanto®. À l'instar d'un nombre inquiétant de résidents de la zone, sa femme est décédée des suites d'un cancer.

Lee Roy Muck at his home in the Poca Basin, close to one of the Monsanto® illegal dump sites. Like an alarming number of residents in the area, his wife suffered a cancer-related death.

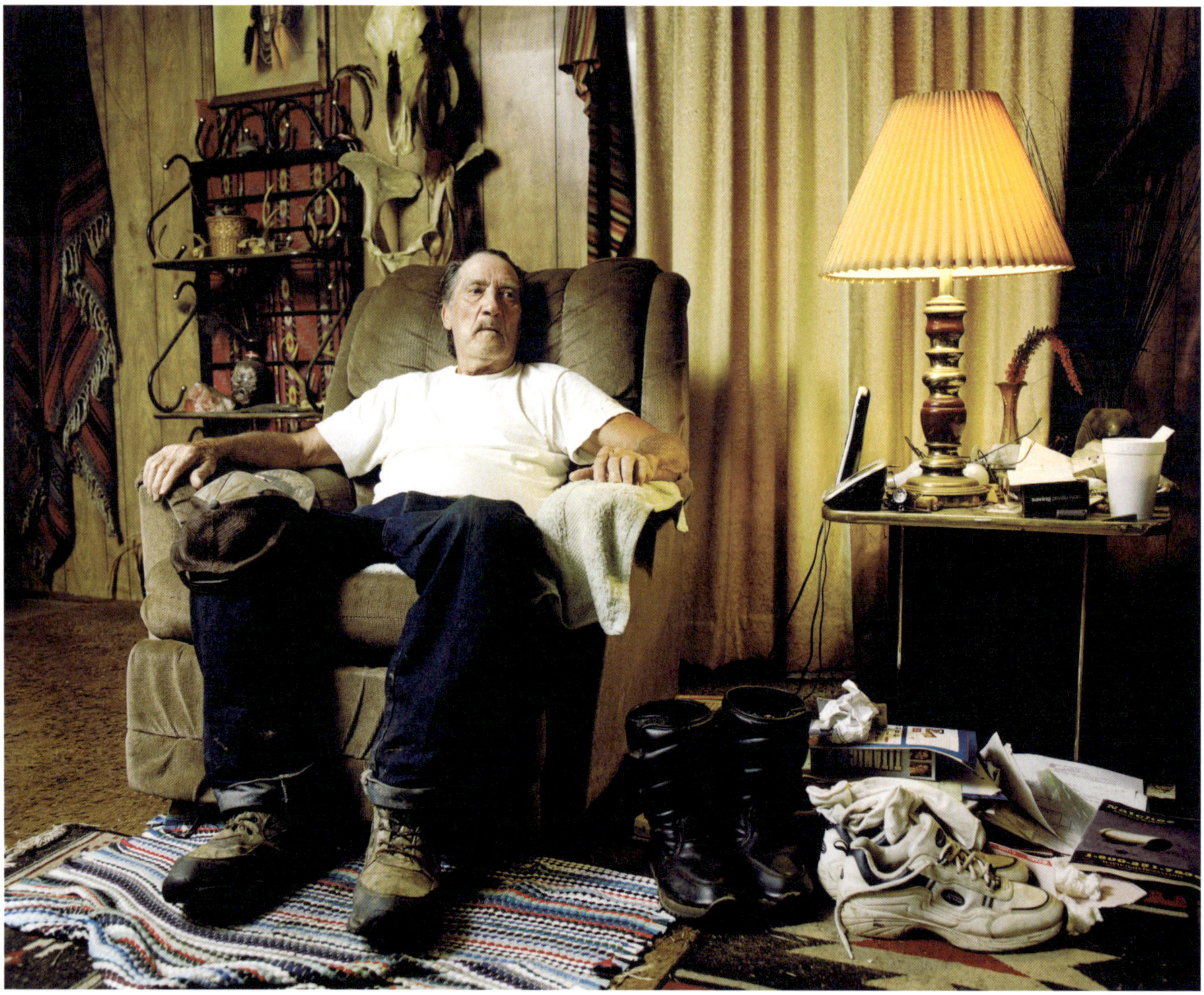

BASSIN DE LA POCA RIVER / POCA RIVER BASIN, VIRGINIE-OCCIDENTALE / WEST VIRGINIA. 2012

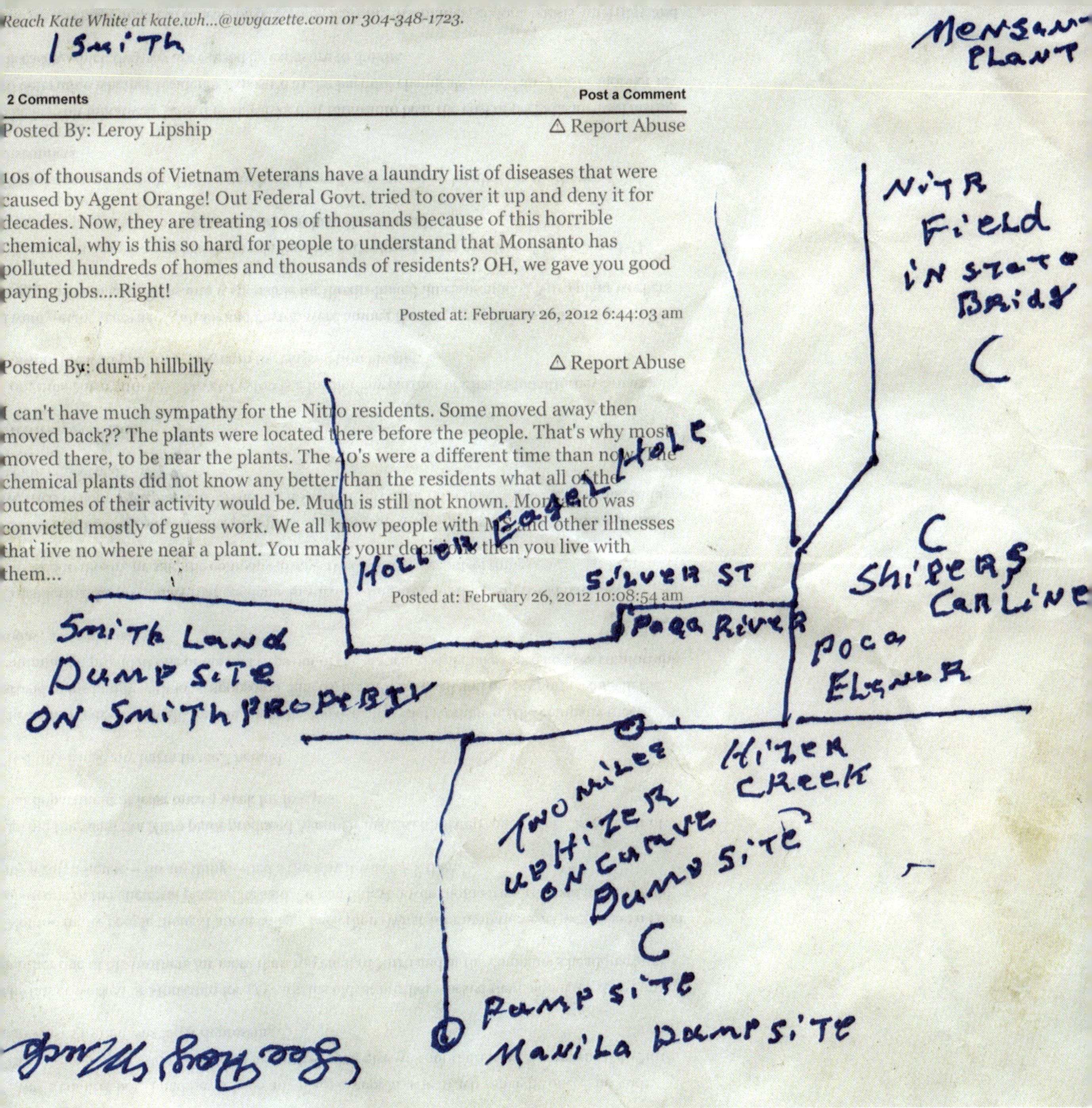

Reach Kate White at kate.wh...@wvgazette.com or 304-348-1723.

2 Comments **Post a Comment**

Posted By: Leroy Lipship △ Report Abuse

10s of thousands of Vietnam Veterans have a laundry list of diseases that were caused by Agent Orange! Out Federal Govt. tried to cover it up and deny it for decades. Now, they are treating 10s of thousands because of this horrible chemical, why is this so hard for people to understand that Monsanto has polluted hundreds of homes and thousands of residents? OH, we gave you good paying jobs....Right!

Posted at: February 26, 2012 6:44:03 am

Posted By: dumb hillbilly △ Report Abuse

I can't have much sympathy for the Nitro residents. Some moved away then moved back?? The plants were located there before the people. That's why most moved there, to be near the plants. The 40's were a different time than now. The chemical plants did not know any better than the residents what all of the outcomes of their activity would be. Much is still not known. Monsanto was convicted mostly of guess work. We all know people with MS and other illnesses that live no where near a plant. You make your decisions then you live with them...

Posted at: February 26, 2012 10:08:54 am

Carte dessinée par Lee Roy Muck indiquant l'emplacement des sites d'enfouissement illégaux.

Map by Lee Roy Muck, pointing to the illegal dumps.

Photographies de la femme de Lee Roy Muck.

Lee Roy Muck's photographs of his wife.

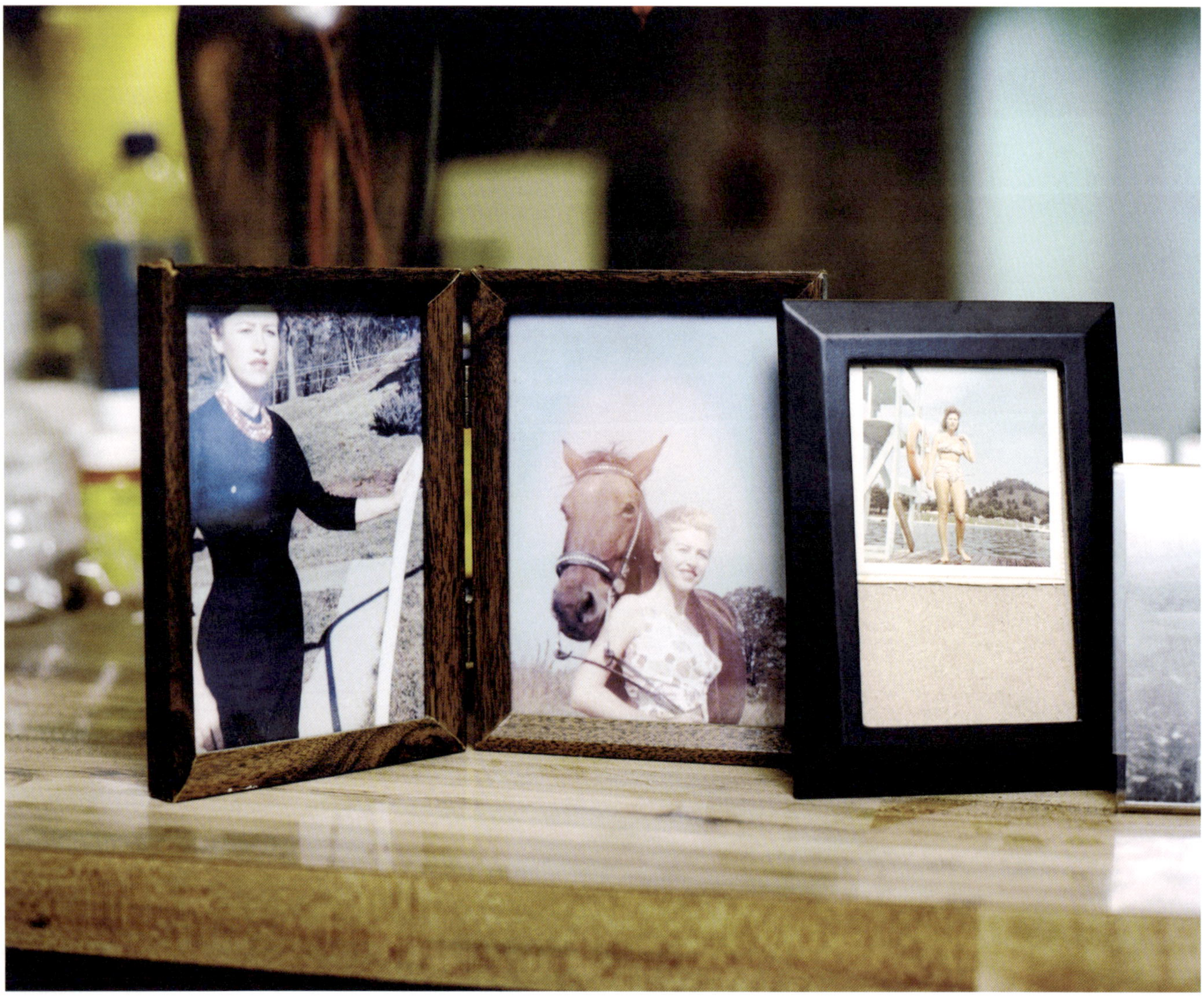

BASSIN DE LA POCA RIVER / POCA RIVER BASIN, VIRGINIE-OCCIDENTALE / WEST VIRGINIA. 2012

Amber Beller montrant une photographie de sa mère, Shirley Beller, décédée d'un cancer des ovaires en 2006.

Amber Beller holds a photograph of her mother, Shirley Beller, who died of ovarian cancer in 2006.

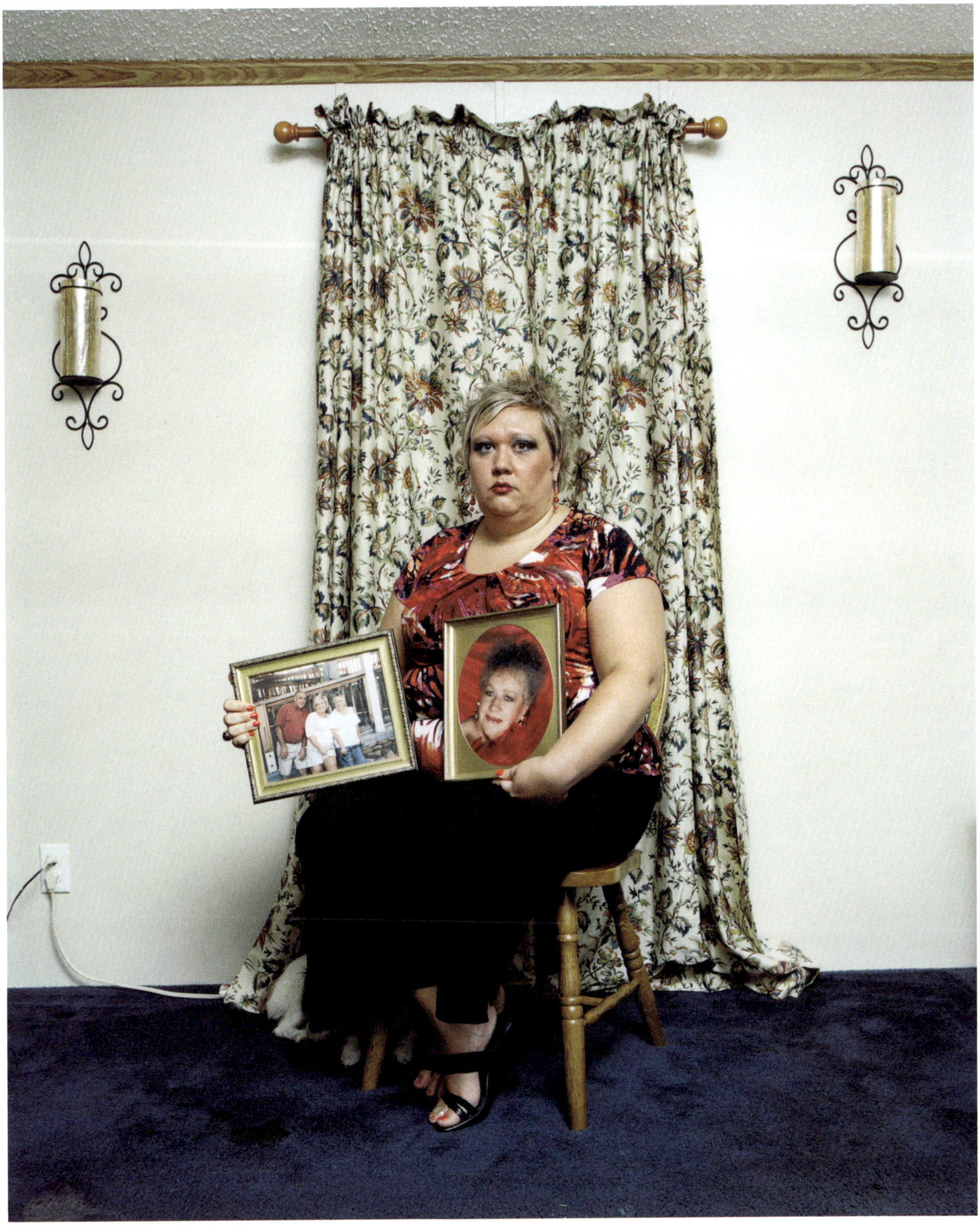

 BASSIN DE LA POCA RIVER / POCA RIVER BASIN, VIRGINIE-OCCIDENTALE / WEST VIRGINIA. 2012

Ciment recouvrant un site d'enfouissement illégal.
Les effets de cette méthode visant à bloquer la contamination sont vivement contestés.

Cement on top of an illegal dump.
The effects of this method to contain and seal contamination are highly disputed.

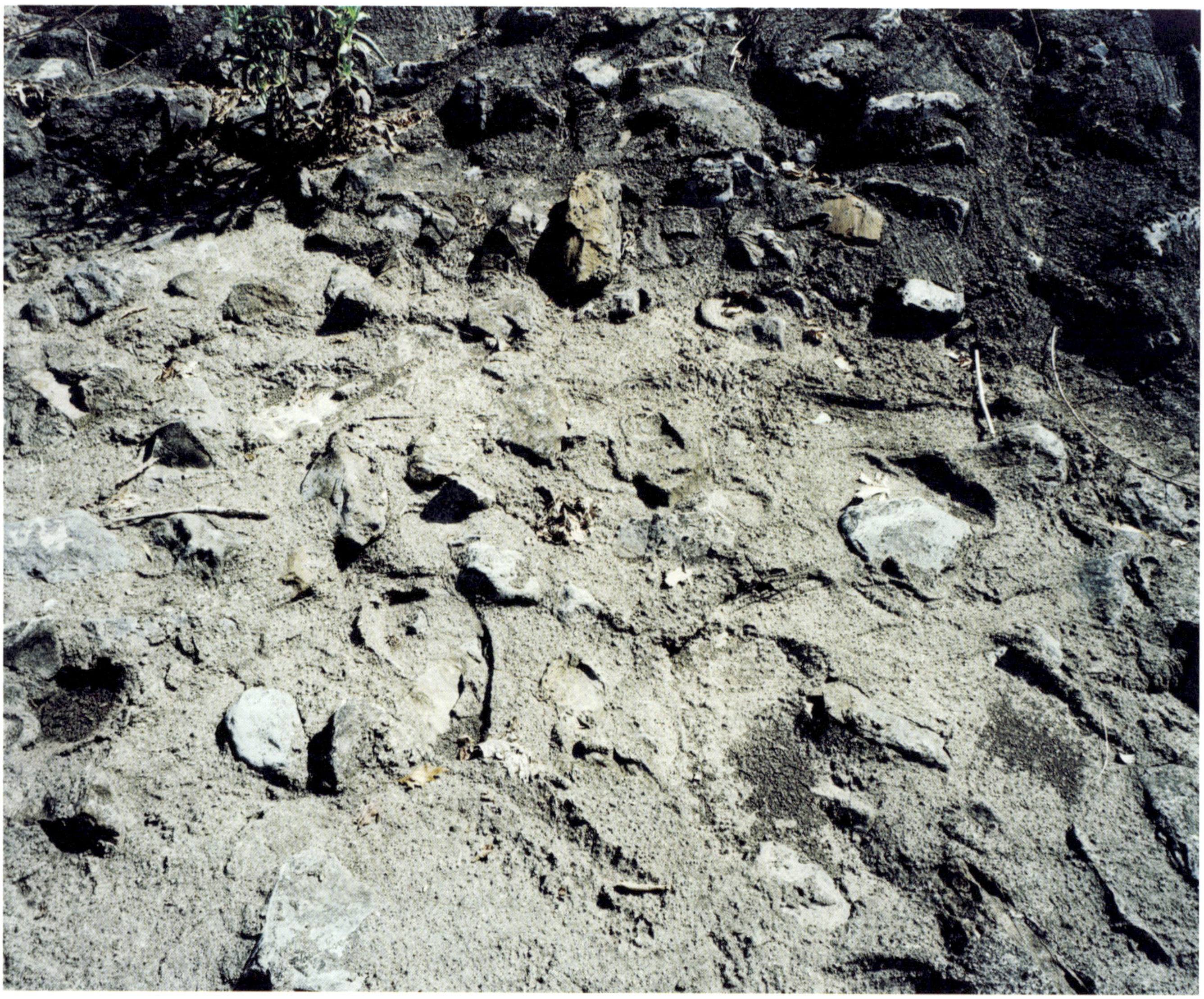

BASSIN DE LA POCA RIVER / POCA RIVER BASIN, VIRGINIE-OCCIDENTALE / WEST VIRGINIA. 2012

L'opération Ranch Hand – d'abord nommée Hadès (le dieu des Morts) mais abandonnée car trop explicite – débute officiellement le 13 janvier 1962 sous la présidence de John F. Kennedy. Il s'agit d'aider l'armée du Viêtnam du Sud contre le Viêtnam du Nord communiste. Un avion de l'US Air Force décolle de la base militaire de Tan Son Nhut avec à son bord plus de 800 litres d'« Agent violet ». Les couleurs de l'arc-en-ciel sont déclinées pour nommer les herbicides à base de dioxine 2,4-D, 2,4,5-T ou d'arsenic contenus dans des bidons en provenance des usines de sept compagnies américaines, dont Monsanto®. L'Agent orange, introduit à partir de 1965, est un mélange de 2,4-D et de 2,4,5-T : c'est le plus toxique. Jusqu'en 1971, plus de 80 millions de litres de défoliants sont ainsi déversés jour après jour sur les plaines vietnamiennes. 366 kilos de dioxine. Une étude de 2003 montre que la dissolution de 80 grammes de dioxine dans un réseau d'eau potable peut éliminer une ville de 8 millions d'habitants[16].

Encore très vives au Viêtnam, les répercussions de l'opération Ranch Hand le sont tout autant pour les vétérans de l'armée américaine. Environs 3 millions de soldats effectuent leur « travail » au nom de la liberté vendue par le gouvernement de Washington. Au maximum des forces en présence en 1969, ils sont plus de 550 000 au Viêtnam et beaucoup ne reviennent pas. Parmi les survivants, certains sont gravement affectés par les épandages de défoliants, et leurs descendants également. Les soldats ne savent pas que les herbicides sont nocifs et il y a lieu de penser que le Gouvernement américain ne le sait pas avant la fin des années 1960[17]. Mais les concepteurs de ces produits ne pouvaient pas, eux, l'ignorer.

En 1978, à l'initiative de Paul Reutershan, s'ouvre la *class action* des vétérans du Viêtnam contre les producteurs de l'Agent orange, Monsanto® et Dow Chemicals® en tête. Le 7 mai 1984, peu avant l'ouverture du procès, les « pères » de l'Agent orange versent 180 millions de dollars. Un règlement de l'affaire « à l'amiable », pour solde de tout compte avec les vétérans. Monsanto® s'appuie sur trois études médicales publiées entre 1980 et 1984 dans des revues scientifiques de référence concluant qu'aucun lien n'existe entre le 2,4,5-T et le cancer[18]. Et déboute ainsi la class action des vétérans du Viêtnam. Il faut attendre le procès « Kemner *vs* Monsanto® » (1984-1987) pour découvrir que les études menées par le Dr Raymond Suskind, mandaté par Monsanto®, étaient truquées. Cette découverte est confirmée en 1990 par une étude de Greenpeace[19].

Après des essais d'épandage fructueux dans le Viêtnam du Sud en 1959 où « 90 % des arbres et buissons ont été détruits sur deux ans[20] », l'opération Ranch Hand de l'armée américaine est lancée le 13 janvier 1962. Un avion Fairchild C-123 s'envole de la base américaine de Saigon pour larguer sa cargaison de 800 litres d'herbicide.

Les estimations les plus fiables[21] précisent que, jusqu'en 1971, 83 millions de litres de défoliants (dont 65 % contiennent de la dioxine) sont déversés sur les forêts et les zones rurales, certaines zones ayant été aspergées plus de dix fois, détruisant les cultures vivrières et l'écologie de la jungle, tout en faisant des milliers de victimes civiles et militaires. 10 % du territoire sud-vietnamien[22] est contaminé par la dioxine, soit 1,68 million d'hectares (16 797 kilomètres carrés), principalement des terres agricoles où sont implantés 3 181 villages. 2,1 à 4,8 millions de Vietnamiens ont été directement exposés à l'Agent orange, auxquels il faut ajouter des Cambodgiens et des Laotiens, ainsi que les troupes américaines et leurs alliés.

Les chiffres donnent le vertige. Toutefois, ils sont certainement supérieurs et ne cessent d'augmenter. En effet, la dioxine est « bioaccumulatrice » : elle se transmet dans la chaîne alimentaire (viande, œufs, poissons, lait et lait maternel). Elle est également tératogène, provoquant des malformations de l'embryon : plus de 500 000 bébés sont nés difformes, le nombre de fausses couches et d'enfants mort-nés étant difficile à déterminer. Il erre dans les couloirs du service de pédiatrie de l'hôpital Tû Dû à Hô Chí Minh-Ville[23] un sentiment d'impuissance et de malaise devant ces « enfants martyrs[24] », malgré le profond dévouement du personnel soignant. La dioxine est responsable de 33 maladies différentes : plus de 2 millions de personnes souffrent de cancer ou de maladies liées à l'exposition chimique[25]. 400 000 sont mortes ou handicapées. Peut-on décemment nier la guerre chimique au Viêtnam ?

En janvier 2004, l'Association vietnamienne des victimes de l'Agent orange porte plainte contre les onze fabricants du produit, dont Monsanto®. La requête est rejetée par la Cour suprême des États-Unis en février 2009[26], les producteurs jouissant d'une immunité d'État en tant que fournisseurs du Gouvernement. En août 2012, pour la première fois, le Viêtnam et les États-Unis entreprennent ensemble des opérations de décontamination à Danang (ancienne base militaire américaine), un des sites les plus pollués du pays. Coût : 43 millions de dollars, majoritairement financés par les États-Unis[27]. Une aide humanitaire, à défaut d'une reconnaissance de responsabilités et de réparations conséquentes.

16 *Le Monde*, 26 avril 2005 : étude de l'université de Columbia, New York, 2003.
17 Diane Courtney, op. cit. *A priori*, la version « agriculture » du 2,4,5-T pour laquelle il y a eu accord avec le Gouvernement contenait moins de dioxine que celles utilisées pour les épandages au Viêtnam.
18 Judith A. Zack et Raymond R. Suskind, « The Mortality Experience of Workers Exposed to Tetrachlorodibenzodioxin in a Trichlorophenol Process Accident », *Journal of Occupational Medicine*, vol. 22, n° 1, 1980 ; Judith A. Zack et William R. Gaffey, « A Mortality Study of Workers Employed at the Monsanto Company Plant in Nitro, West Virginia », *Environmental Science Research*, vol. 26, 1983 ; Raymond R. Suskind et Vicki S. Hertzberg, « Human Health Effects of 2,4,5-T and Its Toxic Contaminants », *Journal of the American Medical Association*, vol. 251, n° 18, 1984.
19 Joe Thornton, *Science for Sale*, Greenpeace, 29 novembre 1990.
20 Service audiovisuel de l'armée américaine, *in* Marie-Monique Robin, *op. cit.*
21 Jeanne Mager Stellman, « The Extent and Patterns of Usage of Agent Orange and Other Herbicides in Vietnam », *Nature*, vol. 422,17 avril 2003.
22 Le Viêtnam, réunifié en 1976, a une superficie de 331 211 kilomètres carrés.
23 Nouveau nom pour Saigon en 1976.
24 William Bourdon, *in* André Bouny, op. cit.
25 *Veterans and Agent Orange*, Institute of Medicine, National Academy Press, Washington, 1997.
26 André Bouny, *op. cit.*
27 AFP et *Le Monde*, 9 août 2012.

On January 13, 1962, Operation "Ranch Hand" — originally entitled "Operation Hades" (the God of the Dead) but abandoned for its overly explicit tone — officially begins, under the presidency of John F. Kennedy. The operation aims to assist the South Vietnamese army in its fight against communist North Viet Nam. On this day, a US Air Force plane takes off from the Tan Son Nhut military base, carrying over 800 liters of "Agent Violet." Herbicides with bases of dioxins 2,4-D, 2,4,5-T or arsenic, named after the colors of the rainbow, are supplied by seven American companies, including Monsanto®. Agent Orange, a mix of 2,4-D and 2,4,5-T, the most toxic of the herbicides, is introduced in 1965. From the beginning of the operation until 1971, more than 80 million liters of defoliants are sprayed over the Vietnamese forests — a total of 366 kilograms of dioxin. A 2003 study demonstrates that dissolving just 80 grams of dioxin in a potable water supply could eliminate a city of eight million inhabitants.[16]

The repercussions of Operation "Ranch Hand" remain ever present, both in Viet Nam and for US army veterans. Approximately three million soldiers fulfilled their "duty" in the name of the concept of freedom promoted by the government in Washington. At the height of the conflict, in 1969, over 550,000 military personnel were stationed in Viet Nam. Many would never return home. Many of the survivors, as well as their descendants, have been severely impacted by defoliant contamination. At the time, the soldiers were unaware that the herbicides were harmful; there is reason to believe that the American government did not realize the dangers they presented until the end of the 1960s.[17] But the creators of these products, for their part, could not have been ignorant of the risks.

In 1978, following the initiative of veteran Paul Reutershan, the Viet Nam veterans launch a class action suit against the producers of Agent Orange, with Monsanto® and Dow Chemicals at the head. On May 7, 1984, just before the trial, the "fathers" of Agent Orange agree to a $180 million settlement. An "amicable" resolution, to settle all accounts with the veterans. Monsanto®'s defense is based on three medical studies published in the scientific literature between 1980 and 1984, which conclude that there is no link between 2,4,5-T and cancer.[18] Later, during the Kemner v. Monsanto® case (1984-1987), it is revealed that the studies, led by Dr. Raymond Suskind, commissioned by Monsanto®, were falsified. This discovery is confirmed in 1990 in a study by Greenpeace.[19]

Following successful trials in South Viet Nam in 1959, which result in "90% of the trees and bushes" being "destroyed for two years,"[20] Operation "Ranch Hand" is launched on January 30, 1962. A Fairchild C-123 takes off from the American base in Saigon, prepared to jettison its cargo of 800 liters of herbicide. The most reliable estimates[21] show that by 1971, 83 million liters of defoliants (of which 65% contained dioxin) have been spread over forests and rural areas, with some zones treated 10 times or more. The operations destroy subsistence crops and the ecology of the jungle and result in thousands of civil and military victims. Ten per cent of the South Vietnamese territory,[22] or 1.68 million hectares (16.797 KM²), are contaminated with dioxin, primarily agricultural regions where a total of 3,181 villages are situated. Between 2.1 million to 4.8 million Vietnamese are directly exposed to Agent Orange, as well as Cambodians and Laotians, and American and allied troops. The numbers are staggering. However, the real impact is certainly even higher. Dioxin is bioaccumulative, meaning it is transmitted along the food chain (through meat, eggs, fish, dairy and breast milk). It is also teratogenic, provoking malformations of the embryo: over 500,000 babies were born with birth defects; the number of miscarriages and stillbirths is difficult to determine. Victims crowd in the pediatric ward of the Tû Dû Hospital in Ho Chi Minh City.[23] Faced with these "child martyrs,"[24] a sense of helplessness and unease prevails, despite the palpable dedication of the hospital personnel. Dioxin is responsible for 33 different illnesses, and over two million people suffer from cancer or other diseases linked to chemical exposure.[25] Four hundred thousand are dead or disabled. Can we, in all decency, deny that Viet Nam is a victim of chemical warfare?

In January 2004, the Vietnamese Association for Victims of Agent Orange initiates legal proceedings against the product's 11 producers, including Monsanto®. The request is rejected by the Supreme Court of the United States in February 2009;[26] the producers, as suppliers to the government, are protected by sovereign immunity. In August 2012, for the first time, Viet Nam and the United States embark on a joint decontamination operation in Danang (a former American military base), one of the most polluted sites in the country. The $43 million cleanup is financed mainly by the United States.[27] They gave humanitarian aid instead of recognizing their responsibility and giving consequent compensation.

16 *Le Monde*, April 26, 2005: study by Columbia University, New York, 2003.
17 Diane Courtney, op. cit. A priori, the "agricultural" version of 2,4,5-T, for which there was a government agreement, contained lower levels of dioxin than those used for defoliation operations in Viet Nam.
18 Judith A. Zack and Raymond R. Suskind, "The mortality experience of workers exposed to tetrachlorodibenzodioxin in a trichlorophenol process accident," *Journal of Occupational Medicine*, vol. 22, N°1, 1980; Judith A. Zack and William R. Gaffey, "A mortality study of workers employed at the Monsanto company plant in Nitro, West Virginia," *Environmental Science Research*, vol. 26, 1983; Raymond R. Suskind and Vicki S. Hertzberg, "Human health effects of 2,4,5-T and its toxic contaminants," *Journal of the American Medical Association*, vol. 251, N°18, 1984.
19 Joe Thornton, *Science for Sale*, Greenpeace, November 29, 1990.
20 U.S. Army audiovisual service, in Marie-Monique Robin, op.cit.
21 Jeanne Mager Stellman, "The extent and patterns of usage of Agent Orange and other herbicides in Viet Nam," *Nature*, vol. 422, April 17, 2003.
22 Viet Nam, reunified in 1976, has a surface area of 331.211 km².
23 Saigon was renamed Ho Chi Minh City in 1976.
24 William Bourdon, in André Bouny, op. cit.
25 *Veterans and Agent Orange*, Institute of Medicine, National Academy Press, Washington,1997.
26 André Bouny, op. cit.
27 AFP and *Le Monde*, August 9, 2012.

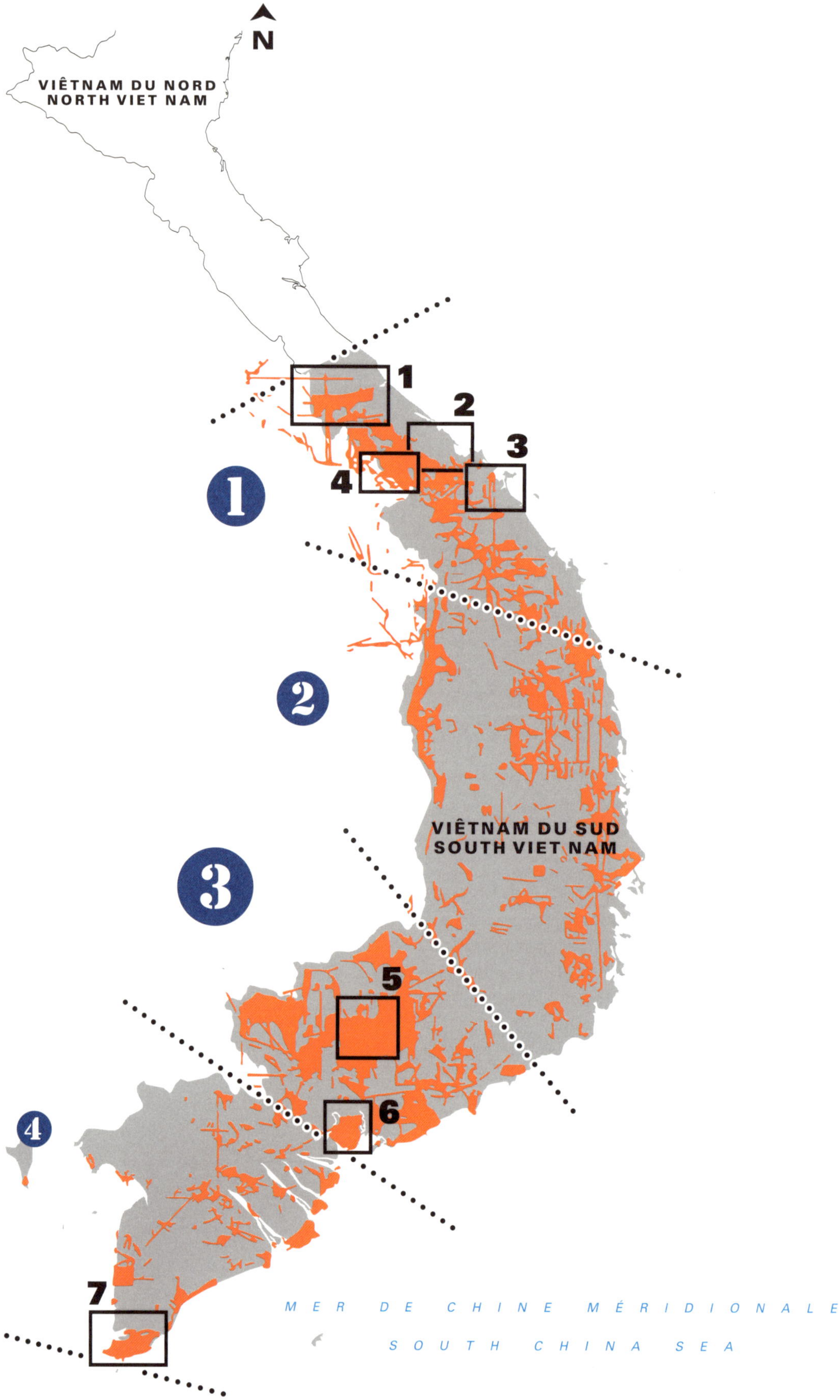
N
VIÊTNAM DU NORD
NORTH VIET NAM
1
2
3
4
1
2
3
VIÊTNAM DU SUD
SOUTH VIET NAM
5
6
4
7
MER DE CHINE MÉRIDIONALE
SOUTH CHINA SEA

Missions aériennes de pulvérisation d'herbicides dans le Sud-Ouest du Viêtnam de 1965 à 1971

Aerial herbicide spray missions in southern Viet Nam, 1965 to 1971

Domaines examinés au cours du programme Dicodin et Radarsat de la vallée de Luoi, de 1994 à 1996 / Areas examined during the A Luoi Valley Dicodin and RADARSAT program,1994 to 1996:

1 Quang Tri
2 Huê
3 Danang
4 A Luoi
5 Ma Da
6 Rung Sat
7 Ca Mau

Zone tactique des us Corps / US Corps Tactical Zones

Limites approximatives des zones tactiques des us Corps / Approximate boundaries of US Corps Tactical Zones

Missions de pulvérisation / Spray missions

L'utilisation militaire d'herbicides au Viêtnam a commencé en 1961, s'est étendue en 1965 et en 1966 et a atteint un pic de 1967 à 1969. Le nom de code pour le programme global d'herbicides était Trail Dust. Le nom de code Ranch Hand a spécifiquement mentionné le projet de pulvérisation d'herbicides C-123. Cette carte est une représentation des missions de pulvérisation d'herbicides au Viêtnam. Elle ne représente que la pulvérisation par avion à voilure fixe et ne comprend pas la pulvérisation par hélicoptère de périmètre ni d'autres méthodes de pulvérisation. La zone tactique des us Corps n° 3 a reçu les plus fortes concentrations de pulvérisation, suivie par Corps n° 1, Corps n° 2 et Corps n° 4.

The military use of herbicides in Viet Nam began in 1961, was expanded during 1965 and 1966, and reached a peak from 1967 to 1969. The code name for the overall herbicide program was "Trail Dust." The code name "Ranch Hand" specifically referred to the C-123 herbicide-spraying project. This map is a representation of herbicide spray missions in Viet Nam. This map only represents fixed-wing aircraft spraying, and does not include helicopter spraying of perimeters or other spray methods. The Corps Tactical Zone #3 received the heaviest concentrations of spraying, followed by Corps #1, Corps #2 and Corps #4.

SOURCE : DÉP. DE L'ARMÉE AMÉRICAINE / US DEPT. OF THE ARMY

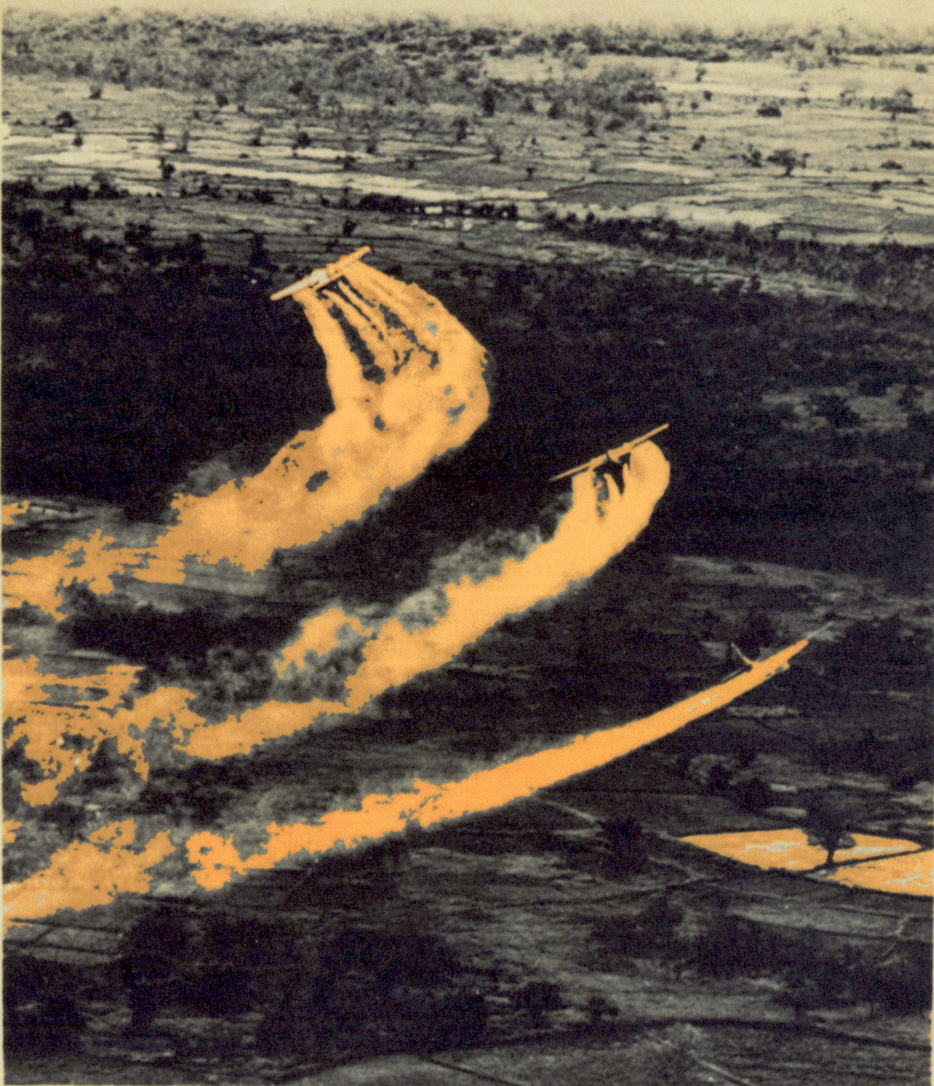

(FOR USE WITH TODAY'S FOCUS STORY ON AGENT ORANGE)
(NY 29-JAN. 21)--AGENT ORANGE DELIVERY--U.S. Air Force planes spray the defoliant chemical Agent Orange over a jungle area in South Vietnam in 1966 as part of a program to seek out Viet Cong. Thousands of ex-GIs are now insisting that the government test them to find out whether they carry in their bodies one of the world's deadliest chemicals, dioxin, which made up part of the Agent Orange.(AP LASERPHOTO)

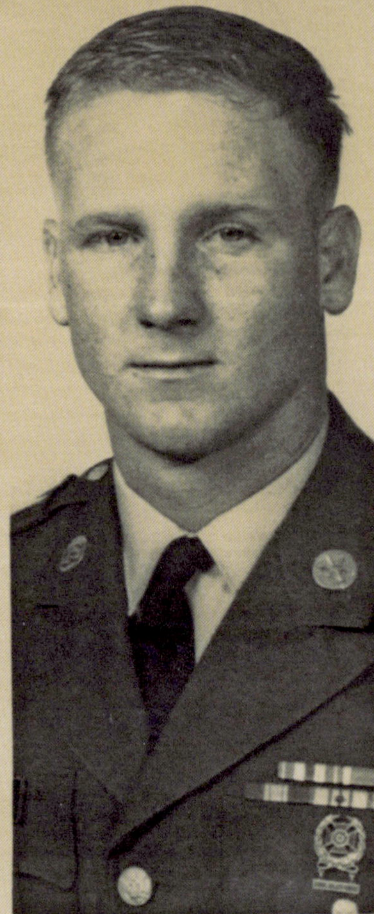

(NY53-July 12)SAYS AGENT ORANGE KILLING HIM--Sammy Lee Davis, 36-year-old West York, Ill. resident and winner of the Medal of Honor from the Vietnam War, told the House Veterans Affairs subcommittee on compensation on Tuesday in Washington that he believes he is dying from the effects of Agent Orange.(AP Laserphot (em32015fls)(EDS: This is a 1968 file photo)1983 Slug: Agent Orange

Documents d'archives.
Photo de gauche : © Bettmann, Getty Images, 2017.
Photos de droite : © Herbicide Assessment Commission, États-Unis.

Archival material:
Left photo: © Bettmann, Getty Images, 2017.
Right photo: © US Herbicide Assessment Commission.

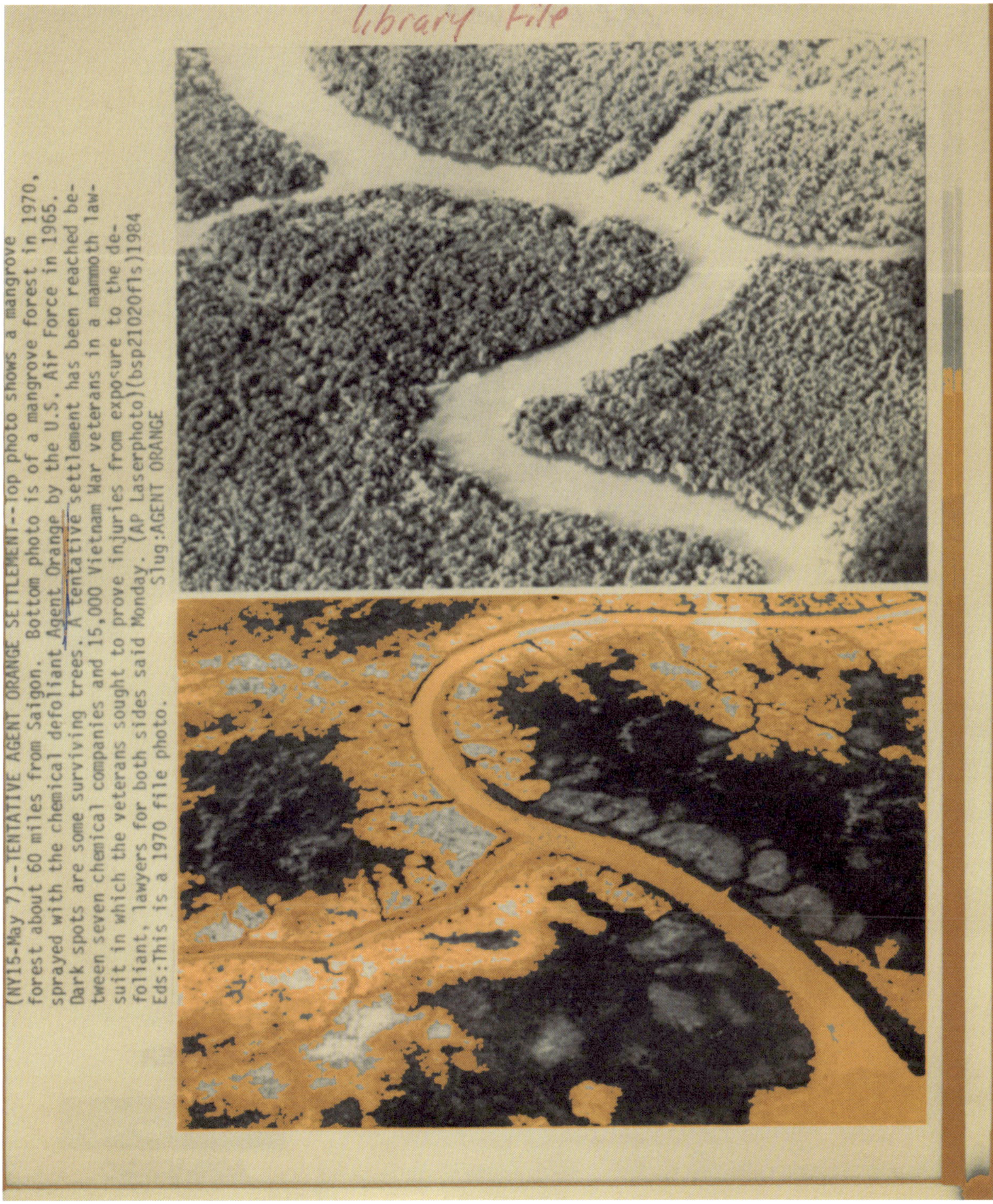

Heather Bowser se décrit comme une « enfant de l'Agent orange ». Elle est née avec plusieurs doigts et une partie de la jambe droite manquants. Son père, Bill Morris, s'est trouvé en contact avec l'Agent orange en combattant au Viêtnam.

Heather Bowser describes herself as a child of Agent Orange. She was born with several fingers and part of her right leg missing. Her father, Bill Morris, fought in Viet Nam and was exposed to Agent Orange.

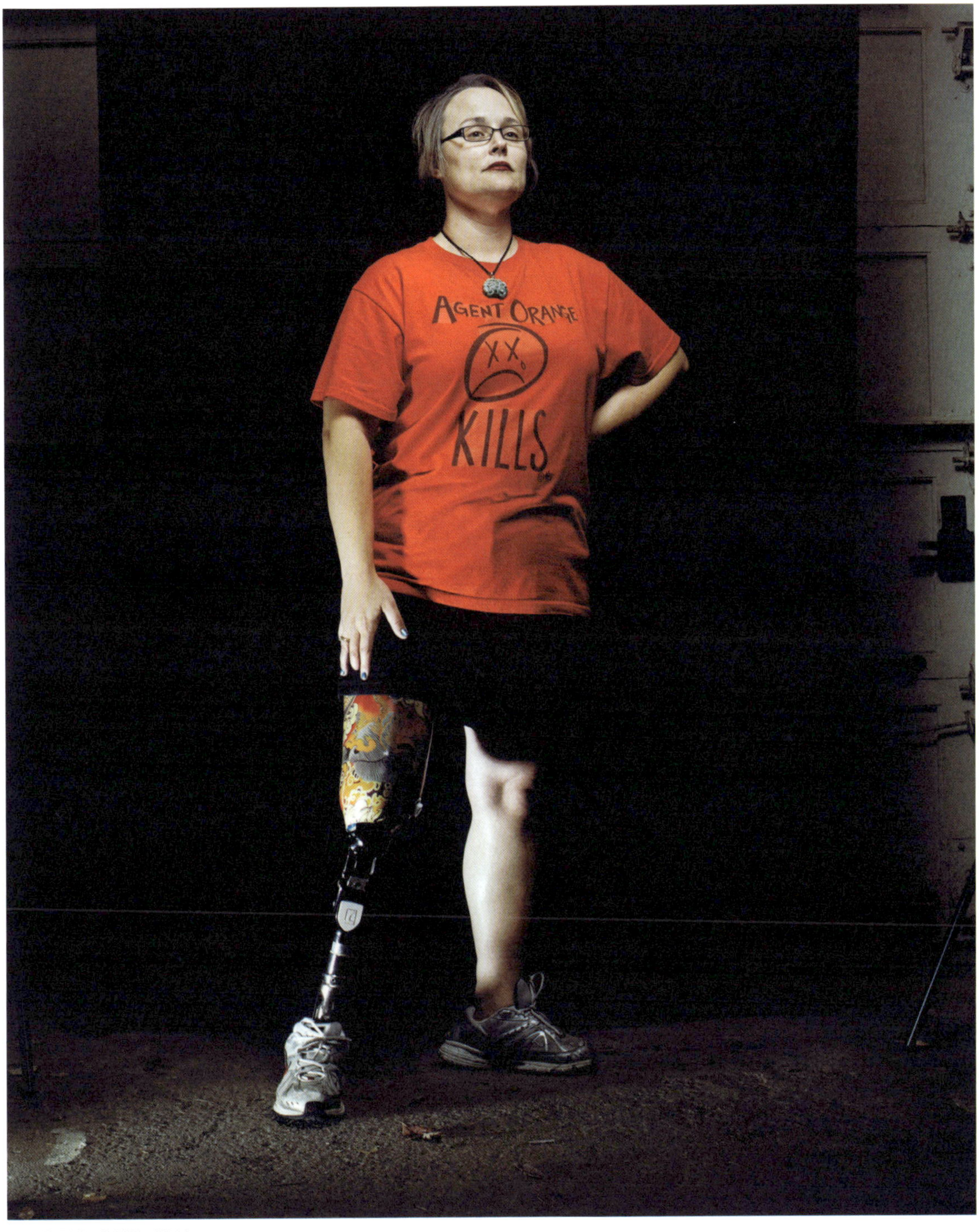

CANFIELD, OHIO. 2012

Heather Bowser montrant une photographie de son père. Bill Morris était en poste dans des zones aspergées d'Agent orange lors de son service. Ses nombreux problèmes de santé étaient directement liés à l'exposition à l'Agent orange. Il est mort le 11 mars 1998.

Heather Bowser holds a photograph of her father. Morris served in Viet Nam in areas that were sprayed with Agent Orange while he was stationed there. Morris's many health problems were directly linked to exposure to Agent Orange. Bill Morris passed away on March 11, 1998.

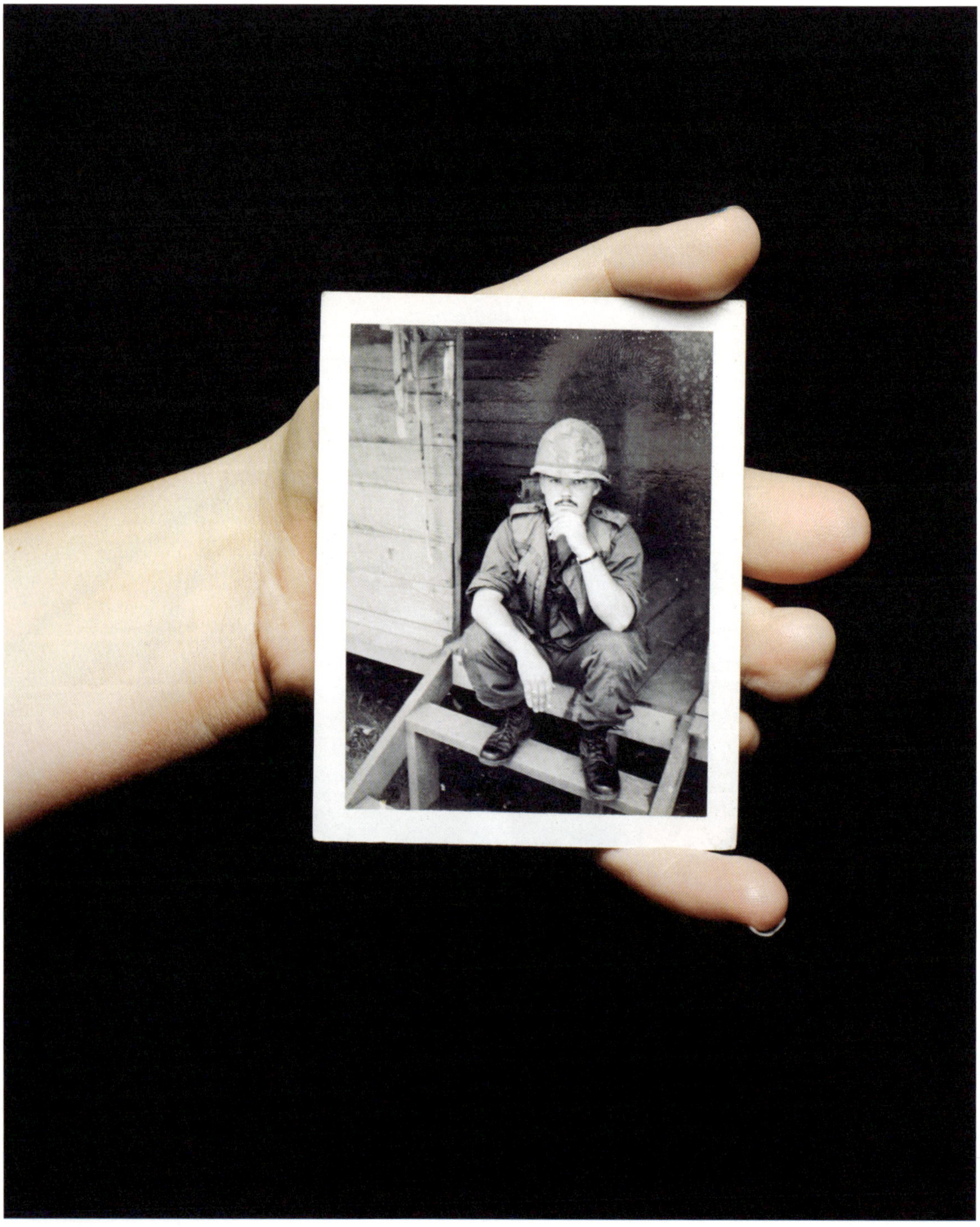

CANFIELD, OHIO. 2012

Photographie de Heather dans ses premières années.

Heather as an infant.

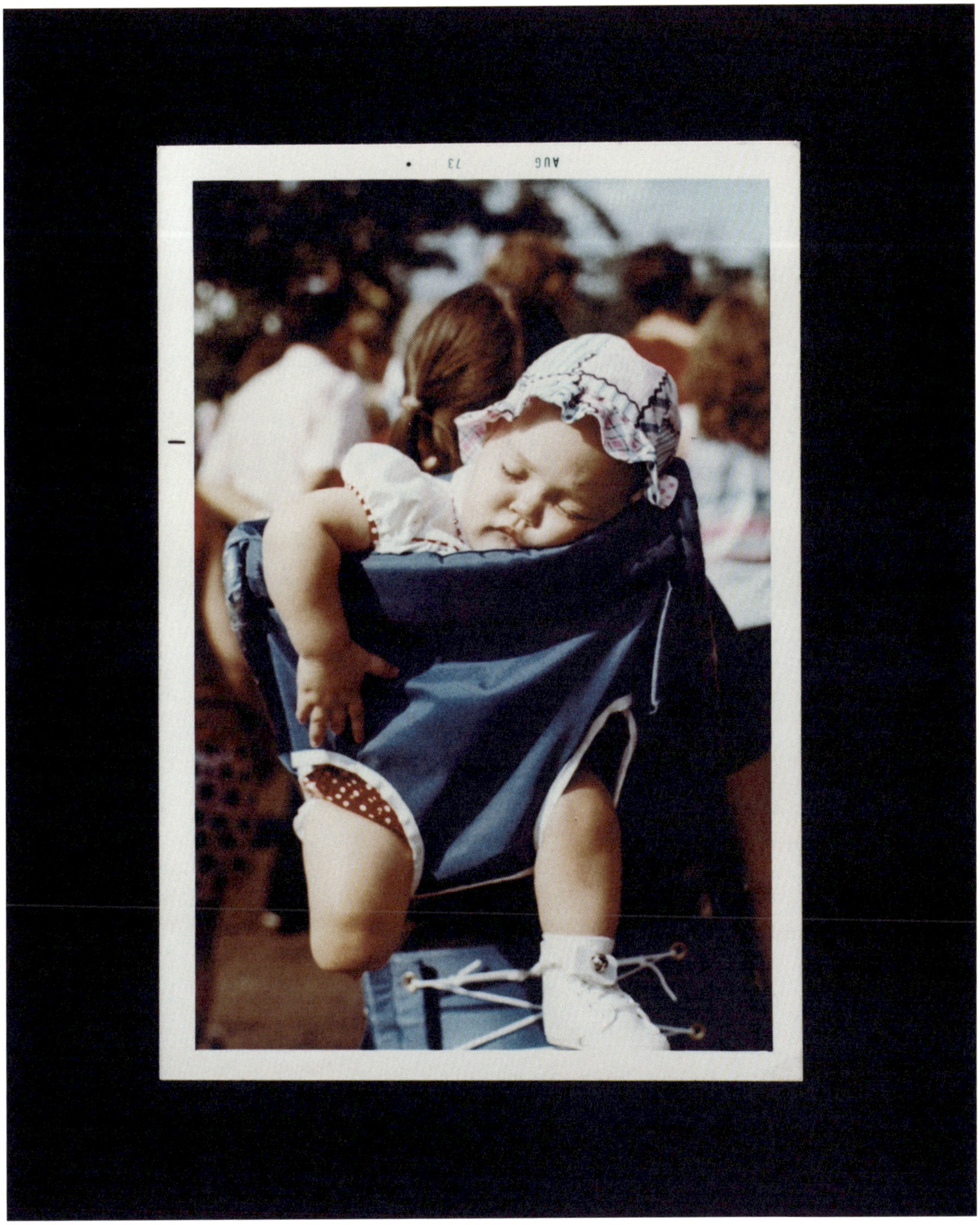

Kelly L. Derricks est la fille du vétéran Harry C. Mackel Jr., mort en 1982 à l'âge de 37 ans des suites de l'exposition à l'Agent orange lors de ses deux périodes de service au Viêtnam. Kelly est aux prises depuis toujours avec de graves problèmes de santé. Parmi une liste de 32 pathologies soupçonnées d'être liées aux effets intergénérationnels de l'Agent orange, elle souffre d'insuffisance rénale chronique, de la maladie de Crohn, d'insuffisance surrénalienne primaire, d'hyperplasie congénitale des surrénales, de cystite interstitielle et de discopathie dégénérative. En 2000, Kelly a été reconnue invalide permanente et a dû cesser son activité de psychothérapeute.

Kelly L. Derricks is the daughter of deceased Viet Nam veteran Harry C. Mackel Jr. Her father died in 1982 at 37, after having been exposed to Agent Orange while serving two tours in Viet Nam. Kelly has battled severe health issues all her life. Some of her illnesses, presumed to be associated with the intergenerational effects of Agent Orange, include chronic kidney disease, Crohn's disease, Addison's disease, congenital adrenal hyperplasia, interstitial cystitis and degenerative disk disease. The complete list consists of 32 illnesses. In 2000, Kelly became permanently disabled and had to retire from her job as a psychiatric therapist.

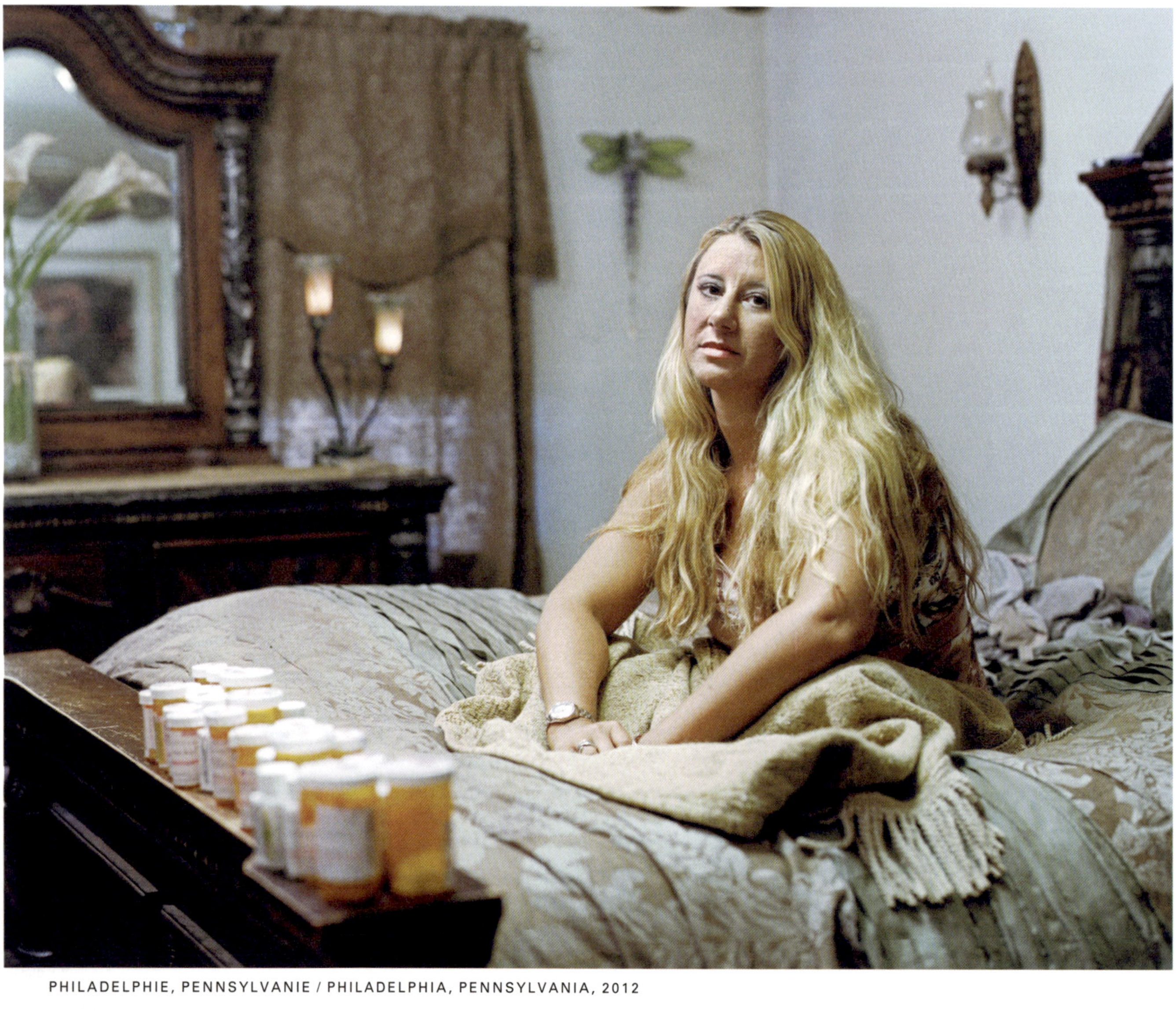

PHILADELPHIE, PENNSYLVANIE / PHILADELPHIA, PENNSYLVANIA, 2012

Le traitement quotidien de Kelly.

Kelly's daily medication.

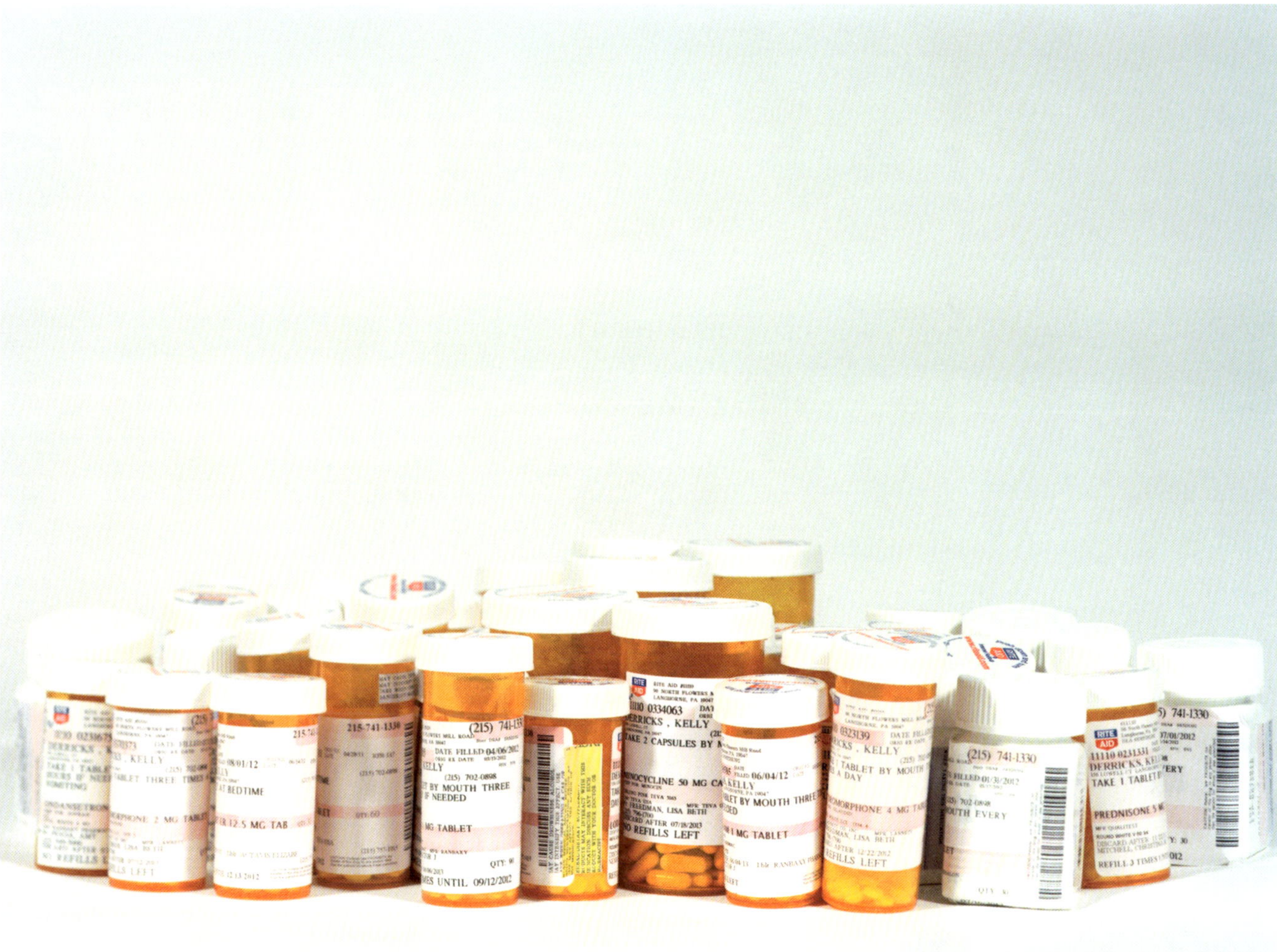

Harry C. Mackel Jr., père de Kelly.

Harry C. Mackel Jr., Kelly's father.

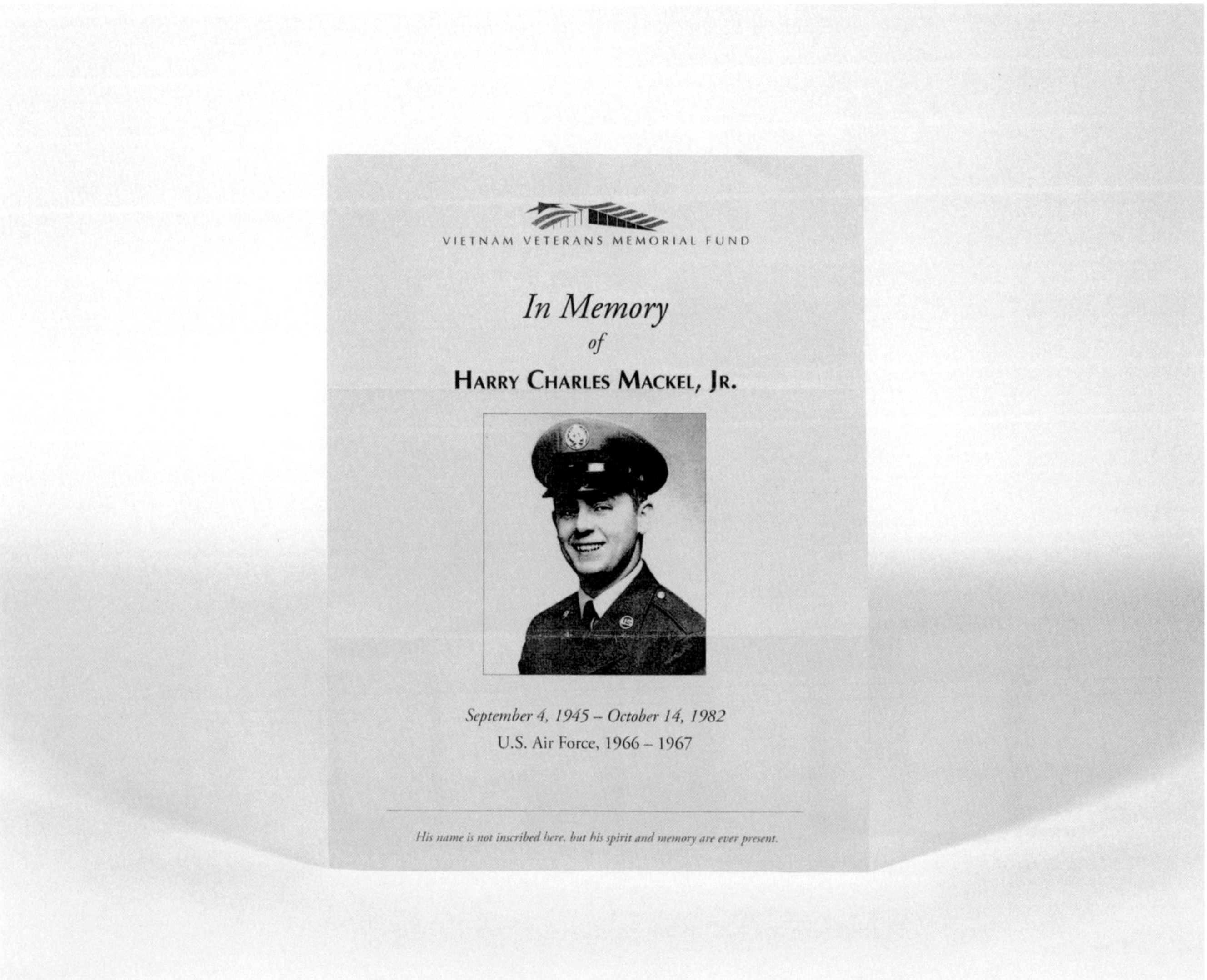

PHILADELPHIE, PENNSYLVANIE / PHILADELPHIA, PENNSYLVANIA, 2012

Lettre écrite par Kelly enfant à son père :
« Papa, j'espèr que tu sai que je sui triste. Je veu pas que tu meure. Mon Dieu, prend soin de mon papa. »

A letter Kelly wrote to her father as a child.

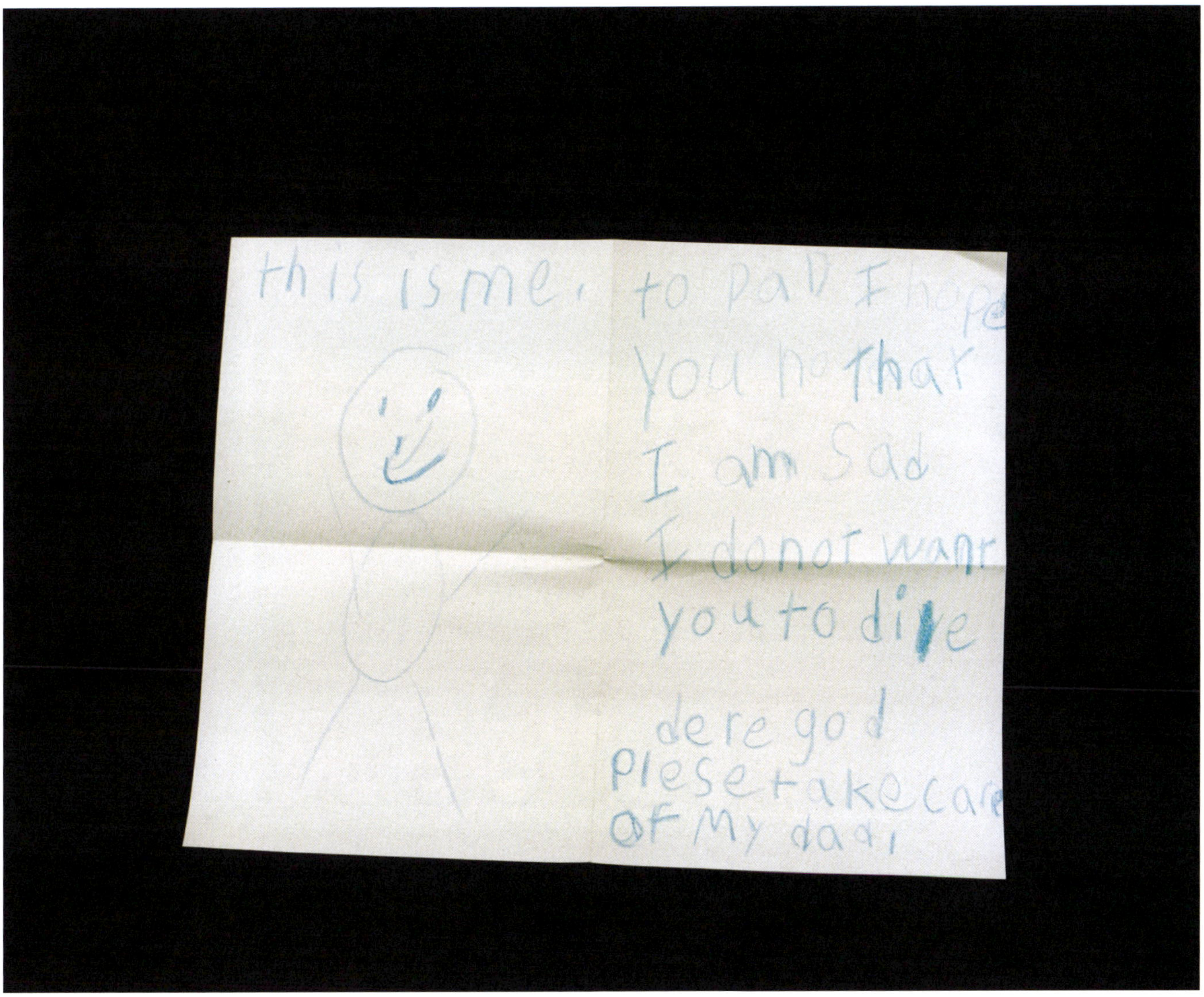

this is me.

to pa I hope
you no that
I am sad
I do not want
you to die

dere god
plese take care
of my dad.

À l'hôpital obstétrique Tû Dû (Hô Chí Minh-Ville, Viêtnam), des embryons contaminés par l'Agent orange sont conservés dans des bocaux en vue de recherches scientifiques.

At Tû Dû Obstetrics Hospital, Ho Chi Minh City, Viet Nam, some Agent Orange affected infants were saved in glass containers for science.

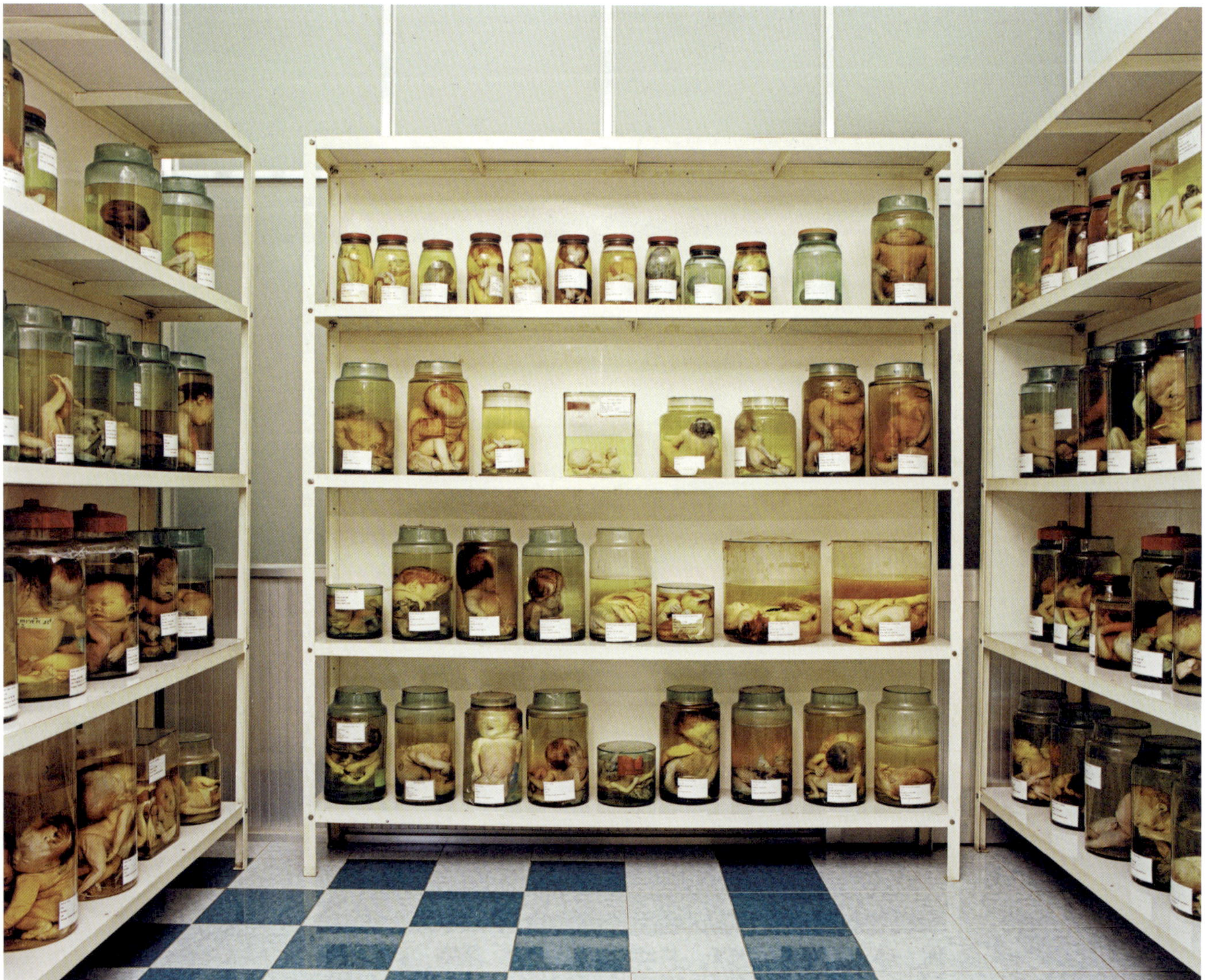

HÔPITAL OBSTÉTRIQUE TÛ DÛ. HÔ CHÍ MINH-VILLE, VIÊTNAM. 2015
TÛ DÛ OBSTETRICS HOSPITAL, HO CHI MINH CITY, VIET NAM, 2015

Nguyên Thanh Hiêp Nam, 34 ans. Multiples troubles et malformations génétiques.

Nguyên Thanh Hiêp Nam, 34 years old. Multiple genetic disorders and malformations.

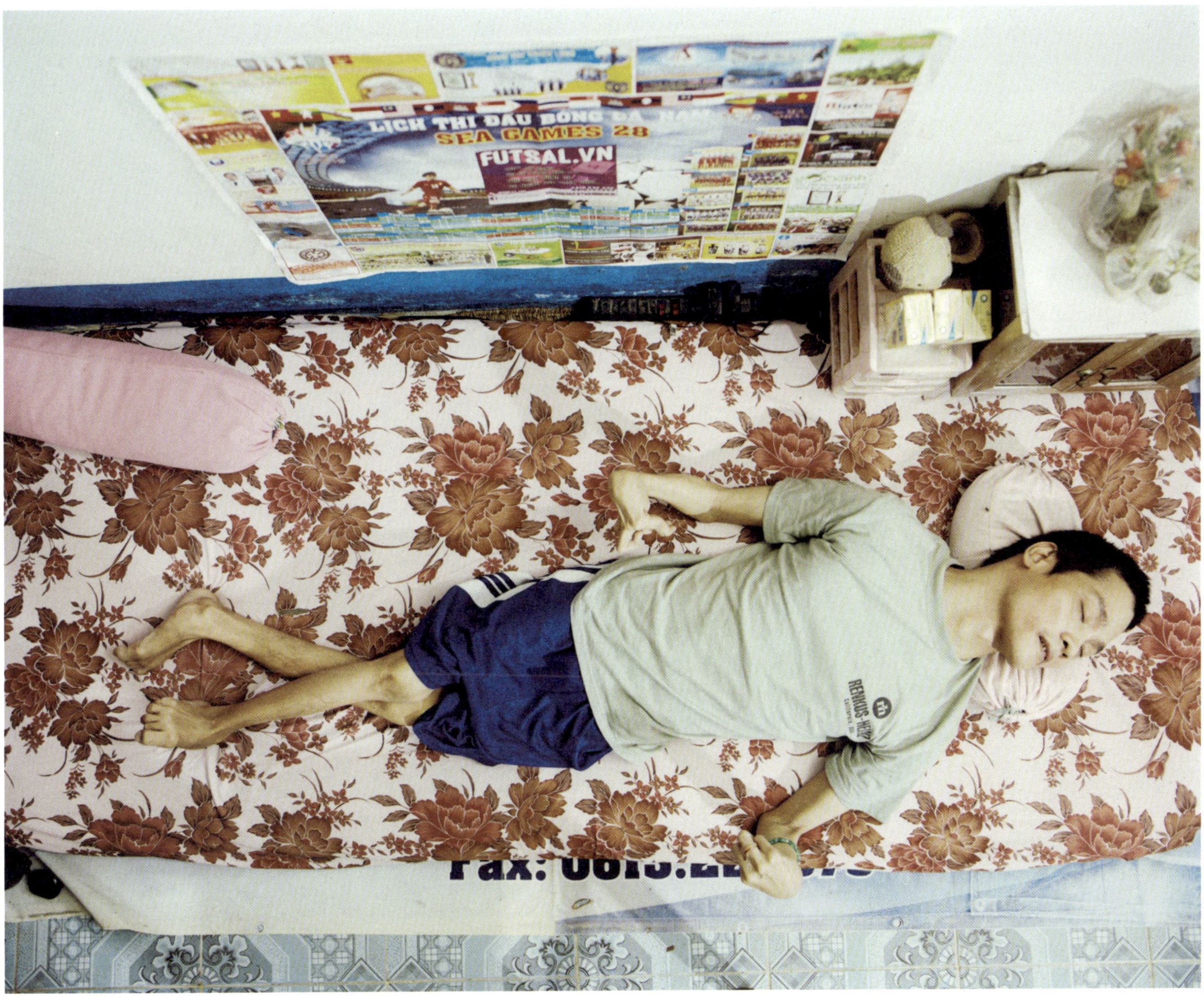

QUARTIER TÂN PHONG, BIÊN HÒA, ĐÔNG NAI, VIÊTNAM. 2015
TÂN PHONG WARD, BIÊN HOÀ, ĐÔNG NAI, VIET NAM, 2015

Nguyên Lê Phu'o'ng Quýnh dans ses premières années.

Nguyên Lê Phu'o'ng Quỳnh as an infant.

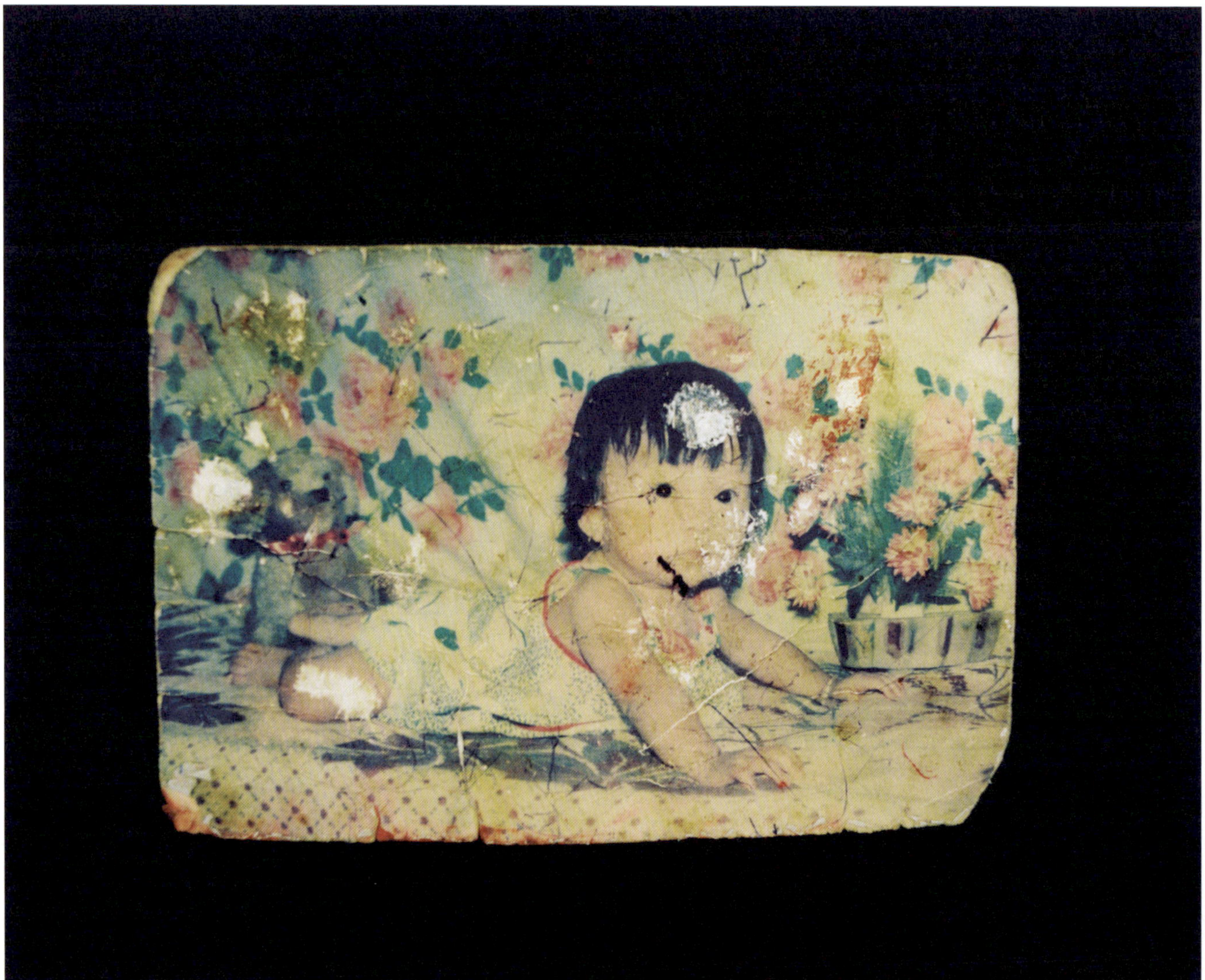

QUARTIER TÂN PHONG, BIÊN HÒA, ĐÔNG NAI, VIÊTNAM. 2015
TÂN PHONG WARD, BIÊN HOÀ, ĐÔNG NAI, VIET NAM, 2015

Nguyên Lê Phu'o'ng Quýnh à 27 ans. Multiples troubles et malformations génétiques.

Nguyên Lê Phu'o'ng Quỳnh, 27 years old. Multiple genetic disorders and malformations.

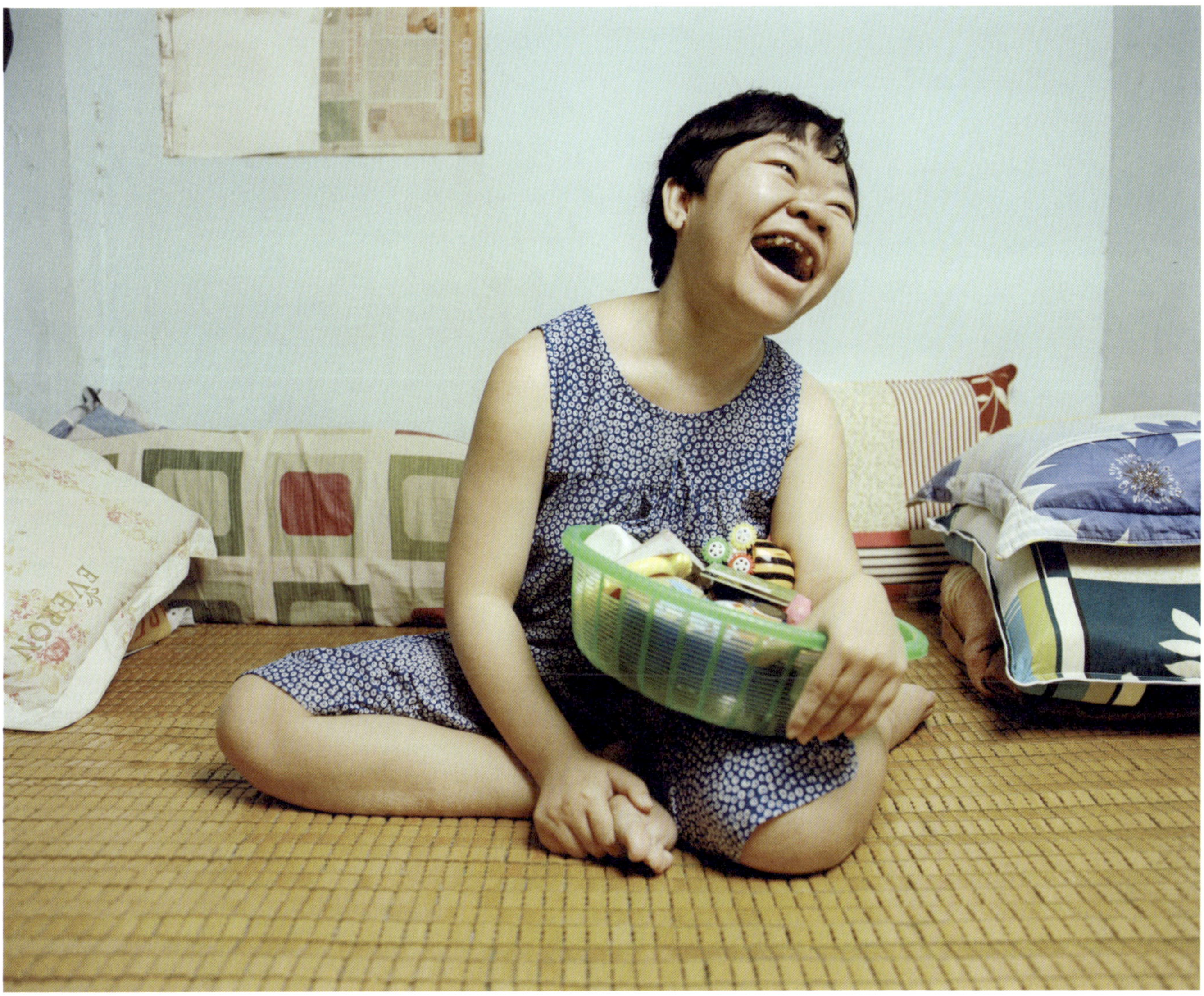

QUARTIER TÂN PHONG, BIÊN HÒA, ĐÔNG NAI, VIÊTNAM. 2015
TÂN PHONG WARD, BIÊN HOÀ, ĐÔNG NAI, VIET NAM, 2015

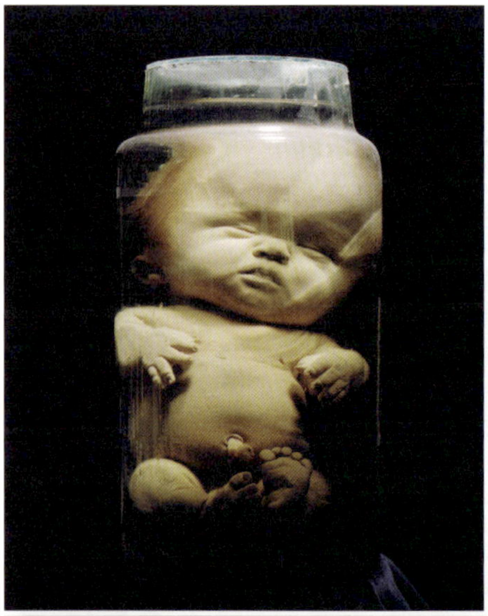

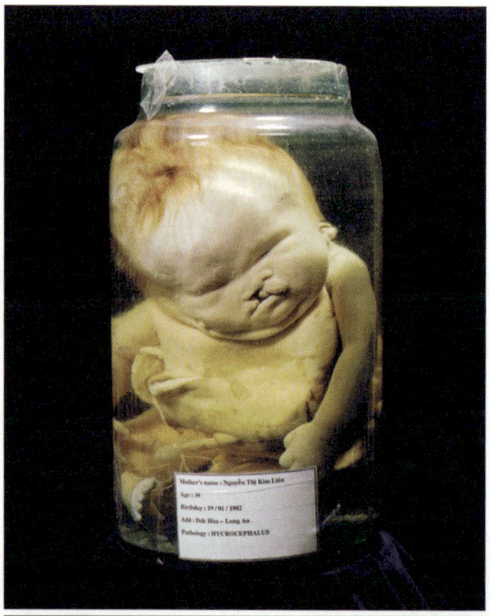
Mother's name : Nguyễn Thị Kim Liên
Birthday : 19 / 01 / 1982
Add : Đức Hòa – Long An
Pathology : HYCROCEPHALUS

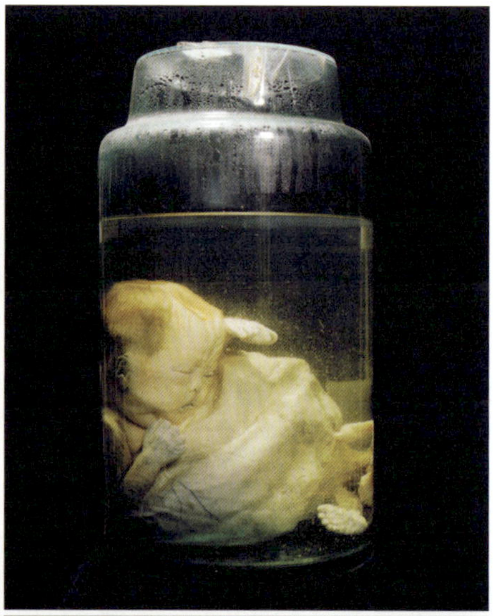

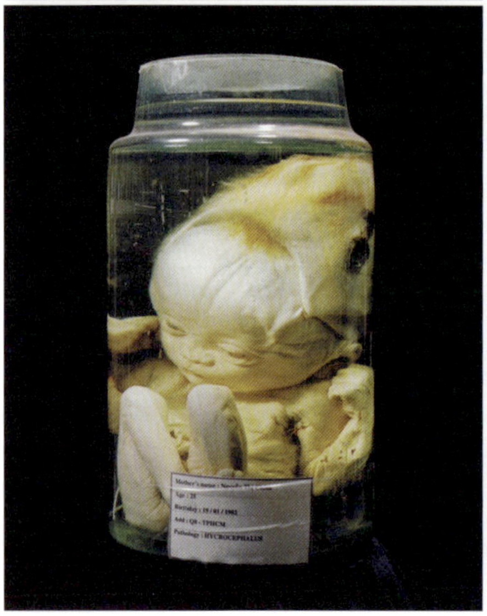
Add : Q8 - TPHCM
Pathology : HYCROCEPHALUS

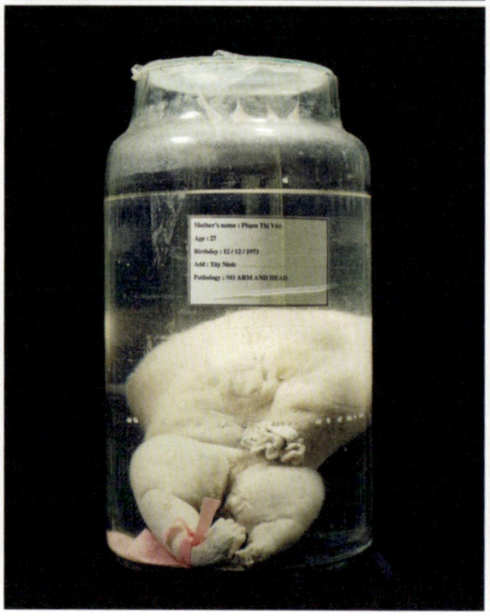
Mother's name : Phạm Thị Vân
Age : 27
Birthday : 12 / 12 / 1973
Add : Tây Ninh
Pathology : NO ARM AND HEAD

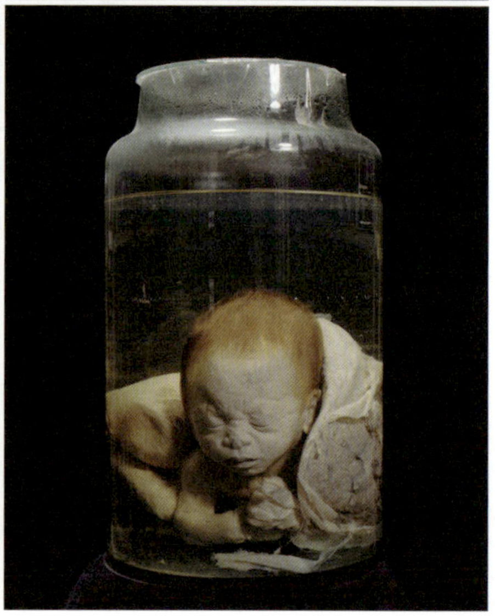

Bocaux contenant des fœtus malformés à la suite des opérations de guerre à base d'herbicide (Agent orange) menées par les États-Unis. Hôpital obstétrique Tû Dû, Hô Chí Minh-Ville.

View of glass jars at Tû Dû Hospital that contain fetuses deformed as a result of the United States' herbicidal warfare (Agent Orange) program during the Viet Nam War.

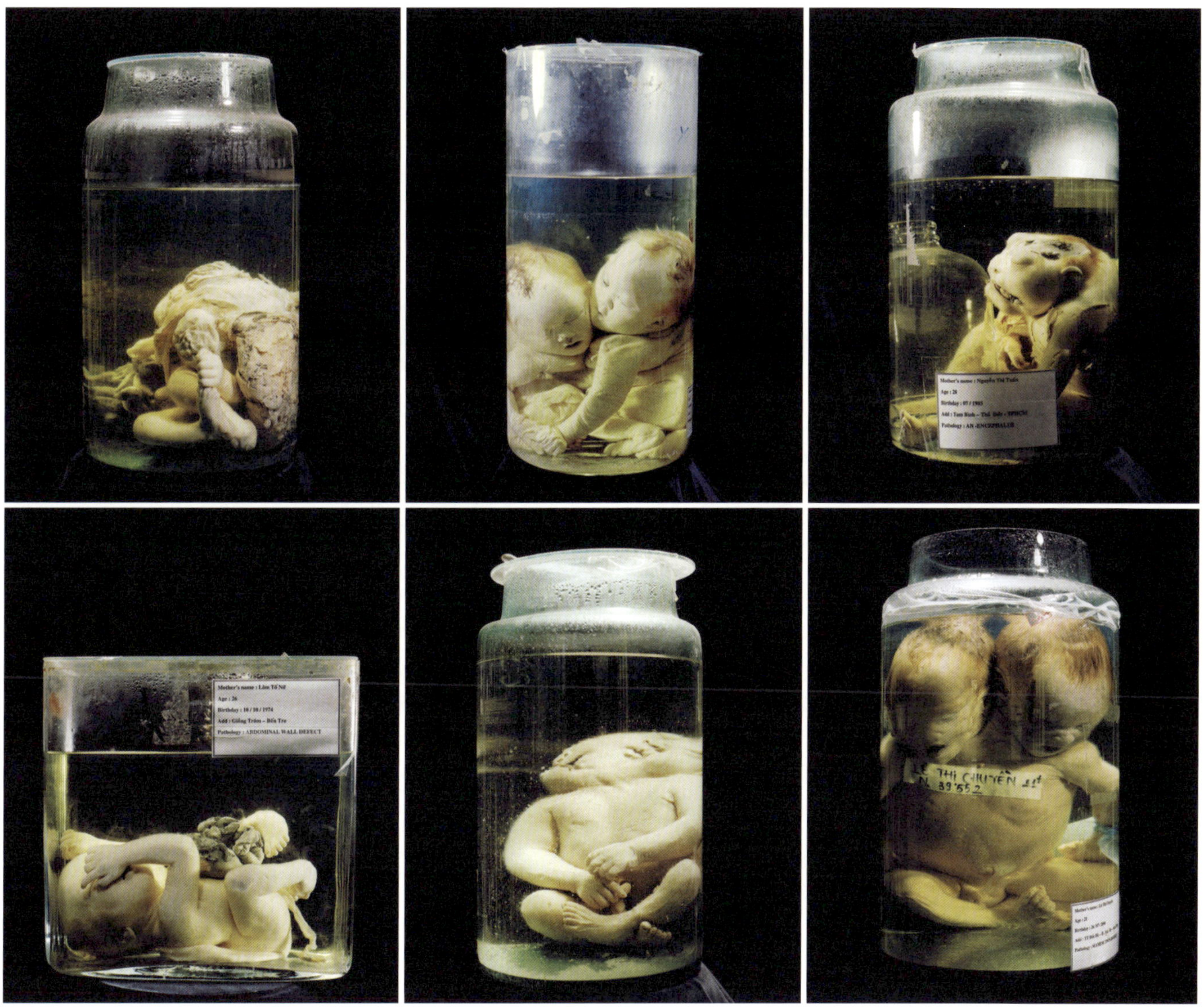

HÔPITAL OBSTÉTRIQUE TÛ DÛ. HÔ CHÍ MINH-VILLE, VIÊTNAM. 2015
TÛ DÛ OBSTETRICS HOSPITAL, HO CHI MINH CITY, VIET NAM, 2015

Th'o'ng Sinh, 14 ans. Multiples troubles et malformations génétiques.

Th'o'ng Sinh, 14 years old. Multiple genetic disorders and malformations.

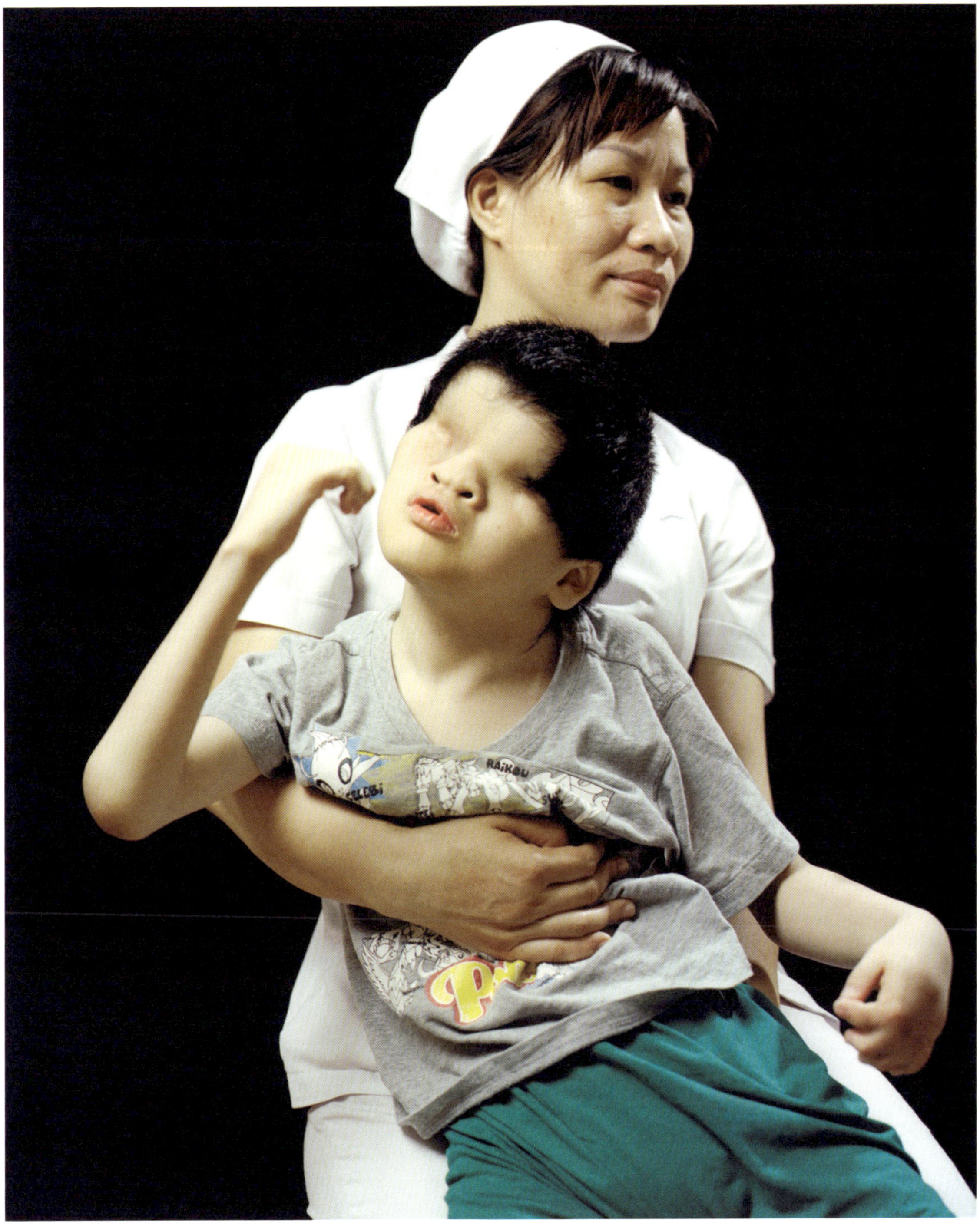

HÔPITAL OBSTÉTRIQUE TÛ DÛ. HÔ CHÍ MINH-VILLE, VIÊTNAM. 2015
TÛ DÛ OBSTETRICS HOSPITAL, HO CHI MINH CITY, VIET NAM, 2015

Thu Huyen, 8 ans. Multiples troubles et malformations génétiques.

Thu Huyen, eight years old. Multiple genetic disorders and malformations.

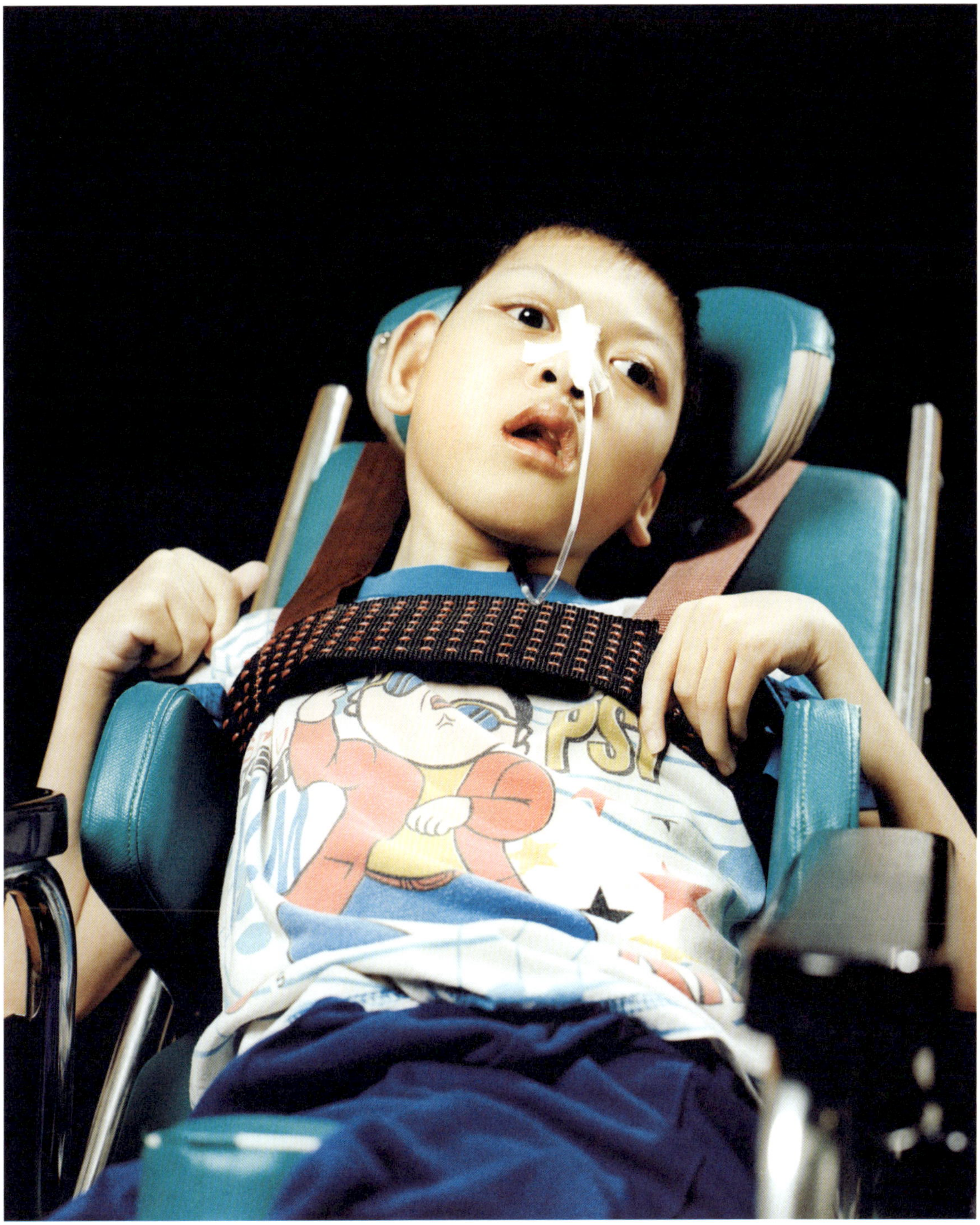

HÔPITAL OBSTÉTRIQUE TÛ DÛ. HÔ CHÍ MINH-VILLE, VIÊTNAM. 2015
TÛ DÛ OBSTETRICS HOSPITAL, HO CHI MINH CITY, VIET NAM, 2015

Minh So'n, 17 ans. Multiples troubles et malformations génétiques.

Minh So'n, 17 years old. Multiple genetic disorders and malformations.

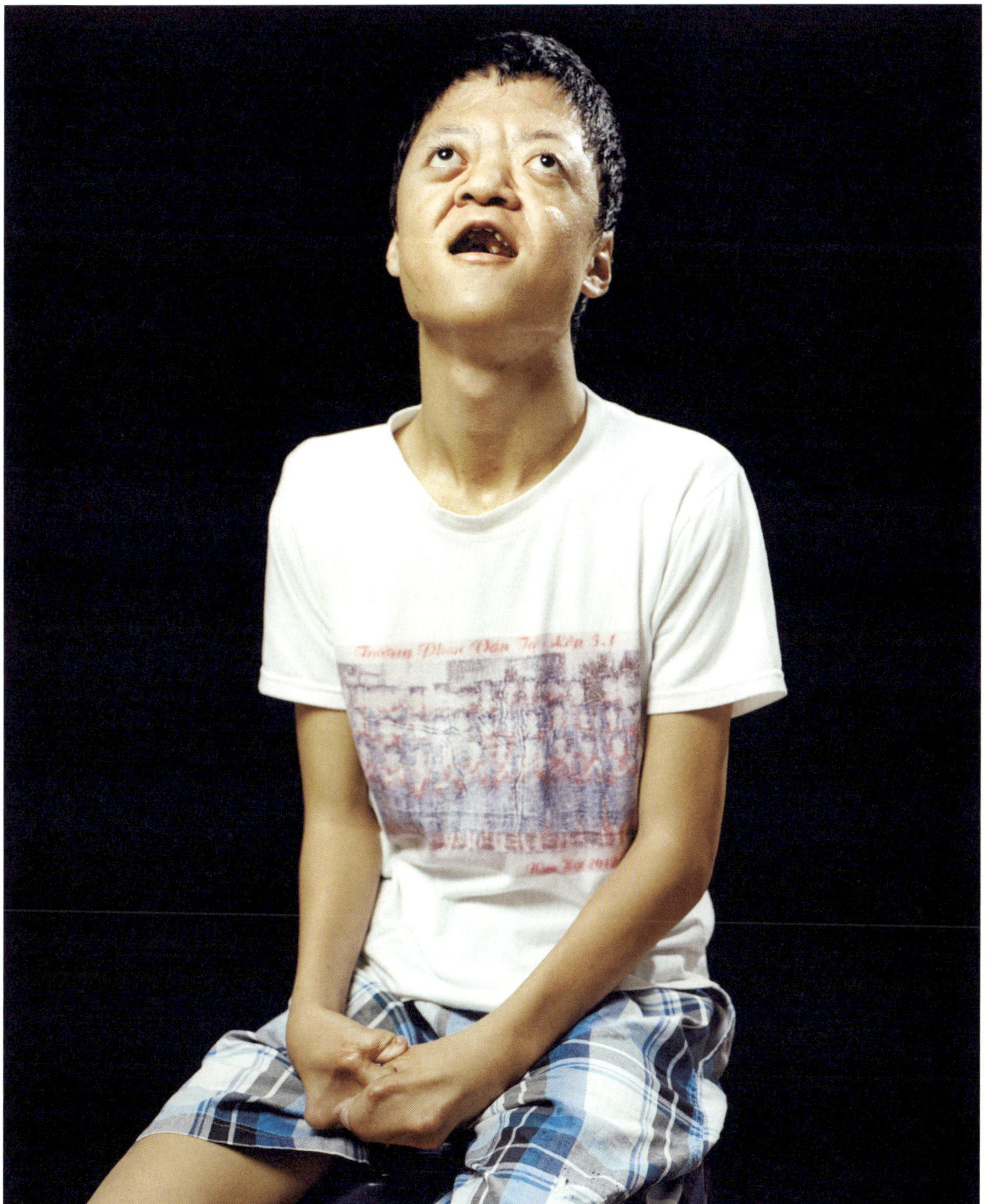

HÔPITAL OBSTÉTRIQUE TÛ DÛ. HÔ CHÍ MINH-VILLE, VIÊTNAM. 2015
TÛ DÛ OBSTETRICS HOSPITAL, HO CHI MINH CITY, VIET NAM, 2015

Thuỷ Linh dans ses premières années.

Thuỳ Linh as an infant.

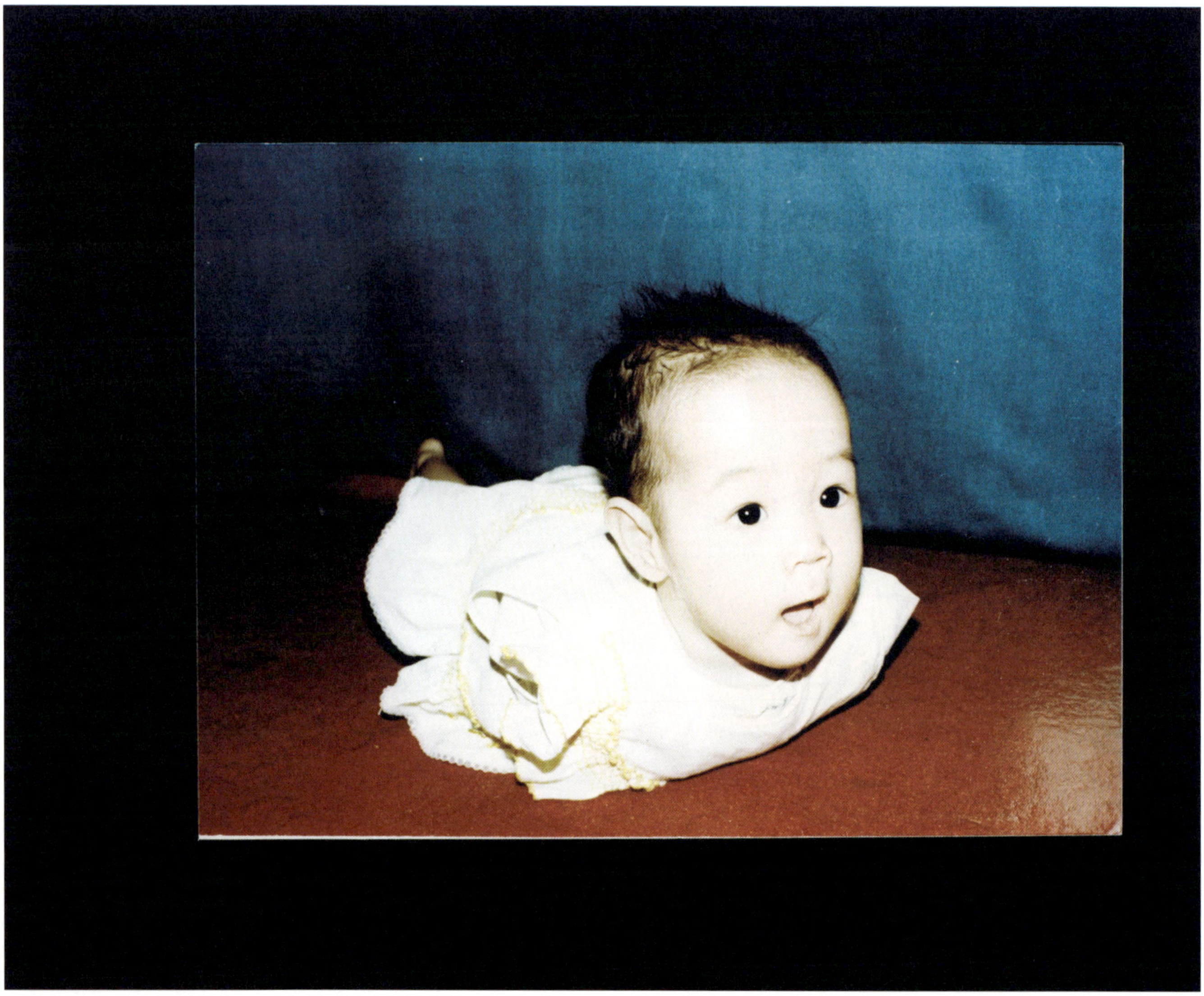

HÔ CHÍ MINH-VILLE, VIÊTNAM. 2015
HO CHI MINH CITY, VIET NAM, 2015

Thuỷ Linh, à 21 ans. Troisième génération de victimes de l'Agent orange souffrant de malformation génétique ; née sans bras. Thuỷ Linh a terminé le lycée il y a deux ans. Elle a envoyé des demandes d'inscription à plusieurs universités, mais aucune ne l'a acceptée à cause de son handicap. Sa mère a fini par lui trouver une école qui voulait bien d'elle. Elle a fini sa formation en design il y a quelques mois. Elle est actuellement à la recherche d'un emploi. Elle est entrée à l'hôpital obstétrique Tû Dû à l'âge de 3 ans et y est restée jusqu'à ses 18 ans.

Thuỳ Linh, 21 years old. Third-generation Agent Orange victim with genetic malformation, born without arms. Thuỳ Linh finished high school two years ago. She applied to many universities to study but most of them didn't accept her because of her missing arms. Her mother finally found a school willing to admit her. She finished her course in design a few months ago. Currently, she is looking for a suitable job. She went to Tû Dû Obstetrics Hospital when she was three years old and stayed until she was 18.

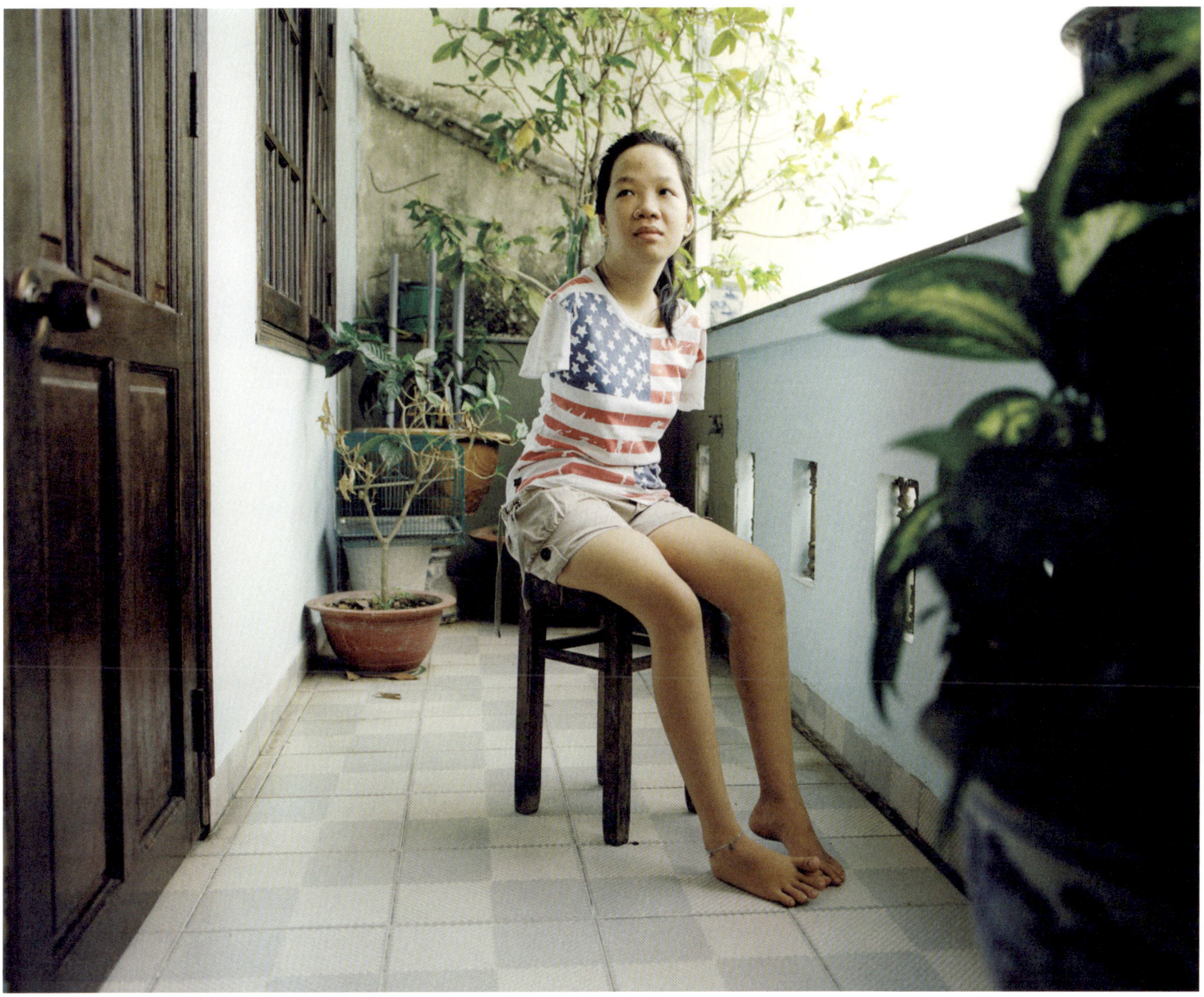

HÔ CHÍ MINH-VILLE, VIÊTNAM. 2015
HO CHI MINH CITY, VIET NAM, 2015

III.

« Dans un nombre croissant de cas, les gestionnaires de l'USDA (ministère de l'Agriculture des États-Unis) interfèrent, intimident, harcèlent et, parfois, punissent les scientifiques de la fonction publique d'avoir fait des travaux qui ont des conséquences néfastes pour l'industrie et pourraient avoir des répercussions directes sur les politiques et la réglementation. »

Jeff Ruch, directeur exécutif Employés publics pour la responsabilité environnementale

"In a growing number of cases, USDA (US Department of Agriculture) managers are interfering, intimidating, harassing and in some cases punishing civil service scientists for doing work that has inconvenient implications for industry and could have direct policy/regulatory ramifications."

Jeff Ruch, Executive Director, Public Employees for Environmental Responsibility

Monsanto® City : Un Paradis Non Régulé

Monsanto® City: An Unregulated Paradise

Le 10 janvier 1979, un train déraille à Sturgeon, Missouri. Il contient 70 000 litres de chlorophénol qui se déversent dans la nature. La cargaison provient de l'usine de Monsanto® à Sauget. Fondée en 1926 sous le nom de Monsanto® City, Sauget[28] se situe dans l'Illinois, sur la rive du Missouri face à Saint Louis, ville natale de Monsanto®. La compagnie veut bénéficier d'un lieu à faibles taxes et à règles environnementales souples pour implanter ses usines chimiques, les dispositions légales étant élaborées par les pouvoirs locaux. Monsanto® s'offre ainsi une zone de non-droit.
« The village », d'une superficie de 4,6 miles carrés — 12 kilomètres carrés —, est aujourd'hui d'une désolation sans bornes où l'empreinte de Monsanto® ne se limite plus aux noms des rues. 153 habitants[29] vivent au milieu d'usines désaffectées et de terrains vagues contaminés, inhalant un air empoisonné décrit dans *Sauget Wind* (Uncle Tupelo, 1992). Selon le maire, Richard Sauget, Monsanto® City a été conçue exclusivement pour être « la décharge de Monsanto® », « un égout » à ciel ouvert[30]. Car, pendant des décennies, Monsanto® y déverse sans honte ni culpabilité ses déchets chimiques et toxiques issus principalement de ses productions de PCB[31]. Monsanto® en effet détient le monopole des PCB aux États-Unis, et l'usine de Sauget est le premier producteur national jusqu'à leur interdiction en 1977. Certes, la décontamination des PCB est délicate : elle se fait par combustion à très haute température dans des incinérateurs. En parallèle, il faut traiter les émissions de dioxine qui s'opèrent durant l'intervention. Elle a surtout un coût. Mais Monsanto®, en toute connaissance de cause, ne prend aucune précaution.
En 1982, l'EPA, l'Agence américaine de protection de l'environnement, réalise des prélèvements dans et autour de la Dead Creek et confirme la présence de plus de 25 produits chimiques[32]. En 2001, Sauget est inscrite sur la liste du Superfund[33] avec deux zones de dépollution (une près de la Dead Creek et une autre le long du Missouri) auxquelles s'ajoute en 2008 celle de l'usine Solutia®, filiale chimique de Monsanto® créée en 1997[34].
« Sauget est un désastre environnemental », déplore Richard Sauget. Après l'accident de Sturgeon en 1979, les prélèvements effectués par l'EPA démontrent que la cargaison du train en provenance de Sauget contient de la dioxine. 65 habitants de Sturgeon portent alors plainte contre Monsanto®. Le procès « Kemner *vs* Monsanto® » s'ouvre le 22 février 1984 et se termine le 22 octobre 1987. C'est le plus long procès civil de l'histoire des États-Unis. Pendant trois ans et demi, 182 témoins et experts se succèdent à la barre et plus de 6 000 documents sont présentés. Si Monsanto® veut établir son sérieux avec ce procès, des voix affirment que la compagnie souhaite dissuader les plaintes futures…
Rex Carr, l'avocat des plaignants, mène une enquête minutieuse qui aboutit à des découvertes ahurissantes : avant 1980, Monsanto® pouvait réduire, voire éliminer, la dioxine présente dans ses PCB en distillant les chlorophénols. De même, elle aurait pu tester et retirer de la vente ses lots contaminés.
Enfin, les études du Dr Raymond Suskind commandées par Monsanto® constituent un réel drame humain. Les risques sanitaires de la catastrophe de Nitro (1949) sont dissimulés pendant trente-cinq ans[35]. Les trois études publiées entre 1980 et 1984 dans des revues scientifiques sont allégrement falsifiées[36]. En se basant sur elles, Monsanto® balaye aisément la *class action* des vétérans du Viêtnam en 1984[37].
Les révélations du procès attestent que Monsanto® connaît depuis longtemps la toxicité des produits qu'il fabrique de 1930 à la fin des années 1970 : PCB, dioxine, 2,4,5-T et Agent orange. Malgré l'interdiction du 2,4,5-T en 1970 et des PCB en 1977 aux États-Unis, les effets sur l'homme et sur l'environnement des substances chimiques créées par Monsanto® subsistent. L'EPA établit en 1988 que la dioxine est un cancérigène possible[38]. En 1996, l'OMS classe la dioxine TCDD parmi les cancérigènes pour l'homme, tout comme les PCB en 2013. Aujourd'hui, 10 % des PCB produits en 1929 sont encore présents dans l'environnement[39].
En 1987, le procès « Kemner *vs* Monsanto® » se termine d'une manière cocasse pour ne pas dire tragique : les plaignants de Sturgeon, ne pouvant pas prouver le lien entre leurs problèmes de santé et l'accident de 1979, reçoivent chacun 1 dollar symbolique de dommages et intérêts. Monsanto® est condamné à 16 millions de dommages punitifs pour son irresponsabilité devant les risques sanitaires liés à la dioxine. Pourtant, la compagnie gagne en appel en 1991[40]. Monsanto® se soustrait de nouveau à ses responsabilités humaines et environnementales.
Toutefois, l'accident de Sturgeon marque un tournant dans l'histoire de Monsanto®. L'opinion publique est maintenant consciente des dangers de ses productions chimiques, dangers qu'il a volontairement masqués pendant des décennies. Pense-t-il redorer son blason en se tournant dorénavant vers l'agroalimentaire ?

28 Ce nom date de 1968 en mémoire de son premier maire, Leo Sauget.
29 Recensement de juin 2014.
30 Scott Beauchamp, « A Short Way to Hell: in Sauget, Illinois, Poisons Mean Profit », *Belt Magazine*, 23 septembre 2015. Richard Sauget est l'arrière-petit-fils de Leo Sauget.
31 Dès 1937, Monsanto® connaît les risques humains et environnementaux liés à la production de PCB (cf. chapitre i).
32 Casey Bukro, « Report Hardly Draws Angry Sniff », *Chicago Tribune*, 5 juillet 1988.
33 Nom donné au CERCLA (Comprehensive Environmental Response, Compensation and Liability Act) de 1980, loi fédérale établie pour nettoyer et réhabiliter les sites les plus pollués.
34 Site de l'EPA : www.epa.gov (région 5 : Sauget Area 1, Sauget Area 2 et Sauget-Solutia Inc.).
35 Cf. chapitre ii ; Raymond R. Suskind, *op. cit.*
36 Marilyn Fingerhut, « Cancer Mortality in Workers Exposed to 2,3,7,8 Tetrachlorodibenzo-p-dioxin », *New England Journal of Medicine*, vol. 34, n° 4, 24 janvier 1991 ; Anthony B. Miller, « Public Health and Hazardous Wastes », *Environmental Epidemiology*, vol. 1, National Academy Press, Washington, 1991.
37 Cf. chapitre II.
38 Cancérigène de groupe 2B selon la classification du CIRC, Centre international de recherche sur le cancer (OMS).
39 J. Maherou, S. Norest et L. Ferrer, « PCB : quels risques pour ma santé ? », ASEF, 16 juin 2014.
40 « Kemner *vs* Monsanto Co. », 22 juillet 1991, www.leagle.com.

On January 10, 1979, a train containing 70,000 liters of chlorophenol derails in Sturgeon, Missouri, its contents spilling into the surrounding environment. The cargo traces back to the Monsanto® plant in Sauget.
Founded in 1926 under the name "Monsanto® City," Sauget,[28] Illinois, is situated on the Missouri river across from Saint Louis, Monsanto®'s founding city. The company selects the location for the construction of chemical factories in order to take advantage of the region's low taxes and flexible environmental restrictions, the legal provisions having been drawn up by local authorities. In this way, Monsanto® creates what is effectively a no-man's land, a city subject only to its own rule of law.
Today, the "village," an area of 4.6 miles² or 12 KM², is a borderless wasteland where Monsanto®'s legacy is no longer limited to the names of the streets. One hundred fifty-three residents[29] live among the derelict factories and contaminated vacant lots, inhaling the noxious air described in "Sauget Wind" (Uncle Tupelo, 1992). According to mayor Richard Sauget, "Monsanto® City" was conceived exclusively as Monsanto®'s "dumping ground," an open-air "sewer."[30] For decades, it was here that, showing neither remorse nor accountability, Monsanto® discharged its toxic chemical waste, originating primarily from PCB production.[31] Monsanto® held an effective monopoly on PCBs in the United States, and the Sauget plant was the nation's primary production site until PCBs were banned in 1977. PCB decontamination is indeed a delicate operation: the product must be incinerated at extremely high temperatures, and dioxin emissions released during the incineration process must be treated. The costs are high. But Monsanto®, with full knowledge of the effects, took no such precautions.
In 1982, the Environmental Protection Agency, carrying out sampling analysis in and around Dead Creek, confirms the presence of over 25 chemical pollutants.[32] In 2001, Sauget is registered on the Superfund[33] list. Two decontamination zones are identified (one near Dead Creek, the other along the Missouri River), to which the Solutia plant, a Monsanto® subsidiary created in 1997,[34] is added in 2008.
"Sauget is an environmental disaster," deplores Richard Sauget. Following the accident in Sturgeon in 1979, samples taken by the EPA reveal that the shipment originating in Sauget contained dioxin. Sixty-five inhabitants of Sturgeon initiate legal proceedings against Monsanto®. The Kemner v. Monsanto® trial begins on February 22, 1984, and ends on October 22, 1987. It is the longest civil jury trial in American history. Over a period of three-and-a-half years, 182 witnesses and experts address the court, and over 6,000 documents are presented. Monsanto® shows that it takes the case seriously, while discouraging future complaints.
The meticulous investigation by Rex Carr, the plaintiffs' attorney, leads to bewildering discoveries. Before 1980, Monsanto® had the ability to reduce and even eliminate dioxins present in its PCBs through the distillation of chlorophenols. Furthermore, it could have tested and pulled its contaminated lots from the market. Finally, the studies commissioned by Monsanto® and undertaken by Dr. Raymond Suskind constitute a veritable human tragedy. The health risks of the Nitro catastrophe of 1949 were covered up for 35 years.[35] The three studies published between 1980 and 1984 in the scientific reviews were falsified.[36] In basing its case on these studies, Monsanto® easily swept aside the class action suit of the Viet Nam veterans in 1984.[37]
The trial reveals that Monsanto® has long been aware of the toxicity of its products produced between 1930 and the end of the 1970s, including PCBs, dioxin, 2,4,5-T and Agent Orange. Although 2,4,5-T has been banned in the United States since 1970 and PCBs since 1977, the effects of these chemical substances on human health and the environment persist. In 1988, the EPA establishes that dioxin is a possible carcinogen.[38] In 1996, the WHO classifies TCDD dioxin as a human carcinogen, followed by PCB in 2013. Today, 10% of the PCBs produced in 1929 are still present in our environment.[39]
In 1987, the Kemner v. Monsanto® case comes to a disparaging end. The Sturgeon plaintiffs, unable to prove the link between their health issues and the 1979 accident, each receive $1 as symbolic compensation for damages. Monsanto® is charged $16 million in punitive damages for its irresponsibility regarding the health risks of dioxin. The company appeals the decision, winning its case in 1991.[40] Once again, Monsanto® evades its human and environmental responsibilities.
Nonetheless, the Sturgeon accident marks a turning point in Monsanto®'s history. Public opinion is now conscious of the dangers of chemical production, dangers that the company kept hidden for decades. In turning toward the food industry, is Monsanto® attempting to restore its tarnished image?

28 The name dates to 1968 in memory of the city's first mayor, Leo Sauget.
29 Census of June 2014.
30 Scott Beauchamp, "A Short Way to Hell: in Sauget, Illinois, Poisons Mean profit," *Belt magazine*, September 23, 2015. Richard Sauget is the great-grandson of Leo Sauget.
31 Monsanto® was aware of the risks of PCB production on human health and the environment since 1937 (cf. Chapter I).
32 Casey Bukro, "Report hardly draws angry sniff," *Chicago Tribune*, July 5, 1988.
33 Alias for CERCLA (Comprehensive Environmental Response, Compensation, and Liability Act) of 1980, a federal law established for the cleanup and rehabilitation of sites contaminated by hazardous waste.
34 EPA website: www.epa.gov (region 5: Sauget Area 1, Sauget Area 2 and Sauget-Solutia Inc.).
35 Cf. Chapter II; Raymond R. Suskind, *op. cit.*
36 Marilyn Fingerhut, "Cancer mortality in workers exposed to 2,3,7,8 tetrachlorodibenzo-p-dioxin," *New England Journal of Medicine*, vol. 34, N°4, January 24,1991; Anthony B. Miller, "Public health and hazardous wastes," *Environmental Epidemiology*, vol.1, National Academy Press, Washington,1991.
37 Cf. Chapter II.
38 Group 2B carcinogen according to the classification of the International Agency for Research on Cancer (WHO).
39 J. Maherou, S. Norest and L. Ferrer, "PCB: quels risques pour ma santé?" (PCB: What are the risks to my health?), ASEF, June 16, 2014.
40 Kemner v. Monsanto Co., July 22, 1991, www.leagle.com.

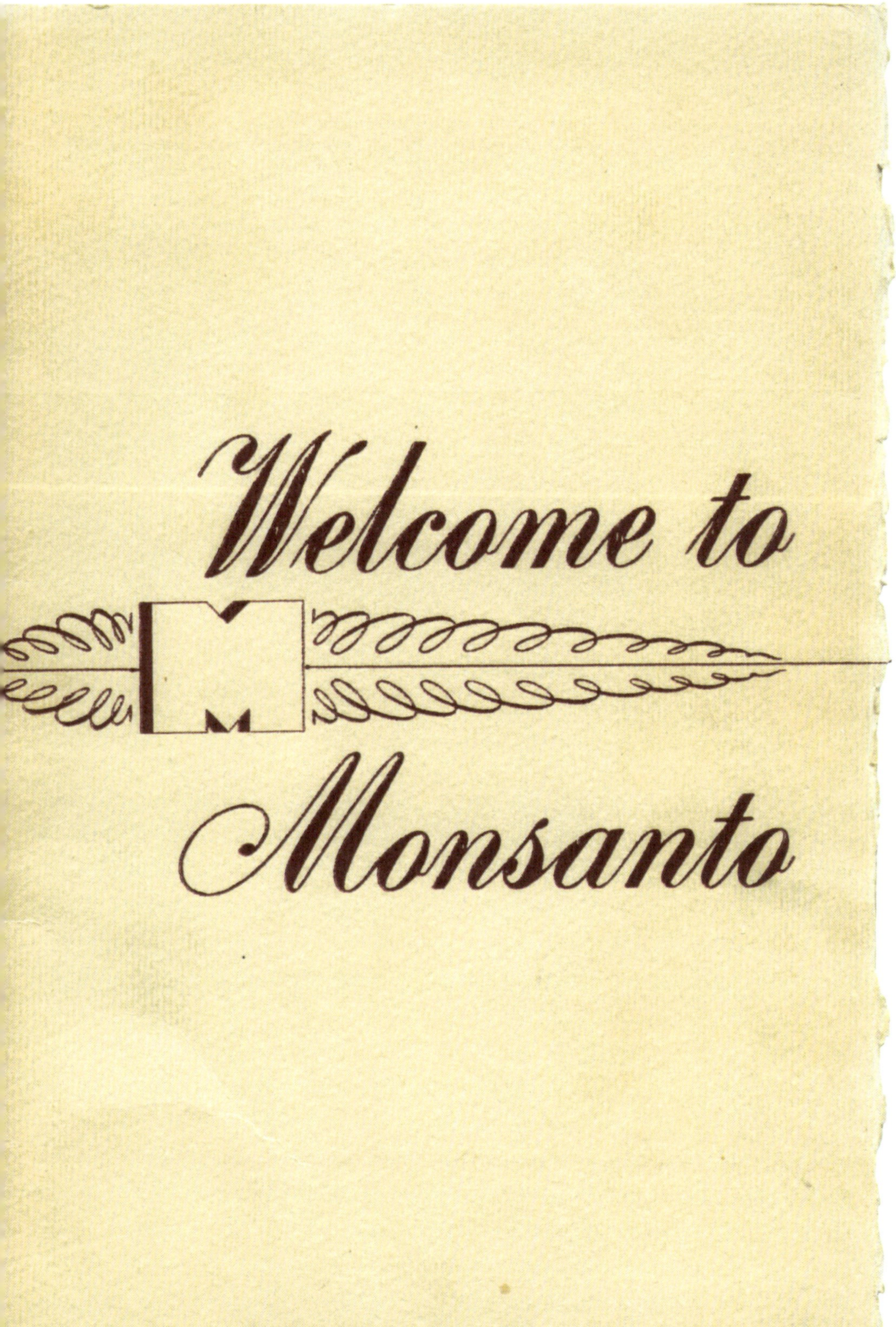

BROCHURE DU 30ᵉ ANNIVERSAIRE DE MONSANTO®. 1947
MONSANTO®'S 30TH ANNIVERSARY BOOKLET. 1947

Two thousand people were working . . .

when this photograph was taken. This air view of Monsanto, Illinois, wa taken from the south. The road running north and south at upper left

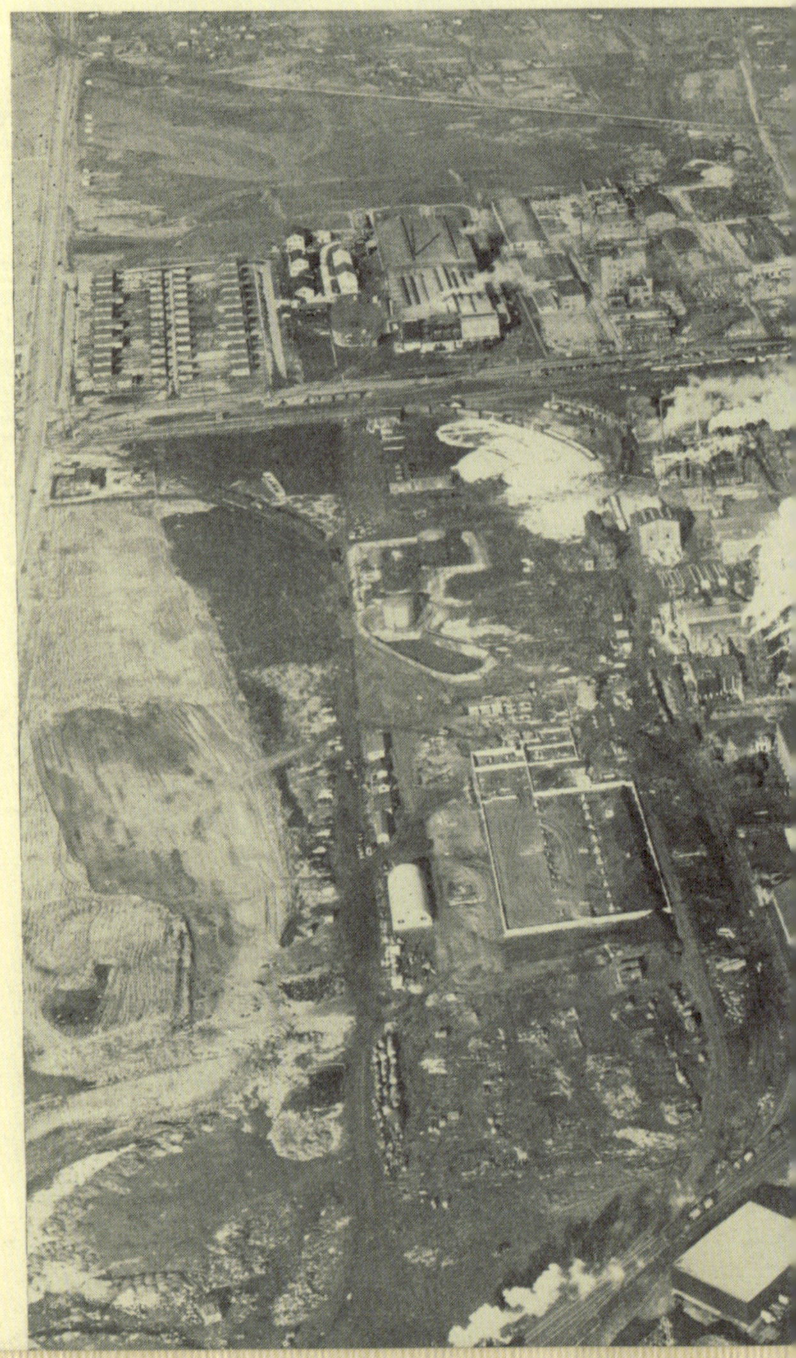

oute 3, and Mississippi Avenue can be seen branching from it to the right. he office building is between the white steam of the phenol unit and ie darker smoke of the power plant near the center of the picture.

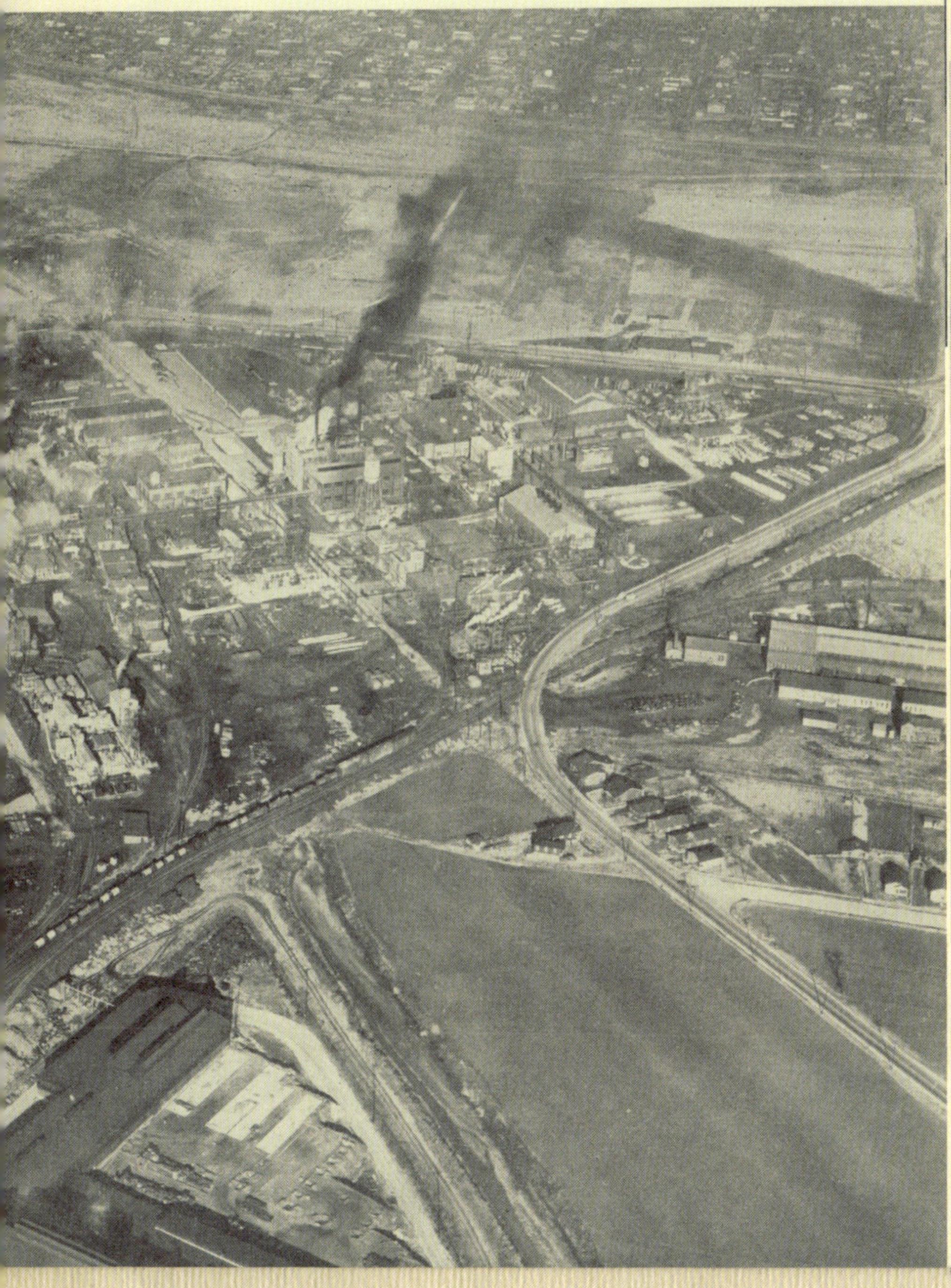

La ville de Sauget, créée en 1926, était alors nommée Monsanto® City. À cette époque où la réglementation sur l'environnement se durcissait, Monsanto® City offrait un cadre plus souple et des incitations fiscales aux usines de Monsanto®. L'usine Monsanto® de Sauget fut le premier producteur de PCB – un produit chimique cancérigène – du pays. Des études ont révélé une très forte concentration de dioxine et de PCB sur une portion de plus de 3 kilomètres d'un cours d'eau situé au milieu d'une zone résidentielle de Sauget. La présence de ces substances toxiques était liée à la production de composants chimiques par l'usine de Monsanto®. En 2001, après des années d'enquête, l'Agence américaine de protection de l'environnement (EPA) a classé les alentours de Dead Creek en « zone toxique » (Superfund Site : classification fédérale autorisant l'EPA à effectuer elle-même des opérations de nettoyage des sites à risque).

The city of Sauget was founded in 1926 and was known as "Monsanto® City." In a time of strict environmental regulations, "Monsanto® City" provided a liberal regulatory environment and low taxes for the Monsanto® chemical plants. Monsanto®'s plant in Sauget was the nation's largest producer of PCBs, a cancer-causing chemical. High concentrations of dioxin and PCBs were detected in a two-mile stretch of a local creek, located within a residential area of Sauget. Toxic substances were associated with chemical products and wastes from the Monsanto® facilities. In 2001, after years of investigation, the US Environmental Protection Agency (EPA) has designated the plant site along Dead Creek as a Superfund Site.

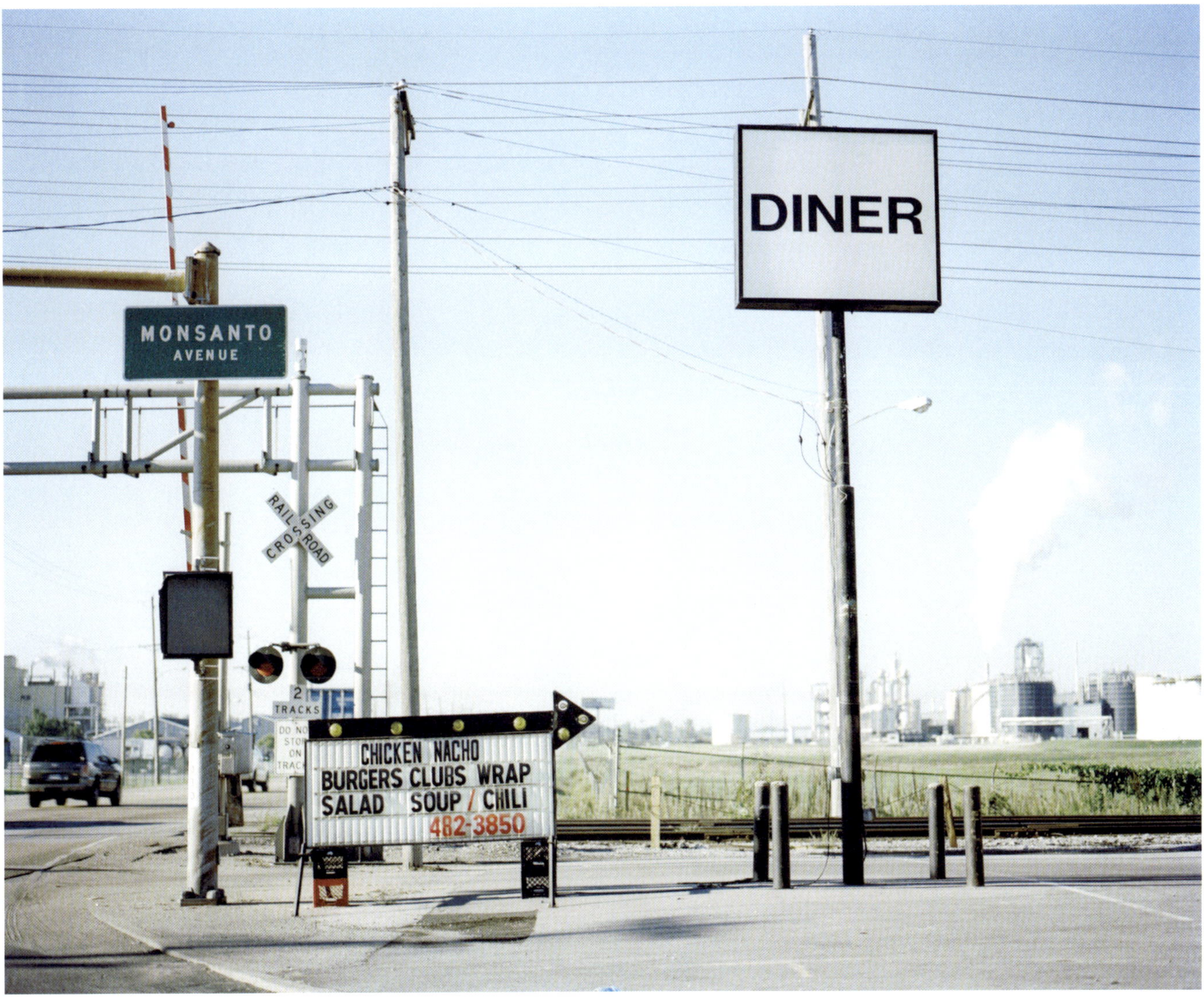

 SAUGET, ILLINOIS. 2012

Quartiers défavorisés à quelques pas de la zone toxique de Sauget. Derrière les grilles au bout de la route se trouve un des sites les plus pollués des États-Unis.

Low-income neighborhood located a few steps from Sauget's Superfund Site. At the end of this road and behind the gates lies one of the most polluted places in the US.

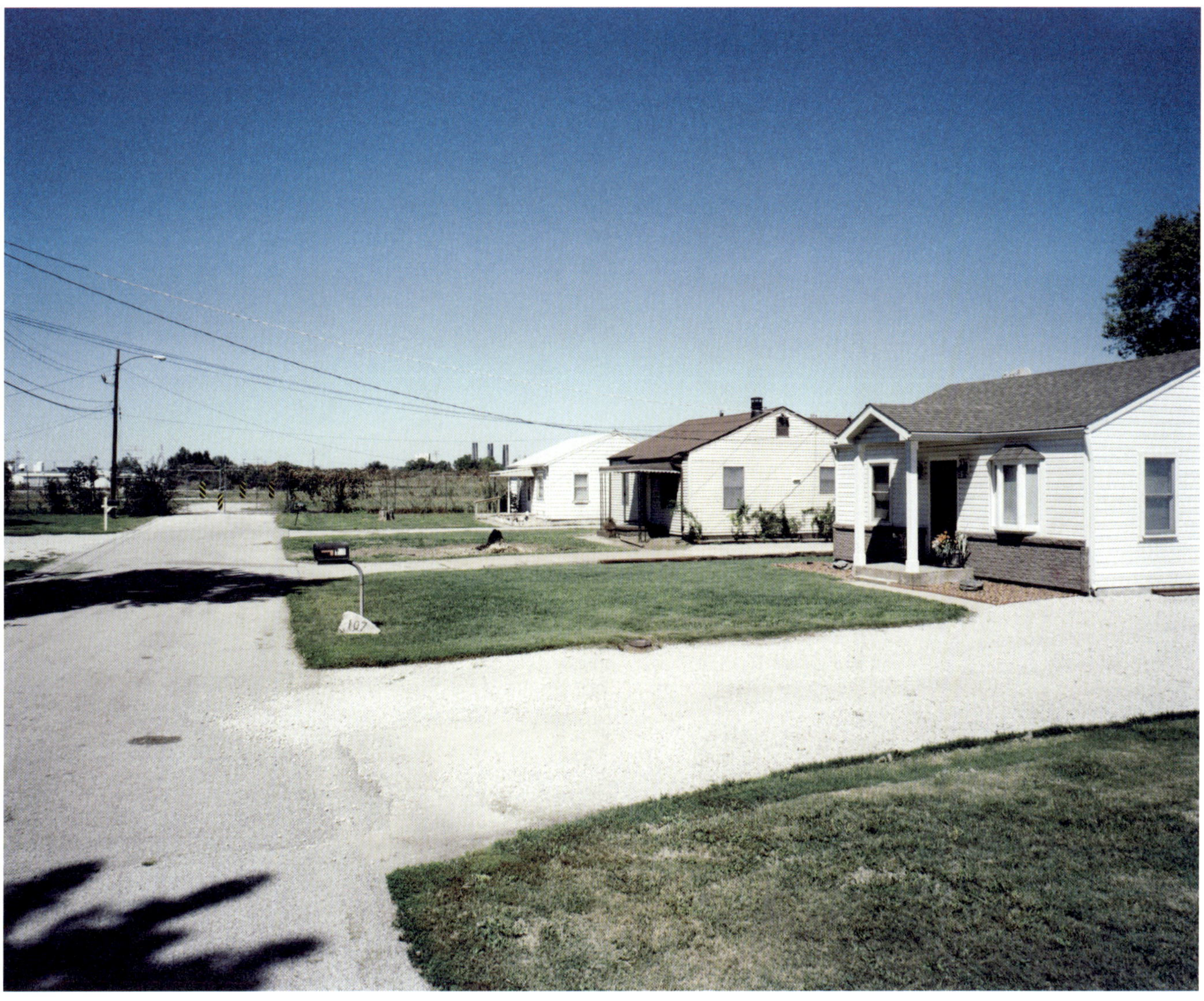

The Centralia Fireside Guard

Vol. 111, No. 10 | Wednesday, February 7, 1979 | Centralia, Mo. 65240 | 20 Cents

Water bond issue passes

☒ Yes 487 76% ☐ No 152

19th State Senatorial District - Boone County results only

☒ Roger Wilson 8075 ☐ Jerry Epple 4806

☒ Boone Retirement Center issue passes

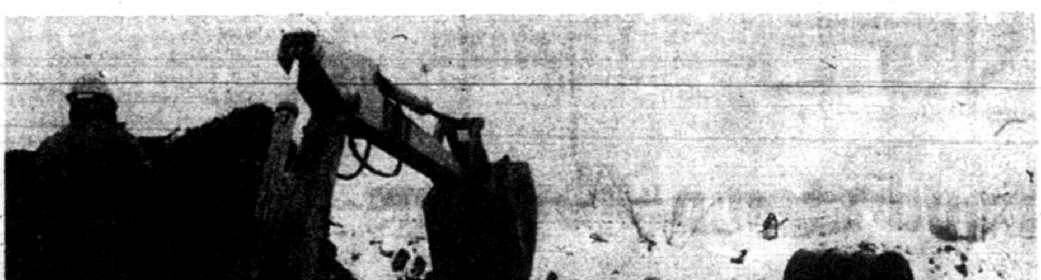

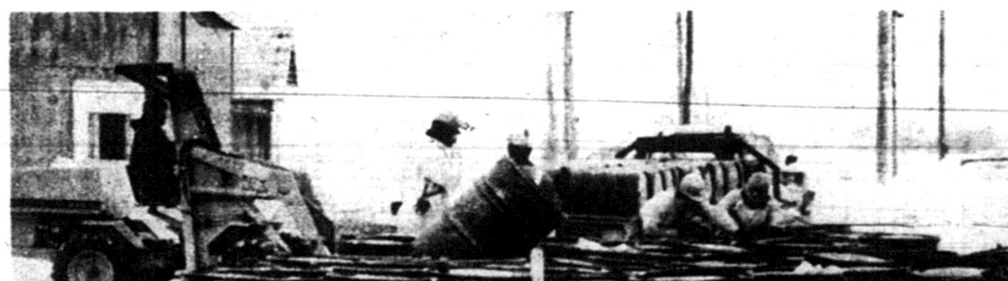

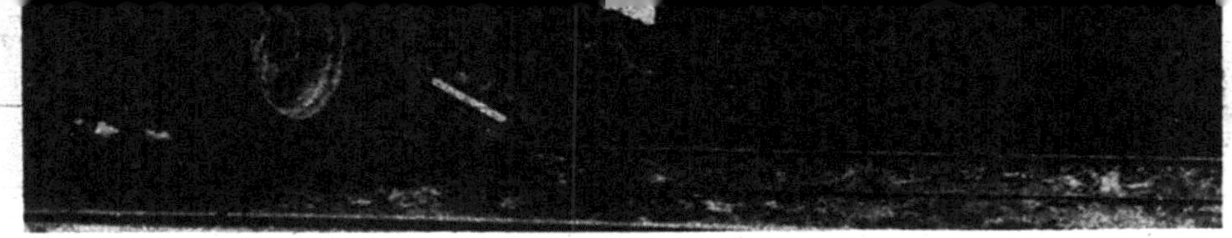

Chemical experts called for second Sturgeon meeting

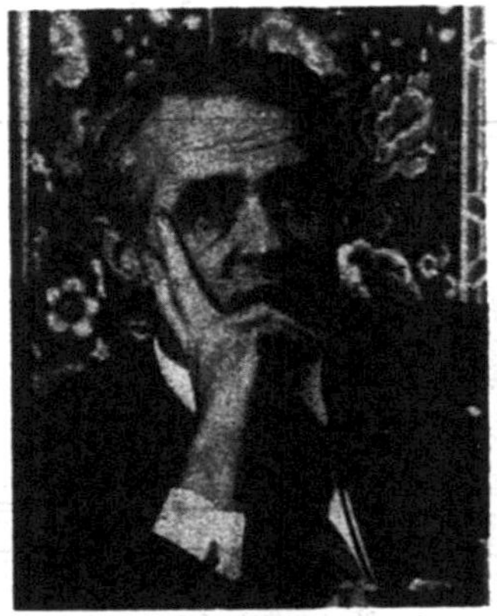

Senator Thomas Eagleton admits the incident is a mystery to him too, during a press conference last week.

by Virginia Haux

STURGEON — Another town meeting to allow questions and answers about orthochlorophenol will be held this Thursday, February 8, 7:30 at the Sturgeon Youth Center, hopefully to arrest fears of residents about the chemical's effects, or at least to give detailed information.

An imposing group of specialists is expected to be at the meeting. They include:

Dr. Joseph Seifter, a medical science adviser to the Environmental Protection Agency, Washington, D.C.;

William Deichmann of the University of Miami;

Charles Pool Washington, D.C.;

Emanuel Landau, American Public Health Association;

Dr. Denny Donnell, Missouri Division of Public Health;

Dr. John Doull of the University of Kansas Medical Center;

John Neuberger, School of Public Health, Epidemiology, University of Kansas Medical Center;

From Monsanto Chemical Co., Dr. George Paget, Joseph Metcalf, and Joseph Wolfberger;

Mike Sanford, Boone County Public Health.

Announcement of Dr. Seifter's attendance was made last week by Sen. Tom Eagleton, who said he requested an expert to visit Sturgeon after news of the previous town meeting.

In Sturgeon, work is continuing on barreling the ballast (the original congealed chemical, contaminated roadbed, snow and ice) and cleaning of the track area. The sealed barrels are being shipped to an area near Wichita which is an approved disposal site for such material.

Additional roadbed material is being removed, as tests have shown penetration of the chemical to a greater depth than expected.

Nearly 12 inches will be removed, and this roadbed rock and cinders are to be taken to a site in the Wright City area, one of two places in Missouri approved for this type of disposal. (The other is near St. Joseph.)

A trench has been dug alongside the affected track to allow operation of an "undercutter" which will remove the roadbed from under the tracks as the tracks themselves are shimmed up. Nearly every day during the past week, a crane loaded tons of the trench material and roadbed into dozens of long open 18-wheel trucks, which were tarp-covered to haul this material out.

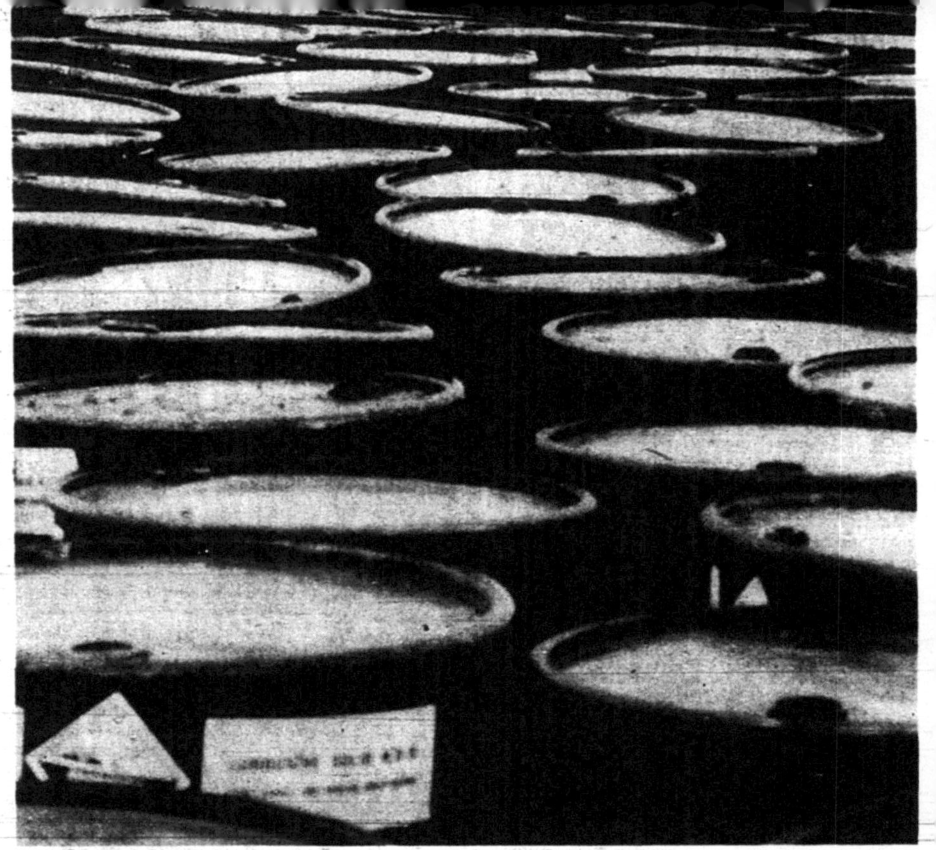

Workmen carry barrels, top left, to an area where they will be loaded with material contaminated with orthochlorophenol. Thousands of the sealed barrels are labeled and stored above awaiting transportation to Wichita.

The undercutter was expected to have arrived this past Monday.

Last Wednesday night, one of the men working to clean up the spill, Walter Kidwell of Columbia, was taken to the hospital after developing respiratory problems and coughing up some blood. Harry Gilmer of the EPA has said Kidwell apparently let some of the material contaminated with the chemical come in contact with his skin.

The odor continues to plague residents living nearby the area, and on especially bad days or nights, they leave home. Regardless of the temperature, the cleanup also stirs up the material and raises the odor level.

One dog reported ill, belonging to Ellis Huskey whose auto repair business is near the tracks, has been determined to have a high level of lead in the dog's blood. It is not yet known whether traces of the chemical are in its blood.

Raymond Barnes, whose home is near the railroad area, says his dog is sick also, however. City Superintendent Dean Connolly says there have been several dead rabbits along the area, who presumably came in contact with the chemical.

Two of Bill Kemner's cattle have aborted, and a hog has respiratory problems, Kemner said. (Once the chemical-spilling tanker was out of the city, the spill occurred on railroad right-of-way adjacent to Kemner land. Material was stockpiled near a pit dug on his land for treatment purposes.-

Cette décharge, juste à côté du fleuve Mississippi, fut utilisée par Monsanto® pour se débarrasser de ses déchets chimiques de 1957 à 1977.

The landfill is located directly next to the Mississippi River and was used by Monsanto® to dispose of chemical waste from 1957 to 1977.

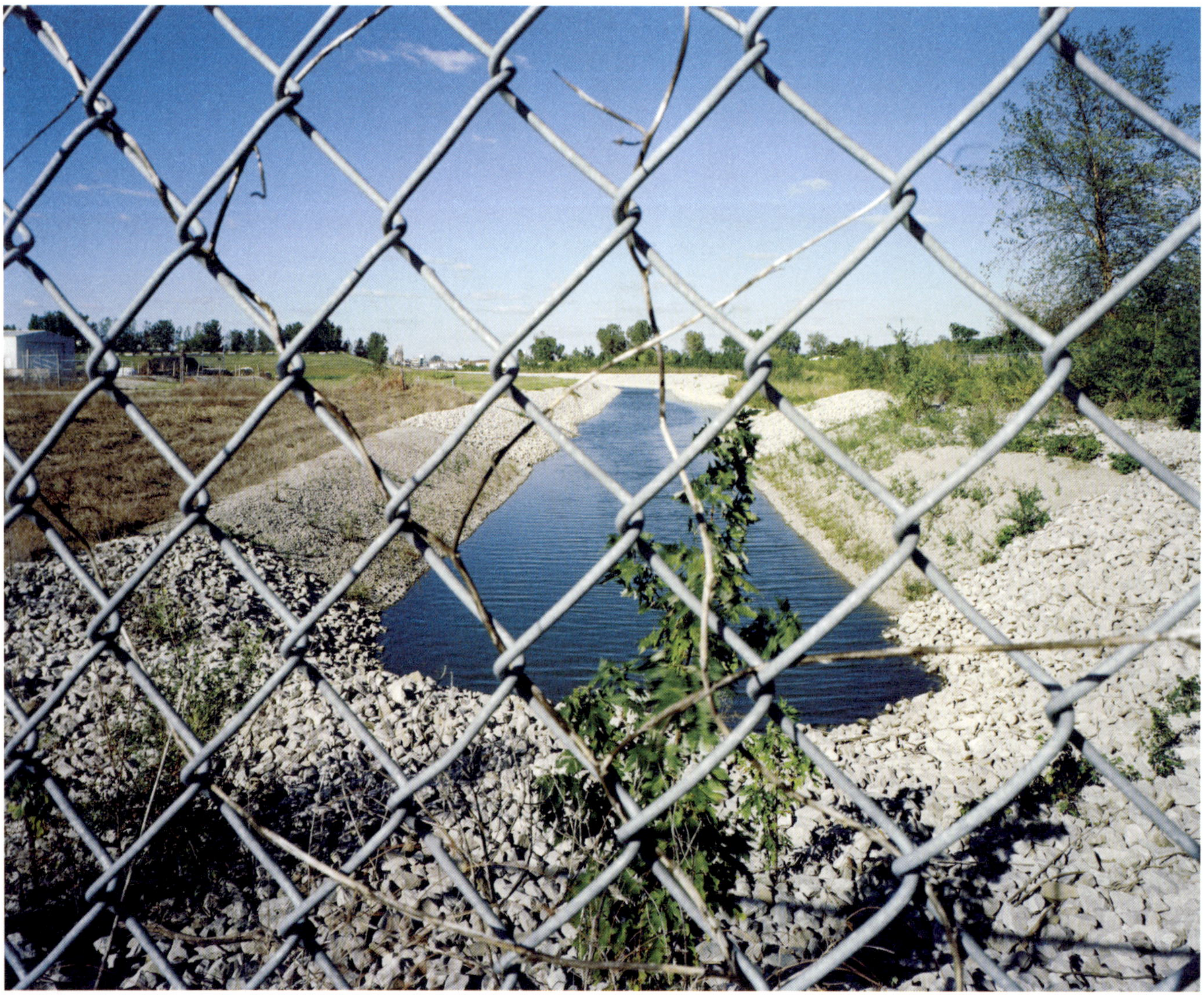

SAUGET, ILLINOIS. 2012

Le fleuve Mississippi.

Mississippi River.

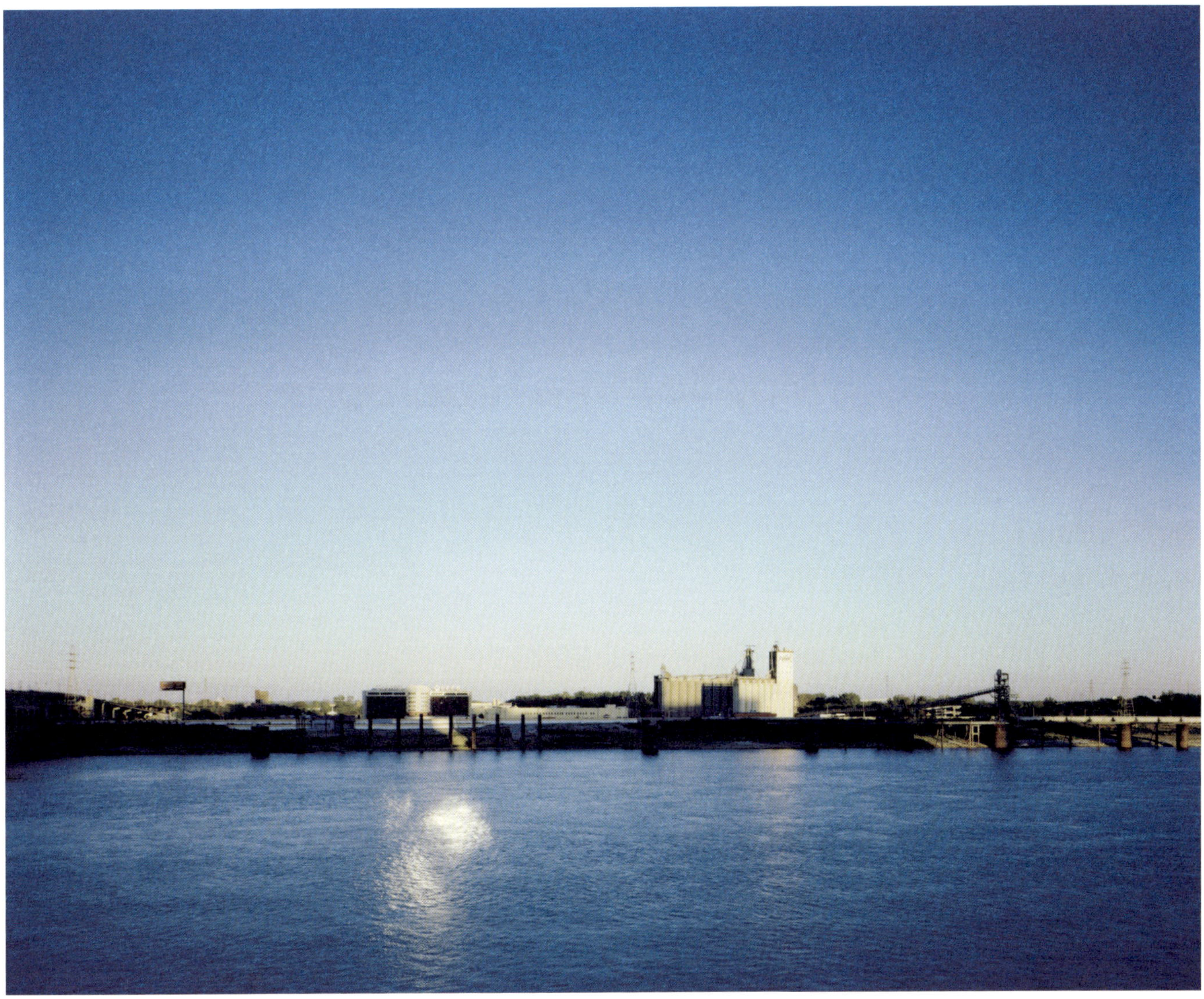

Carthage Press Photo by Steve Christy

THE BIG LICK — Recreation Center receptionist Jeanie Baum, 703 East Second St., does not have to go far from her desk for a snack break — as long as the weather stays cold she can dart out the center's front door and take a lick from the huge icicle on the Big Smith, Inc. building next door to the center.

LITTLE ENCOURAGEMENT ON PROGRAM...

Leaders Buck Carter On Inflation

By MICHAEL DOAN
Associated Press Writer

WASHINGTON (AP) — Urban officials and the Senate leader of the president's own party are giving the Carter administration little encouragement on its anti-inflation program as prices continue to rise.

Alfred E. Kahn, who heads the anti-inflation program, told the National Urban Coalition Wednesday that "the prescribed medicine for inflation is restraint" by government and the public.

As part of the anti-inflation effort, he said, more money cannot be spent to fight unemployment, to rebuild the cities or to pay for universal medical care.

His audience was not pleased.

"What kind of restraint would you suggest for an elderly woman living alone who cannot afford medical care and enough food to eat?" asked Donald McCullum, an Oakland, Calif., judge.

Kahn responded, "I would, if I could, impose a minimum level below which a sacrifice would not be imposed."

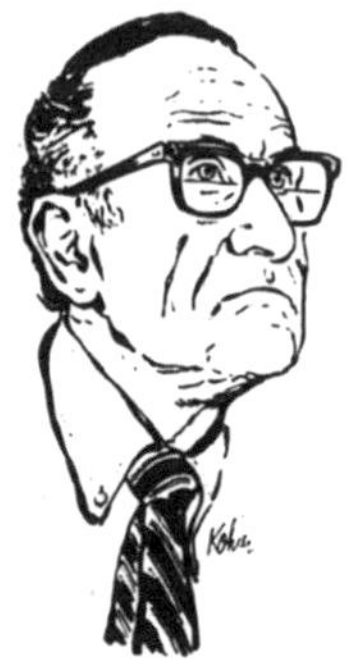

ALFRED E. KAHN

Joseph Rhodes, a state representative from Pennsylvania, told Kahn he could "kiss goodbye" to the anti-inflation program if the military budget is increased while other countries are making what he called inadequate contributions to NATO.

Meanwhile, Senate Majority Leader Robert C. Byrd, DW.Va., said he hasn't detected much support on Capitol Hill for President Carter's proposal to offer "inflation insurance" to workers who limit pay increases to less than 7 percent.

"The reaction has been rather bland ... not enthusiastic," Byrd said.

Workers who comply with the 7 percent limit on wage increases would be eligible for a tax credit of up to 1 per cent of their first $20,000 in wages for each percentage point the cost of living rises above 7 percent.

The Council on Wage and Price Stability, which Kahn heads, said Wednesday private wage-insurance plans similar to Carter's federal proposal will not be allowed under the administration's voluntary guidelines.

Cost-of-living increases granted employees by companies were to be included under the 7 percent pay-hike limit, but the council had approved a Minnesota company's wage-insurance plan which have circumvented requirement, the council That approval will stand, b council's new rules forbid companies from following su

Also Wednesday, the Ba America, the world's largest mercial bank, issued a r predicting a 7.5 percent to cent inflation rate this year.

INFLATION MAINTAINS MOMENTUM...

Wholesale Prices Rise 0.8 Percent Last Month

By MICHAEL DOAN
Associated Press Writer

WASHINGTON (AP) — Rising costs of gasoline, food and machinery pushed wholesale prices up 0.8 percent in December as inflation kept up its momentum, the Labor Department said today.

For all of 1978, wholesale prices rose 9.1 percent, the biggest such increase since an 18.3 percent jump in 1974, the department said. In 1977, prices went up 6.6 percent.

The wholesale price figures are important because they are an early sign of what consumers can expect in the way of price changes in the next few months.

The 0.8 percent increase for December was the same as in November and about average for the past four months. If averaged out over an entire year it would amount to 10 percent — slightly above the inflation rate of about 9 to 9.5 percent for 1978.

Wholesale food prices, which had eased in November, resumed their climb last month,, rising 0.9 percent.

Beef and veal prices turned up in December after declining in November, but pork prices slipped.

Prices were higher for processed poultry, fruit and vegetables, dairy products and candy. Prices of eggs dropped 4 percent.

***

BULLETIN

TEHRAN, Iran (AP) — A mob hauled down and burned the American flag today in front of the U.S. consulate in Shiraz, toppled three statues of the shah and stormed the secret police headquarters, residents reported. between two and eight persons were killed.

*

BANGKOK, Thailand (AP) — A Thai helicopter whisked former Cambodian Deputy Premier Ieng Sary from his homeland to safety today as Vietnamese tanks were reported closing in, and the ousted official then flew out of Bangkok for Hong Kong, Thai airlines officials said.

***

The price of gasoline, sold at the refinery, rose 4 percent in December, and kerosene rose in price by 2.8 percent.

The report measured finished goods, or the price of products just before they are sold to consumers. The Producer Price Index for Finished Goods stood at 202.4, meaning that wholesale products that cost $100 in the base period of 1967 cost $202.40 last month.

The report was released as urban officials and the Senate leader of President Carter's party were giving the administration little encouragement on its anti-inflation program.

At earlier stages of production, there were some signs of improvement. The cost of intermediate goods rose 0.6 percent and the cost of crude goods, the earliest stage of production, slowed markedly to 0.4 percent because of a decline in crude food prices. However, food at the intermediate level was still a high 1.2 percent.

The administration is trying to cut its budget and promote its wage and price standards as a way to fight inflation.

F*OR* Y*OUR* I*NFORMATION*

Weather and Forecast

FORECAST — Travelers advisory tonight. Occasional snow tonight, possibly mixed briefly with sleet or freezing rain. Snow accumulation of one to three inches expected. Low tonight 10-15. Good chance for freezing rain or snow Friday with the high near 30. Winds southeasterly 10-20 mph tonight. Probabilities of measurable precipitation 60 percent tonight, 50 percent Friday.

1 p.m....21	9 p.m.... 17	5 a.m....20
2 p.m....21	10 p.m....17	6 a.m....20
3 p.m....20	11 p.m....17	7 a.m....20
4 p.m....20	Midnight..17	8 a.m....21
5 p.m....19	1 a.m....17	9 a.m....22
6 p.m....18	2 a.m....18	10 a.m....23
7 p.m....17	3 a.m....19	11 a.m....24
8 p.m....18	4 a.m....20	Noon....25
Maximum 25	Minimum 17	Precipitation .03"

EXTENDED OUTLOOK — Snow ending Saturday. Clear to partly cloudy Sunday and Monday. Lows from zero to 5 above north to 15-20 in the Bootheel. Highs from 15-20 north and 20s south.

LAKE LEVELS — Grand Lake—734.64, no change; Table Rock—906.47, drop of .23; Bull Shoals—651.53, drop of .18; Beaver—1.109.62, drop of .04; Stockton—861.58, drop of .01; Taneycomo—700.60, rise of .15.

On Promoting Downtown

Today's edition of The Carthage Press starts a new monthly feature, the Downtown Carthage Page. The page is devoted to downtown business — the people that make it happen, special sales events, customer reactions. It represents a unified effort by 36 progressive local retailers, working with The Press, to promote and expand the downtown business community. See page 5 for details.

Downtown Carthage Page sponsors include Bank of Carthage, Belk-Simpson, Ben Franklin, Bowers Annex, Brownsberger's, Cantrell Seed House, Carthage Cablevision, Carthage Hardware, The Chinese Connection, College Pharmacy, Dan's Linoleum and Carpet, Davison Shoes, Firestone, Fran's Galary, Gay's Fashions and Gays Jewelers.

Also, Goodyear Service Store, Gray-Krummel Drug Co., Harry's Shoes, M.F.A. Insurance, Mode O'Day, Morgan's Studio & Frame Shop, Murray-Duncan Drug Co., Orient Express, OTASCO, J.C. Penney, Ramsays, Rogers Office Products, Sears, the Shoe Center and Smith's Town and Country.

Also, United Missouri Bank of Carthage, vanPerk's, Westco, Western Auto and Ernie Williamson's Music House.

News Digest

From The Associated Press

JEFFERSON CITY, Mo. — Gov. Joseph Teasdale's plan to cut $53 million in state income taxes next December may go to the Senate soon, Ways and Means Committee Chairman John Schneider said Wednesday: Schneider hopes to get a committee vote on the bill by noon Thursday.

SEATTLE — The Rev. A.A. Lemieux, a Jesuit priest who served as president of Seattle University for 17 years and who was named the school's chancellor in 1976, died Wednesday at age 70.

ATHENS, Greece — Defying opposition from women's rights groups, hundreds of women enlisted Wednesday in Greece's first-ever female volunteer army.

ESSEN, West Germany — Steel workers in West Germany's industrial Rhur region were returning to work today after endorsing a new contract that ended the area's first strike in 50 years.

MANAGUA, Nicaragua — Troops sealed off all highway entrances to Managua and patrolled the capital in force following anti-government protests in which seven demonstrators were shot and wounded.

ANKARA, Turkey — U.S. Deputy Secretary of State Warren Christopher is in Turkey for talks aimed at helping the Ankara government ease its staggering $15 billion foreign debt.

ROME — A feud between rightist and leftist militants came to a boil in Rome as marauders from both camps rampaged through the streets of the capital firebombing buildings, overturning cars and causing huge traffic jams.

CHICAGO — John Wayne Gacy Jr. stood silently as his attorney entered innocent pleas to charges of murder, mute as a judge ordered he be examined by a psychiatrist.

KNOXVILLE, Tenn. — The Rev. Clifford Barbour, 83, a former head of the Presbyterian Church in the United States of America, died Wednesday. He also served as president of the Pittsburg Theological Seminary.

TEL AVIV, Israel — Brig. Gen. Zeev Almog has been named commander of Israel's navy, replacing Adm. Michael Barkai who was fired after being acquitted of an attempted rape charge.

WASHINGTON — A scientific society says a solar power satellite system may someday be able to supply all of the nation's energy needs — but the idea must be studied at length.

SPRINGFIELD, Ill. — Gov. James R. Thompson said today he will ask the state to sell $18 million worth of bonds

NEW SURGEON GENERAL'S REPORT...

Caution: Smoking May Be More Hazardous

WASHINGTON (AP) — The surgeon general says he has "overwhelming" evidence that smoking causes death and disease. What he doesn't have is a way to help people stop.

Those were among the conclusions in a 1,200-page report issued today by Surgeon General Julius Richmond in a "review and reappraisal" of research accumulated over the past 15 years.

"This document reveals, with dramatic clarity, that smoking is even more dangerous — indeed, far more dangerous — than was supposed in 1964," said HEW Secretary Joseph A. Califano Jr.

"It is hoped that in another 15 years we will not have to say, 'We still don't know what works!'" in helping people stop smoking, said Richmond.

Califano contended the report "demolishes" claims by cigarette manufacturers that there is no proven link between smoking and cancer and chronic diseases.

Commenting before the report was released, the Tobacco Institute predicted it would be "more rehash than research" and issued its own 168-page report saying the "preoccupation with smoking may be both unfounded and dangerous...because evidence on many critical points is conflicting...(and it) diverts attention from other suspected hazards."

The new surgeon general's report is based on no specific new research and contained no startling new conclusions. Its thrust is that the volume of research carried out since the initial surgeon general's report 15 years ago makes all the more certain the conclusion that smoking contributes to cancer, heart disease, bronchitis, emphysema and other ills.

That first report created a furor and led to the now-famous warning printed on each pack of cigarettes sold in the United States: "Warning: The Surgeon General has Determined That Cigarette smoking Is Dangerous to Your Health."

Unlike the initial report, the main findings in the new study generally have been reported separately as the research which led to them was completed. Much of the material incorporated in the new report was contained in 10 earlier reports to Congress, the most recent one last fall on the sharp increase in lung cancer among women.

Among the findings re-emphasized in the latest report:

—That smokers, male and female, die from a variety of ailments at a rate two-thirds higher than nonsmokers.

—The risk goes up as the amount smoked goes up. For example, two-pack-a-day smokers have a death rate twice as high as nonsmokers. And a 30 to 35-year-old smoker can expect to die eight or nine years earlier than a nonsmoker.

—Women are dying from lung cancer at a rate three times as high as in 1964. The disease may overtake breast cancer as the leading cause of cancer deaths in women "if present trends are not reversed during the next decade."

—Here is a summary of conclusions:

—The overall death rate for current cigarette smokers is 70 percent higher than for nonsmokers. It increases with the amount smoked, but ten to 15 years after they quit, the ex-smokers' death rate is about the same as nonsmokers'.

—Cigar and pipe smokers have "slightly higher" mortality rates than nonsmokers, but "substantially lower" than cigarette smokers.

Peptic Ulcers May Be Inherited Trait

BOSTON (AP) — The peptic ulcer, long thought to be a symptom of the stresses of modern life, may actually be inherited in many cases, according to a new study.

California researchers say that more than half of all ulcers may be passed on from generation to generation, although drinking, diet and stress can make the disease appear sooner.

For the first time, the doctors said, they have found a specific, genetically-determined trait that can be measured to figure out who is in danger of developing an ulcer of the duodenum, the most common form of this intestinal ailment.

One researcher said the discovery may make it possible for doctors to spot youngsters who risk ulcers and help them avoid the disease.

A report on the research, conducted at Harbor-UCLA Medical Center in Torrance, Calif., was published in today's New England Journal of Medicine.

The doctors discovered that, in some families, people whose stomachs secrete unusually large amounts of an enzyme called pepsinogen are likely to have ulcers.

The researchers said they are not sure whether pepsinogen always means an inclination to develop ulcers. Other studies, however, have shown that two-thirds of people with duodenal ulcers also have high levels of this enzyme.

Peptic ulcers occur in 8 percent to 12 percent of American adults.

Nothing Fishy About State Funds Request

JEFFERSON CITY, Mo. (AP) - Fishermen will find an "adequate" supply of trout in Missouri lakes and streams in future years if legislators approve a request by the state Department of Conservation for a $57 million appropriation in fiscal 1980, a conservation official says.

Larry Gale, director-designate of the conservation department, told the House Appropriations Committee Wednesday night that the $57 million includes money that will be used to complete an expansion project at the Shepherd of the Hills Hatchery at Branson, the state's largest trout hatchery.

"Completion of the three-yearold project, which is expected this year, will double the output of the hatchery and enable conservation officials to "keep up" with the ever-increasing number of

UMC Medical Workers Avert Infant Tragedy

COLUMBIA, Mo. (AP) — Workers in the neonatal care unit of the University of Missouri Medical Center worked feverishly for several hours early today to keep newborn infants breathing after compressors powering both a main and backup central air unit failed.

About 25 babies were in the unit when the compressors broke down shortly after midnight, according

some cases, manually helped the babies breathe through the use of plastic bags.

Horn said things were back to normal within two hours, and all the infants were doing well.

The Missouri Highway Patrol used its emergency airplane to bring a prenatal ventilator to the hospital from the Cox Medical Center in Springfield, Mo. Two other units were brought to the

Teasdale Budget Cut Cuts MSSC Growth Too

The four percent increase recommended by Gov. Joe Teasdale will not allow for "any growth whatever" at Missouri Southern State College, Dr. Paul Shipman, interim executive vice president and vice president for financial affairs, said today.

Although the governor recommended a four percent increase in 1979-1980 to $6,201,735, the amount is $600,558 less than the college requested for its 1979-80 funding. The higher amount also was endorsed by the state coordinating Board on Higher Education.

There had been small increases each year in the general revenue budget, Dr. Shipman said. The cut this year will be in the student services portion of the budget. Student services includes student health services, registrar, admissions, counseling and guidance as well as the entire athletic

and the legislature remains to be seen, Dr. Shipman stated. However, with the presently recommended four percent increase, "it is assumed by the governor that there will be sufficient funds for 5 percent salary increases. It is not totally clear whether colleges will be treated as some other state agencies have been in that respect," he said. "Under the governor's austerity program, college administrators will find more controls on the ways in which appropriations may be expended," Dr. Shipman added.

One of the governor's staff members has said that the governor is "strongly dedicated to the austerity budget," Shipman concluded.

The MSSC Board of Regents regular monthly meeting is scheduled for 1 p.m. Friday and

'Gypsy' Tickets Go On Sale Friday, Shows Jan. 18-20

Tickets for the forthcoming musical production of "Gypsy," sponsored by the Carthage Council on the Arts and Carthage Music Club, will go on sale Friday morning.

The $3 general admission tickets will be available at the Bank of Carthage, United Missouri Bank of Carthage and Rogers Office Products on the square. Reserved seat tickets, $3.50 each, will be available at College Pharmacy.

Curtain time will be at 7:30 p.m. Thursday, Friday, and Saturday, Jan. 18, 19, and 20. The gala

The Centralia Fireside Guard

Vol. 111, No. 9 | Wednesday, January 31, 1979 | Centralia, Mo. 65240 | 20 Cents

Water bond .op priority 'or city voters

:entralians will go to the polls t Tuesday, February 6, to accept or ect a water improvement bond posal totaling $1,800,000. The pro- will include a lime softening plant, r 3,000 feet of new water lines and a ,000 gallon storage tower.

Along with the water bond issue, tralians will join the rest of the ers in District 19 in deciding on a te senator to fill the vacancy of rren Welliver, who was appointed he State Supreme Court earlier this r. Roger Wilson, (D) and Jerry ole, (R), are the candidates in that e.

:ity officials are optimistic about voter turnout, according to John at" McDonald, city administrator. ie senatorial race coupled with the er bond issue makes us optimistic a better than average voter turn- ."

Another issue that involves Cen- lia and Boone County voters is the 300,000 special bond election for a bed expansion of the Boone County rsing Home.

/oting places for Centralians are same as in the past. Ward I will e at the Chance Elementary School; rd II at Centralia High School; and rd III and Centralia Township will e at the City Hall.

Hallsville voters will vote at the llsville Community Center and rgeon voters will vote at the rgeon City Hall. Polls will be open m 6:00 a.m. until 7:00 p.m. at these ces also.

Absentee ballots may be obtained til 5:00 p.m. Monday, February 5. t if you live in out-county and plan use the mails there probably uldn't be time after you read this to ain and return an absentee ballot. e best way would be to go to the unty Clerk's office in Columbia, fill a request form for an absentee lot, after which you may vote mediately.

Workers at the polls are:

Ward I, Mrs. Virginia Green and Mrs. Elizabeth Woolfolk, Democrats; No one has been confirmed yet for the Republican workers in Ward I;

Ward II, Marvin "Sparky" Hombs, and Mrs. Urith Kinkead, Democrats, and Mrs. Marge Bevard and Mrs. Delilah Houseworth, Republicans;

Ward III, Mrs. Shirley Burnett and Mrs. Helen Brown, Democrats, and Chester Sperflage and William Roth, Republicans; Township, Mrs. Carl McManama, and Mrs. Nadine Reams, Democrats, and Mrs. Georgia Meadows and Mrs. Esther Heaton, Republicans.

Hallsville, Mrs. Linda McKenzie and Mrs. Irene Burnett, Democrats, and Mrs. Rita Hibbs and Mrs. Kathryn Durk, Republicans; Sturgeon, Mrs. Bufa Mae Bowne and Mrs. Margaret Robinson, Democrats, and Mrs. Virginia Judy and Mrs. Dorothy Davenport, Republicans.

Issues that involve the city of Columbia are:

Sewerage system revenue bonds in the amount of $4.5 million for the purpose of extending and improving the existing public sewerage system of Columbia, including constructing outfall sewers and waste water treatment facilities;

Special obligation bonds in the amount of $750,000 for the purpose of extending and improving the waterworks system of the Columbia Public Water Supply District No. 2.

Industrial revenue bonds in the amount of $3,000,000 for the purpose of purchasing and constructing an industrial plant to be leased and otherwise disposed of to the American Air Filter Company, Inc., a Delaware corporation, for manufacturing and industrial development purposes, including real estate, buildings, improvements, fixtures, machinery and equipment.

Harrisburg residents will be voting on a $35,000 school bond issue for the purpose of constructing a lighted baseball field.

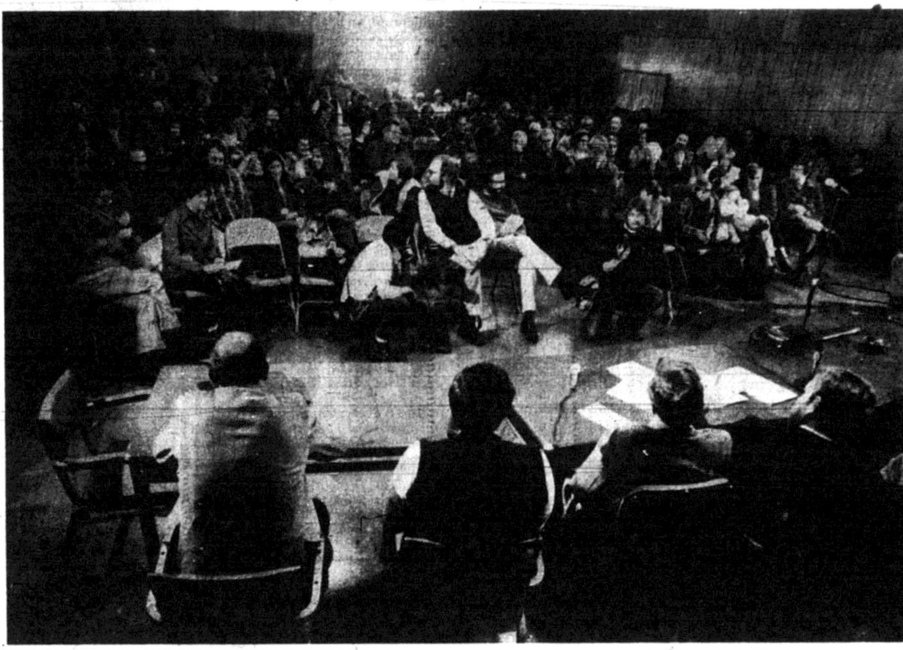

Environmental and railroad officials take the heat from a full house Monday at the Youth Center.

Sturgeon residents ask tough cleanup questions

They think officials are stonewalling

by Virginia Haux

More than 100 people attended a town meeting at the Sturgeon Youth Center Monday night concerning the recent chemical spill caused by a railroad tank car derailment. It was a meeting arranged by the city board of aldermen so the townspeople could ask of the invited involved officials the questions they had been asking their own city leaders.

As the meeting was ending, nearly two-and-one-half hours later, with many having left one by one, Sturgeon resident Dan Daigle stood and summed it all up, saying, "It looks as if after all this time, everyone is leaving knowing just about what they knew when they came in."

Or as another man put it more privately afterward, and rather more earthly, "What is it they say? 'If you can't astonish 'em with your knowledge, baffle 'em with some bull'."

Almost without exception Sturgeon residents came away with their questions unsatisfied, and a shaken confidence in those in positions meant to provide some protection or relief.

All members of the city council were seated at the officials' table — T. J. Carr, Johnny Robinson, Larry Brooks, along with City Clerk Cora Neal and City Attorney Paul Nettleton.

Mayor D. C. White was unable to attend, and Alderman Jerry Robinson, mayor pro tem, introduced city officials and: Harry Gilmer of the Environmental Protection Agency; Roland Miller of Western Environmental Sanitation (conducting the cleanup); Robert Robinson of the Department of Natural Resources; a representative of Norfolk and Western Railroad; the railroad's attorney; and Bob White, Senator Thomas Eagleton's secretary, who was present to observe on behalf of the senator.

Nearly all questions were fielded by Gilmer of EPA, except for a few answers by Miller, and two or three from the railroad attorney.

The first question was from Bill McGrath, who wondered what he should do about continuing health problems since missing a day of work because of illness after returning home from the evacuation.

Gilmer said, "Air tests at the end of the spill showed levels of toxicity which did not constitute a hazard as far as respiratory problems were concerned and subsequent tests confirmed that decision." "Today," he said, "we initiated additional tests each 24 hours at each of three stations" in the area. Gilmer added some people may be more susceptible than others and suggested Bridges — and any others — see his doctor.

Mrs. Raymond Barnes, who lives near the heaviest spill site and near the cleanup operation, asked "If air is being tested, how about testing our homes where so much odor has penetrated? We can't get the fumes out of the house, they've made us sick, we've had to leave home when it's very bad. What can we do about the odor in our homes?"

Gilmer replied, "We don't have the authority to test homes; the odor will gradually wear out. We know of no way to get rid of it." He added, "Based on the opinion of our toxicologist, there's no toxic danger."

To another's question of "What do we do while we wait for the smell to go away if we can hardly stand it?" Gilmer shrugged and said monitoring would continue to be sure there's no hazard.

Close questioning on how many parts per million were in the air now, how recent was the information on which safety estimates were based, yielded the concession that knowledge of the pollutant's effects are incomplete.

To a question on when damages would be paid, the railroad's attorney said, "We are still investigating what caused the accident, and don't know what the results will be or when they will be known."

Questions such as what led authorities to believe the substance still in Sturgeon is safe, or "What does toxic mean? That it can't kill you but can make you sick?" or "What will be the effect a year or 10 years from now?" and "What will be the effects for those who are pregnant?" drew silence.

Jim Stockton spoke of his baby who developed bronchitis the day after returning home, with some symptoms still lingering, and asked what was the time period for the chemical to fade away. Gilmer could not "say how long... tests indicate the level has decreased."

Charles Hubble, Jr., asked "Why did you decide to put the residue in barrels? Why is the EPA man answering all the questions instead of the railroad? Why did EPA give permission to dig a trench to keep it here instead of removing it? If it hadn't been for the Department of Natural Resources, might it have always remained here?"

His questions drew the first applause.

Gilmer said the quantity and extent of the spill had not at first been fully realized.

Last Tuesday morning, Western Environment expected to treat all residue in a washing operation which would supposedly remove the orthochlorophenol and dump it into a pit dug on adjacent land. Chemical and roadbed material was being moved by gondola cars to the site and stockpiled on the ground for treatment.

By Wednesday morning, operations had ceased due to notification from the DNR that this means of treatment was prohibited, and giving a 30-day period for removal. (A later question brought the answer that the 30-day period is to date from January 23, which is 12 days after the spill).

The Department of Natural Re-

(Continued on page 3)

Board plans opening of Bicentennial Park

Looking to the time when the snows gone and outdoor recreation is ain possible, the Centralia Park ard met Tuesday at the Centralia untry Club.

The main topic of discussion was nning for the opening of Bicentenl Park. Scheduling of the various ojects for development and setting proximate completion dates are in hopper now. Any group wishing to unteer labor is asked to contact ard President Bill Kirtley.

Wally Schramm reported that he s received the last proof for the olet to be placed in the new park, ting names of people and organizations who made donations of $100 or more to the development of Bicentennial Park.

Don Johnson, chairman of Winter Recreation, brought a report of continued interest in the program — despite the weather.

The board's annual budget will be presented at the February meeting.

Those present at the luncheon meeting were Kirtley, Schramm, Johnson, Stan Fadler, Jr., Harell Aderton, John Malloy, Mrs. J. E. Houseworth, and Mrs. N. A. Toalson of the board. Roy Shilharvey represented the City Council.

City stickers due today

City stickers for vehicles and ... number, make and year of vehi-

Cannon Dam project 81 per cent complete

President Carter's budget for the next fiscal year includes $12.6 million for the Cannon Dam and lake project in ... mated to be 81 per cent completed and is slated for completion in the next two years.

The lake has also made possible enlargement of the Mark Twain State Park from 1200 to 2,000 acres. The ...

parts although considered as one. The first will be located slightly north of Highway 154 roughly between the ...

Le 10 janvier 1979, à la suite d'un accident de train de fret, des milliers de litres de chlorophénol, un produit de traitement pour le bois, furent déversés à cette intersection. La marchandise provenait de l'usine Monsanto® de Sauget où étaient fabriqués des PCB jusqu'à récemment. Monsanto® tenta de nier la présence de dioxine (la substance chimique artificielle la plus toxique) dans le liquide renversé : en vain, puisque les tests de l'EPA révélèrent la présence d'un fort taux de dioxine. Monsanto® a été reconnu coupable de n'avoir pas informé les habitants de Sturgeon des risques entraînés par l'accident.

On January 10, 1979, at this intersection, a freight train accident in Sturgeon spilled thousands of gallons of the wood preservative Chlorophenol. The cargo came from Monsanto®'s chemical plant in Sauget, where it had until recently been manufacturing its PCBs. Monsanto® tried to deny the presence of dioxin (the most toxic man-made chemical) in the spill. However, EPA-testings confirmed high levels. Monsanto® was found liable for failing to warn Sturgeon residents about the risks of this spill.

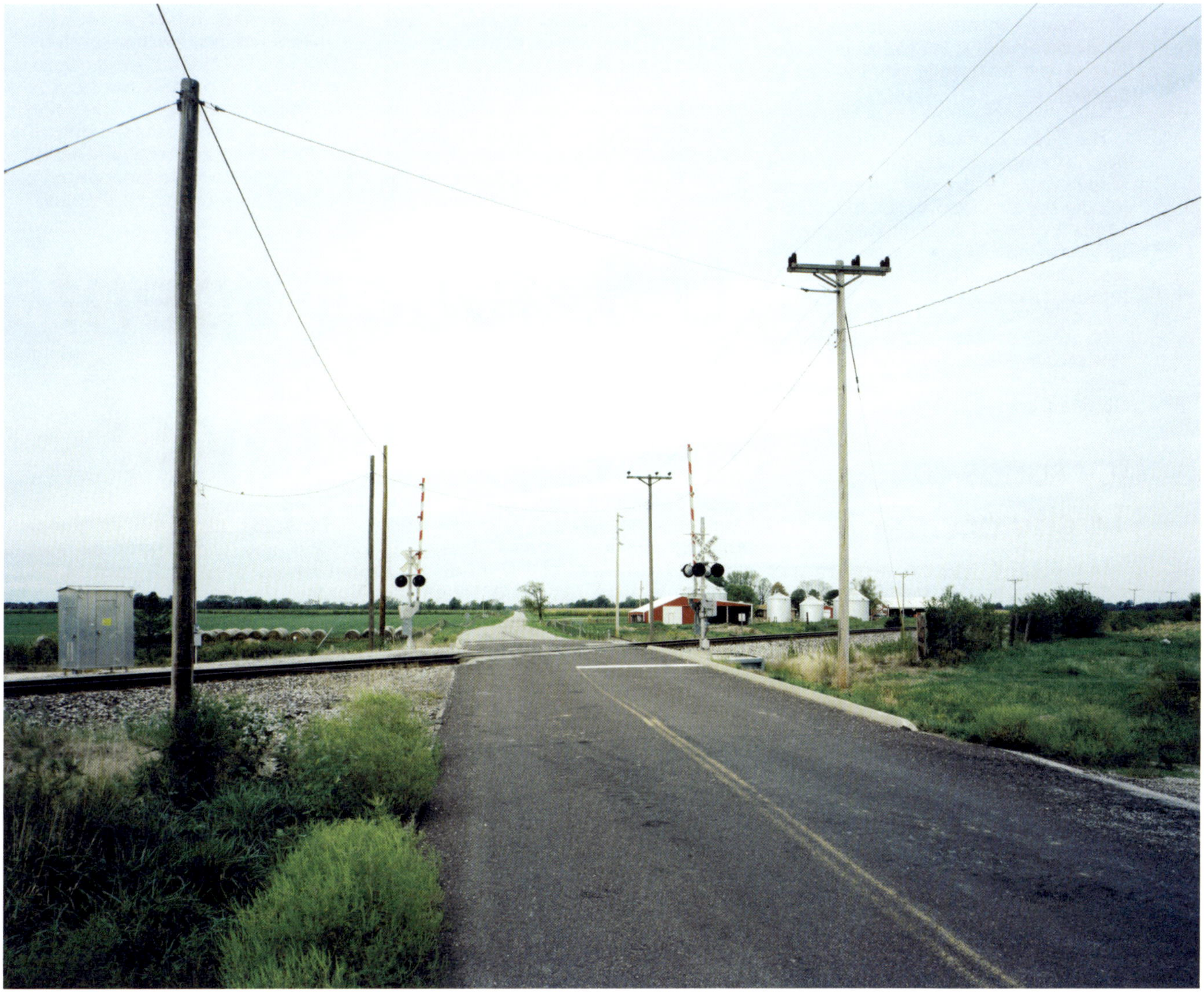

 STURGEON, MISSOURI. 2013

administrative assistant and was given the responsibility of handling bookkeeping duties for the department.

Cole County Prosecuting Atty. Tom Brown had hoped to file additional charges today, but he said he is having trouble in getting some private firms to

alleged theft of a combination AM-FM and CB radio. As in the Jinson case, the radio was allegedly purchased with city funds.

The preliminary hearing on another charge — the theft of a stereo and speaker set on Nov. 2, 1976 — was continued until a later date because of a conflict that

at $20,442 be

According be account special bank and travel with the una

Recount order seen

Missouri House leaders of both parties say they expect little difficulty in the full House ordering a recount of the general election ballots in the race that saw Republican Norbert Plassmeyer of Freeburg win by four votes.

"I wouldn't expect any significant opposition against a recount," said House Republican Floor Leader Russell Brockfeld of Warrenton. "But I may have a different response depending on what happens after the recount is finished."

Democratic Floor Leader Joe Holt said the full House would probably act on the recount recommendation next week so the more than 11,000 ballots in Osage, Maries and Gasconade counties can be counted.

The House Elections Committee made the unanimous recommendation Wednesday, with four Republicans joining the nine Democrats, based on a request from Democrat Gregory Stratman of Vienna, who lost the election according to the official election returns, 5,715 to 5,711.

Stratman's request and another by Joe McCracken of Springfield, who lost by 13 votes to Willard Republican John Hoffman, are the first to be filed with the Legislature since the state's new election code took effect last year. The House Elections Committee will consider McCracken's request next week.

Hoffman was the first House member in decades ousted from his seat in an election contest when the heavily Democratic House voted in 1975 to seat his Democratic opponent Harry Blackwell even though five recounts by election officials showed Hoffman winning or tying.

The latest recount will be conducted by people selected by the committee from lists of candidates submitted to the panel by the election opponents. The committee has yet to determine who should pay for the costs of the recount.

In granting Stratman's request, the committee rejected attempts by Plassmeyer and his attorney to dismiss the action on the grounds that Stratman failed to provide proper notice of the request and document the reasons a recount was necessary.

"We are not alleging any kind of fraud at this point," said Stratman's lawyer Brad Lochenvitz. "We're not alleging any kind of wrongdoing. We're just asking for a recount as a matter of right."

The new law provides for a recount in elections where the margin of victory is less than 1 percent.

The committee also rejected a suggestion that it had no authority in considering the recount, adhering to recent decisions of the state Supreme Court that the Legislature is the sole judge of the qualifications of its members and their election results.

This General Assembly is the third in a row in which the House has been faced with election challenges. In the previous ones, the candidates, including Hoffman, who were originally seated as House members were both ousted as a result of challenges to their election.

Icy roads cause 14 city accidents

Ice-glazed roads apparently contributed to 14 traffic accidents reported Wednesday afternoon and evening in the city.

City police said the accidents were reported between 2 and 8:30 p.m. Wednesday in different sections of the city. None of the accidents resulted in injuries, police said.

Only two accidents were reported before 10 a.m. today.

U.S. funds spent to pay lobbyist

KANSAS CITY, Mo. (AP) — It is "patently outrageous" that the Mid-America Health Systems Agency is paying $25,000 in federal funds to a lobbyist to push for a bill before the legislature, a member of the agency's board says.

Donald Flora, the five-county health planning agency's executive director, says it was necessary to hire Kenneth Hill because Missouri could lose millions of dollars in federal public health grants if the General Assembly doesn't pass the bill.

The bill would give Missouri's blessing to strict federal rules on the expansion of hospitals.

"To spend that kind of money is overkill and unnecessary on such a meritorious piece of legislation," said Gordon Hurlbut, a member of the agency's board. He said it was outrageous to pay the money to Hill for the 5½-month session because the bill probably would be passed anyway.

Hill, a longtime Demoratic party worker and Jimmy Carter's pre-convention campaign chairman in Missouri, said he would "spend as much time as needed" to lobby for the bill and would probably spend 40 hours a week or more in the capital.

Candidates for city office

A 10-cent reduction in the property tax rate, the location of a new animal control shelter and the hiring of a city administrator were all touched upon

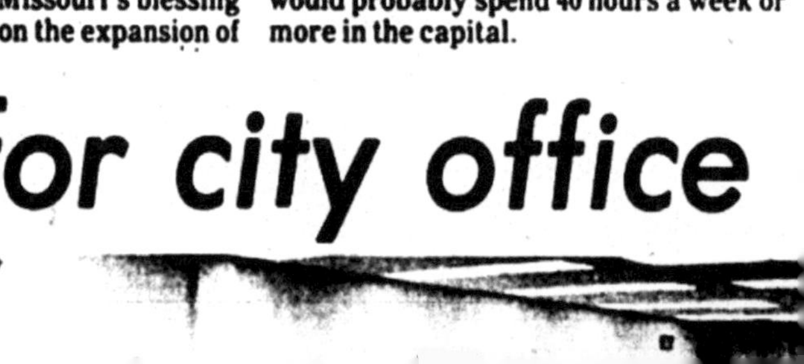

ounted for.
udit, more than $40,000 could not
hen unaccounted for funds in
s and unaccounted for training
ements were lumped together
for items and supplies.

ick action
ves babies

UMBIA, Mo. (AP) — Workers in
natal care unit of the University
souri Medical Center worked
ly for several hours early today
newborn infants breathing after
ssors powering both a main and
central air unit failed.
25 babies were in the unit when
mpressors broke down shortly
idnight, according to Jack Horn,
al administrator. Workers
d the babies to bottled air and, in
ases, manually helped the babies
through the use of plastic bags.
said things were back to normal
two hours, and all the infants
ing well.
Missouri Highway Patrol used its
ncy airplane to bring a prenatal
or to the hospital from the Cox
Center in Springfield, Mo. Two
nits were brought to the medical
y a rental firm.
said he did not know what caused
akdown. He added that he had
with some physicians in the unit
d the emergency had no adverse
n the babies' health.

Snow

One to three inches of
snow tonight with the
low around 10. Weather
details on page 5.

Inside today

Train wheel came loose causing accident and resulting in carbolic acid leak.

Tanker ruptures; 800 evacuated

STURGEON, Mo. (AP) — The 800 residents of this Central Missouri town were evacuated before dawn today after a railroad tank car carrying a caustic, flammable substance collapsed and ruptured.

Jim Patty, Boone County civil defense director, said the 20,000 gallons of chlorophenol leaked from the tank car and became semisolidified by the cold air. Residents said the substance smelled "like the brakes on your car burning."

John Spano, a spokesman for Monsanto Chemical Co. of St. Louis which shipped the substance, said chlorophenol is a type of carbolic acid which is used in the production of wood preservatives. He said it is irritating to the eyes and respiratory system and can burn the skin on contact.

Spano called the evacuation a precautionary move.

Representatives of Monsanto met at the scene after dawn with an environmental cleanup crew to determine the best way to remove the chlorophenol. Patty said the substance had become thick and pasty and there was no danger of it running into any nearby streams.

Patty said some firefighters at the scene had gotten some of the substance on their hands and clothing but were not injured. He said no injuries were reported.

The evacuation was ordered a short time after a wheel of the tank car — which was part of an 87-car Norfolk and Western freight train headed from St. Louis to Kansas City — apparently became disengaged from its mounting. The car fell and broke open about a block north of the city limits.

Volunteer firemen and others went from door to door in the town, located about 20 miles north of Columbia, and advised them to leave their homes. Patty said a bus firm helped evacuate the residents of a nursing home.

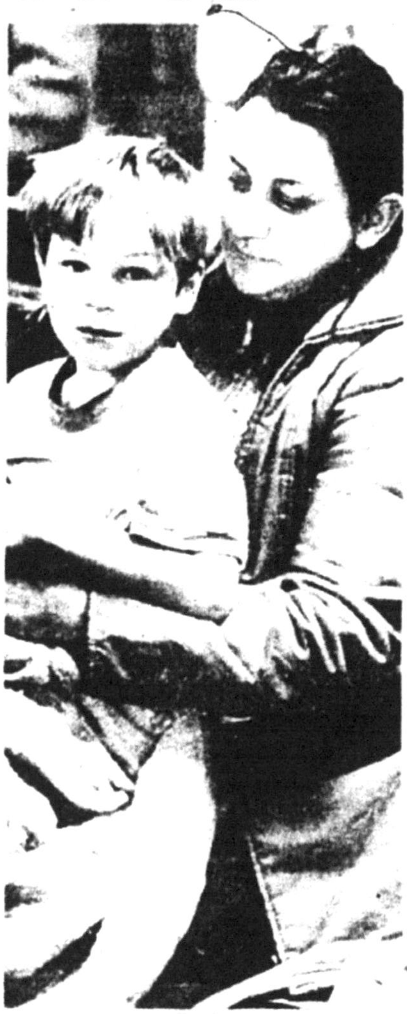

Sturgeon residents Mrs. Roger Wilson and her son Jimmy Thomas at an evacuation shelter.

The evacuated residents were taken to schools, churches and other facilities in nearby communities. "Everything seems to be going smoothly," said Patty. "There were no problems at all. The evacuation went smoothly."

r views on varied issues

Hartsfield's opponent for the Democratic nomination, Kenneth Bell, also said he favored an administrator over a city manager since a manager

centered on the need for the state to pay its share in Jefferson City. Bell noted the Harry S Truman office building has

s if Iran

upplies

regularly deal with the news media on his behalf and serve as his interpreters.

Sadegh Ghotbzadeh said in the interview that if a military coup is permitted, the long-range consequences for the American strategic position in the Persian Gulf would be incalculable because the main-stream opposition to the shah would have been proven wrong in its belief that it could oust the regime without communist support.

Khomaini said in an interview with Italian state television yesterday that he fears the general plan to take over the country on the shah's behalf when he leaves the country.

Ghotbzadeh said Khomaini had alerted the population and urged it to stock as many arms as possible to resist the army and, in the aide's words, "to blow everything up if there is a coup." That seemed to be a call to sabotage Iran's oil industry, the basis of its wealth and of its economic interest to the West.

The Khomaini aide rated as 50-50 the chances that the military plot would be carried out and implied that this depends largely on the U.S. attitude. He dismissed the chances for success of the civilian government of Bakhtiar, who has been rejected by Khomaini.

In a thinly veiled hint that the ayatollah's movement would be forced to turn to the neighboring Soviet Union for help in case of a coup, he said, "if we are defeated by a military coup, the argument that we need money, weapons and external support becomes valid. Then the Communists will be accepted. This is the real danger."

The aides said that Iranian Communists always have argued with members of Khomaini's movement that to win out over "American and British imperialism," the backing of the only viable counterforce, the Soviets, was necessary. Khomaini's followers consistently rejected this view, Ghotbzadeh said.

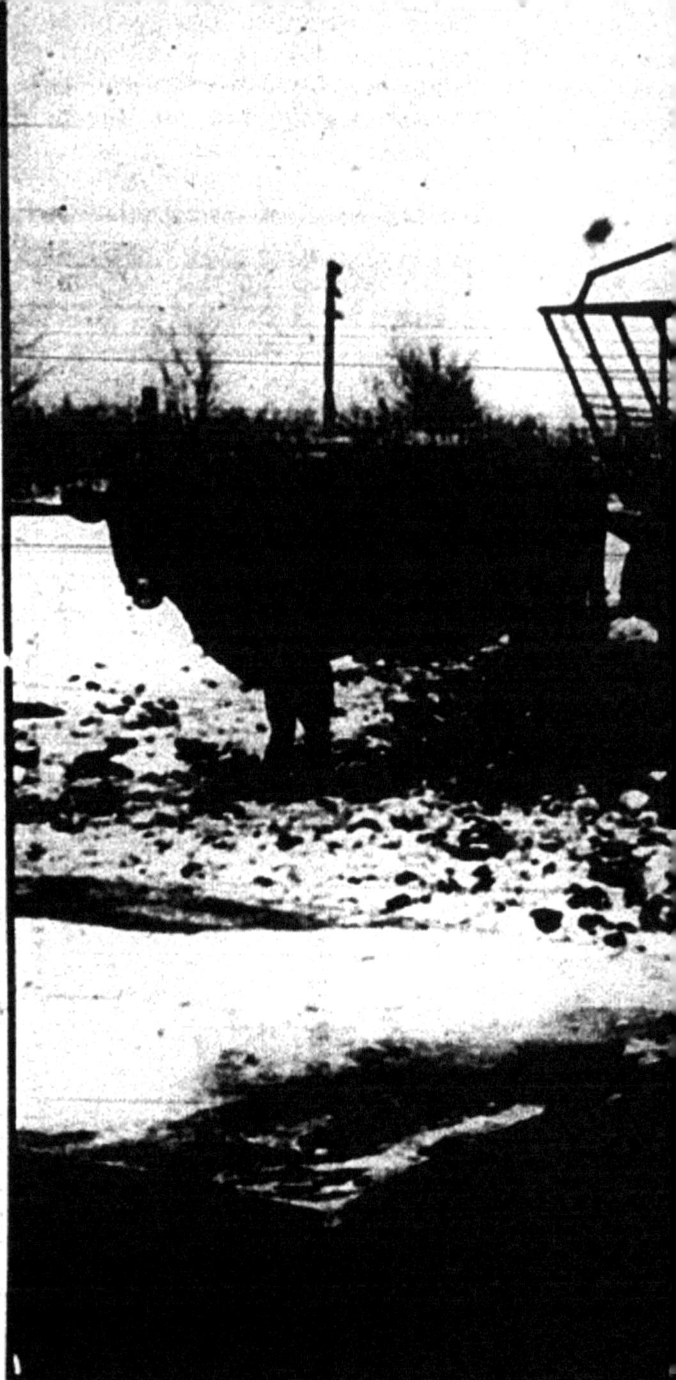

About 75 head of cattle owned by Bill Kemners yards from the toxic chemical spill. And in tow norm. At right, Harold Phillippe cuts Marshall B

Toxic smell subsi linger after 40-ho

By KEN FUSON
of the Tribune's staff

STURGEON — The smell practically is gone, a people are back

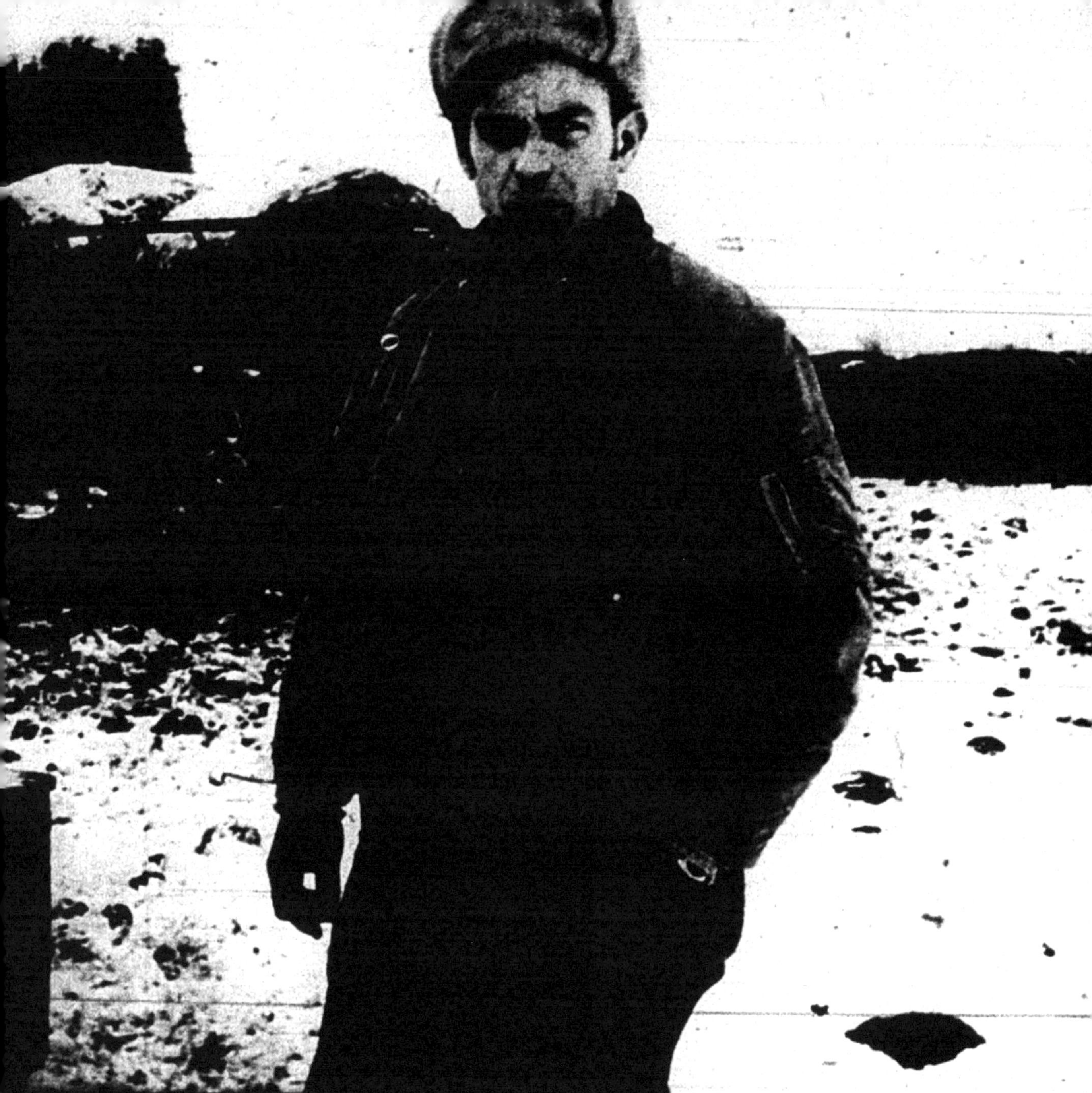

, began grazing today a few hundred e chores like a haircut became the s hair.

Keith McMiflin p

, yet memories Sturgeon ordeal

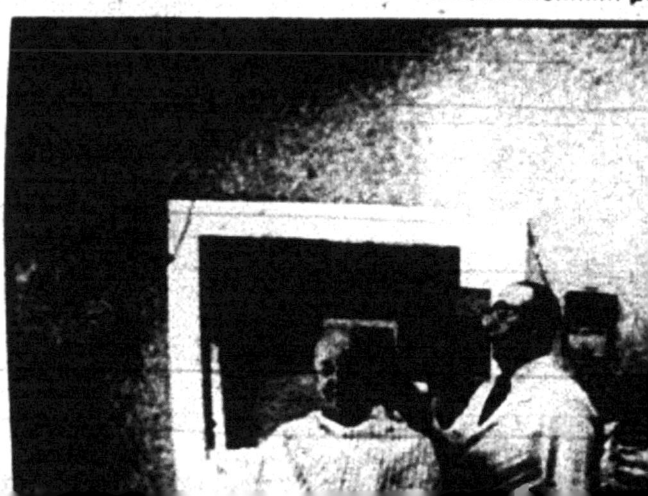

isiness community opened shortly after officials ave the all-clear notice yesterday.

Residents who filtered through the area traded xperiences with talk of the spill, caused when a orfolk and Western Railroad tank car containing

Lecteur de microfilms et pellicules contenant les articles sur l'accident de Sturgeon. Société historique de l'État du Missouri, université du Missouri, Columbia.

The State Historical Society of Missouri at the University of Missouri in Columbia. Microfilm machine and cartridge with the Sturgeon accident headline.

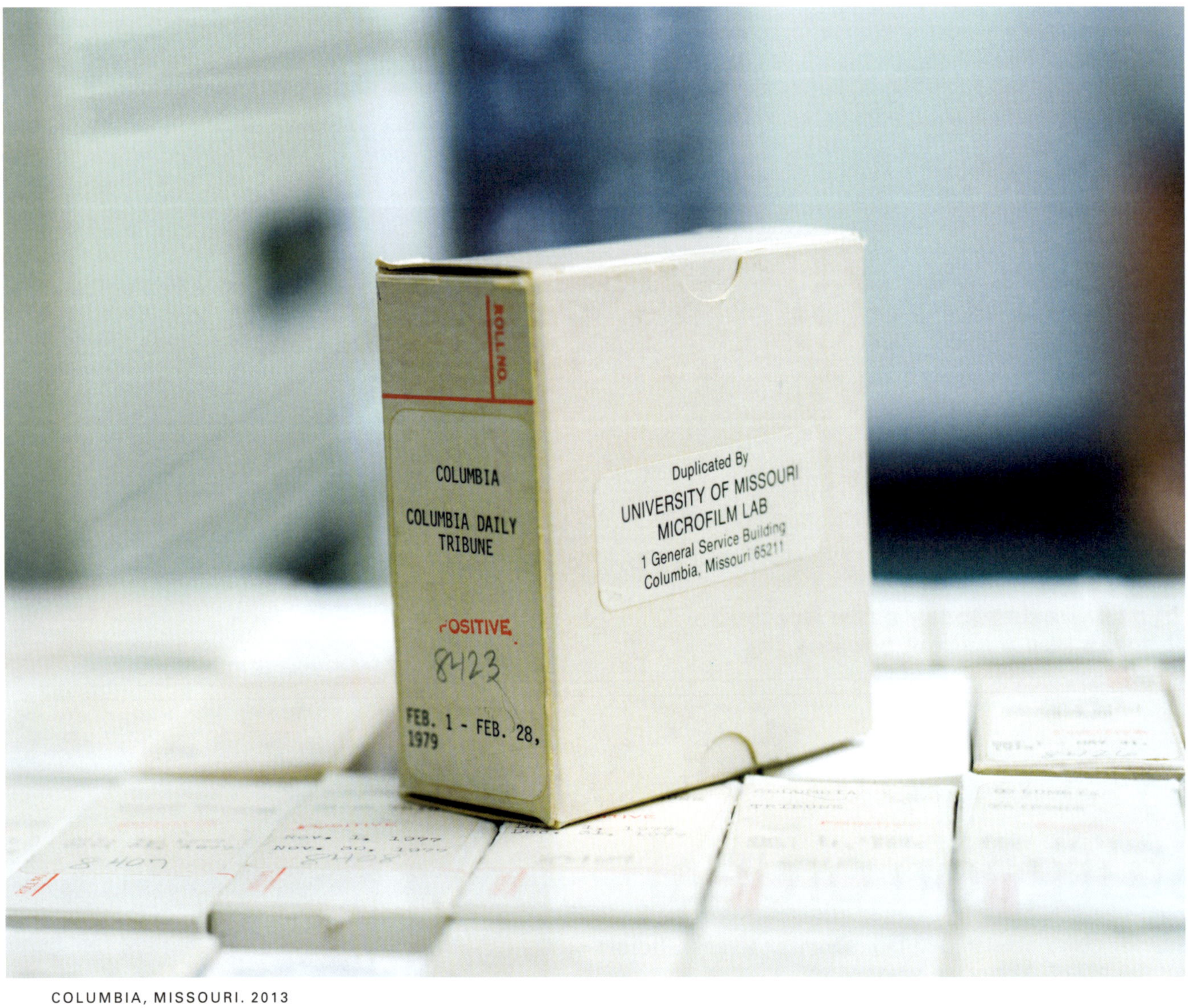

COLUMBIA, MISSOURI. 2013

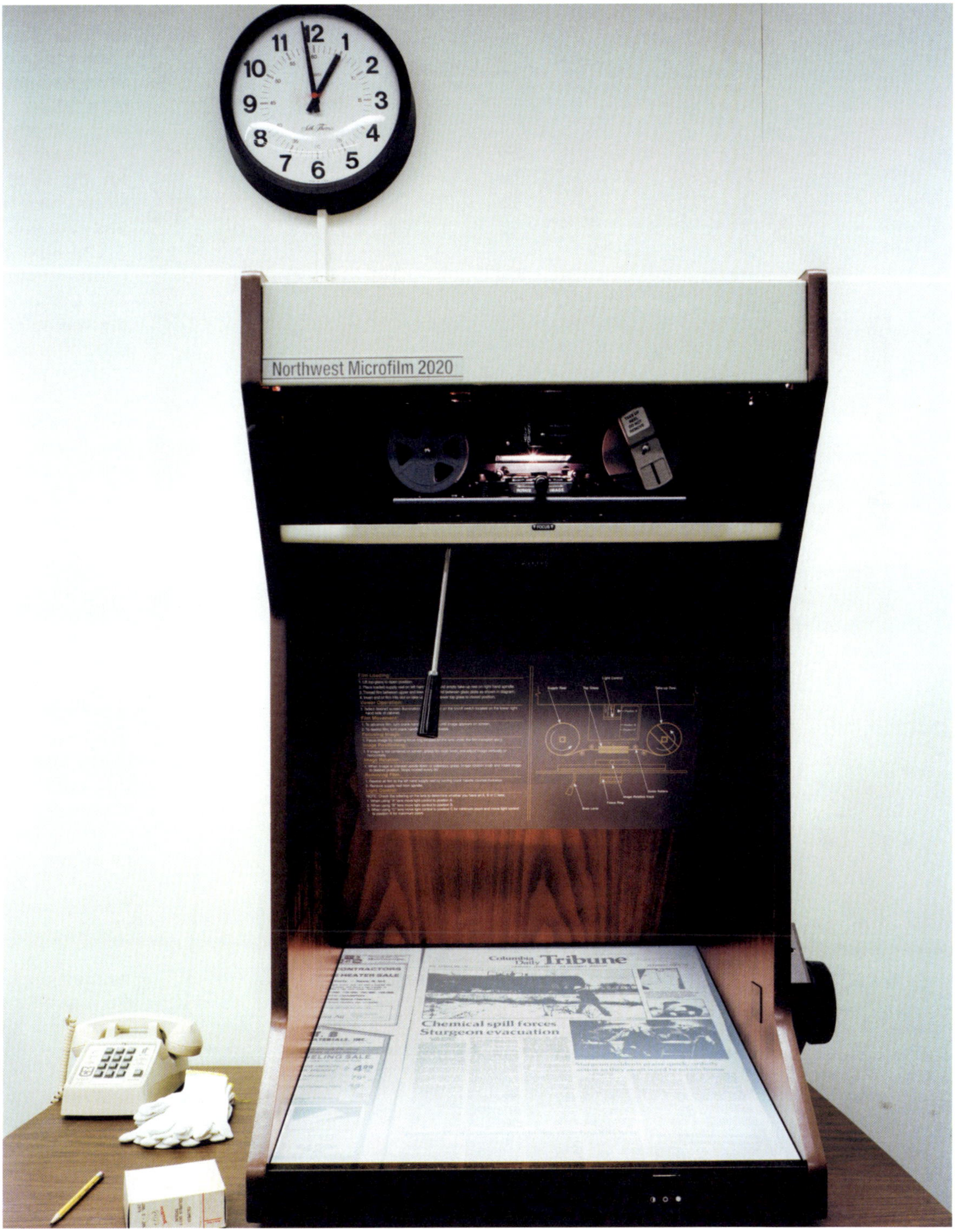

COLUMBIA, MISSOURI. 2013

Sturgeon ev

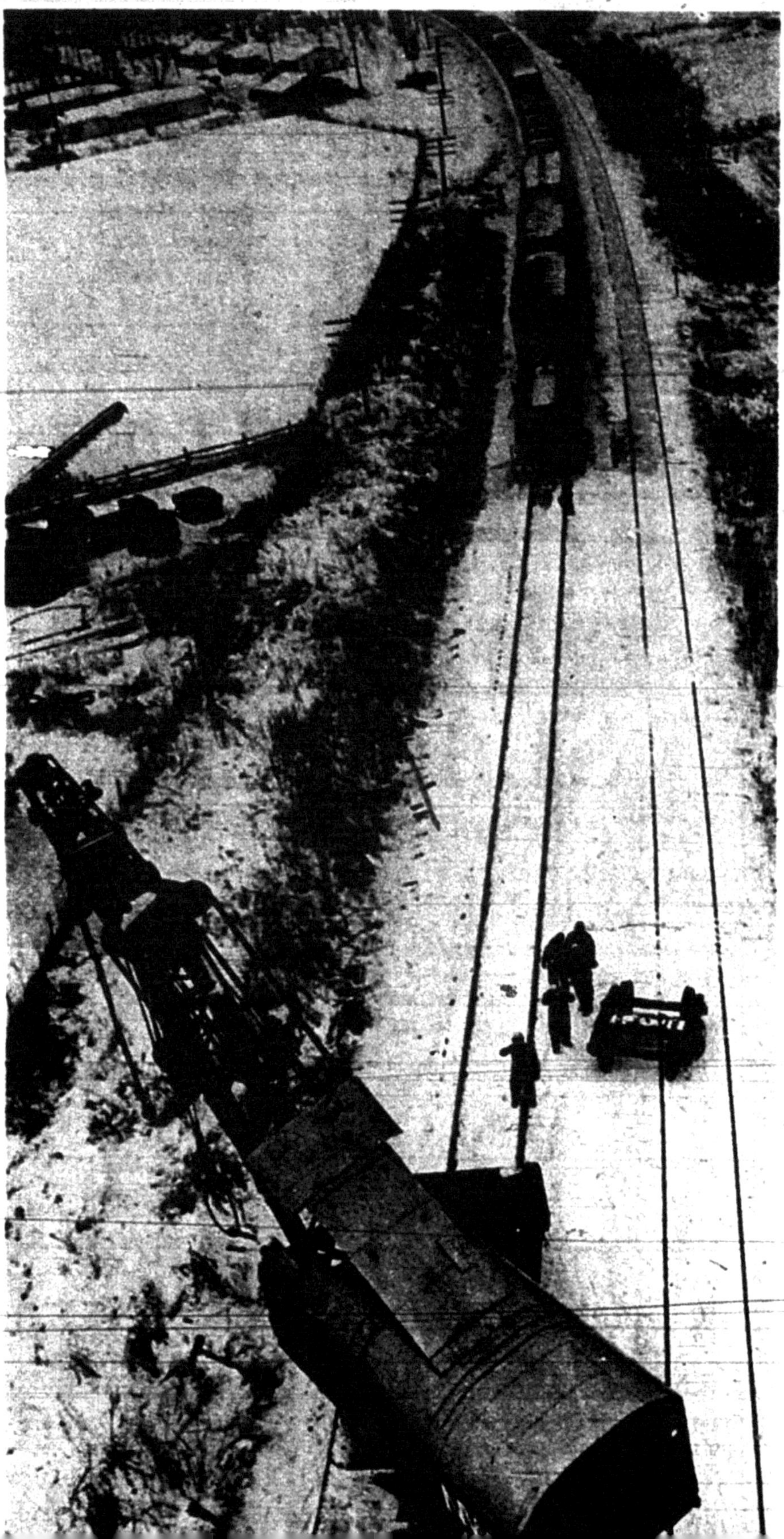

(Continued from page 1)

said she had arrived home and wa retiring for the night when news accident and expected arrival fl on the screen. She gathered up q crackers and cheese and three po of coffee (and cups from an awak Quentin Thompson) and had a come waiting, as she and Daisy B Sturgeon dispensed coffee and from about 1:30 when the evac began to stream in.

Howard Burton, civil defense tor for Centralia, announced a Cross truck would be coming witl and cots.

The Rev. Edwin Burris of the tralia Baptist Church and the Don Carter of the Christian Ch arrived to invite Sturgeon peop their churches, and many went to of those places, where they spen rest of the night, comforted by c food, and the concern of their hosts voluntarily and warmly fed housed them through the next day night. Church members and Red volunteers left their homes and rived at the church to prepare both night and day. The county Cross was alerted by 5 a.m., and of those volunteers arrived short

From the first, a sort of che camaradarie was evident, a "toge ness," in spite of eventual tired Some had taken their pets, some livestock or horses left at hom worry about. Families worried a the welfare of men who remain Sturgeon.

People played cards, visited. next-door neighbors who are sis Mrs. John Moynihan and Mrs. A Boothe, had not seen each other the first of the year, as Mrs. Bo said she'd had a cold and h wanted her sister to catch it. "I've fussing because I had to stay in, now I'm already homesick," laughed.

A Red Cross worker took four school boys with her to buy provis partly to give these caged young something to do. The Sturgeon master called Columbia to ask Sturgeon's mail be left in Centr where he sorted and delivered as n as possible.

In the meantime, a command

cuated after acid spill

been set up at the Sturgeon Fire ion. Gary Scott said that eventu- 36 different organizations were esented by people inside, possibly t once. "I look back on it now," t said, "and can't imagine all those le being in there." Organizations ided three Environmental Protec- Agency offices, fire departments, railroad, Monsanto Chemical ch was shipping the chemical edient for a wood preservative), ty health department, Red Cross, ation Army, Western Environ- t (handling the cleanup opera- , county road department, county t, and others.

e station's three phones were in nuous use, Scott said. For the inder of the first night no one , but by the second night people rying to get brief stretches of sleep op of fire trucks, in trucks, in rs, couches, army cots, on nearly object that didn't move.

ott said all the firemen did an llent job, and no one complained t the task. He termed their opera- a "textbook case of proper handl- " and added the firemen "espe- y appreciate the people's coopera- and are so thankful to them for ing their homes so well without cting, because that's what made gs go so smoothly." He also men- ed the community could feel fortu- the tanker had not contained ething like LP gas or vinyl ride which could have caused nsive damage from fire.

reman Bill Littrell agreed that ple, especially the older people, wonderful — they just got dres- didn't question, were very good t it." He was of the opinion that all many agencies performed as well ey could, given the responsibility had of thinking of the welfare of some people.

nerally, he said, the firemen were usy to think of the strangeness of g in an empty town, as they stood y with medical or emergency aid, ted with clean up, relieved law rcement efforts, and other ac- ies. He mentioned the help of the ty court in providing trucks to k roads, freeing law enforcement people from that added duty.

Mayor D.C. White said one of his main concerns had been policing the area, but between the county road district and the fire department and other volunteer, and later the county sheriff's department and highway patrol, it would have been impossible for anyone to get into town except with approval, and that for only a short time.

Littrell also expressed gratitude to the Salvation Army which arrived at the fire station not long after the mishap, bringing coffee, hot chocolate and rolls, and furnishing hot meals therafter until noon Friday, with sandwiches Friday night. He spoke of the before-departure help of Sturgeon merchants: Charlie Hubble who opened the store to let the men get some supplies; Stugeon Oil Company who let the men have access to its gas pumps; Ritchie Hardware for providing a key to the store so supplies could be obtained there.

Working steadily during all the evacuation and all the cleanup efforts also were Bob Jesse and Dean Connolly, who were covering the spill with lime to neutralize it. Connolly loaded lime for Jesse to haul and spread that first night, all day, and the next night, with others of the men present alternating.

In the initial cleanup, the spilled chemical was scraped up and put in sealed barrels for transport out. By Sunday, and into the early part of this week, the material was being loaded into railroad gondola cars to be hauled out for some type of cleaning operation.

Drainage ditches are being dug in case of rain or a thaw, to allow any resulting liquid to run off. Jesse said there may be some ground penetration, but none very deep unless it's deeper by the tanker's stopping place. The smell still surrounds any area where spillage still lays. Liming was still underway Monday. The first two or three inches of ground is being removed, between the tracks and on farther along the tracks. The affected area is blocked off.

The tanker wheels were hauled out Friday. The sealed car, now in Moberly, was patched Sunday, as residents there were complainig about the smell.

David Ritchie, chief of the Sturgeon Fire Department, BCFPD Station 6, said EPA representatives and cleanup men are still in town, and may be working at the continuing cleanup all this week and into next week. Efforts are being made to try to get Monsanto Chemical to return and continue some air testing from time to time. Ritchie also said he understood some type of steam machine will be brought in to wash out the area in a sort of vacuuming operation.

Shortly after 10:30 a.m. Friday, about 36 hours after it all began, an air sampling indicated the worst of the hazard was over, the announcement was made, barricades lifted, and residents returned one after another to their homes, burrowing thankfully in: thankful to their erstwhile hosts, thankful to the men who had remained in Sturgeon through it all, and just plain thankful to be home again — before Friday night's snowstorm.

Four firemen were taken to the hospital at various times to check on possible effects from the chemical: Gary Scott, Gary Jennings, David White and Buster Adkisson. All appeared to be all right, but Adkisson is still experiencing some effects.

Chief Ritchie said a totaling had been made of the man hours spent by 18 men in the Sturgeon Fire Department through the whole ordeal. For these Sturgeon firemen alone, the total is 674 hours. Including men from the Columbia and Hallsville stations and the University fire training division, the total should probably rise to over 1,?00 hours, plus all the hours spent by other volunteers.

As long ago as 1975 the Sturgeon firemen began to attend seminars and study the handling of hazardous materials, always considering the proximity of the railroad to the community, and knowing something of the nature of various materials that undoubtedly came rolling through town, not just by the railroad but, by trucks on nearby highways. Their foresight and preparedness has been fortunate for the community.

IV.

« En vertu des accords de Monsanto®, les agriculteurs ne peuvent plus conserver leurs graines pour une utilisation ultérieure, ce qui met fin à une tradition agricole de dix mille ans. »
Centre pour la sécurité alimentaire

"Under Monsanto®'s agreements, farmers can no longer save their seeds for later use, ending a 10,000-year-old farming tradition." Center for Food Safety

Le Contrat

The Contract

En 1993, Monsanto® dépose le brevet de son premier OGM résistant au Roundup : le soja RR (Roundup Ready) et demande sa mise sur le marché en 1994. Vingt ans plus tard, 181 millions d'hectares de plantes transgéniques sont cultivés dans le monde dont 73 millions aux États-Unis, 42 millions au Brésil, 24 millions en Argentine, 11 millions en Inde et au Canada[41]. Monsanto® à lui seul totalise 90 % des semences transgéniques du monde : soja, maïs, coton et colza. 80 % du maïs américain proviennent de cultures transgéniques de Monsanto®. Les OGM, initialement créés pour permettre de meilleurs rendements aux agriculteurs et limiter la faim dans le monde, contiennent un transgène — un gène pesticide — qui supporte le Roundup. Les cultures agricoles ainsi parées courent peu de risques lors des épandages : 70 % des OGM résistent au Roundup. Depuis l'introduction des OGM dans les cultures, les ventes mondiales du Roundup ont explosé.

À partir de 1974, Monsanto® impose le Roundup sur les marchés américain et européen. L'herbicide annoncé « 100 % biodégradable » et « bon pour l'environnement » s'inscrit dans les préoccupations de l'époque : en 1970, la création de l'EPA (Agence américaine de protection de l'environnement) répond aux demandes insistantes du public désireux de disposer d'un environnement propre. Le Roundup — nom commercial du glyphosate de Monsanto® — est dérivé d'un acide aminé (la glycine) découvert à la fin des années 1960. Qualifié de « total » ou « non sélectif », le désherbant permet de bloquer la croissance végétale et de détruire la plante. Dans les années 1970, des laboratoires privés, dont Industrial Bio-Test (IBT) et Craven, effectuent des tests sur les pesticides, le glyphosate et le Roundup et transmettent leurs résultats à l'EPA. Ces études, concluant qu'il n'y a pas de résidus de pesticides dans les aliments, l'eau ou les sols, permettent l'homologation du Roundup et sa mise sur le marché[42]. En 1983, l'EPA découvre que IBT a manipulé ses données et ses résultats « manifestement (...) pour satisfaire (ses) clients[43] ». *Idem* pour Craven en 1991[44]. Les responsables des laboratoires sont condamnés pour fraude à cinq ans de prison. Monsanto® et les bénéficiaires de ces études biaisées ne sont pas poursuivis.

Impassiblement, l'usage des pesticides — en tête le Roundup — progresse dans le monde. Selon Julie Marc, 25 millions de tonnes de pesticides sont répandues annuellement sur les cultures mondiales : « 0,3 % entre en contact avec les organismes cibles, ce qui veut dire que 99,7 % des substances déversées s'en vont "ailleurs" dans l'environnement, dans le sol et les eaux[45] ». En 1996, Monsanto® est condamné par le tribunal de New York pour publicité mensongère sur la biodégradabilité du Roundup. En 2012, Monsanto® réalise un chiffre d'affaires de 13,5 milliards de dollars, soit 14 % de croissance par rapport à 2011. Il atteint 14,9 milliards de dollars en 2013. Des profits sûrement insuffisants pour Monsanto®, qui propose un « contrat » spécifique aux agriculteurs. Selon le principe commercial de la vente liée, Monsanto® vend à la fois ses semences brevetées OGM et son herbicide Roundup. Le contrat stipule que les agriculteurs doivent racheter chaque année les semences à planter. Le génie de Monsanto® a même créé des plantes stériles — *Terminator* — pour garantir ces achats annuels, les plantes n'étant utilisées qu'une seule fois[46]. Un moratoire de l'ONU en 1999 empêche toutefois l'utilisation de ce procédé au nom de la biodiversité. Avec ces contrats, Monsanto® s'assure des revenus réguliers alors que les agriculteurs s'endettent inexorablement.

D'après David Snively, vice-président et avocat de Monsanto®, la compagnie investit 2,6 millions de dollars par jour en recherche-développement. Pour protéger ses brevets « qui bénéficient aux agriculteurs et aux consommateurs », elle a mené plus de 140 procès — au nom du droit de la propriété intellectuelle — « contre les fermiers qui volent ou réutilisent leurs semences[47] ». Monsanto® a même recruté une « police des graines » qui traque les OGM « illégaux » chez les agriculteurs. Or les OGM infestent les champs par dissémination naturelle (vent ou insectes), le soja transgénique s'autoféconde, les semenciers revendent des graines OGM aux agriculteurs qui n'ont pas signé de contrat avec Monsanto®... Les agriculteurs sont sans recours : le contrat dégage Monsanto® de la responsabilité des contaminations mais il lui permet de poursuivre un agriculteur qui cultive involontairement une graine transgénique. Le débat sur le brevetage du vivant est, certes, sujet à polémiques. En attendant des solutions claires et mondiales, les paysans sont ruinés.

En 2004, des *superweeds*[48] résistantes au Roundup envahissent les États-Unis et prolifèrent à tel point que des agriculteurs abandonnent la culture transgénique quand d'autres délaissent leurs champs. Après avoir « créé son poison, Monsanto® invente son antidote[49] » : le 15 janvier 2015, le ministère de l'Agriculture américain autorise la commercialisation de semences OGM nommées Roundup Ready Extend qui supportent deux herbicides combinés, le Roundup et le dicamba[50].

Une nouvelle génération d'OGM aux conséquences environnementales et sociales dramatiques pour toutes les zones du monde qui les utilisent : États-Unis, Brésil, Argentine, Inde et Canada principalement. La dépendance des OGM aux pesticides est indéniable, les rendements agricoles ne sont pas meilleurs, la faim dans le monde n'a pas cessé, mais Monsanto® et comparses s'enrichissent toujours, en limitant les choix de productions agricoles, en contrôlant les prix sur les marchés mondiaux et en laissant leurs traces sur la planète. Même si fin 2015 Monsanto® enregistre une perte nette de 253 millions de dollars et voit ses ventes de semences transgéniques reculer de 13,7 %[51].

En mars 2015, l'OMS classe le glyphosate — principe actif du Roundup — cancérigène probable pour l'homme[52]. Le 12 novembre 2015, l'Autorité européenne de sécurité des aliments (EFSA) juge le risque improbable[53], une fois le produit réévalué par l'Institut fédéral allemand d'évaluation des risques (le BFR) où « le tiers des membres du comité sont directement salariés... par des géants de l'agrochimie ou des biotechnologies[54] ».

Le 9 mars 2016, Bruxelles reporte pourtant le vote sur le renouvellement de l'autorisation du glyphosate en Europe[55].

41 Clive James, « Global Status of Commercialized Biothec / GM Crops: 2014 », *ISAAA Brief*, n° 49, New York, 2014.

42 EPA, *Data Validation. Memo from K. Locke, Toxicology Branch, to R. Taylor, Registration Branch*, Washington, 9 août 1978.

43 EPA, Office of Pesticides and Toxic Substances, *Summary of the IBT Review Program, Washington*, juillet 1983 ; Marie-Monique Robin, op. cit., p. 33.

44 EPA, Communication and Public Affairs, *Note to Correspondents*, Washington, 1er mars 1991.

45 Julie Marc, *Effets toxiques d'herbicides à base de glyphosate sur la régulation du cycle cellulaire et le développement précoce en utilisant l'embryon d'oursin*, Université de biologie de Rennes, 10 septembre 2004.

46 Technologie développée en 1998 par la firme Delta & Pine Land (rachetée par Monsanto® en 2006).

47 Conger Beasley Jr., « Defending Monsanto, David Snively Doesn't Mind the Stress », *Super Lawyers*, septembre 2009.

48 Environ quinze plantes, dont la robuste et prolifique amarante, résistent au Roundup. Elles s'adaptent à tout type de climat et concernent plus de 50 000 hectares, *in* agriculture.greenpeace.fr, 11 août 2010.

49 Julien Goetz, « Monsanto, sa vie, son empire », *Datagueule*, France Télévision, 19 juin 2014.

50 Herbicide provoquant des perturbations hormonales chez la plante.

51 *Le Monde* et AFP, 6 janvier 2016.

52 Cancérigène de groupe 2A selon la classification du circ, Centre international de recherche sur le cancer (OMS).

53 *Le Monde* et AFP, 12 novembre 2015.

54 *Le Monde*, 25 mars 2015.

55 *Le Monde*, 8 mars 2016.

MONSANTO® CONTRE LES AGRICULTEURS

Estimation du nombre de « piratages de semences » par région/État et des sommes versées par les agriculteurs à Monsanto®.

Région ou État	Nombre de comtés	Nombre minimum de cas	Nombre maximum de cas	Mise à jour du piratage de semences	Règlement moyen	Règlement maximum	Minimum perçu	Maximum perçu
CAROLINE DU NORD ET DU SUD	58	289	505	JUIN 2006	72 229 $	919 068 $	20 874 181 $	36 475 645 $
MISSOURI ET KANSAS	114	422	785	JUIN 2006	28 442 $	195 636 $	12 002 524 $	22 326 970 $
ILLINOIS	81	307	564	JUIN 2006	34 476 $	200 000 $	10 584 132 $	19 444 464 $
MINNESOTA, DAKOTA DU NORD ET DU SUD	100	291	574	JUIN 2006	32 317 $	136 333 $	9 404 247 $	18 549 958 $
MICHIGAN ET OHIO	89	312	584	MAI 2006	28 111 $	96 400 $	8 770 632 $	16 416 824 $
INDIANA	74	223	434	JUIN 2006	33 934 $	225 000 $	7 567 282 $	14 727 356 $
KENTUCKY	23	68	131	JUIN 2006	83 867 $	230 000 $	5 702 956 $	10 986 577 $
IOWA	90	276	532	JUIN 2006	20 536 $	175 000 $	5 667 936 $	10 925 152 $
VIRGINIE, MARYLAND, DELAWARE, NEW JERSEY ET PENNSYLVANIE	39	80	175	JUIN 2006	37 671 $	52 073 $	3 013 680 $	6 592 425 $
NEBRASKA	43	123	247	JUIN 2006	16 797 $	48 139 $	2 066 031 $	4 148 859 $
TOTAL	711	2 391	4 531	--	--	--	85 653 601 $	160 594 230 $

Dix documents intitulés « Piratage de semences : Mise à jour locale [État/région] » ont été téléchargés l'été 2006 du site www.monsantoperformance.com pour les États/régions donnés (voir annexe II). Tous les documents sont datés de juin 2006, à l'exception de ceux concernant le Michigan et l'Ohio, datés de mai 2006. Depuis le 24 octobre 2007, les documents ne sont plus en ligne. Méthodologie : sur chaque mise à jour du piratage de semences par État ou région, Monsanto® fournit une carte des « affaires de piratage de semences » par comté. Sur la carte, les codes couleurs indiquent 1 à 3, 4 à 7, 8 à 13, 14 à 23 ou 24 à 36 affaires de piratages de semences par comté. Si on additionne les chiffres les plus bas pour chaque comté, on obtient le nombre minimum de cas pour un État ou une région donnés, de même que si on additionne les chiffres les plus élevés pour chaque comté, on obtient le nombre maximum de cas. La multiplication du nombre minimum ou maximum de cas de piratage de semences par le « règlement moyen » pour l'État/région donne les montants minimum et maximum des règlements pour l'État/région dont il est question. La somme de ces chiffres pour les dix mises à jour « Piratage de semences » donne une estimation du nombre minimum de règlements (2 391), du nombre maximum de règlements (4 531), et la fourchette des montants des règlements pour les 19 États dont traitent les dix documents. Tous les cas impliquent les graines de soja Roundup Ready.
SOURCE : http://www.centerforfoodsafety.org/files/cfsmonsantovsfarmerreport11305.pdf

In 1993, Monsanto® files the patent for its first Roundup-resistant GMO, Roundup Ready (RR) soybeans, and requests the approval for commercialization the following year. Twenty years later, 181 million hectares of transgenic plants are cultivated around the world: 73 million hectares in the United States, 42 million hectares in Brazil, 24 million hectares in Argentina, and 11 million in India and Canada.[41] Monsanto® alone accounts for 90% of the world's transgenic seeds: soybeans, maize, cotton and colza. Eighty per cent of American maize is cultivated from transgenic seeds originating from Monsanto®. The genetically modified organisms (GMO), initially created to increase crop yields and reduce world hunger, contain transgenes that render them resistant to Roundup. Seventy per cent of GMO crops are Roundup-resistant, making them immune to harm during herbicide application. Since the introduction of GMO crops, Roundup sales have exploded.

Roundup is introduced onto the American and European markets in 1974. The herbicide is lauded as "100% biodegradable" and "good for the environment," consistent with the concerns of the time: in 1970, the Environmental Protection Agency is created to respond to increasing public demand for a clean environment. Roundup, the commercial name for Monsanto®'s glyphosate, is derived from an amino acid (glycine) discovered at the end of the 1960s. Qualified as "total" or "non-selective," the herbicide inhibits vegetative growth, eventually destroying the plant. In the 1970s, private laboratories including Industrial Bio-Test (IBT) and Craven perform studies on glyphosate and Roundup and transmit their results to the EPA. The tests conclude that no pesticide residues are found in food products, water or soil, clearing the way for Roundup's approval for sale.[42] In 1983, the EPA discovers that IBT manipulated its data and the results of its studies, seemingly to satisfy its clients.[43] Likewise for Craven in 1991.[44] Several key officials are charged with fraud and sentenced to five years imprisonment. Monsanto® and the other beneficiaries of the falsified studies are never pursued.

Little by little, pesticide use is progressing throughout the world, with Roundup in the lead. According to Julie Marc, of the 25 million tonnes of pesticides applied to crops annually, "0.3% reach their target organisms; 99.7% of the applied substances end up 'elsewhere' in the environment, in the soil and water."

In 1996, the Attorney General of New York takes legal action against Monsanto® for false advertising regarding Roundup's biodegradability.

In 2012, Monsanto® generates revenues of $13.5 billion, representing a 14% increase as compared to 2011. This figure reaches $14.9 billion in 2013. Apparently this profit is insufficient for Monsanto®, which now proposes a "contract" to farmers. According to the commercial principle of tied selling, Monsanto® sells its patented GM seeds along with its herbicide Roundup. The contract stipulates that farmers must purchase new seeds each year for planting. Monsanto®'s engineers go so far as to create sterile plants, a technology known as Terminator, in order to ensure its annual sales, as the seed can be used only once.[46] In 1999, the United Nations imposes a moratorium on this practice in the name of biodiversity. The contract ensures Monsanto®'s revenues, while inexorably indebting farmers. According to David Snively, Monsanto®'s Vice President and General Counsel, the company invests $2.6 million per day in research and development that "benefits farmers and consumers." In the name of intellectual property, the company has filed over 140 patent infringement cases against farmers "to ensure that its seeds are not stolen or reused."[47] However, GMOs overtake fields in natural dissemination by wind or insects, transgenic soybeans self-fertilize, and seed companies resell GMO seeds to farmers who have not signed Monsanto®'s contract. The farmers are without recourse, as Monsanto®'s contract clears the company of responsibility for crop contamination while allowing it to pursue farmers who involuntarily cultivate transgenic seeds.

The patent of living organisms is naturally subject to debate. As we await clear, global solutions, farmers fall into financial ruin. In 2004, Roundup-resistant superweeds[48] storm across the United States, proliferating with such force that some farmers abandon transgenic plants while others leave their fields barren. Monsanto® responds by "selling the poison and the antidote."[49] On January 15, 2015, the United States Department of Agriculture announces the deregulation of the next generation of GM seed, Roundup Ready 2 Xtend, which is tolerant to two herbicides, Roundup and Dicamba.[50]

This new generation of GMOs comes with dramatic environmental and social consequences for all the regions of the world where they are cultivated, principally the United States, Brazil, Argentina, India and Canada. The dependence of GMO crops on pesticides is undeniable; since their emergence, crop yields are no higher, and world hunger continues to rise. Although at the end of 2015, Monsanto® registered a net loss of $253 million and saw its transgenic seed sales reduced by 13.7%,[51] the company and its cohorts continue to enrich themselves, limiting choice in agricultural production and controlling world market prices, leaving their mark around the globe.

In March 2015, the WHO classified Roundup's principle ingredient, glyphosate, as a probable human carcinogen.[52] On November 12, 2015, the European Food Safety Authority judged the risk improbable[53] after the product was reevaluated by the German Federal Institute for Risk Assessment (the BFR), where "a third of the committee members are paid directly... by the giants of agrochemical or biotech industries."[54] On March 9, 2016, Brussels postponed the vote to renew the authorization for the use of glyphosate in Europe.[55]

41 Clive James, "Global Status of Commercialized Biotech / GM Crops: 2014," ISAAA Brief N°49, New York, 2014.

42 EPA, Data Validation, *Memo from K. Locke, Toxicology Branch, to R. Taylor, Registration Branch*, Washington, August 9, 1978.

43 EPA, Office of Pesticides and Toxic Substances, *Summary of the IBT Review Program*, Washington, July, 1983; Marie-Monique Robin, op. cit., p. 33.

44 EPA, Communication and Public Affairs, Note to Correspondents, Washington, March 1, 1991.

45 Julie Marc, "Effets toxiques d'herbicides à base de glyphosate sur la régulation du cycle cellulaire et le développement précoce en utilisant l'embryon d'oursin," (Toxic effects of glyphosate-based herbicides on the regulation of the cell cycle and early development), Université de Rennes, September 10, 2004.

46 Technology developed in 1998 by the firm Delta & Pine Land (purchased by Monsanto® in 2006).
47 Conger Beasley Jr., "Defending Monsanto, David Snively doesn't mind the stress," *Super Lawyers*, September 2009.
48 Approximately 15 plants, including the robust and prolific amaranth, are resistant to Roundup. They adapt to all climate types and affect over 50,000 hectares. In Agriculture.greenpeace.fr, August 11, 2010.
49 Julien Goetz, "Monsanto, sa vie, son empire," (Monsanto, its life, its empire), *Datagueule*, France Télévision, June 19, 2014.
50 Herbicide that provokes hormonal disruptions of the plant.
51 *Le Monde* and AFP, January 6, 2016.
52 Group 2A carcinogen according to the classification of the International Agency for Research on Cancer (WHO).
53 *Le Monde* and AFP, November 12, 2015.
54 *Le Monde*, March 25, 2015.
55 *Le Monde*, March 8, 2016.

MONSANTO® *VS.* US FARMERS
Estimates of number of "Seed Piracy Matters" by region/state and sums paid by farmers to Monsanto®.

Region/State	Number of Counties	Minimum number of cases	Maximum number of cases	Seed Piracy Update	Average settlement	Maximum settlement	Minimum collected	Maximum collected
NORTH & SOUTH CAROLINA	58	289	505	JUNE 2006	$72,229	$919,068	$20,874,181	$36,475,645
MISSOURI & KANSAS	114	422	785	JUNE 2006	$28,442	$195,636	$12,002,524	$22,326,970
ILLINOIS	81	307	564	JUNE 2006	$34,476	$200,000	$10,584,132	$19,444,464
MINNESOTA, NORTH & SOUTH DAKOTA	100	291	574	JUNE 2006	$32,317	$136,333	$9,404,247	$18,549,958
MICHIGAN & OHIO	89	312	584	MAY 2006	$28,111	$96,400	$8,770,632	$16,416,824
INDIANA	74	223	434	JUNE 2006	$33,934	$225,000	$7,567,282	$14,727,356
KENTUCKY	23	68	131	JUNE 2006	$83,867	$230,000	$5,702,956	$10,986,577
IOWA	90	276	532	JUNE 2006	$20,536	$175,000	$5,667,936	$10,925,152
VIRGINIA, MARYLAND, DELAWARE, NEW JERSEY & PENNSYLVANIA	39	80	175	JUNE 2006	$37,671	$52,073	$3,013,680	$6,592,425
NEBRASKA	43	123	247	JUNE 2006	$16,797	$48,139	$2,066,031	$4,148,859
TOTAL	711	2 391	4 531	--	--	--	$85,653,601	$160,594,230

Ten documents entitled "Seed Piracy: [State/Region] Local Update" were downloaded in the summer of 2006 from www.monsantoperformance.com for the given states/regions (see Appendix II). All documents dated 06/06 except Michigan-Ohio (05/06). As of October 24, 2007, documents no longer posted. Methodology: For each state/regional Seed Piracy Update, Monsanto® provides a map of "Seed Piracy Matters" by county. The map is color-coded by county for 1-3, 4-7, 8-13, 14-23 or 24-36 Seed Piracy Matters. Adding together the lower-bound figures for each county provides the minimum number of cases, while adding together the upper-bound figures for each county provides the maximum number of cases, for the given state or region. Multiplication of the minimum and maximum Seed Piracy Matters by the "average settlement" for the state/region gives the minimum and maximum settlement amounts for the given state/region. Summation of these figures for all 10 "Seed Piracy" updates gives the estimated minimum number of settlements (2,391), the maximum number of settlements (4,531), and the range of settlement amounts for the 19 states covered by the 10 documents. All cases involved Roundup Ready soybeans. SOURCE: http://www.centerforfoodsafety.org/files/cfsmonsantovsfarmerreport11305.pdf

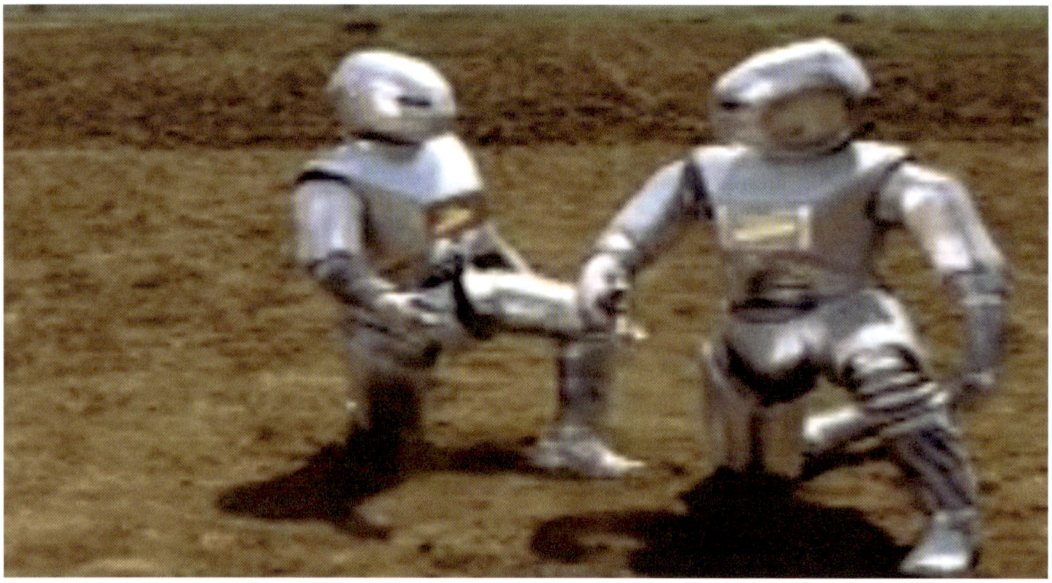

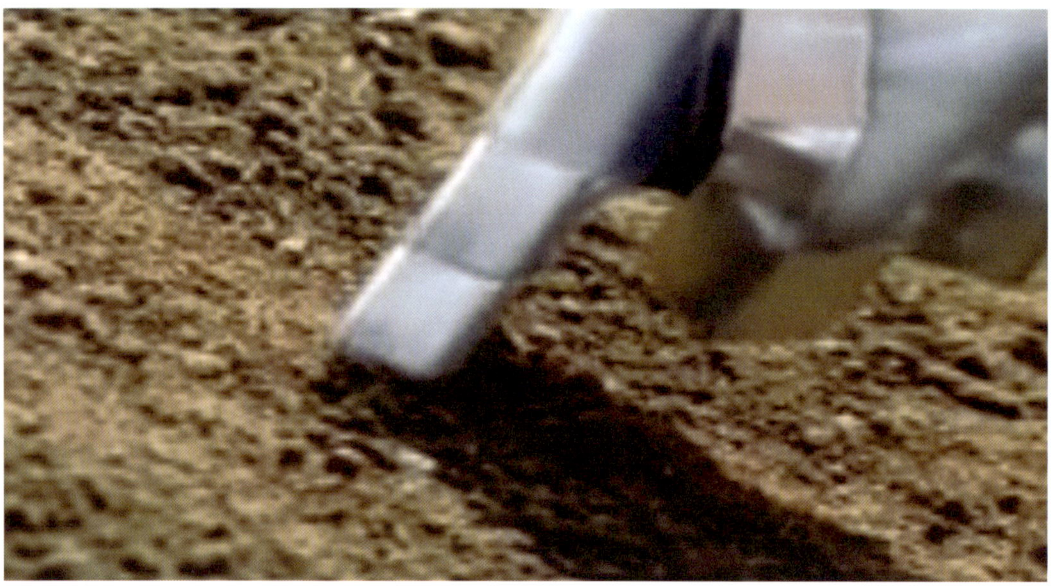

Capture d'écran d'un spot publicitaire pour les produits Monsanto® destiné au marché indien.

Screenshot from a Monsanto® TV commercial produced for India.

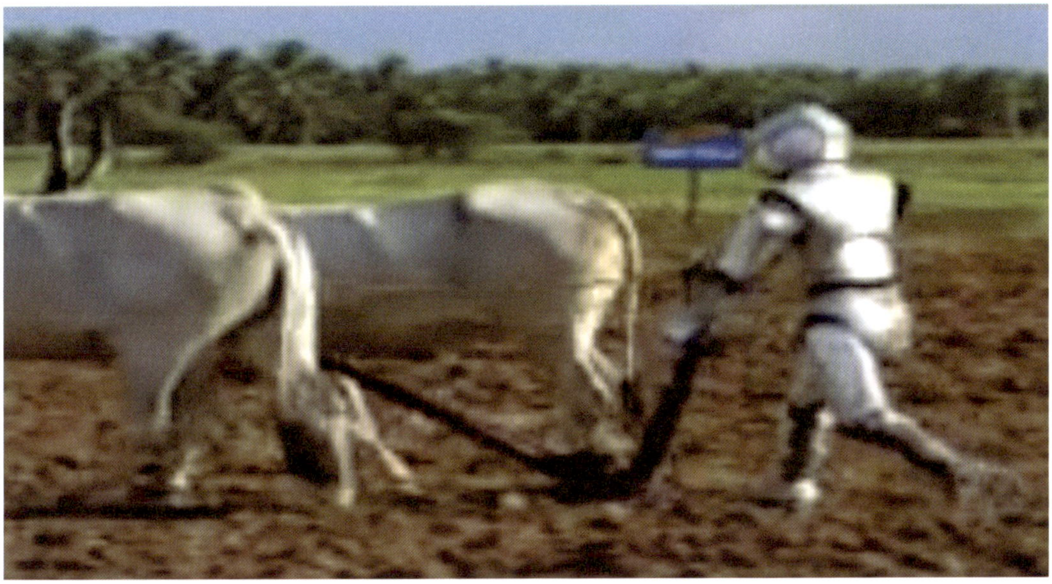

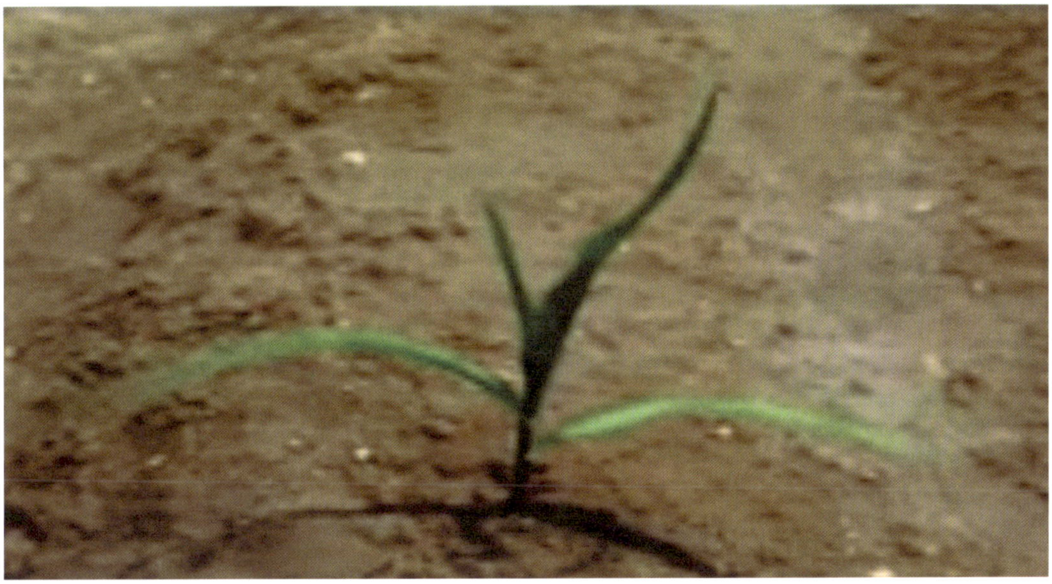

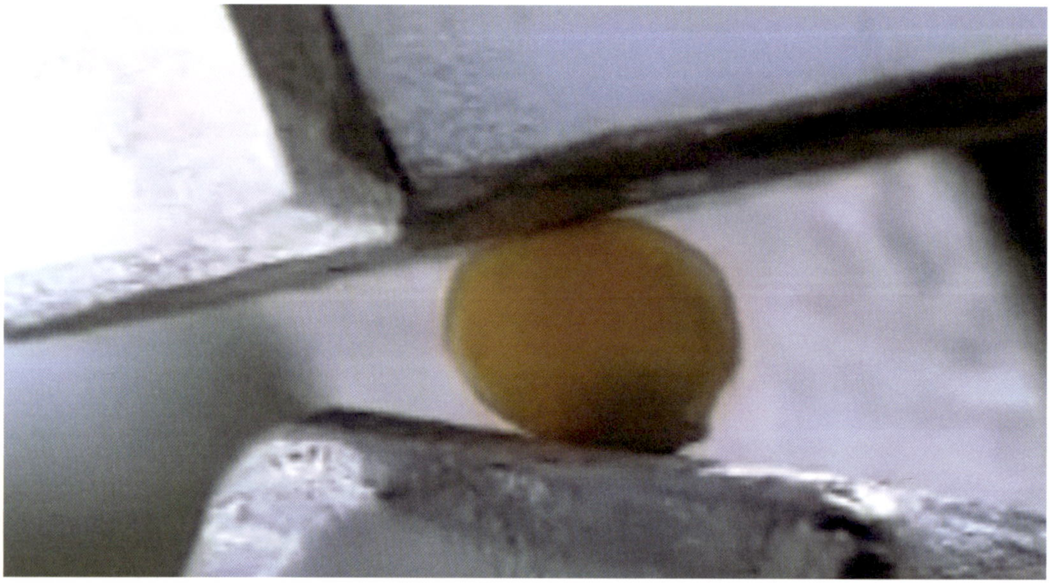

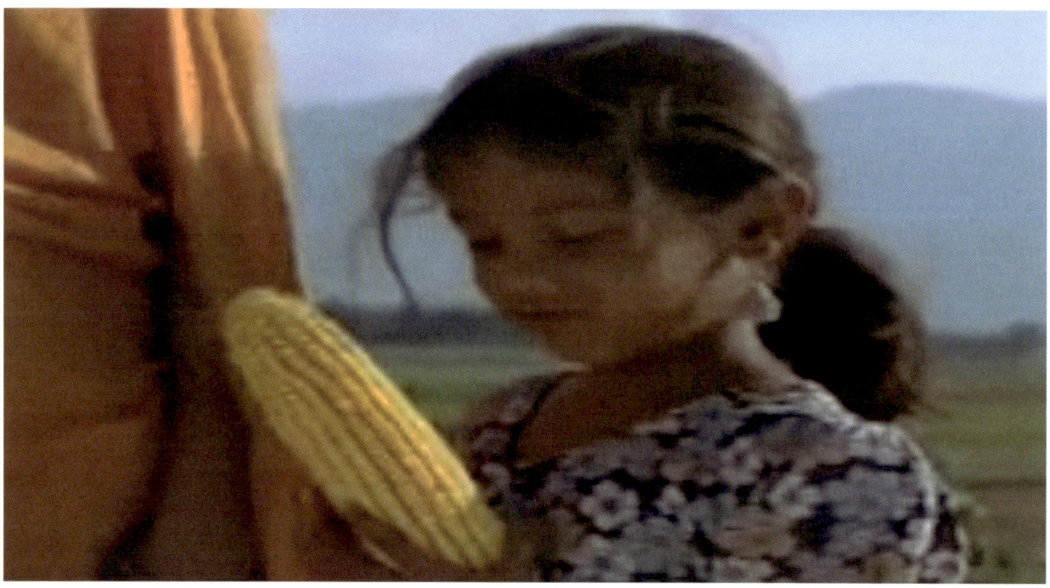

Capture d'écran d'un spot publicitaire pour les produits Monsanto® destiné au marché indien.

Screenshot from a Monsanto® TV commercial produced for India.

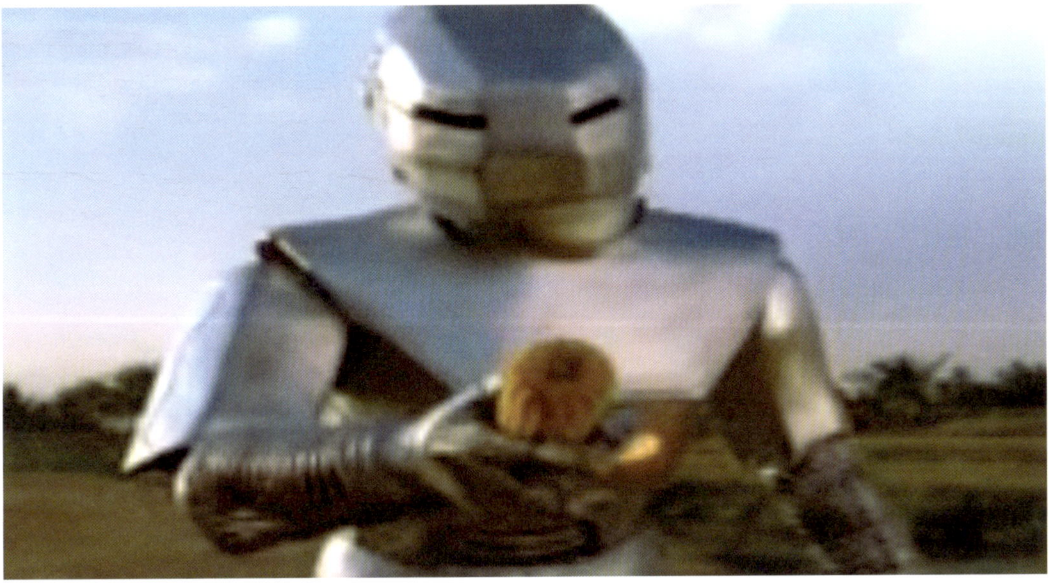

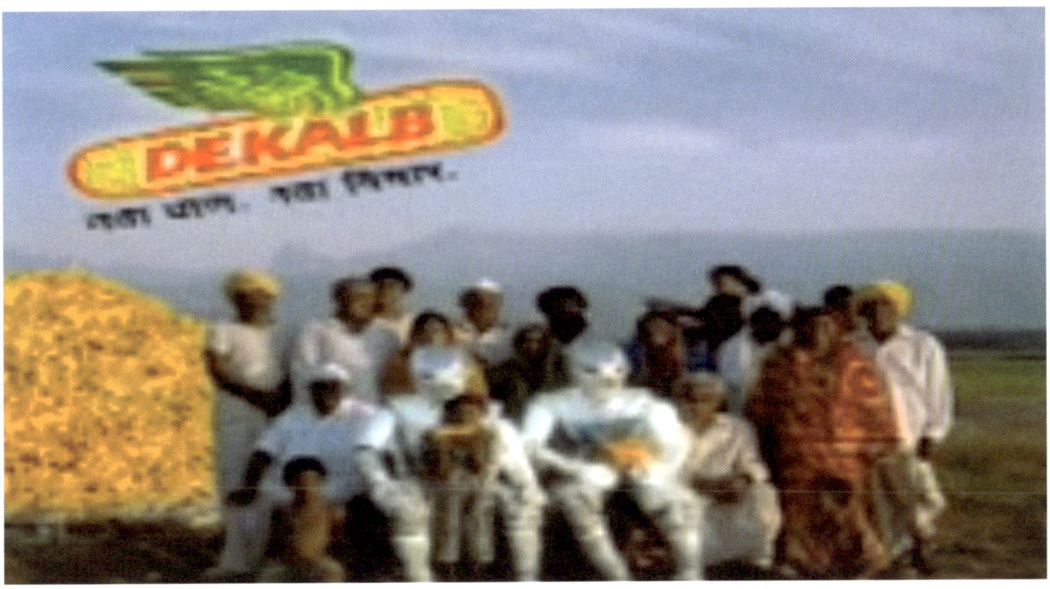

En 1996, Monsanto® introduit ses premières semences transgéniques. Il fait en sorte que les fermiers ne puissent pas récupérer les graines, ne faisant ni plus ni moins que les déposséder de leurs propres semences. Conséquence, le pouvoir passe aux mains des grands groupes, qui détiennent aujourd'hui environ 80 % du marché du maïs transgénique et 93 % de celui du soja transgénique. Les fermiers doivent désormais racheter des semences aux grands groupes chaque année. Pire, ils sont forcés de se conformer à la réglementation qui leur est imposée, évidemment à leur désavantage.

In 1996, Monsanto® introduced its first GMO seeds. It ensured that farmers could not save the seeds and essentially lost the ownership of their seeds. Consequently, the power balance shifted away from the farmers to corporations who now own about 80% of GM corn and 93% of the GM soy market. Now farmers not only have to buy the seeds from the corporations year after year, but they are also forced to comply with the rules and regulations embedded in the contracts, which are designed to put the farmers at a juridical disadvantage.

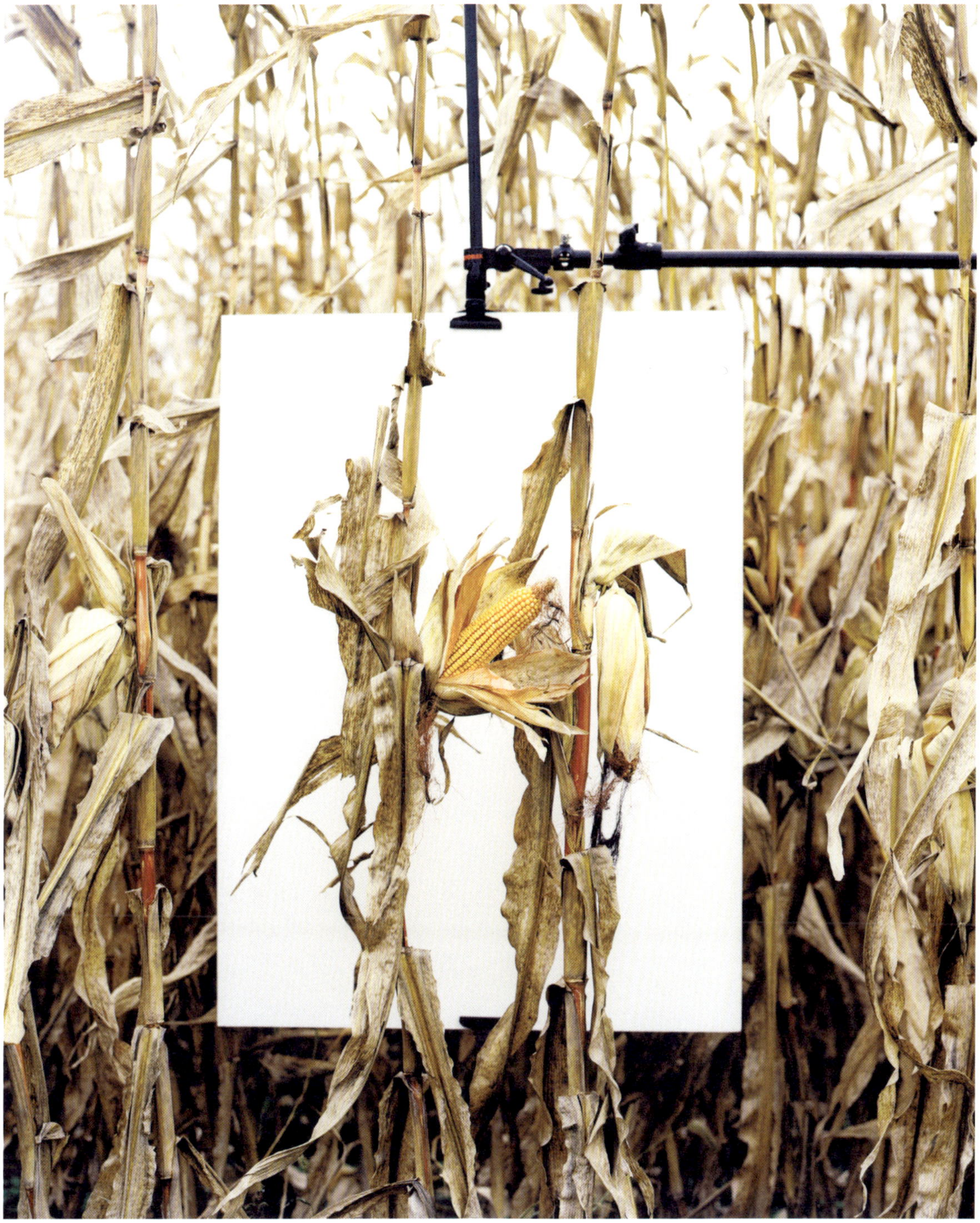

 VAN BUREN, INDIANA. 2013

Dans les années 1970, Monsanto® introduit le glyphosate sous la marque Roundup. Avec l'usage massif de cet herbicide en agriculture, la résistance des mauvaises herbes au glyphosate devient problématique. Si le glyphosate et les formules de type Roundup ont été approuvés par les agences de régulation du monde entier, de forts doutes subsistent quant à leur dangerosité pour l'être humain et l'environnement. En mars 2015, le Centre international de recherche sur le cancer et l'Organisation mondiale de la santé (OMS) classent le glyphosate dans la catégorie des « cancérigènes probables ». Ils évoquent également « des risques accrus de lymphome non hodgkinien ».

In the 1970s, Monsanto® introduced glyphosate under the trade name Roundup. With its heavy use in agriculture, weed resistance to glyphosate is a growing problem. While glyphosate and formulations such as Roundup have been approved by regulatory bodies worldwide and are widely used, concerns about their effects on humans and the environment persist. In March 2015, the International Agency for Research on Cancer and the WHO (World Health Organization) said glyphosate, the active ingredient in the Monsanto® herbicide Roundup, was classified as "probably carcinogenic to humans." It also stated that there was "limited evidence" that glyphosate was carcinogenic in humans for non-Hodgkin lymphoma.

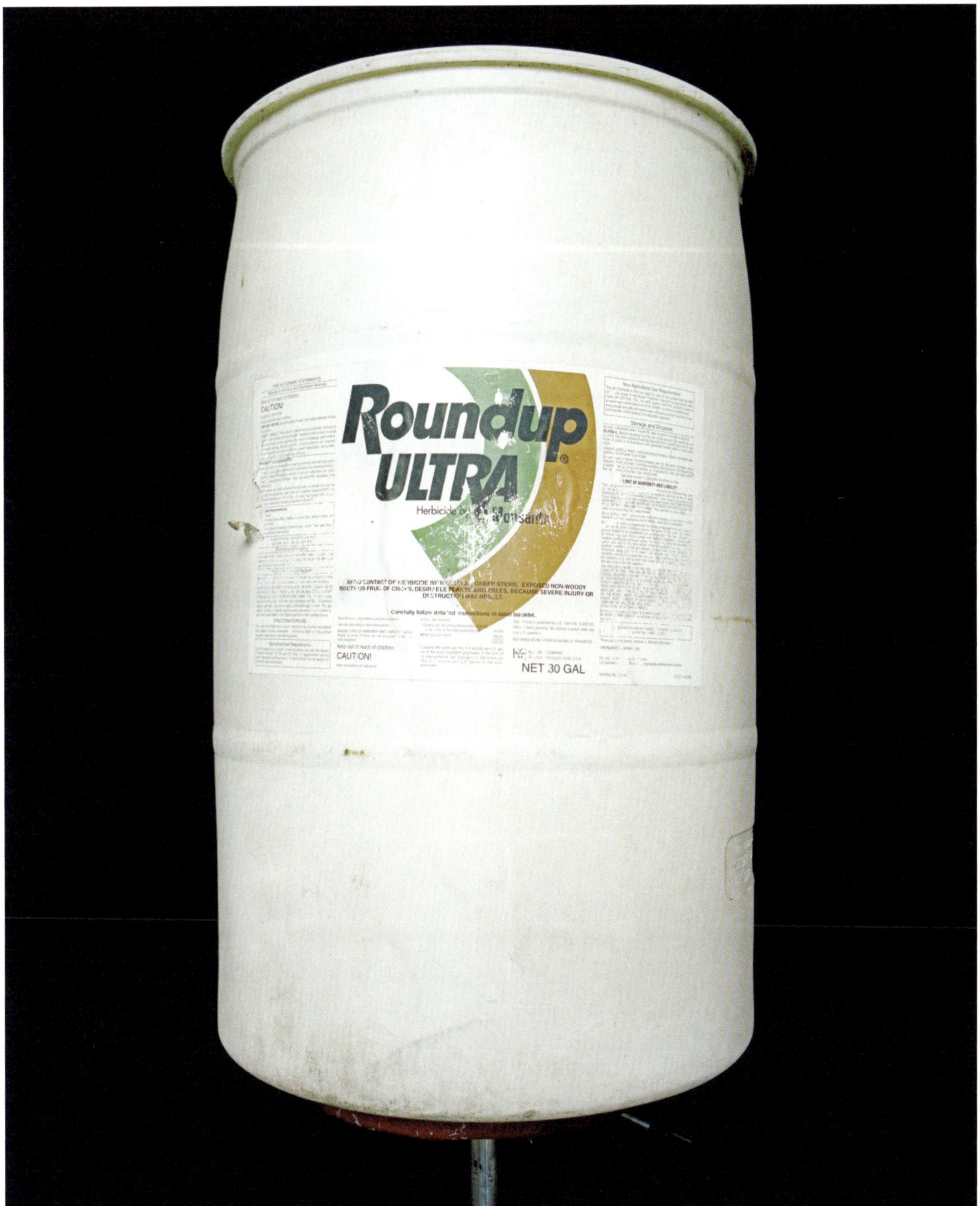

 GENEVA, INDIANA. 2013

Semences transgéniques de Monsanto®.

Monsanto® GMO seeds.

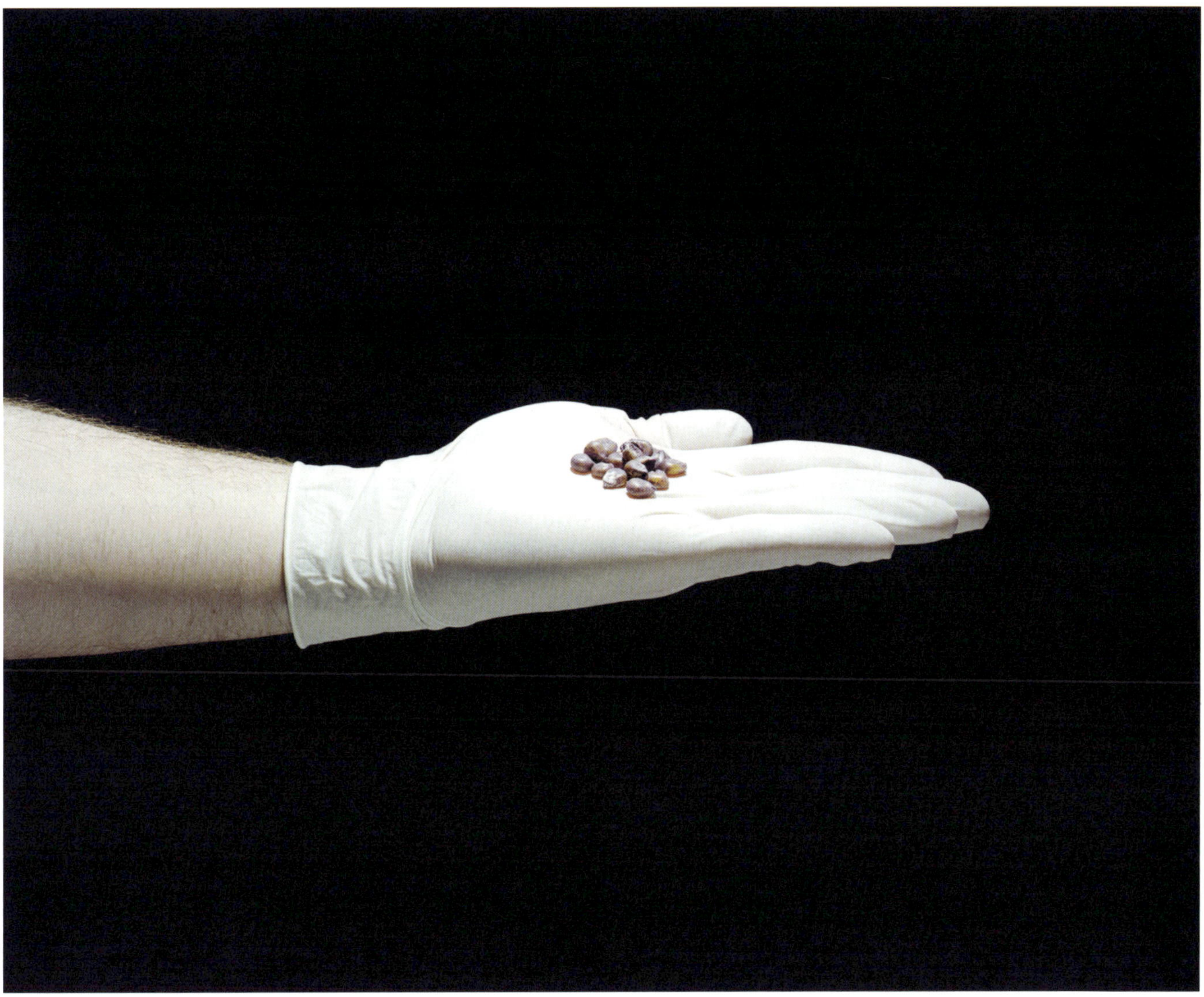

Troy Roush, fermier accusé à tort d'avoir conservé des semences. La bataille juridique contre Monsanto® lui a coûté 390 000 dollars en frais d'avocats. Il a alors commencé à réaliser en quoi le système est en train de dévaster l'agriculture traditionnelle. « Les cultures transgéniques détruisent le tissu social de nos communautés rurales », affirme-t-il. Roush ne pourrait sans doute pas revenir à des récoltes conventionnelles, même s'il parvenait à trouver de bonnes semences : une fois l'ADN Monsanto® implanté dans un champ, il est impossible de l'en retirer. Et, avec la police des graines de la firme qui effectue des contrôles réguliers, les agriculteurs ne peuvent se permettre de prendre le moindre risque.

Troy Roush, a farmer, was wrongly accused of saving seeds. The legal fight against Monsanto® cost him $390,000 in lawyers' fees. Since then, he has begun to see the way the system is devastating traditional farming. "Genetically modified crops are destroying the social fabric of our rural communities," he says. Roush probably couldn't go back to conventional crops even if he could find good conventional seeds. Once Monsanto®'s DNA is in a field, it is almost impossible to get it out. And with the corporate DNA police regularly checking, farmers can't afford to take a chance.

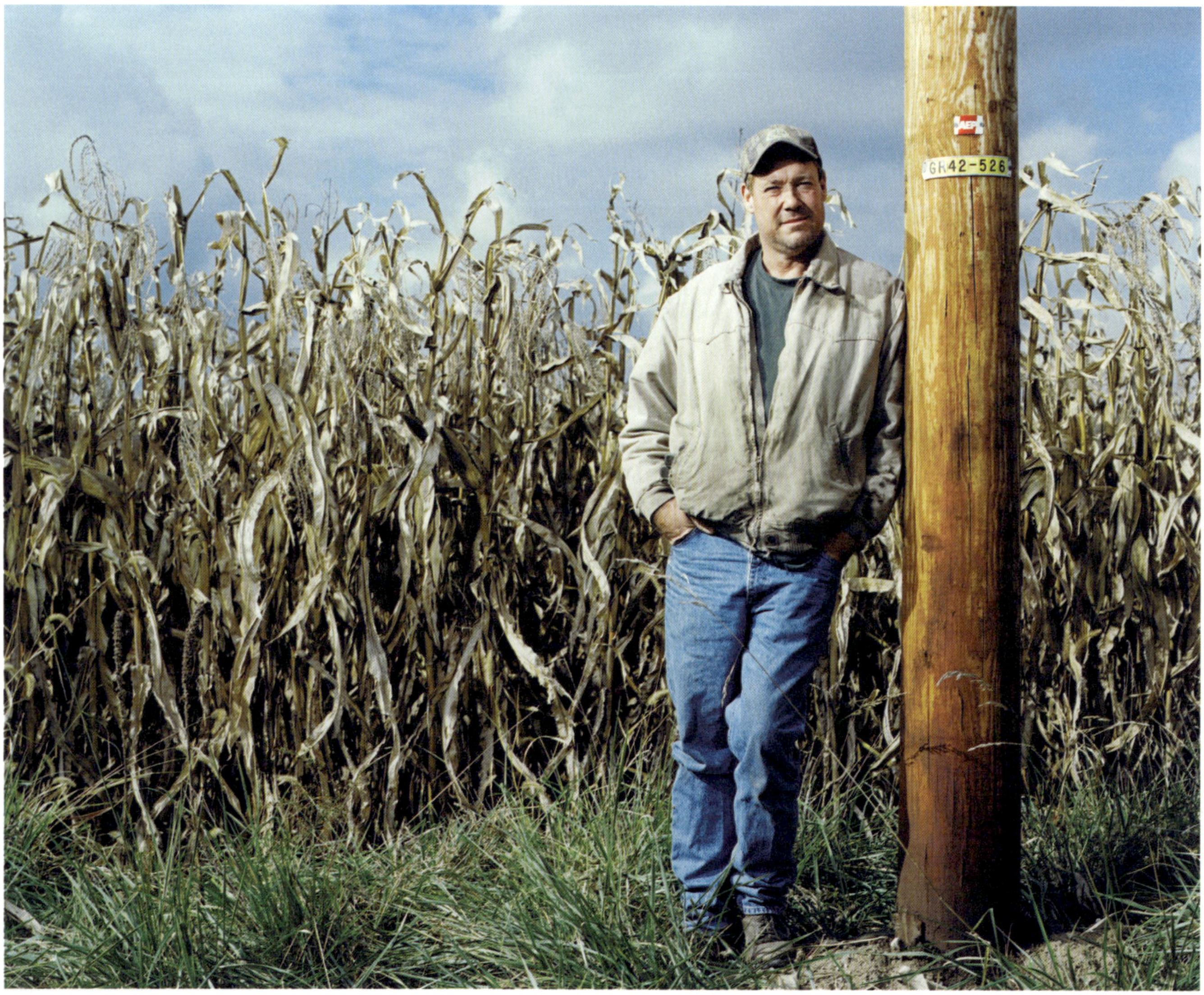

VAN BUREN, INDIANA. 2013

Mo Parr, 74 ans, est trieur de semences. Il est engagé par des fermiers pour séparer les mauvaises graines de celles à replanter. Monsanto® l'a attaqué en justice pour « complicité avec des fermiers dans l'usurpation de brevets ». La firme a ordonné la production des relevés bancaires de Mo Parr sans qu'il en ait connaissance, et a trouvé qui étaient ses clients. Après avoir reçu des appels de Monsanto®, certains fermiers ont cessé toute relation avec lui. Monsanto® a gagné son procès contre Mo Parr.

Seventy-four-year-old Mo Parr is a seed cleaner. He is hired by farmers to separate debris from the seeds to be replanted. Monsanto® sued him, claiming he was "aiding and abetting" farmers, helping them to violate the patent. The company subpoenaed Parr's bank records without his knowledge and found his customers. After receiving calls from Monsanto®, some of the farmers stopped talking to him. Monsanto® won its legal case against Parr.

SOURCE: WWW.CBSNEWS.COM/NEWS/AGRICULTURAL-GIANT-BATTLES-SMALL-FARMERS.

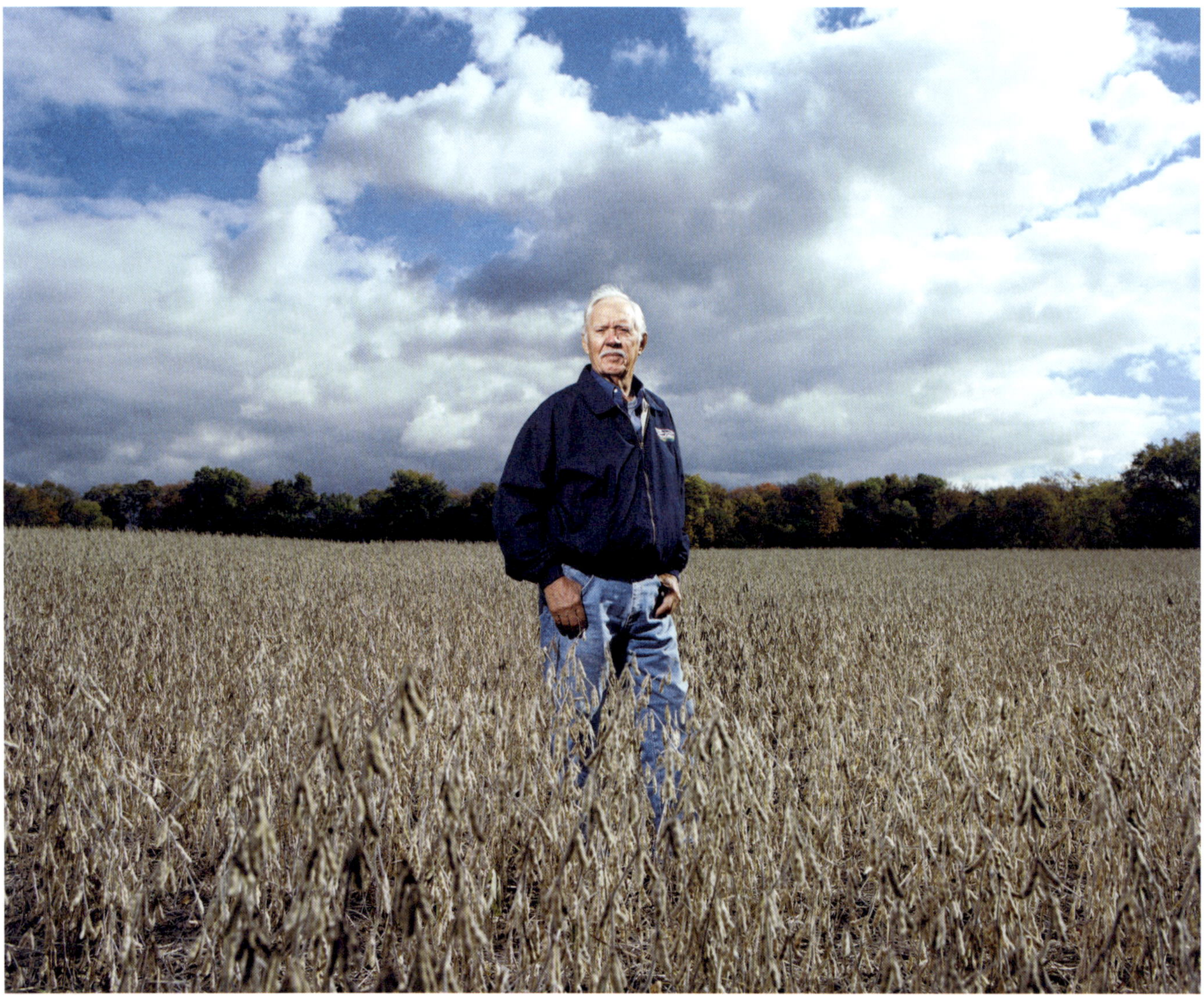

ROLLING PRAIRIE, INDIANA. 2013

2012 MONSANTO TECHNOLOGY/STEWARDSHIP AGREEMENT
(Limited Use License)

Form Number
120572441

PLEASE MAIL THE SIGNED 2012 MONSANTO TECHNOLOGY/STEWARDSHIP AGREEMENT TO: Grower Licensing, Monsanto, 622 Emerson Road, Suite 150, St. Louis, MO 63141

GROWER INFORMATION (please print)

Please complete this section with your business information. To sign this Monsanto Technology/Stewardship Agreement ("Agreement") you must be the **operator/grower** for all fields that will grow plants from Seed (as defined below). You represent that you have full authority to and do hereby bind to this Agreement yourself, all entities for which you obtain Seed, all individuals and entities having an ownership interest in any entities for which you obtain Seed, and that Monsanto Company has not barred any of those individuals or entities from obtaining this limited-use license. Your name must be filled in and must match the signature below. This Agreement becomes effective if and when Monsanto issues the Grower a license number from Monsanto's headquarters in St. Louis, Missouri. Monsanto does not authorize seed dealers or seed retailers to issue a license of any kind for Monsanto Technologies.

Please check one of the following: **NEW LICENSE** ☐ **RENEWAL** ☐

Grower's Full Legal Name (First/Middle/Last) ☐ Dr. ☐ Mr. ☐ Mrs. ☐ Ms. Suffix (Sr, Jr, II, III)

Farm Business Name

Grower's Mailing Address (no P.O. Boxes)

Farm Physical Address (as listed with the FSA)

Grower's City **State** **Zip**

Farm City **State** **Zip**

Area Code **Home Phone** **Fax**

Last Four of Social Security # XXX-XX-

Role ☐ Operator ☐ Owner/Operator ☐ Farm Manager ☐ Other

Area Code **Cell Phone** **Email**

If the above information changes, Grower agrees promptly to notify Monsanto of the changes by calling the Grower Licensing Team at 1-800-768-6387, Option #3.

SEED SUPPLIER

Business Name **Area Code** **Phone**

City **State** **Zip**

THIS SPACE FOR MONSANTO OFFICE USE ONLY, PLEASE LEAVE THIS SECTION BLANK:

Lic. #: Batch #: Date:

This Monsanto Technology/Stewardship Agreement is entered into between you ("Grower") and Monsanto Company ("Monsanto") and consists of the terms on this page and on the reverse side of this page.

This Monsanto Technology/Stewardship Agreement grants Grower a limited license to use Genuity® Bollgard II® cotton, Genuity® Bollgard II® with Roundup Ready® cotton, Genuity® Bollgard II® with Roundup Ready® Flex cotton, Genuity® Roundup Ready 2 Yield® soybeans, Genuity® Roundup Ready® Canola, Genuity® Roundup Ready® Alfalfa, Roundup Ready® Corn 2 corn, Roundup Ready® Cotton, Genuity® Roundup Ready® Flex cotton, Roundup Ready® Soybeans, Genuity® Roundup Ready® Sugarbeets, YieldGard® Corn Borer corn, YieldGard® Corn Borer with Roundup Ready® Corn 2 corn, Genuity® VT Double PRO™ corn, YieldGard VT Rootworm/RR2® corn, YieldGard VT Triple® corn, Genuity® VT Triple PRO™ corn, Performance Series™ Sweet Corn, Vistive® low linolenic soybeans, Genuity® SmartStax® corn, Genuity® SmartStax® RIB Complete™ corn, Monsanto patented germplasm and Monsanto Plant Variety Protection rights ("Monsanto Technologies"). Seed containing Monsanto Technologies are referred to herein as ("Seed"). This Agreement also contains Grower's stewardship responsibilities and requirements associated with the use of Seed and Monsanto Technologies.

1. **GOVERNING LAW:** This Agreement and the parties' relationship shall be governed by the laws of the State of Missouri and the United States (without regard to the choice of law rules).

2. **BINDING ARBITRATION FOR COTTON-RELATED CLAIMS MADE BY GROWER:** Any claim or action made or asserted by a cotton Grower (or any other person claiming an interest in the Grower's cotton crop) against Monsanto or any seller of cotton Seed containing Monsanto Technology arising out of and/or in connection with this Agreement or the sale or performance of the cotton Seed containing Monsanto Technology other than claims arising under the patent laws of the United States must be resolved by binding arbitration. The parties acknowledge that the transaction involves interstate commerce. The parties agree that arbitration shall be conducted pursuant to the provisions of the Federal Arbitration Act, 9 U.S.C. Sec 1 et seq. and administered under the Commercial Dispute Resolution Procedures established by the American Arbitration Association ("AAA"). The term "seller" as used throughout this Agreement refers to all parties involved in the production, development, distribution, and/or sale of the Seed containing Monsanto Technology. In the event that a claim is not amicably resolved within 30 days of Monsanto's receipt of the Grower's notice required pursuant to this Agreement any party may initiate arbitration. The arbitration shall be heard in the capital city of the state of Grower's residence or in any other place as the parties decide by mutual agreement. When a demand for arbitration is filed by a party, the Grower and Monsanto/sellers shall each immediately pay one half of the AAA filing fee. In addition, Grower and Monsanto/sellers shall each pay one half of AAA's administrative and arbitrator fees as those fees are incurred. The arbitrator(s) shall have the power to apportion the ultimate responsibility for all AAA fees in the final award. The arbitration proceedings and results are to remain confidential and are not to be disclosed without the written agreement of all parties, except to the extent necessary to effectuate the decision or award of the arbitrator(s) or as otherwise required by law.

3. **FORUM SELECTION FOR NON-COTTON-RELATED CLAIMS MADE BY GROWER AND ALL OTHER CLAIMS:** THE PARTIES CONSENT TO THE SOLE AND EXCLUSIVE JURISDICTION AND VENUE OF THE U.S. DISTRICT COURT FOR THE EASTERN DISTRICT OF MISSOURI, EASTERN DIVISION, AND THE CIRCUIT COURT OF THE COUNTY OF ST. LOUIS, MISSOURI, (ANY LAWSUIT MUST BE FILED IN ST. LOUIS, MO) FOR ALL CLAIMS AND DISPUTES ARISING OUT OF OR CONNECTED IN ANY WAY WITH THIS AGREEMENT AND/OR THE USE OF THE SEED OR THE MONSANTO TECHNOLOGIES, EXCEPT FOR COTTON-RELATED CLAIMS MADE BY GROWER. THE PARTIES WAIVE ANY OBJECTION TO VENUE IN THE EASTERN DIVISION OF THE U.S. DISTRICT COURT FOR THE EASTERN DISTRICT OF MISSOURI, INCLUDING THOSE BASED, IN WHOLE OR IN PART, ON THE DIVISIONAL VENUE LOCAL RULE(S) OF THE U.S. DISTRICT COURT FOR THE EASTERN DISTRICT OF MISSOURI.

   THIS AGREEMENT CONTAINS A BINDING ARBITRATION PROVISION FOR COTTON RELATED CLAIMS PURSUANT TO THE PROVISIONS OF THE FEDERAL ARBITRATION ACT, 9 U.S.C. §1 ET SEQ., WHICH MAY BE ENFORCED BY THE PARTIES.

4. **GROWER AGREES:**
   - To accept and continue the obligations of this Monsanto Technology/Stewardship Agreement on any new land purchased or leased by Grower that has Seed planted on it by a previous owner or possessor of the land; and to notify in writing purchasers or lessees of land owned by Grower that has Seed planted on it that the Monsanto Technology is subject to this Monsanto Technology/Stewardship Agreement and they must have or obtain their own Monsanto Technology/Stewardship Agreement.
   - To read and follow the applicable Technology Use Guide ("TUG") and the Insect Resistance Management Grower Guide ("IRM Grower Guide") which are incorporated into and are a part of this Agreement, for specific requirements relating to the terms of this Agreement, and to abide by and be bound by the terms of the TUG and the IRM Grower Guide as they may be amended from time to time.
   - To implement an Insect Resistance Management ("IRM") program as specified in the applicable Genuity® Bollgard II® cotton, Genuity® corn and YieldGard® corn sections of the most recent IRM Grower Guide and to cooperate and comply with these IRM programs.
   - To acquire Seed containing these Monsanto Technologies only from a seed company with technology license(s) from Monsanto for the applicable Monsanto Technology(ies) or from a licensed company's dealer authorized to sell such licensed Seed.
   - To acquire Seed from authorized seed companies (or their authorized dealers) with the applicable license(s).
   - To use Seed containing Monsanto Technologies solely for planting a single commercial crop.
   - Not to save or clean any crop produced from Seed for planting, not to supply Seed produced from Seed to anyone for planting, not to plant seed for production other than for Monsanto or a Monsanto licensed seed company under a seed production contract.
   - Not to transfer any Seed containing patented Monsanto Technologies to any other person or entity for planting.
   - To plant and/or clean Seed for Seed production, if and only if, Grower has entered into a valid, written Seed production agreement with a Seed company that is licensed by Monsanto to produce Seed. Grower must either physically deliver to that licensed Seed Company or must sell for non-seed purposes or use for non-seed purposes all of the Seed produced pursuant to a Seed production agreement.
   - Grower may not plant and may not transfer to others for planting any Seed that the Grower has produced containing patented Monsanto Technologies for crop breeding, research, or generation of herbicide registration data. Grower may not conduct research on Grower's crop produced from Seed other than to make agronomic comparisons and conduct yield testing for Grower's own use. Monsanto makes available separate license agreements to academic institutions for research.
   - To direct crops produced from Seed to appropriate markets as necessary. Any grain or material produced from Seed can only be exported to, or used, processed or sold in countries where all necessary regulatory approvals have been granted. It is a violation of national and international law to move material containing biotech traits across boundaries into nations where import is not permitted.
   - Grower agrees to lawfully plant Genuity® Roundup Ready® Alfalfa, to direct any product produced from a Genuity® Roundup Ready® Alfalfa seed or crops (including hay and hay products) only to those countries where regulatory approvals have been granted, and to grow and manage Genuity® Roundup Ready® Alfalfa in accordance with the TUG. Pending import approvals in China, Grower agrees not to export Genuity® Roundup Ready® Alfalfa seed or crops (including hay or hay product) to China. In addition, due to the unique cropping practices Grower agrees not to plant Genuity® Roundup Ready® Alfalfa in Imperial County, California, pending import approvals in China and until Monsanto grants express permission for such planting.
   - Grower agrees: 1) not to export Genuity® Roundup Ready® Flex Pima cotton seed, meal, linters, or gin trash to Korea pending import approval; 2) to deliver cotton to an Arizona, California, New Mexico, or Texas gin that is on Monsanto's approved list (available at www.genuity.com under the Commodity Marketing section of the Stewardship tab) or to a third party who agrees in writing (copy to Monsanto) to use products for domestic feed use; and 3) not to market cotton seed, meal, linters or gin trash from Genuity® Roundup Ready® Flex Pima to a third party who may send such products to countries where those products are not approved.
   - To pay all applicable fees due to Monsanto that are a part of, associated with or collected with the Seed purchase price or that are invoiced for the seed. If Grower fails to pay Monsanto for cotton related Monsanto Technologies, Grower agrees to pay Monsanto default charges at the rate of 14% per annum (or the maximum allowed by law whichever is less) plus Monsanto's reasonable attorneys' fees, court costs and all other costs of collection.
   - To provide Monsanto copies of any records, receipts, or other documents that could be relevant to Grower's performance of this Agreement, including but not limited to, Summary Acreage History Report, Form 578 (producer print), Farm and Tract Detail Listing and corresponding aerial photographs, Risk Management Agency claim documentation, and dealer/retailer invoices for seed and chemical transactions. Such records shall be produced following Monsanto's actual (or attempted) oral communication with Grower and not later than seven (7) days after the date of a written request from Monsanto.
   - To identify and to allow Monsanto and its representatives access to land farmed by or at the direction of Grower (including refuge areas) and bins, wagons, or seed storage containers used or under the control or direction of Grower, for purposes of examining and taking samples of crops, crop residue or seeds located therein. Such inspection, examination or sampling shall be available to Monsanto and its representatives only after Monsanto's actual (or attempted) oral communication with Grower and after at least seven (7) days prior written request by Monsanto to Grower.

[The Agreement continues on the reverse side of this page.]

GROWER SIGNATURE AND DATE REQUIRED ▶

Name ____________________ Date ____________________

Distribution: White to Monsanto, Yellow to Dealer, Pink to Grower

- To allow Monsanto to obtain Grower's internet service provider ("ISP") records to validate Grower's electronic signature, if applicable.

Performance Series™ Sweet Corn

- To read and follow the Sweet Corn Technology Use Guide for Performance Series™ Sweet Corn and to abide by and implement Insect Resistance Management requirements on the product tag.
- To direct any fresh produce from this product for sale or use in the US, Canada and Mexico. It is a violation of national and international laws to move material containing biotech traits across boundaries into nations where import is not permitted. Grower must talk to Grower's buyers to confirm their uses of this product.
- To use on crops containing Roundup Ready® or Roundup Ready® 2 Technology only a labeled Roundup® agricultural herbicide or other authorized non-selective herbicide which could not be used in the absence of the Roundup Ready® gene (see TUG for details on authorized non-selective products). Use of any selective herbicide labeled for the same crop without the Roundup Ready® gene is not restricted by this Agreement. MONSANTO DOES NOT MAKE ANY REPRESENTATIONS, WARRANTIES OR RECOMMENDATIONS CONCERNING THE USE OF PRODUCTS MANUFACTURED OR MARKETED BY OTHER COMPANIES WHICH ARE LABELED FOR USE IN ROUNDUP READY® CROP(S). MONSANTO SPECIFICALLY DISCLAIMS ALL RESPONSIBILITY FOR THE USE OF THESE PRODUCTS IN ROUNDUP READY® OR GENUITY® ROUNDUP READY® 2 YIELD® CROP(S). ALL QUESTIONS AND COMPLAINTS ARISING FROM THE USE OF PRODUCTS MANUFACTURED OR MARKETED BY OTHER COMPANIES SHOULD BE DIRECTED TO THOSE COMPANIES.

5. GROWER RECEIVES FROM MONSANTO COMPANY:

- A limited use license to purchase and to plant Seed in the United States except in any state or county where the products do not have all the necessary approvals and to apply Roundup® agricultural herbicides and other authorized non-selective herbicides over the top of Roundup Ready®, Genuity® Roundup Ready® or Performance Series Sweet Corn crops. Check with your local Monsanto representative if you have questions about the approval status in your state. Monsanto retains ownership of the Monsanto Technologies including the genes (for example, the Roundup Ready® gene) and the gene technologies. Grower receives the right to use the Monsanto Technologies subject to the conditions specified in this Agreement.
- Monsanto Technologies are protected under U.S. patent law. Monsanto licenses the Grower under applicable U.S. patents listed below (other than the Dow AgroSciences Patent Rights), to use Monsanto Technologies subject to the conditions listed in this Agreement. Dow AgroSciences LLC and Agrigenetics, Inc. (collectively "Dow AgroSciences") licenses the Grower under its applicable U.S. patents listed below (the "Dow AgroScience Patent Rights") to use Dow AgroSciences' Event TC 1507 and Event DAS 59122-7 to the extent either is present in any SmartStax Seed being obtained by Grower pursuant to this Agreement, Monsanto being authorized to act on Dow AgroSciences' behalf for this Agreement, subject to the conditions listed in this Agreement. These licenses do not authorize Grower to plant Seed in the United States that has been purchased in another country or plant Seed in another country that has been purchased in the United States. Grower is not authorized to transfer Seed to anyone outside of the U.S.
- Enrollment for participation in Roundup Ready PLUS™ Weed Management Solutions.
- A limited use license to prepare and apply on glyphosate-tolerant soybean, cotton, alfalfa, or canola crops (or have others prepare and apply) tank mixes of, or sequentially apply (or have others sequentially apply), Roundup® agricultural herbicides or other glyphosate herbicides labeled for use on those crops with quizalofop, clethodim, sethoxydim, fluazifop, and/or fenoxaprop to control volunteer Roundup Ready® Corn 2 corn in Grower's crops for the 2012 growing season. However, neither Grower nor a third party may utilize any type of co-pack or premix of glyphosate plus one or more of the above-identified active ingredients in the preparation of a tank mix.

6. GROWER UNDERSTANDS:

- **Monsanto Company is a member of Excellence Through Stewardship® (ETS).** Monsanto products are commercialized in accordance with ETS Product Launch Stewardship Guidance, and in compliance with Monsanto's Policy for Commercialization of Biotechnology-Derived Plant Products in Commodity Crops. These products have been approved for import into key export markets with functioning regulatory systems. Any crop or material produced from these products can only be exported to, or used, processed or sold in countries where all necessary regulatory approvals have been granted. It is a violation of national and international law to move material containing biotech traits across boundaries into nations where import is not permitted. Growers should talk to their grain handler or product purchaser to confirm their buying position for these products. Excellence Through Stewardship® is a registered trademark of Biotechnology Industry Organization.
- Performance Series™ Sweet Corn and Genuity® Roundup Ready® Alfalfa are subject to specific product export requirements.
- Insect
- Insect Resistance Management: When planting any YieldGard® brand corn products, Genuity® brand corn products or Genuity® Bollgard II® cotton products, Grower must implement an IRM program according to the size and distance guidelines specified in the IRM Grower Guide, including any supplemental amendments. Grower may lose Grower's limited use license to use these products if Grower fails to follow the IRM program required by this Agreement. When planting Performance Series Sweet Corn growers must implement the IRM program outlined on the product tag.
- Crop Stewardship & Specialty Crops: Refer to the section on Coexistence and Identity Preservation in the TUG for applicable information on crop stewardship and considerations for production of identity preserved crops.
- Corn Trait Performance: All hybrids containing Monsanto corn traits (YieldGard® brand corn products, Performance Series Sweet Corn and Roundup Ready® Corn 2 corn) have been screened for the presence of the appropriate protein and have passed that screening prior to commercial sale. YieldGard® Rootworm corn and YieldGard® Plus corn hybrids have achieved industry leading success rates in excess of 99%. A small number of these hybrids may infrequently demonstrate variable levels of performance in fields and not meet grower expectations.

7. SPECIAL LIMITATIONS ON PRODUCTS CONTAINING MON 863 (ie. YieldGard® Rootworm corn, YieldGard® Plus corn, YieldGard® Rootworm with Roundup Ready® Corn 2 corn, YieldGard® Plus with Roundup Ready® Corn 2 corn): The U.S. EPA has prohibited the sale, distribution, and planting of seed containing the MON 863 Event, which includes the Monsanto products YieldGard® Rootworm, YieldGard Rootworm with Roundup Ready® Corn 2, YieldGard® Plus and YieldGard Plus® with Roundup Ready® Corn 2 seed. Any remaining inventory of seed containing the MON 863 Event must be handled in accordance with legal and regulatory requirements (non-treated seed can be sold as grain, and treated seed must be disposed of properly). It is a violation of federal law to sell or distribute an unregistered pesticide.

8. GENERAL TERMS:

Grower's rights may not be transferred to anyone else without the written consent of Monsanto. If Grower's rights are transferred with Monsanto's consent or by operation of law, this Agreement is binding on the person or entity receiving the transferred rights. If any provision of this Agreement is determined to be void or unenforceable, the remaining provisions shall remain in full force and effect.

Grower acknowledges that Grower has received a copy of Monsanto's TUG and the IRM Grower Guide and/or Performance Series Sweet Corn TUG and IRM Grower Guide on the product tag. To obtain additional copies of the TUG and/or the IRM Grower Guide, contact Monsanto at 1-800-768-6387 or go to www.monsanto.com. Once effective, this Agreement will remain in effect until either the Grower or Monsanto choose to terminate the Agreement, as provided in Section 9 below. Information regarding new and existing Monsanto Technologies, including any additions or deletions to the U.S. patents licensed under this agreement, and any new terms will be mailed to you each year. Continuing use of Monsanto Technologies after receipt of any new terms constitutes Grower's agreement to be bound by the new terms.

9. TERMINATION:

Grower may choose to terminate this Agreement in its entirety effective immediately by delivering written notice to Monsanto. Monsanto may choose to terminate this Agreement in whole or in part by delivering written notice to Grower. Grower must deliver the notice of termination to Grower Licensing, Monsanto, 622 Emerson Road, Suite 150, St. Louis, MO 63141. If this Agreement is terminated pursuant to such a notice, Grower's responsibilities and the other terms herein shall survive (such as but not limited to Grower's obligation to use Seed for a single commercial crop) as to Seed previously purchased by the Grower.

In the event Grower violates the terms of this Agreement, then the Grower's rights under this Agreement shall automatically terminate. However, Grower's responsibilities and the other terms herein shall survive as to all Seed purchased or used by the Grower (such as but not limited to Grower's obligation to use Seed for a single commercial crop, Grower's obligation to pay Monsanto for its attorneys' fees, costs and other expenses incurred in enforcing its rights under this Agreement, and Grower's agreement to the choice of law and forum selection provisions contained herein). Further, Grower shall not be entitled to obtain a future limited-use license from Monsanto unless Monsanto provides Grower with specific written notice expressly recognizing the prior breach and prior termination of the limited-use license and expressly granting and/or reissuing the limited-use license previously obtained (and terminated) pursuant to this Agreement. Grower expressly acknowledges that Grower's submission of a new Monsanto Technology Stewardship Agreement and Monsanto's issuance of a new license number shall not satisfy the specific written notice reference above and that any such action shall have no legal effect. If Grower is found by any court to have breached any term of this Agreement and/or to have infringed one or more of the U.S. patents listed below, Grower agrees that, among other things, Monsanto and Dow Agrosciences, as appropriate, shall be entitled to preliminary and permanent injunctions enjoining Grower and any individual and/or entity acting on Grower's behalf or in concert therewith from making, using, selling, or offering Seed for sale. Additionally, Grower agrees that any such finding of infringement by Grower shall entitle Monsanto and Dow Agrosciences, as appropriate, to patent infringement damages to the full extent authorized by 35 U.S.C. § 271 et. seq. Grower will also be liable for all breach of contract damages. If Grower is found by any court to have infringed one or more of the U.S. patents listed below or otherwise to have breached this Agreement, Grower agrees to pay Monsanto and the licensed Monsanto Technology provider(s) and Dow AgroSciences, as appropriate, their attorneys' fees and costs and other expenses incurred in enforcing rights under this Agreement including, but not limited to, expenses incurred in the investigation of the breach of this Agreement and/or infringement of one or more of the U.S. patents listed herein.

Grower accepts the terms of the following NOTICE REQUIREMENT, LIMITED WARRANTY AND DISCLAIMER OF WARRANTY AND EXCLUSIVE LIMITED REMEDY by signing this Agreement and/or opening a bag of Seed. If Grower does not agree to be bound by the conditions of purchase or use, Grower agrees to return the unopened bags to Grower's seed dealer.

10. NOTICE REQUIREMENT:

As a condition precedent to Grower or any other person with an interest in Grower's crop asserting any claim, action, or dispute against Monsanto and/or any seller of Seed regarding performance or non-performance of Monsanto Technologies or Seed, Grower must provide Monsanto a written, prompt, and timely notice (regarding performance or non-performance of the Monsanto Technologies) and to the seller of any Seed (regarding performance or non-performance of the Seed) within sufficient time to allow an in-field inspection of the crop(s) about which any controversy, claim, action, or dispute is being asserted. The notice will be timely only if it is delivered 15 days or less after the Grower first observes the issue(s) regarding performance or non-performance of the Monsanto Technology and/or the Seed. The notice shall include a statement setting forth the nature of the claim, name of the Monsanto Technology, and Seed hybrid or variety. Grower must deliver the notice to Grower Licensing, Monsanto, 622 Emerson Road, Suite 150, St. Louis, MO 63141.

11. LIMITED WARRANTY AND DISCLAIMER OF WARRANTIES:

Monsanto warrants that the Monsanto Technologies licen sed hereunder will perform as set forth in the TUG when used in accordance with directions. This warranty applies only to Monsanto Technologies contained in planting Seed that has been purchased from Monsanto and seed companies licensed by Monsanto or the seed company's authorized dealers or distributors. EXCEPT FOR THE EXPRESS WARRANTIES IN THE LIMITED WARRANTY SET FORTH ABOVE, MONSANTO MAKES NO OTHER WARRANTIES OF ANY KIND, AND DISCLAIMS ALL OTHER WARRANTIES, WHETHER ORAL OR WRITTEN, EXPRESS OR IMPLIED INCLUDING THE IMPLIED WARRANTIES OF MERCHANTABILITY AND FITNESS FOR PARTICULAR PURPOSE.

12. GROWER'S EXCLUSIVE LIMITED REMEDY:

THE EXCLUSIVE REMEDY OF THE GROWER AND THE LIMIT OF THE LIABILITY OF MONSANTO OR ANY SELLER FOR ANY AND ALL LOSSES, INJURY OR DAMAGES RESULTING FROM THE USE OR HANDLING OF SEED (INCLUDING CLAIMS BASED IN CONTRACT, NEGLIGENCE, PRODUCT LIABILITY, STRICT LIABILITY, TORT, OR OTHERWISE) SHALL BE THE PRICE PAID BY THE GROWER FOR THE QUANTITY OF THE SEED INVOLVED OR, AT THE ELECTION OF MONSANTO OR THE SEED SELLER, THE REPLACEMENT OF THE SEED. IN NO EVENT SHALL MONSANTO OR ANY SELLER BE LIABLE FOR ANY INCIDENTAL, CONSEQUENTIAL, SPECIAL, OR PUNITIVE DAMAGES.

Thank you for choosing our advanced technologies. We look forward to working with you in the future. If you have any questions regarding the Monsanto Technologies or this license, please call the Monsanto Customer Relations Center at: 1-800-768-6387.

13. PLEASE MAIL THE SIGNED 2012 MONSANTO TECHNOLOGY/STEWARDSHIP AGREEMENT TO:

Grower Licensing, Monsanto, 622 Emerson Road, Suite 150, St. Louis, MO 63141.

14. UNITED STATES PATENTS:

The licensed U.S. patents include: for Genuity® Bollgard II® cotton – 5,362,865; 5,659,122; 5,717,084; 5,728,925; 6,489,542; 6,943,282; 7,064,249; 7,223,907; 7,700,830; for Genuity® Bollgard II® with Roundup Ready® cotton – 5,362,865; 5,659,122; 5,717,084; 5,728,925; 6,051,753; 6,083,878; 6,489,542; 6,943,282; 7,064,249; 7,223,907; 7,700,830; 7,807,357; 7,820,392; RE39247; for Genuity™ Bollgard II® with Roundup Ready® Flex Cotton – 5,362,865; 5,659,122; 5,717,084; 5,728,925; 6,051,753; 6,083,878; 6,489,542; 6,660,911; 6,943,282; 6,949,696; 7,064,249; 7,112,725; 7,141,722; 7,223,907; 7,381,861; 7,700,830; RE39247; for Genuity™ Roundup Ready 2 Yield® Soybeans – 5,717,084; 5,728,925; 6,051,753; 6,660,911; 6,949,696; 7,141,722; 7,608,761; 7,632,985; RE39247; for Genuity® Roundup Ready® Alfalfa – 5,362,865; 5,659,122; 5,717,084; 5,728,925; 6,051,753; 7,566,817; RE39247; for Genuity® Roundup Ready® Canola – 5,463,175; 5,717,084; 5,728,925; 6,051,753; 6,083,878; 7,306,909; 7,718,373; RE38825; RE39247; for Roundup Ready® Corn 2 – 5,554,798; 5,593,874; 5,641,876; 5,717,084; 5,728,925; 5,859,347; 6,025,545; 6,083,878; 6,825,400; 7,582,434; RE39247; for Roundup Ready® Cotton – 5,717,084; 5,728,925; 6,051,753; 6,083,878; 7,807,357; 7,820,392; RE39247; for Genuity® Roundup Ready® Flex Cotton – 5,717,084; 5,728,925; 6,051,753; 6,083,878; 6,660,911; 6,949,696; 7,112,725; 7,141,722; 7,381,861; RE39247; for Roundup Ready® Soybeans – 5,717,084; 5,728,925; RE39247; for Genuity™ Roundup Ready® Sugarbeets – 5,717,084; 5,728,925; 6,051,753; 6,083,878; 7,335,816; RE39247; for YieldGard® Corn Borer corn – 5,484,956; 5,593,874; 5,859,347; 6,180,774; for YieldGard® Corn Borer with Roundup Ready® Corn 2 – 5,484,956; 5,554,798; 5,593,874; 5,641,876; 5,717,084; 5,728,925; 5,859,347; 6,025,545; 6,083,878; 6,180,774; 6,825,400; 7,582,434; RE39247; for YieldGard® Rootworm corn – 5,484,956; 6,063,597; 6,501,009; 7,408,096; 7,544,862; 7,705,216; for YieldGard® Plus corn – 5,484,956; 5,593,874; 5,859,347; 6,063,597; 6,180,774; 6,501,009; 7,408,096; 7,544,862; for YieldGard® Plus with Roundup Ready® Corn 2 - 5,484,956; 5,554,798; 5,593,874; 5,641,876; 5,717,084; 5,728,925; 5,859,347; 6,025,545; 6,063,597; 6,083,878; 6,180,774; 6,501,009; 6,825,400; 7,408,096; 7,554,862; 7,582,434; RE39247; for YieldGard® Rootworm with Roundup Ready® Corn 2 – 5,484,956; 5,554,798; 5,593,874; 5,641,876; 5,717,084; 5,728,925; 5,859,347; 6,025,545; 6,063,597; 6,083,878; 6,501,009; 6,825,400; 7,408,096; 7,544,862; 7,582,434; 7,705,216; RE39247; for YieldGard VT PRO™ – 6,051,753; 6,489,542; 6,645,497; 6,713,063; 6,962,705; 7,064,249; 7,070,982; 7,250,501; 7,304,206; 7,618,942; 7,700,830; 7,927,598; for Genuity® VT Double PRO™ – 5,554,798; 5,593,874; 5,641,876; 5,717,084; 5,728,925; 5,859,347; 6,025,545; 6,051,753; 6,083,878; 6,489,542; 6,645,497; 6,713,063; 6,825,400; 6,962,705; 7,064,249; 7,070,982; 7,250,501; 7,304,206; 7,582,434; 7,618,942; 7,700,830; 7,927,598; RE39247; for YieldGard VT Rootworm/RR2® – 5,554,798; 5,641,876; 5,717,084; 5,728,925; 6,025,545; 6,063,597; 6,083,878; 7,544,862; RE39247; for YieldGard VT Triple® – 5,484,956; 5,554,798; 5,593,874; 5,641,876; 5,717,084; 5,728,925; 5,859,347; 6,025,545; 6,063,597; 6,083,878; 6,180,774; 7,544,862; RE39247; for Genuity® VT Triple PRO™ and Performance Series™ Sweet Corn – 5,554,798; 5,641,876; 5,717,084; 5,728,925; 6,025,545; 6,051,753; 6,063,597; 6,083,878; 6,489,542; 6,645,497; 6.713;063; 6,962,705; 7,064,249; 7,070,982; 7,250,501; 7,304,206; 7,544,862; 7,618,942; 7,700,830; 7,927,598; RE39247; for tank mix - 6,239,072 ; for Drought – 5,641,876; 7,786,353; for Genuity® SmartStax®– 5,550,318; 5,554,798; 5,641,876; 5,717,084; 5,728,925; 6,025,545; 6,051,753; 6,063,597; 6,083,878; 6,489,542; 6,645,497; 6,713,063; 6,962,705; 7,064,249; 7,070,982; 7,112,665; 7,250,501; 7,304,206; 7,544,862; 7,618,942; 7,927,598; RE39247;

Dow AgroScience Patent Rights for Genuity® SmartStax® – 5,510,474; 6,083,499; 6,127,180; 6,218,188; 6,340,593; 6,548,291; 6,624,145; 6,893,872; 6,900,371; 6,943,282; 7,956,246.

Based on the decision of the U.S. Department of Agriculture (USDA) on January 27, 2011, Genuity® Roundup Ready® Alfalfa seed is available for sale and distribution by authorized Seed Companies or their dealers for use in the United States. This seed may not be planted outside of the United States, or for the production of seed, or sprouts.

ALWAYS READ AND FOLLOW PESTICIDE LABEL DIRECTIONS. Roundup Ready® crops contain genes that confer tolerance to glyphosate, the active ingredient in Roundup® brand agricultural herbicides. Roundup® brand agricultural herbicides will kill crops that are not tolerant to glyphosate. Bollgard II®, Genuity and Design®, Genuity Icons, Genuity®, Respect the Refuge and Cotton Design®, RIB Complete™, Roundup Ready 2 Technology and Design®, Roundup Ready 2 Yield®, Roundup Ready®, Roundup®, SmartStax®, Vistive®, VT Double PRO™, VT Triple PRO™, YieldGard VT Rootworm/RR2®, YieldGard VT Triple®, YieldGard VT®, and YieldGard® are trademarks of Monsanto Technology LLC. Ignite® and LibertyLink® and the Water Droplet Design® are registered trademarks of Bayer. Herculex® is a registered trademark of Dow AgroSciences LLC. Respect the Refuge and Corn Design® and Respect the Refuge® are registered trademarks of National Corn Growers Association. All other trademarks are the property of their respective owners. ©2011 Monsanto Company. [22908Apgd] SA9E115789

Distribution: White to Monsanto, Yellow to Dealer, Pink to Grower

L'accord, à prendre ou à laisser, comporte des clauses qui placent les fermiers en position très désavantageuse. Nul besoin d'être populiste pour comprendre que les accords entre Monsanto et les fermiers constituent des contrats d'adhésion qui rendent les fermiers responsables en cas de violation de l'accord, de contamination d'une récolte voisine ou d'usurpation des brevets de la firme. Dans le cas de Monsanto, on peut bel et bien affirmer que la plume est plus forte que l'épée.

1. INTERDICTION DE RÉCUPÉRER LES SEMENCES

Avec cette mesure, Monsanto s'assure un client régulier année après année. Peu importe que cela aille à l'encontre de l'essence même de l'agriculture telle que pratiquée partout dans le monde depuis des siècles. Une clause similaire interdit aux fermiers d'utiliser les semences à des fins de croisement ou de recherche, de manière à ce que toute nouvelle découverte soit le seul fait de Monsanto, et non de l'innovation des fermiers.

2. INSPECTION DES REGISTRES

L'accord imposé par Monsanto autorise la firme à accéder à tous les registres du fermier ainsi qu'à s'informer à son sujet auprès d'un tiers, comme l'Agence de régulation du département de l'Agriculture (USDA), au travers de son registre des surfaces arables. En général, l'accès aux documents de la Farm Service Agency (FSA), une branche de l'USDA, est protégé par la loi sur le respect de la vie privée ; en signant un accord avec Monsanto, le fermier « renonce » à cette protection. Comme tu vois, cher fermier, le nouveau Big Brother s'associe avec l'ancien pour mieux t'observer. À en croire les groupes de consommateurs et les membres du groupe d'aide juridique aux agriculteurs, auteurs du Guide des ogm pour le fermier, Monsanto est capable de déterminer le nombre de sacs de semences vendus par un agriculteur et le nombre d'hectares plantés pour une culture en particulier à partir des relevés du département de l'Agriculture et des photographies aériennes correspondantes. (On peut d'ailleurs légitimement se demander, étant donné les nombreux dysfonctionnements de l'USDA évoqués précédemment, si Monsanto n'est pas plus efficace dans son utilisation des informations sur les fermiers que l'USDA elle-même). Le plus inquiétant est qu'il n'existe aucune limite à cette clause. En d'autres termes, il est envisageable que Monsanto tente d'obtenir des documents concernant un agriculteur à l'avenir – et parvienne à ses fins –, même après que ce dernier a cessé de cultiver des semences Monsanto.

3. MONSANTO, UNE DIVISION DE L'EPA ?

Afin que les plantes transgéniques produisent des pesticides dans leurs cellules, l'EPA exige que les agriculteurs plantent des variétés « refuges » non transgéniques ne contenant pas de pesticides à côté des cultures ogm. L'objectif de ces « zones refuges » est d'empêcher le développement de superbactéries qui pourraient développer une résistance aux pesticides à l'intérieur des plants transgéniques. Au-delà de la question de l'efficacité de ces zones refuges, c'est la question du contrôle du respect de ces normes qui se pose. En général, c'est l'EPA qui est chargée de superviser l'application du règlement. En l'occurrence, le Guide du fermier indique que l'accord de Monsanto avec les fermiers délègue la compétence de contrôle de l'EPA à la firme. Une compétence qui va de pair avec un droit d'inspection des champs. On peut dès lors douter que la firme applique le règlement (même si elle encourt une amende de 5 000 dollars pour chaque violation de l'obligation de disposer de zones refuges) si elle peut se permettre de s'en abstenir afin de réaliser plus de profits. Quand bien même la firme appliquerait le règlement, sa participation au processus de supervision est contestable. Comment être à la fois producteur de semences et chargé de l'application de la réglementation sur les cultures ? En matière d'action publique, c'est un choix étrange. Quant à la communication de l'administration, il est désastreux d'utiliser Monsanto, étant donné ses états de service passés et présents, comme une branche de l'administration et de lui confier le contrôle du bon respect des lois par les agriculteurs.

4. LIMITATION DE LA RESPONSABILITÉ DE MONSANTO EN CAS DE DOMMAGES

Les contrats de Monsanto découragent également les fermiers de remettre en cause la qualité des produits Monsanto (par exemple, des rendements pas aussi hauts que prévu) en limitant le remboursement au prix payé pour la quantité de semences, ou, à la discrétion de la firme, au simple remplacement des semences. Si l'applicabilité de ce type de clauses reste à prouver, le Guide du fermier indique que Monsanto n'hésitera pas à plaider devant un tribunal qu'en signant l'accord le fermier avait préalablement accepté ces conditions.

5. CHOIX DE LA LOI APPLICABLE, CLAUSES ATTRIBUTIVES DE COMPÉTENCE ET ARBITRAGE OBLIGATOIRE

Alors même que Monsanto a les moyens de s'offrir les meilleurs services juridiques dans n'importe quel État, son accord avec les fermiers stipule que (à part dans le cas du coton) le règlement des éventuels différends sera soumis au droit de l'État du Missouri (où se situe le siège de Monsanto) et non à celui de l'État du fermier ; attribution de juridiction est par ailleurs donnée au Tribunal de première instance du Missouri. Ce genre de clauses, habituelles dans de nombreux contrats et généralement validées par les tribunaux, n'en sont pas moins extrêmement dissuasives pour les fermiers qui envisagent de poursuivre Monsanto en justice, surtout ceux venant d'autres États ; elles constituent par ailleurs un fardeau supplémentaire pour les fermiers attaqués par Monsanto pour violation contractuelle. Ces clauses viennent s'ajouter à la limite imposée par Monsanto sur le remboursement d'éventuels dommages : il est dès lors clair que Monsanto s'est quasiment immunisé contre toute poursuite engagée sur des accusations de mauvais résultats de ses produits. Les clauses contractuelles relatives à la production de coton imposent aux fermiers la résolution d'éventuels différends par l'intermédiaire d'un arbitrage contraignant rendu dans la capitale de l'État du fermier. L'arbitrage contraignant obligatoire est aussi coûteux qu'une procédure classique, avec des honoraires supplémentaires à verser à l'arbitre ou au panel d'arbitres, même si le contrat précise que ces honoraires seront à la charge conjointe de la firme et du fermier. Le Guide du fermier note en outre que ces clauses ne vont pas dans l'intérêt du fermier, puisqu'elles limitent les recours à sa disposition. Il faut également noter que les clauses d'arbitrage de Monsanto imposent la confidentialité des procédures et des décisions, empêchant ainsi le fermier de partager avec ses homologues placés dans la même situation les enseignements qu'il a pu tirer de ce processus.

6. MONSANTO ET LES DOMMAGES ET INTÉRÊTS

La stratégie agressive de Monsanto se retrouve dans les dommages et intérêts que la firme réclame aux fermiers. D'abord, Monsanto interdit à vie au fermier condamné l'usage de toute semence Monsanto. Sachant que Monsanto dispose d'un quasi-monopole sur le marché des semences, ayant breveté plus de 90 % des semences et de leur composition génétique et continuant de racheter les compagnies indépendantes les unes après les autres, ce genre de clauses complique grandement la tâche du fermier qui souhaite racheter des semences. Ensuite, Monsanto cherche à obtenir le maximum de dommages et intérêts et à imposer au fermier le règlement des frais d'avocats et de procédure. Si la firme se dédouane contractuellement de toute responsabilité vis-à-vis du fermier en cas de mauvais rendement de ses produits, les indemnisations qu'elle cherche à obtenir des fermiers sont, sans surprise, très élevées et conçues pour les assécher financièrement.

Il n'est pas étonnant que nombre des agriculteurs ayant essayé de s'opposer à Monsanto se retrouvent en situation de faillite.

GUERRE D'USURE

Ah, autre chose : Monsanto considère qu'un fermier a « accepté » les termes de l'accord s'il a

1) signé le contrat OU

2) ouvert un sac de semences.

Vous avez bien lu, la simple curiosité engage la responsabilité.

Il fait peu de doute que les contrats entre Monsanto et les agriculteurs soient fondamentalement injustes pour ces derniers.

Ici, David ne s'en sort pas très bien face à Goliath. Mais ces accords sont également injustes pour la société dans la mesure où, à moins que vous ne cultiviez vos propres produits, ce que fait pousser l'agriculteur est ce que vous retrouvez dans votre assiette.

En d'autres termes, si le contrat est bien conclu entre Monsanto et un fermier, nous, en tant que population, sommes la troisième partie non représentée à ce contrat, puisque nous consommons les produits de l'accord. La nourriture étant la pierre angulaire de notre existence, ne revient-il pas à nos gouvernements d'agir au nom de tous pour empêcher cette inégalité de droit ?

DENIZA GERTSBERG.
SOURCE : www.gmo-journal.com

The take-it-or-leave-it agreement contains clauses that place farmers at a great disadvantage. One does not have to be a populist to understand that the Monsanto-farmer agreements are adhesion contracts which leave farmers facing substantial liability for violations of such contracts, contamination of neighbors' crops, or infringement of the companies' patents. In the case of Monsanto's contracts, the pen is indeed mightier than the sword.

1. NO SEED SAVING ALLOWED

With this prohibition Monsanto ensures that it gets a repeat customer the next year. Never mind that it goes against the very essence of farming practices cultivated for centuries by farmers around the world. A related clause prohibits farmers from using seeds for breeding or research purposes thus ensuring that any new developments come only from Monsanto and not farmers' innovation.

2. INSPECTION OF RECORDS

Monsanto's agreements give the company access to virtually all of farmer's records as well as the right to seek information about a farmer from third-parties, like the USDA Farm Service Agency's ("FSA") Summary Acreage History Report. Ordinarily, FSA information is protected by the Privacy Act but by signing an agreement with Monsanto a farmer "waives" that protection. So the New Big Brother is teaming up with the Old Big Brother and is watching you, dear farmer. According to Consumer Food Safety Report and Farmers' Legal Aid Group/Rural Advancement Foundation International-USA, authors of the Farmers' Guide to GMOs ("Farmers' Guide"), accessing USDA's Summary Acreage History Report and corresponding aerial photographs, helps Monsanto to determine how many bags of seed a farmer was sold and how many acres of a particular crop were planted. (As an interesting aside, given themany cited failures of the USDA that I wrote about previously, it would not be surprising if Monsanto was better at using USDA's information on farmers than USDA itself). More alarming is that there is no time limit on this clause. In other words, it is possible that Monsanto could attempt to obtain and review a farmer's documents at any point in the future, even after the farmer stops growing Monsanto's seeds.

3. MONSANTO—AN ARM OF THE EPA?

For plants that are genetically modified to produce pesticides in their cells, the Environmental Protection Agency ("EPA") requires that such farmers establish "refuges" of non-GM varieties that do not contain pesticides to be grown along side with the GM crops. The purpose of establishing such refuges is to act as a deterrent to the development of superbugs that may have become resistant to the pesticide inside the GM crop. Putting aside the question of whether such refuges are successful at deterring the development of superbugs, the fact remains that ordinarily, EPA monitors compliance with the refuge requirement. The Farmers' Guide, however, reports that Monsanto's agreement with farmers delegates the EPA's monitoring authority to the company.

This delegation comes with a right to inspect fields. Whether Monsanto enforces the refuge requirement is questionable (even if the company is fined $5,000 per violation of the refuge requirement) as there is little incentive to enforce that which does not contribute to its bottom line. Even if Monsanto was to enforce this requirement, however, Monsanto's involvement in the enforcement just feels wrong. Monsanto the seed producer is also the rule enforcer? It is an unwise policy decision and from a purely government PR perspective, having Monsanto, with its past and current controversial practices, act like an arm of the government, policing and controlling farmers to ensure compliance with the law is unacceptable.

4. LIMITING MONSANTO'S LIABILITY AND DAMAGE

Monsanto's contract also discourages farmers' challenges to the performance of Monsanto's products, say, lower than expected yields, by limiting the recovery to the price paid for the quantity of the seeds, or, at Monsanto's election, replacement of the seed. While the enforceability of such clauses remains questionable, as the Farmer's Guide indicates, Monsanto will go to court arguing that by signing the agreement a farmer agreed to be bound by these limitations.

5. CHOICE OF LAW, FORUM SELECTION CLAUSES AND MANDATORY ARBITRATION

Despite the fact that Monsanto could afford hiring a top-notch legal team in any state, its agreement with farmers nonetheless specifies that (other than cotton), legal disputes are to be resolved according to the laws of the state of Missouri (Monsanto headquarters) and not the state of the farmer and such disputes must also be resolved in a particular court, in this case, the Missouri District court. Such clauses, although common in many contracts and routinely upheld by courts, nonetheless create an enormous suing disincentive, particularly for farmers in other states, and places an extra heavy burden on farmers when Monsanto sues them for alleged violation. And when this clause is combined with Monsanto's self-created limitation on damages to price paid for the commodity or replacement of seeds, it becomes clear that Monsanto has virtually isolated itself from any suit by farmers for performance based reasons. Contract clauses concerning cotton requires farmers to resolve the disputes through a binding arbitration to be held in the capital of the farmer's state. Mandatory binding arbitration is as expensive as litigation but with an additional cost of paying for the arbitrator or a panel of arbitrators, even if the contract indicates that arbitrators' fees will be split between the company and the farmer. Additionally, as the Farmer's Guide notes, such clauses are generally detrimental to the farmer because they limit the remedies available. Furthermore, Monsanto's arbitration clause requires that all proceedings and results be kept confidential, thereby preventing the farmer from sharing the knowledge and insight gained with other farmers facing similar difficulties.

6. MONSANTO REMEDIES AND DAMAGES

Monsanto is aggressive about everything, including the damages it extracts from farmers. First, Monsanto cuts violators off forever from the use of any Monsanto seed products. Given that Monsanto has a nearly monopolizing control over the seed market, having patented control over 90 percent of seeds and seed genetics and continually acquiring independent seed companies, this clause could make obtaining seeds difficult.

Next, Monsanto will seek to extract as damages injunction, attorneys' fees, and costs of enforcing the agreement. While Monsanto attempts to contractually insulate itself from liability it may owe to farmers for poor product performance, the damages it seeks from farmers, are, with little surprise, expansive and designed to financially drain the farmer. It is no wonder that many farmers who try to stand up to Monsanto face bankruptcies.

ATTRITION WARFARE, ANYONE?

Oh, and, did we mention that Monsanto considers that a farmer "accepts" the terms of the agreement when a farmer does one of two things: 1) signs the contract; or 2) opens a bag of seeds. That's right, liability stems from curiosity. There is little doubt that Monsanto-farmer contracts are fundamentally unfair to the farmers. In this case, David does not fair well against Goliath. But are such agreements also fundamentally unfair to society because, unless you grow it yourself, what the farmer grows is what you eat. In other words, while the immediate contract may be between Monsanto and a farmer, we the people are the third unrepresented party to such a contract because we end up consuming the products of this agreement. As food is the corner stone of our existence, should the government take action on behalf of us all, to prevent such an uneven distribution of rights?

DENIZA GERTSBERG.
SOURCE: www.gmo-journal.com

En juillet 2004, David Runyon et sa famille sont devenus victimes des persécutions de Monsanto® contre les fermiers. Accusé à tort d'avoir fait usage de semences brevetées par Monsanto®, David a été contraint par les avocats de Monsanto® à leur remettre tous ses registres commerciaux, dossiers fiscaux compris.

In July 2004, David Runyon and his family became victims of Monsanto®'s persecution of farmers. Wrongly accused of using Monsanto®'s patented seeds, David was coerced by Monsanto®'s lawyers to turn over all his business records, including taxes.

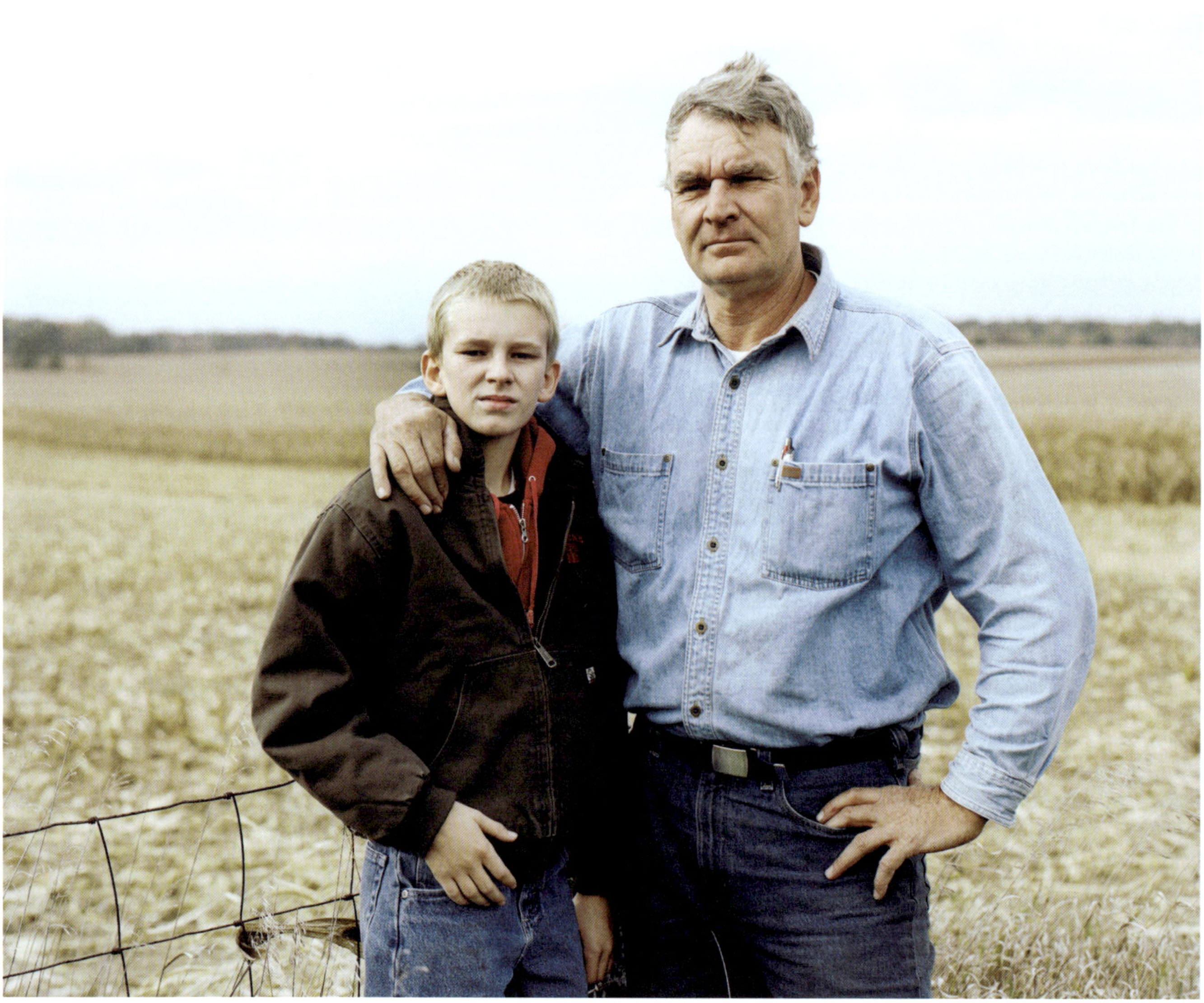

GENEVA, INDIANA. 2013

Au 28 novembre 2012, Monsanto® avait engagé 142 procédures judiciaires contre des fermiers pour violation de ses accords technologiques ou de ses brevets sur les semences génétiquement modifiées. 410 agriculteurs et 56 petites exploitations sont concernés.

As of November 28, 2012, Monsanto® had filed 142 lawsuits against farmers for alleged violations of its Technology Agreement and/or its patents on genetically engineered seeds. These cases have involved 410 farmers and 56 small farm businesses.

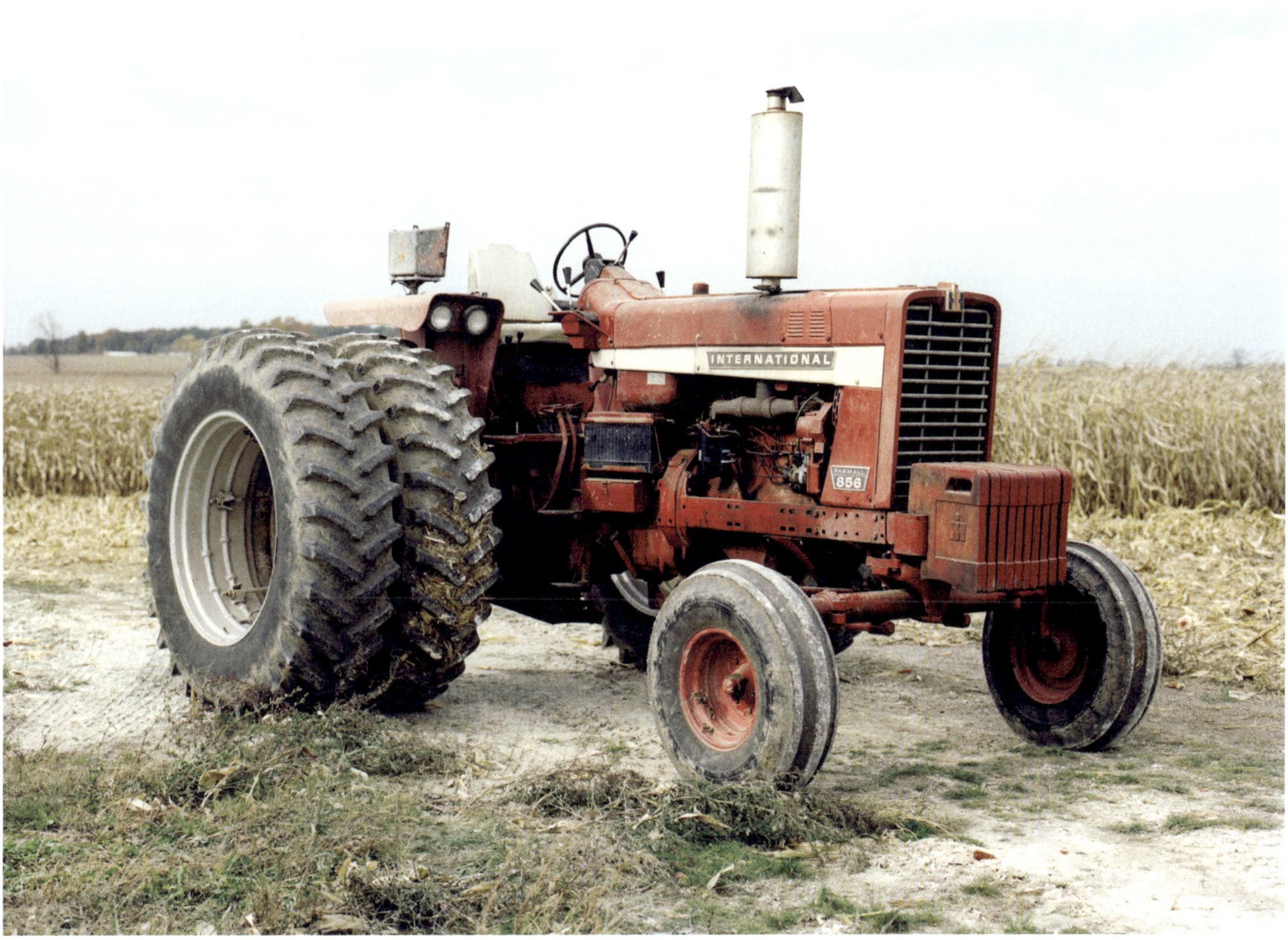

 GENEVA, INDIANA. 2013

L'exploitation de David Runyon.

David Runyon's farm.

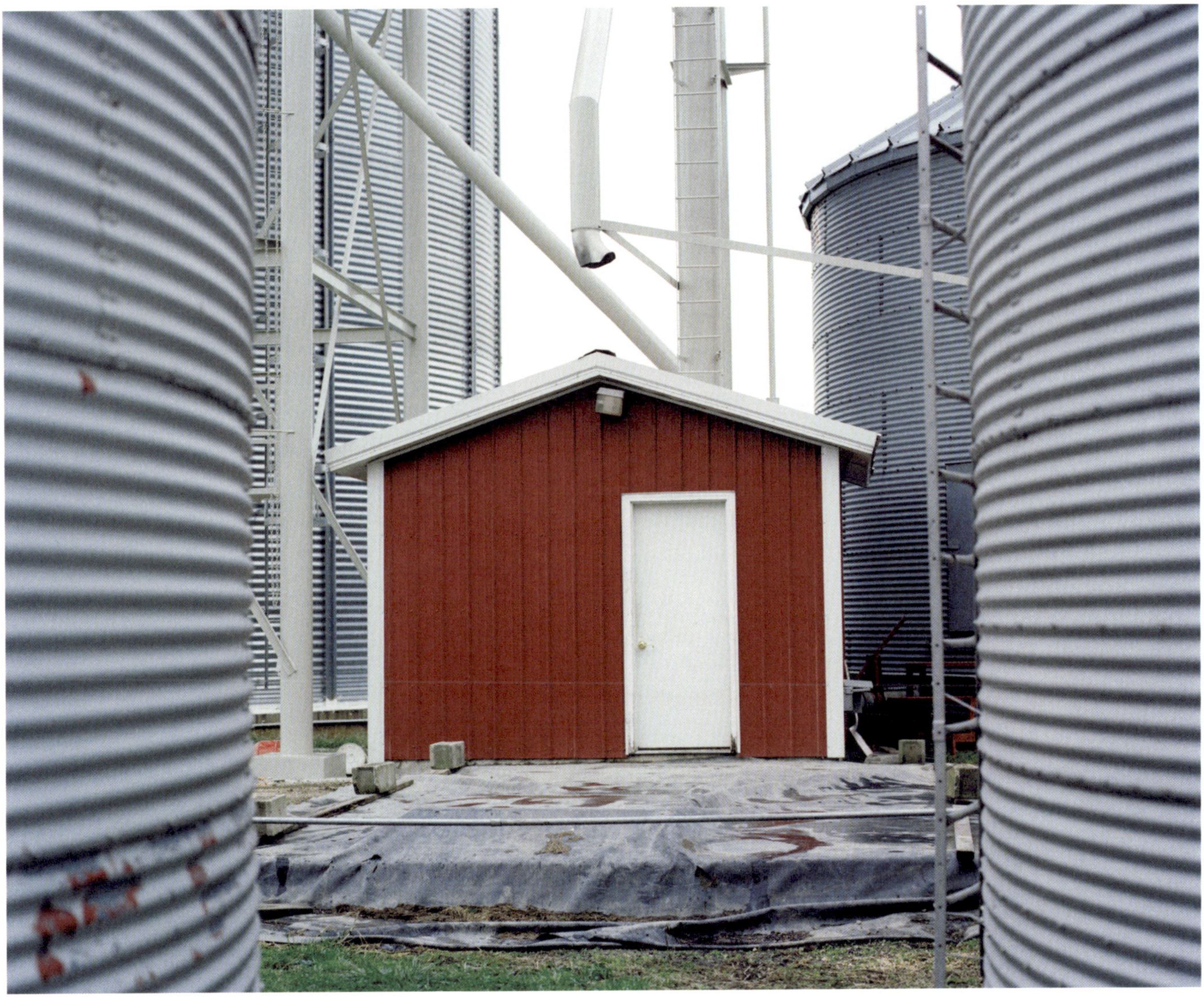

V.

« Monsanto® a déclaré avoir dépensé 4 600 000 dollars en lobbying à Washington DC en 2016. »
"Monsanto® declared $4.6 million in lobbying expenses in Washington, DC, in 2016."

Source: www.opensecrets.org/lobby/clientsum.php?id=d000000055&amp.

« On peut raisonnablement estimer que le chiffre réel des activités de lobbying de Monsanto® auprès de l'Union européenne dépasse les 399 999 euros annoncés. »
"It is reasonable to conclude that the actual amount of money Monsanto® spends on lobbying activitie in the European Union exceeds the reported €399,999."

Source: https://corporateeurope.org/power-lobbies/2017/11/eu-lobby-register-still-failing-live-transparency-promise.

Le marché boursier

The Stock Market

La relation entre les agriculteurs et Monsanto® tient du combat de David contre Goliath. Guidés par une expérience millénaire, les agriculteurs ont toujours craint et respecté la nature et la météo qui avaient tout pouvoir sur leurs cultures. Mais ils redoutent désormais d'autres entités : les nouveaux souverains de leurs semences. En effet, l'époque où ils utilisaient leurs propres semences est révolue. Le marché mondial est aujourd'hui contrôlé par une oligarchie composée des Américains Corteva® (ancien Dow-DuPont®), entré en Bourse en juin 2019, et Monsanto®, racheté par Bayer® en juin 2018, du Suisse Syngenta®, absorbé en 2017 par ChemChina®, et du Français Limagrain® avec sa filiale Vilmorin®[56]. Pour ces groupes tentaculaires, la satisfaction des actionnaires supplante de loin celle des agriculteurs ou des consommateurs.

En 2016, le géant allemand de l'agrochimie Bayer® formule une offre de rachat de Monsanto®. Bien plus connu pour son Aspirine™ et son Alka-Seltzer®, Bayer® est déjà un acteur important du secteur des semences avec 2 % du marché mondial, dont Monsanto® détient à lui seul près d'un quart (23 %). L'offre est la suivante : Bayer® déboursera 66 milliards de dollars pour racheter Monsanto®. Une transaction en numéraire dépassant la plus grosse acquisition de ce type jusqu'alors, la fusion des géants de la bière Anheuser® et InBev® en 2008. Selon les termes de l'accord, Bayer® s'acquittera de 128 dollars par action Monsanto®. Le 9 mai 2016, jour de l'offre, ce montant représente une prime de 44 % par rapport à la valeur du titre. La fusion, telle que présentée au monde, sera bénéfique pour les deux sociétés. D'une part, elle catapultera Bayer® au sommet du marché semencier — un marché dont la prospérité est assurée tant qu'il y aura des hommes à nourrir. D'autre part, elle laissera à Monsanto® les coudées franches pour distancer la concurrence et obtenir un quasi-monopole sur les semences. Selon Werner Baumann, le PDG de Bayer® à l'initiative de cette offre quelques semaines après sa prise de fonctions, la transaction « apporte[ra] une valeur ajoutée considérable aux actionnaires, à nos clients, aux employés et à la société dans son ensemble ». Hugh Grant, PDG de Monsanto®, renchérit : « Nous pensons que cette fusion avec Bayer® représente une très grande valeur pour nos actionnaires, notamment en raison de la nature de la transaction entièrement en espèces. »

Deux déclarations[57] qui mettent en évidence l'objectif premier de notre économie spéculative : servir les volontés court-termistes des actionnaires. Dans le projet initial, Werner Baumann vise une fusion effective pour fin 2017. Entretemps, le tableau s'assombrit. Les obstacles se succèdent. Du fait de la nature transnationale de leurs activités, Bayer® et Monsanto® doivent obtenir le feu vert de trente autorités de régulation de la concurrence à travers le monde. Exaspérée par la lourdeur des procédures, la direction de Bayer® dénonce publiquement un excès de zèle. Werner Baumann évoque les « détails inimaginables » exigés par les enquêteurs de la Commission européenne, auxquels le groupe a remis plus de 4 millions de pages de documents[58]. Bayer® finit par accepter de céder certaines de ses activités de vente de semences et d'herbicides à son rival BASF®. Fin janvier 2018, quatorze autorités ont donné leur accord à cette fusion ; l'Union européenne, les États-Unis et l'Inde suivent au printemps.

Le 6 juin 2018, après deux ans d'attente, Bayer® rachète Monsanto® pour 63 milliards de dollars. Cette transaction s'inscrit dans la logique des grandes manœuvres du secteur semencier en 2017, avec la fusion pour 130 milliards de dollars de Dow Chemical® et DuPont®, donnant naissance à une nouvelle entité, Corteva®, et le rachat du Suisse Syngenta® pour 43 milliards de dollars[59] par le géant chinois ChemChina®, après les tentatives avortées de Monsanto® en 2015[60]. En 2017, le secteur semencier compte une petite dizaine d'acteurs mondiaux dont les trois premiers se partagent 55 % du marché mondial[61]. Avec le rachat de Monsanto® par Bayer® et l'avènement d'un leader pesant 26 milliards de dollars de revenus agricoles cumulés, ils ne sont plus qu'une infime poignée[62]. Dans ce jeu des chaises musicales, les autorités de régulation de la concurrence tentent de contenir la concentration d'un secteur où trois grands groupes se disputent le monopole des semences mondiales. Les autorités semblent pourtant impuissantes face à un avenir incertain où ces groupes continuent de tisser leur toile en rachetant leurs petits concurrents, et jouent du lobbying auprès des organismes publics nationaux et internationaux[63].

Même après avoir cédé l'intégralité de ses semences de coton, de soja et de colza et ses semences potagères, ainsi que son herbicide Liberty (pendant du Roundup de Monsanto®), Bayer® a maintenant accès à plus de 2 000 variétés de semences, notamment pour le maïs, le soja et le blé. Issues du travail de Monsanto® sur les OGM, ces variétés suscitent de vives inquiétudes en Europe et dans le monde où un vent de défiance souffle sur la machine Monsanto®. La FAO (Organisation mondiale de l'alimentation) a fait part de ses inquiétudes[64], rejoignant le mouvement grandissant d'une société civile alarmée par les effets dévastateurs des activités de ces grands groupes. Un mouvement de révolte qui s'exprime aujourd'hui devant les tribunaux. Bayer® a racheté Monsanto® au prix fort pour bénéficier de ses brevets technologiques et de son savoir-faire, mais souhaitait réduire le déficit d'image lié à Monsanto® en supprimant son nom[65]. Or, depuis, ce nom ne cesse de s'afficher sur la scène publique. En août 2018, aux États-Unis, Monsanto® est condamné à payer 289 millions de dollars, ramenés en appel à 78,5 millions en octobre 2018, lors du procès Johnson. En mars 2019, Monsanto® doit verser 80 millions de dollars, ramenés à 25 millions de dollars en juillet 2019, dans l'affaire Hardeman en Californie.

Le 13 mai 2019, c'est une condamnation à 2 milliards de dollars dans l'affaire Pilliod. Plus de 11 200 plaintes sont déposées contre Monsanto® aux États-Unis et 13 400 procédures sont en cours dans le monde : Bayer® s'attend à débourser plus de 10 milliards de dollars de dommages et intérêts[66]. Enfin, le 26 avril 2019, *Le Monde* porte plainte après les révélations de l'existence d'un fichier établi fin 2016 par Fleishman-Hillard, un cabinet de lobbying mandaté par Monsanto® pour l'assister sur le renouvellement du glyphosate en Europe[67]. L'affaire du « fichier Monsanto » concerne 600 personnes dans pas moins de cinq pays d'Europe et pousse Bayer® à mettre fin à sa collaboration avec l'agence Fleishman-Hillard [68].

Dès août 2018, le titre Bayer® perdait 42 % de sa valeur, tirant vers le bas le DAX (indice phare de la Bourse allemande) et soulevant la colère des actionnaires de Bayer®. L'action Bayer® est à 55 euros en avril 2019, son plus bas niveau depuis 2012. Bayer®, qui pesait 136 milliards d'euros en 2015, atteint laborieusement 57 milliards d'euros en mai 2019 : à peine plus que les 56,4 milliards d'euros consentis pour avaler Monsanto®.

56 *Multinationales : hold-up sur nos fruits et légumes*, réalisé par Linda Bendali (France, 2019, 140 mn), Cash investigation, France Télévision, 18 juin 2019.
57 Cf. bayer.fr.
58 Reuters, 29 novembre 2017.
59 Zonebourse.com, 3 juin 2019.
60 *Le Monde*, 8 juin 2015.
61 *Le Temps*, Suisse, 17 novembre 2017.
62 *Le Monde*, 18 juin 2019.
63 *Le Monde*, 4 octobre 2017 et 11 août 2018.
64 *Le Temps*, Suisse, 17 novembre 2017.
65 *Tendances-Trends*, Belgique, 21 mars 2019 ; *Le Figaro*, 4 juin 2018.
66 *Le Parisien*, 28 mars 2019 ; *Libération*, 14 mai 2019.
67 *Le Monde*, 9 mai 2019.
68 *Le Monde*, 17 juin 2019.

The relationship between farmers and Monsanto® is a David vs. Goliath story. Farmers, guided by thousands of years of experience, have always feared and respected nature and the weather, with its almighty power over their crops. But the days when farmers could use their own seeds are over. The global market is now controlled by an oligarchy consisting of the American companies Corteva® (formerly Dow-DuPont®), which became an independent public company in June 2019, and Monsanto®, purchased by Bayer® in June 2018; the Swiss Syngenta®, taken over by ChemChina® in 2017; and the French group Limagrain®, with its subsidiary Vilmorin®.[56] These massive multinationals are far more concerned with satisfying their shareholders rather than working on behalf of farmers and consumers.

In 2016, the German chemical and agricultural giant Bayer® made an offer to purchase Monsanto®. Far better known for its Aspirin® and Alka-Seltzer®, Bayer® was already a major company in the seed market, with a 2% share of the market; Monsanto® alone holds nearly a quarter (23%) of this worldwide market. This was the offer: Bayer® would pay $66 billion to acquire Monsanto®, making the deal the largest cash transaction of this type ever made, outweighing the 2008 merger of beer giants Anheuser® and InBev®. Under the terms of the agreement, Bayer® would pay $128 for each share of Monsanto®. On May 9, 2016, this amount represented a 44% premium over the share price of Monsanto®. The merger, as it was presented to the world, would be advantageous to both companies. On the one hand, it would catapult Bayer® to the top of the seed business — a market that holds a great future for as long as there are people to feed. On the other, it would provide Monsanto® with the deep pockets to acquire a de facto monopoly in seeds, leaving its competition behind. According to Werner Baumann, CEO of Bayer®, who initiated the offer a few weeks after he took up his position, the deal would deliver "substantial value to shareholders, our customers, employers and society at large." Monsanto®'s CEO Hugh Grant added similarly promising words: "We believe that this combination with Bayer® represents the most compelling value for our shareowners, with the most certainty through the all-cash consideration."

Both statements[57] underline what has become the primary goal of the speculative economy: to serve the short-term interests of shareholders. In the first draft of the merger, Baumann predicted that the deal would be completed by late 2017. In the meantime, the outlook shifted as several roadblocks cropped up. Because they run operations in multiple countries, Bayer® and Monsanto® had to obtain approval from 30 anti-trust institutions around the world. Exasperated by the lengthy procedures, Bayer®'s management publicly denounced what they saw as excessively zealous oversight. Baumann described the "unimaginable depths" pursued by the European Commission; the group handed over more than four million pages of documents to its investigators.[58] Bayer® finally agreed to sell some of its seed and herbicide businesses to its rival BASF®. By late January 2018, 14 agencies had given their approval; the EU, the United States and India followed suit in the spring.

On June 6, 2018, after a two-year wait, Bayer® purchased Monsanto® for $63 billion. This deal capped the major reshaping of the crop and seed industry that took place in 2017, with the $130 billion merger between Dow Chemical® and DuPont®, which created a new entity, Corteva®, as well as the acquisition of the Swiss firm Syngenta® for $43 billion[59] by the Chinese giant ChemChina®, after Monsanto® had tried, unsuccessfully, to buy it several times in 2015.[60] In 2017, the seed sector had fewer than a dozen global players, with the leading three firms sharing 55% of the world market.[61] With Bayer®'s purchase of Monsanto®, creating a leader with $26 billion, only a handful of companies remain.[62] In this game of musical chairs, anti-trust regulatory agencies are trying to contain the concentration of a sector in which three major multinationals are vying for a monopoly of the world seed market. Yet authorities seem powerless to act, given an uncertain future in which these groups tighten their grips by purchasing their smaller competitors and by intense lobbying with national and international public institutions.[63]

Even after selling all its cotton, soy, colza and vegetable seeds, as well as its herbicide Liberty (the equivalent of Monsanto®'s Roundup), Bayer® gained access to more than 2,000 varieties of seeds, notably for corn, soybean and wheat. Created through Monsanto®'s research into GMOs, these varieties are viewed with deep suspicion in Europe and throughout the world, where a wave of distrust has overtaken the Monsanto® machine. The Food and Agriculture Organization (FAO) has expressed serious concerns,[64] joining the growing movement of a civil society alarmed by the devastating effects of these groups' activities. It has fueled a rebellion that is now playing out in court. Bayer® paid top dollar for Monsanto® to acquire its technological patents and its expertise, but dropped the Monsanto® name to avoid the image problem linked to the company.[65] Yet it has remained prominent in the public eye. In August 2018, in the United States, Monsanto® was sentenced to pay $289 million, a settlement reduced to $78.5 million on appeal on October 2018, during the Johnson v. Monsanto® trial. In March 2019, Monsanto® was ordered to pay $80 million, lowered to $25 million in July 2019, in the Hardeman case in California. On May 13, 2019, the Pilliod couple was awarded a settlement of $2 billion. More than 11,200 suits have been filed against Monsanto® in the United States, and 13,400 legal proceedings are currently underway around the world. Bayer® expects to pay more than $10 billion in damages and interest.[66] Finally, on April 26, 2019, *Le Monde* filed a complaint after discovering the existence of a file drawn up in late 2016 by Fleishman-Hillard, a PR and marketing firm hired by Monsanto® to support the reauthorization of glyphosate in Europe.[67] The "Monsanto® file" involved 600 people in at least five European countries; Bayer® was compelled to terminate its contract with Fleishman-Hillard.[68]

By August 2018, the share value of Bayer® had dropped 42%, sinking the DAX (the blue-chip German stock market index) and angering the company's shareholders. In April 2019, a Bayer® share was worth €55, its lowest price since 2012. Bayer®, which was worth €136 billion in 2015, struggled to reach €57 billion in May 2019 — just slightly more than the €56.4 billion spent to gobble up Monsanto®.

56 *Multinationales: hold-up sur nos fruits et légumes*, by Linda Bendali (France, 2019, 140 min), Cash investigation, France Télévision, June 18, 2019.
57 Cf. bayer.fr.
58 Reuters, November 29, 2017.
59 Zonebourse.com, June 3, 2019.
60 *Le Monde*, June 8, 2015.
61 *Le Temps*, Switzerland, November 17, 2017.
62 *Le Monde*, June 18, 2019.
63 *Le Monde*, October 4, 2017 and August 11, 2018.
64 *Le Temps*, Switzerland, November 17, 2017.
65 *Tendances-Trends*, Belgium, March 21, 2019; *Le Figaro*, June 4, 2018.
66 *Le Parisien*, March 28, 2019; *Libération*, May 14, 2019.
67 *Le Monde*, May 9, 2019.
68 *Le Monde*, June 17, 2019.

BUY

ACHETER

SELL

VENDRE

2019/02/20
Bayer®aktiengesellschaft (BAYRY) other OTC — other otc delayed price. currency in USD 19.40 +0.15 (+0.78%) at close: february 20 3:59 pm EST

source: https://www.deutsche-boerse.com

20/02/2019
société anonyme Bayer® (BAYRY)
autres marchés OTC – prix différés des autres marchés OTC
monnaie en USD
19,40 + 0,15 (+ 0,78 %)
à la fermeture : 20 février 15 h 59 EST

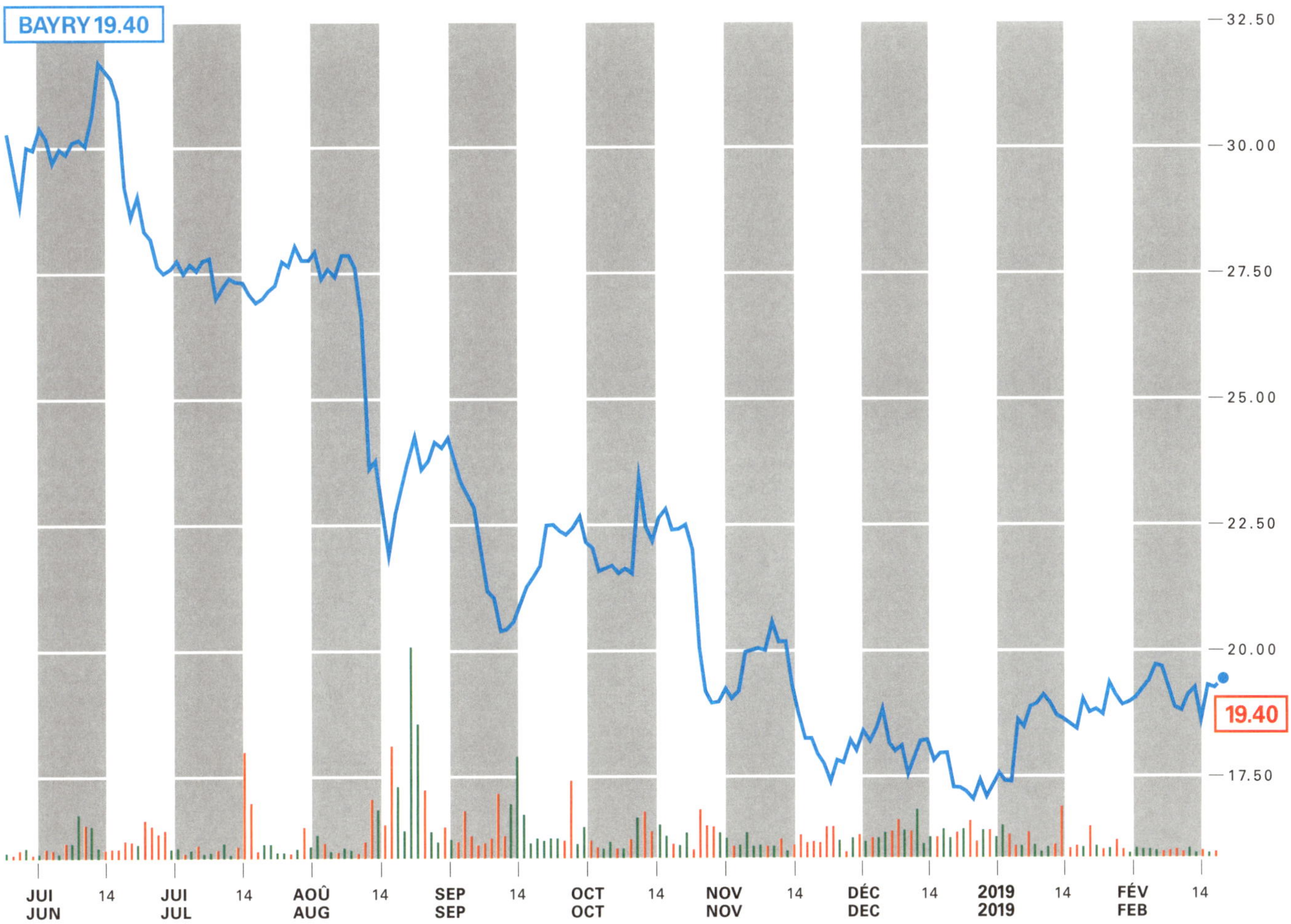

DATE	FERMETURE / CLOSE	VOLUME	OUVERTURE / OPEN	LE PLUS HAUT / HIGH	LE PLUS BAS / LOW
2018/02/20	30.3600	200077.0000	30.4950	30.6600	30.3600
2018/02/21	30.1100	348428.0000	30.3600	30.5400	30.1100
2018/02/22	30.1800	163077.0000	30.1350	30.4613	30.0600
2018/02/23	30.3150	189671.0000	30.1600	30.3600	30.0910
2018/02/26	30.5000	258077.0000	30.2800	30.5300	30.1600
2018/02/27	29.9400	202529.0000	30.2500	30.2800	29.8600
2018/02/28	29.2400	636841.0000	29.2850	29.4300	29.1500
2018/03/01	28.9750	557094.0000	28.8800	29.2500	28.6800
2018/03/02	28.8400	1529208.0000	28.7700	28.8800	28.5000
2018/03/05	29.3600	290733.0000	28.6300	29.4000	28.6300
2018/03/06	29.8100	307397.0000	29.7600	29.8600	29.6400
2018/03/07	30.1700	209431.0000	29.7200	30.2100	29.7200
2018/03/08	29.9700	146310.0000	30.0500	30.2000	29.9400
2018/03/09	30.2000	177745.0000	30.0960	30.2500	30.0300
2018/03/12	30.3250	543836.0000	29.9700	30.3600	29.9500
2018/03/13	29.5600	444282.0000	30.1850	30.1850	29.5000
2018/03/14	29.6300	201009.0000	29.7100	29.7800	29.4600
2018/03/15	29.1650	837532.0000	29.7600	29.9700	29.0000
2018/03/16	29.4700	751063.0000	29.0500	29.5300	29.0300
2018/03/19	28.8850	252094.0000	29.1250	29.1540	28.7600
2018/03/20	28.9800	304149.0000	28.6250	29.0400	28.6100
2018/03/21	28.9200	476998.0000	28.8900	29.0800	28.8200
2018/03/22	28.4100	397697.0000	28.4250	28.6800	28.2900
2018/03/23	27.7500	481429.0000	28.2200	28.2350	27.6000
2018/03/26	28.1350	400262.0000	28.1250	28.2000	27.6500
2018/03/27	27.8700	242233.0000	28.1000	28.2700	27.7200
2018/03/28	27.9100	173719.0000	27.9300	28.1800	27.7700
2018/03/29	28.2550	403524.0000	28.3000	28.4700	28.1400
2018/04/02	28.0000	310521.0000	27.8500	28.8800	27.6300
2018/04/03	28.0100	625132.0000	27.8700	28.0300	27.7100
2018/04/04	28.3500	278023.0000	27.8200	28.3800	27.8100
2018/04/05	28.7700	218494.0000	28.7300	28.9170	28.6800
2018/04/06	28.6500	317933.0000	28.7100	28.8800	28.5200
2018/04/09	29.3000	279519.0000	28.7400	29.8500	28.5400
2018/04/10	30.1800	493727.0000	30.2650	30.4700	30.0500
2018/04/11	30.0000	220991.0000	29.9300	30.1620	29.9013
2018/04/12	30.3600	455692.0000	30.3000	30.3900	30.1700
2018/04/13	30.3900	183314.0000	30.5800	30.5800	30.3000
2018/04/16	30.8400	850757.0000	30.4600	30.9800	30.2300
2018/04/17	31.1900	500533.0000	30.9150	31.2000	30.9000
2018/04/18	31.0800	145166.0000	31.1300	31.1400	31.0100
2018/04/19	30.7600	468136.0000	30.7700	30.8900	30.6600
2018/04/20	30.4350	132230.0000	30.4700	30.5362	30.3500
2018/04/23	30.1500	309363.0000	30.1900	30.2200	30.0000
2018/04/24	29.7700	205307.0000	30.0000	30.0500	29.6400
2018/04/25	29.7800	136120.0000	29.6400	29.7800	29.4340
2018/04/26	29.8500	240234.0000	29.6400	30.1000	29.4400
2018/04/27	29.8400	231927.0000	29.7700	29.8800	29.6100
2018/04/30	29.9050	225280.0000	29.7300	30.0440	29.7300
2018/05/01	29.7700	164907.0000	29.8800	29.9900	29.4400
2018/05/02	29.8200	271309.0000	29.9950	30.0700	29.7700
2018/05/03	30.2000	502003.0000	29.8600	30.2700	29.7700
2018/05/04	30.5700	238810.0000	29.9400	30.6500	29.9400
2018/05/07	30.4200	186501.0000	30.4600	30.5900	30.3500
2018/05/08	30.1900	355570.0000	30.0500	30.2600	30.0000
2018/05/09	30.3700	186000.0000	30.0000	30.4363	29.9700
2018/05/10	30.6700	210361.0000	30.4100	30.6800	30.4100
2018/05/11	30.5800	235652.0000	30.3800	30.5900	30.3800
2018/05/14	30.6600	200408.0000	30.7000	30.7800	30.5700
2018/05/15	30.2900	220212.0000	30.3500	30.3840	30.1800
2018/05/16	30.6600	217778.0000	30.5200	30.7100	30.4550
2018/05/17	30.9300	193848.0000	30.7700	30.9900	30.7250
2018/05/18	30.7700	185596.0000	30.7850	30.9300	30.7500

Historique des cours Monsanto® Co. Première date : 4 janvier 2016. Dernière date : 20 février 2019. Bourse de Francfort
Price history Monsanto® Co. Start date January 4, 2016 / Finish date February 20, 2019. Stock Market Frankfurt

DATE	FERMETURE / CLOSE	VOLUME	OUVERTURE / OPEN	LE PLUS HAUT / HIGH	LE PLUS BAS / LOW
2018/05/21	31.0100	131484.0000	30.7100	31.1900	30.7100
2018/05/22	30.9700	262570.0000	30.8800	31.0900	30.8400
2018/05/23	30.2100	212730.0000	30.1300	30.3500	30.0000
2018/05/24	30.2800	262105.0000	30.2600	30.3200	29.9400
2018/05/25	29.5000	206160.0000	29.4900	29.5000	29.0800
2018/05/29	28.8800	378881.0000	28.8600	29.2838	28.5900
2018/05/30	29.9800	441109.0000	29.9700	30.2300	29.7800
2018/05/31	29.9400	186806.0000	29.7500	30.0900	29.3900
2018/06/01	30.3800	226967.0000	30.3100	30.4900	30.0700
2018/06/04	30.1550	422019.0000	30.1000	30.2400	29.8800
2018/06/05	29.6800	347517.0000	29.6950	30.1100	29.3600
2018/06/06	29.9600	215789.0000	29.8800	30.2000	29.6800
2018/06/07	29.8500	636034.0000	29.8600	30.1000	29.5100
2018/06/08	30.1000	663519.0000	29.9700	30.2400	29.5200
2018/06/11	30.1500	1793579.0000	29.4900	30.4000	29.2200
2018/06/12	30.0150	1383452.0000	29.7550	31.4400	29.7500
2018/06/13	30.6050	1357863.0000	30.1000	30.6800	30.0500
2018/06/14	31.6700	466359.0000	30.5000	31.7900	30.4000
2018/06/15	31.5250	386341.0000	31.4500	31.9000	30.7400
2018/06/18	31.3500	437348.0000	29.9850	31.5200	29.5100
2018/06/19	30.9000	430987.0000	31.0000	32.8000	30.5000
2018/06/20	29.2000	761821.0000	29.0900	29.3700	29.0900
2018/06/21	28.6000	685739.0000	29.0700	29.0700	28.5000
2018/06/22	29.0200	603930.0000	28.7000	29.1400	28.7000
2018/06/25	28.3200	1555784.0000	28.2200	28.4636	28.2000
2018/06/26	28.1650	1352520.0000	28.1800	28.2500	27.9200
2018/06/27	27.6200	1038477.0000	28.0600	28.1900	27.6000
2018/06/28	27.4900	1168365.0000	27.2100	27.5600	27.1300
2018/06/29	27.5800	417726.0000	27.7900	27.8300	27.5500
2018/07/02	27.7400	446620.0000	27.5100	27.8100	27.4800
2018/07/03	27.4800	243483.0000	27.8100	27.8400	27.4800
2018/07/05	27.6800	356668.0000	27.5500	27.7000	27.4800
2018/07/06	27.5350	539401.0000	27.4800	27.5900	27.3300
2018/07/09	27.7500	235987.0000	27.7400	27.7500	27.6300
2018/07/10	27.7900	275685.0000	27.8900	27.9150	27.7600
2018/07/11	26.9900	390807.0000	27.0500	27.2300	26.9850
2018/07/12	27.2200	638908.0000	27.0700	27.2300	27.0100
2018/07/13	27.3900	204597.0000	27.2550	27.4200	27.2000
2018/07/16	27.3200	519884.0000	27.4900	27.5060	27.2700
2018/07/17	27.3100	4293021.0000	26.9700	27.3900	26.9600
2018/07/18	27.0650	2278339.0000	27.1500	27.1600	27.0100
2018/07/19	26.9050	343083.0000	26.7650	26.9500	26.7200
2018/07/20	26.9900	221187.0000	26.8350	27.0600	26.8200
2018/07/23	27.1600	336448.0000	27.1200	27.1700	27.0600
2018/07/24	27.2700	277526.0000	27.3170	27.4800	27.2000
2018/07/25	27.7250	287008.0000	27.1550	27.7400	26.9300
2018/07/26	27.6300	211100.0000	27.6800	27.7400	27.5400
2018/07/27	28.0300	402639.0000	28.1500	28.1700	27.9200
2018/07/30	27.7500	1298045.0000	27.9100	27.9400	27.7200
2018/07/31	27.7500	518642.0000	27.7600	27.8800	27.6400
2018/08/01	27.9100	974037.0000	27.8800	28.0000	27.8400
2018/08/02	27.3750	666258.0000	27.4570	27.4700	27.2900
2018/08/03	27.5800	342228.0000	27.6150	27.6800	27.4700
2018/08/06	27.4200	295047.0000	27.4000	27.4850	27.3300
2018/08/07	27.8500	441999.0000	27.9900	28.0200	27.7900
2018/08/08	27.8450	363077.0000	27.7950	27.9300	27.7500
2018/08/09	27.6000	234080.0000	27.7000	27.7200	27.5600
2018/08/10	26.5900	671369.0000	26.6700	26.7500	26.5100
2018/08/13	23.5850	2421820.0000	23.6700	23.8880	23.5800
2018/08/14	23.7700	1974883.0000	23.9000	23.9800	23.6500
2018/08/15	22.8650	1410241.0000	22.8800	22.9980	22.6600
2018/08/16	21.8600	4541604.0000	21.5550	21.9600	21.5400
2018/08/17	22.7300	2899293.0000	22.4450	22.7500	22.1105

DATE	FERMETURE / CLOSE	VOLUME	OUVERTURE / OPEN	LE PLUS HAUT / HIGH	LE PLUS BAS / LOW
2018/08/20	23.2900	1159005.0000	23.1350	23.2900	22.9992
2018/08/21	23.8150	8537627.0000	23.9500	23.9600	23.7000
2018/08/22	24.2500	5431748.0000	24.2700	24.3100	24.1055
2018/08/23	23.5900	2773032.0000	23.8300	23.8400	23.5000
2018/08/24	23.7700	1109709.0000	23.6400	23.8300	23.6100
2018/08/27	24.1300	673255.0000	23.8900	24.1700	23.8800
2018/08/28	24.0100	1298471.0000	24.0900	24.1700	23.9300
2018/08/29	24.2100	773579.0000	23.9900	24.2400	23.9475
2018/08/30	23.7900	697140.0000	23.8450	24.0100	23.7000
2018/08/31	23.3250	1959528.0000	23.5550	23.6300	23.2360
2018/09/04	23.1000	943929.0000	23.0850	23.2000	23.0000
2018/09/05	22.8300	535649.0000	22.8700	22.9700	22.7000
2018/09/06	21.9600	638359.0000	22.2600	22.3400	21.7500
2018/09/07	21.1700	819210.0000	20.9350	21.3100	20.8900
2018/09/10	21.0400	2631541.0000	21.2150	21.2500	20.9500
2018/09/11	20.3850	925210.0000	20.4350	20.6800	20.3600
2018/09/12	20.4300	2242083.0000	20.3500	20.5300	20.2775
2018/09/13	20.5700	4111456.0000	20.4150	20.6000	20.3296
2018/09/14	20.8900	1807767.0000	20.8150	21.1985	20.7800
2018/09/17	21.2800	628004.0000	21.0700	21.3600	21.0520
2018/09/18	21.4600	817180.0000	21.2200	21.4900	21.2120
2018/09/19	21.6900	725737.0000	21.5800	21.7200	21.5000
2018/09/20	22.4900	810624.0000	22.5200	22.5600	22.3000
2018/09/21	22.5000	835090.0000	22.4500	22.5300	22.3300
2018/09/24	22.3650	747342.0000	22.5300	22.5400	22.3600
2018/09/25	22.2950	3164018.0000	22.4400	22.4400	22.1600
2018/09/26	22.4500	590175.0000	22.3750	22.6000	22.3500
2018/09/27	22.6700	1300909.0000	22.8650	22.8900	22.6200
2018/09/28	22.1400	353397.0000	22.1200	22.3400	22.1000
2018/10/01	22.0400	736865.0000	22.0000	22.1800	21.9100
2018/10/02	21.5750	473302.0000	21.5500	21.6200	21.4500
2018/10/03	21.6250	436542.0000	21.5950	21.8000	21.5800
2018/10/04	21.6900	684405.0000	21.9400	21.9700	21.5800
2018/10/05	21.5300	433525.0000	21.6150	21.6600	21.4100
2018/10/08	21.6300	427991.0000	21.8250	21.8500	21.4200
2018/10/09	21.5200	771667.0000	21.2500	21.6200	21.1400
2018/10/10	23.5000	1661841.0000	21.8000	23.5000	21.5800
2018/10/11	22.4500	1909502.0000	22.5600	22.8900	22.1400
2018/10/12	22.1550	1128802.0000	22.3550	22.3600	21.9000
2018/10/15	22.6400	1381089.0000	22.4950	22.7700	22.4600
2018/10/16	22.8200	904701.0000	22.5570	22.8300	22.5200
2018/10/17	22.3900	600888.0000	22.5700	22.5900	22.3200
2018/10/18	22.4100	569926.0000	22.5850	22.7400	22.3100
2018/10/19	22.4850	1075183.0000	22.3500	22.5200	22.2900
2018/10/22	22.0000	378009.0000	22.1350	22.2100	21.9700
2018/10/23	20.1000	1993429.0000	19.3900	20.1700	19.3800
2018/10/24	19.1800	1349478.0000	19.7600	19.8300	19.0800
2018/10/25	18.9490	1295339.0000	18.7800	19.0400	18.5200
2018/10/26	18.9750	1068980.0000	18.9900	19.0500	18.5100
2018/10/29	19.2350	810093.0000	19.3680	19.5200	19.1000
2018/10/30	19.0550	509059.0000	18.9750	19.1300	18.8800
2018/10/31	19.1900	546803.0000	19.1600	19.3300	19.0800
2018/11/01	19.9650	1046574.0000	19.6100	19.9900	19.5300
2018/11/02	20.0050	521092.0000	20.2050	20.2200	19.7900
2018/11/05	20.0400	552387.0000	20.1050	20.2200	19.9900
2018/11/06	20.0100	494922.0000	20.0700	20.1200	19.9100
2018/11/07	20.5450	518753.0000	20.5450	20.6000	20.4000
2018/11/08	20.1700	770899.0000	20.3100	20.3500	20.1030
2018/11/09	20.1750	313732.0000	20.0550	20.1900	19.9300
2018/11/12	19.3100	564151.0000	19.4700	19.5900	19.2400
2018/11/13	18.7150	956608.0000	18.6800	18.8500	18.5700
2018/11/14	18.2500	627309.0000	18.7250	18.7400	18.1700
2018/11/15	18.2400	698904.0000	18.0600	18.3300	17.8500

DATE	FERMETURE / CLOSE	VOLUME	OUVERTURE / OPEN	LE PLUS HAUT / HIGH	LE PLUS BAS / LOW
2018/11/16	17.9200	652598.0000	17.8300	18.0500	17.7400
2018/11/19	17.7400	1303980.0000	18.0150	18.0200	17.6800
2018/11/20	17.3750	1296998.0000	17.4800	17.5800	17.3500
2018/11/21	17.8250	757116.0000	17.6600	17.8900	17.6000
2018/11/23	17.7650	287657.0000	17.7000	17.8000	17.6650
2018/11/26	18.2200	823706.0000	18.1020	18.4150	18.1000
2018/11/27	18.0000	958957.0000	17.9350	18.0500	17.8000
2018/11/28	18.4100	687620.0000	18.1300	18.4500	18.0100
2018/11/29	18.1750	838101.0000	18.0500	18.2900	17.9200
2018/11/30	18.4270	822479.0000	18.5500	18.5600	18.2500
2018/12/03	18.8600	1072444.0000	18.8750	18.9200	18.6600
2018/12/04	18.1500	1106376.0000	18.6900	18.7000	18.0700
2018/12/06	18.0000	1592178.0000	18.0300	18.1000	17.6400
2018/12/07	18.0950	1161957.0000	17.8600	18.2620	17.5900
2018/12/10	17.5150	1100061.0000	17.7300	17.7700	17.1400
2018/12/11	17.8600	1977637.0000	18.0700	18.0800	17.6300
2018/12/12	18.2001	578453.0000	18.1550	18.3400	18.1200
2018/12/13	18.2200	856600.0000	18.1350	18.2800	18.0500
2018/12/14	17.8100	890008.0000	18.0800	18.1300	17.7700
2018/12/17	17.9600	1220278.0000	17.8150	18.1500	17.7901
2018/12/18	17.9600	853927.0000	18.1100	18.1700	17.8500
2018/12/19	17.2650	1084957.0000	17.8300	17.8700	17.1100
2018/12/20	17.2700	1183785.0000	17.5650	17.6000	17.2600
2018/12/21	17.1900	1537200.0000	17.2300	17.6600	17.1500
2018/12/24	17.0400	689341.0000	17.3200	17.4400	16.9800
2018/12/26	17.4200	1162140.0000	17.1100	17.4300	16.8800
2018/12/27	17.0900	1156072.0000	16.8950	17.0900	16.5800
2018/12/28	17.3100	887908.0000	17.3300	17.4000	17.2300
2018/12/31	17.5700	1346797.0000	17.5500	17.6400	17.4600
2019/01/02	17.4000	966780.0000	17.1950	17.4300	17.1700
2019/01/03	17.3900	521642.0000	17.4300	17.4800	17.3200
2019/01/04	18.6100	523122.0000	18.1950	18.6600	18.1900
2019/01/07	18.4600	1082955.0000	18.3700	18.4900	18.2500
2019/01/08	18.8800	560034.0000	18.8750	18.9500	18.7400
2019/01/09	18.9400	261318.0000	19.0600	19.1100	18.8700
2019/01/10	19.1200	448790.0000	18.8000	19.1300	18.7700
2019/01/11	18.9550	557984.0000	18.6650	18.9800	18.6100
2019/01/14	18.6900	2096220.0000	18.6000	18.7600	18.5800
2019/01/15	18.6300	392256.0000	18.5600	18.7500	18.5360
2019/01/16	18.5300	417383.0000	18.5700	18.6300	18.5000
2019/01/17	18.4300	528462.0000	18.2800	18.5000	18.2000
2019/01/18	19.0400	464107.0000	18.8000	19.0500	18.6100
2019/01/22	18.7600	1290345.0000	18.4800	18.7900	18.4700
2019/01/23	18.8200	499307.0000	18.8050	18.8980	18.7500
2019/01/24	18.7100	371512.0000	18.7050	18.8700	18.6500
2019/01/25	19.3550	404125.0000	19.2300	19.5350	19.2000
2019/01/28	19.1000	751629.0000	19.0600	19.1600	19.0100
2019/01/29	18.9100	380828.0000	18.9400	19.0100	18.8400
2019/01/30	18.9650	233214.0000	18.8050	19.0200	18.7120
2019/01/31	19.0600	411510.0000	18.8650	19.0800	18.7800
2019/02/01	19.2400	383281.0000	19.0850	19.2800	19.0500
2019/02/04	19.3950	350552.0000	19.2700	19.4000	19.1950
2019/02/05	19.7100	341562.0000	19.5350	19.8190	19.5200
2019/02/06	19.6700	291852.0000	19.6700	19.6950	19.6000
2019/02/07	19.2250	329533.0000	19.2300	19.7600	19.0500
2019/02/08	18.8550	350302.0000	18.7950	18.8995	18.6500
2019/02/11	18.7900	267479.0000	18.7900	18.8700	18.7300
2019/02/12	19.1200	415348.0000	19.1300	19.1900	19.0900
2019/02/13	19.2750	242871.0000	19.2350	19.3500	19.1800
2019/02/14	18.5750	301345.0000	18.7550	18.7700	18.4800
2019/02/15	19.3000	225051.0000	19.0400	19.3100	18.9800
2019/02/19	19.2500	261377.0000	19.1800	19.3200	19.1800
2019/02/20	19.4000	212306.0000	19.2500	19.4900	19.2300

We can't afford to lose one dollar of business. Our attitude discussing this subject with our customer will be the decidin factor in our success or failure in retaining all our present business. Good luck.

Nous ne pouvons pas nous permettre de perdre un seul dollar. Notre attitude lors des pourparlers à ce sujet avec notre clien décisive pour le succès ou l'échec du maintien de toute notre activité actuelle. Bonne chance.

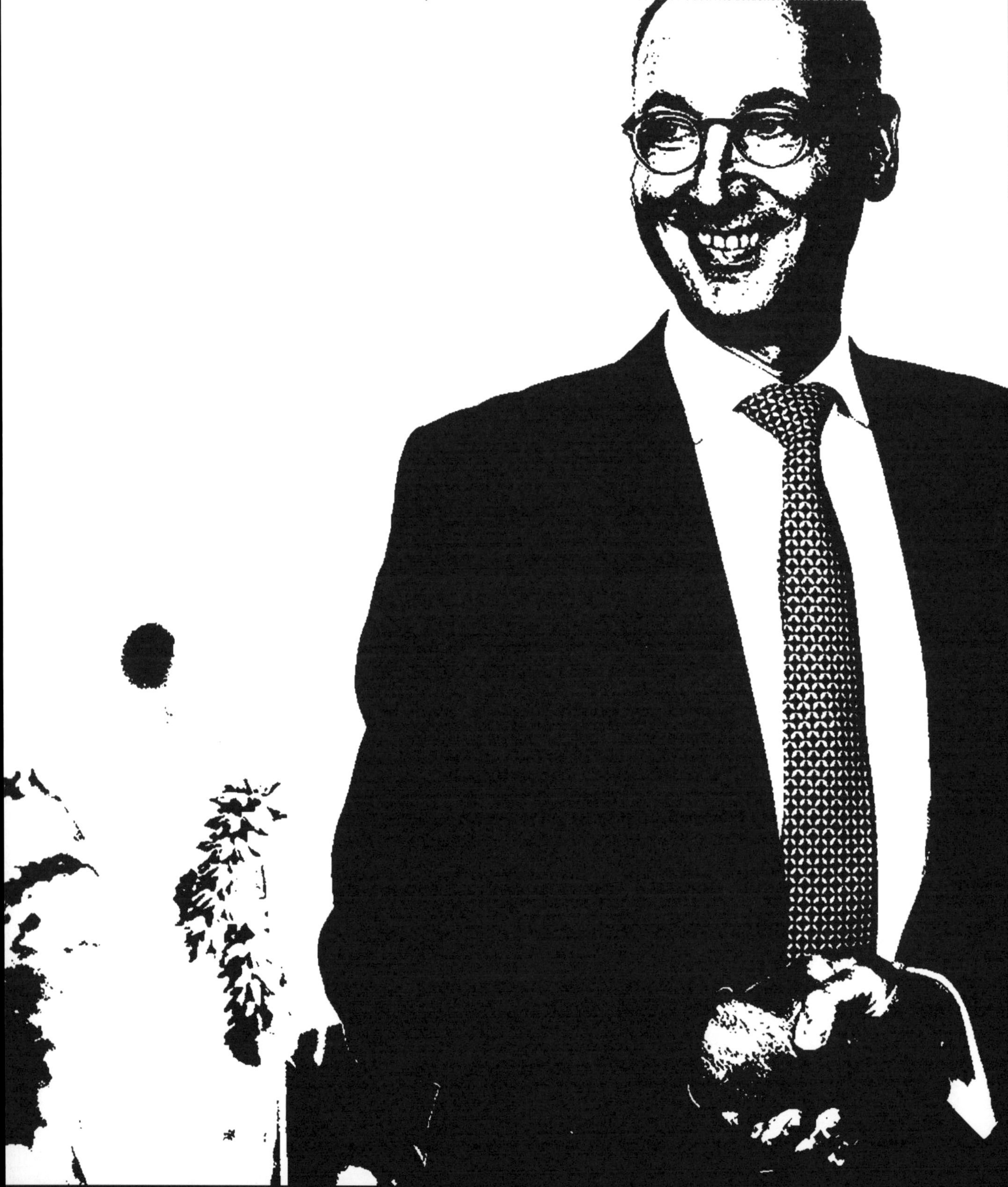

Texte extrait de documents internes datant de 1970 et montrant les tentatives de Monsanto® de tenir le public au courant des faits sur les PCB
Text extracted from internal documents from 1970 showing Monsanto®'s attempts to keep the public in the dark about PCBs.

Bayer® aurait signé un contrat de 66 milliards de dollars pour l'achat de Monsanto® le 14 septembre 2016.

Bayer® reportedly signed a $66 billion deal to buy Monsanto® on September 14, 2016.

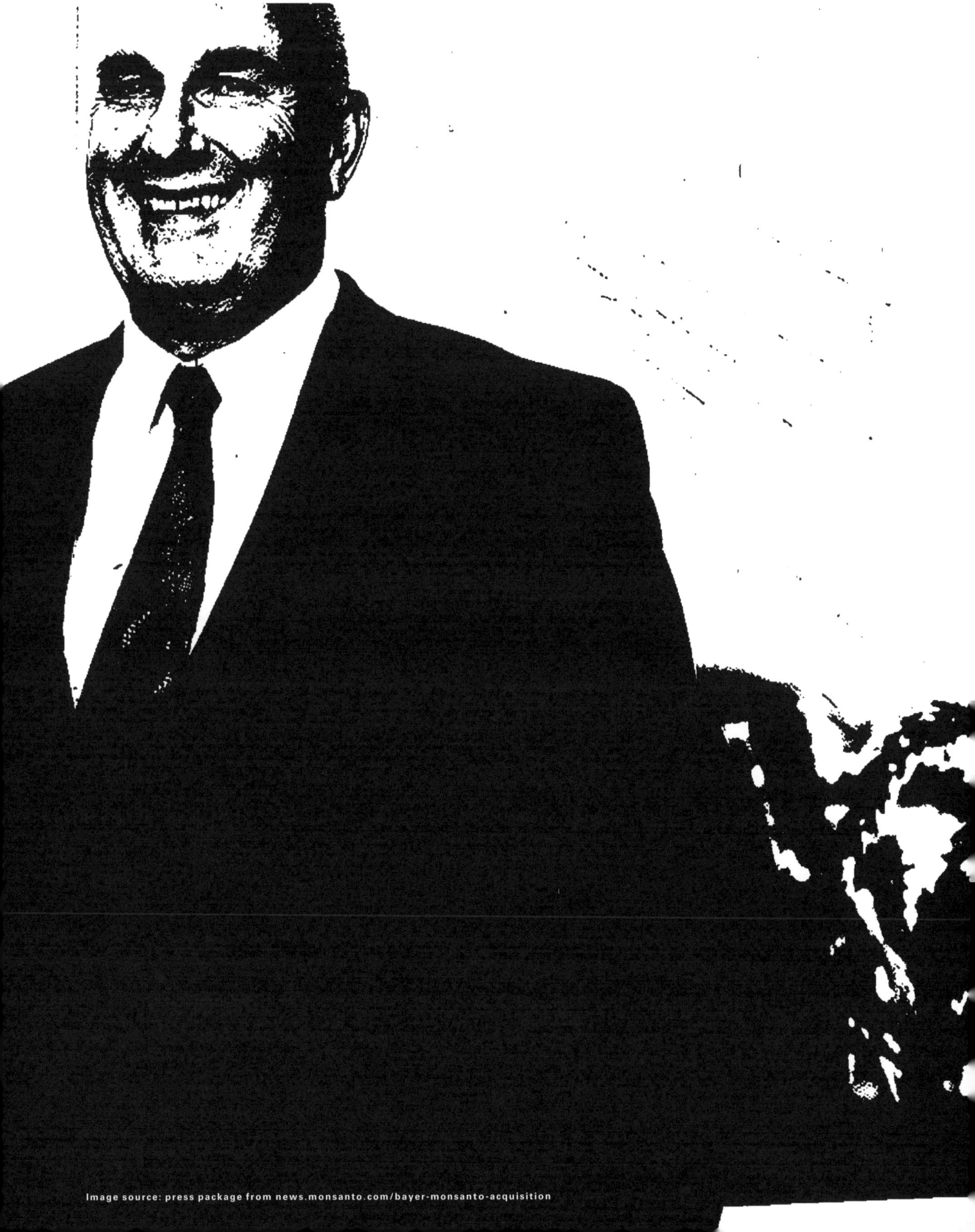

Image source: press package from news.monsanto.com/bayer-monsanto-acquisition

Au cours du dernier cycle électoral (2016), le corps législatif des républicains a reçu 226 000 dollars de Monsanto® Co., tandis que les démocrates ont reçu seulement 90 500 dollars.

In the last electoral cycle (2016), the Republicans in the legislature received US$226,000 from Monsanto® Co., while Democrats received only US$90,500.

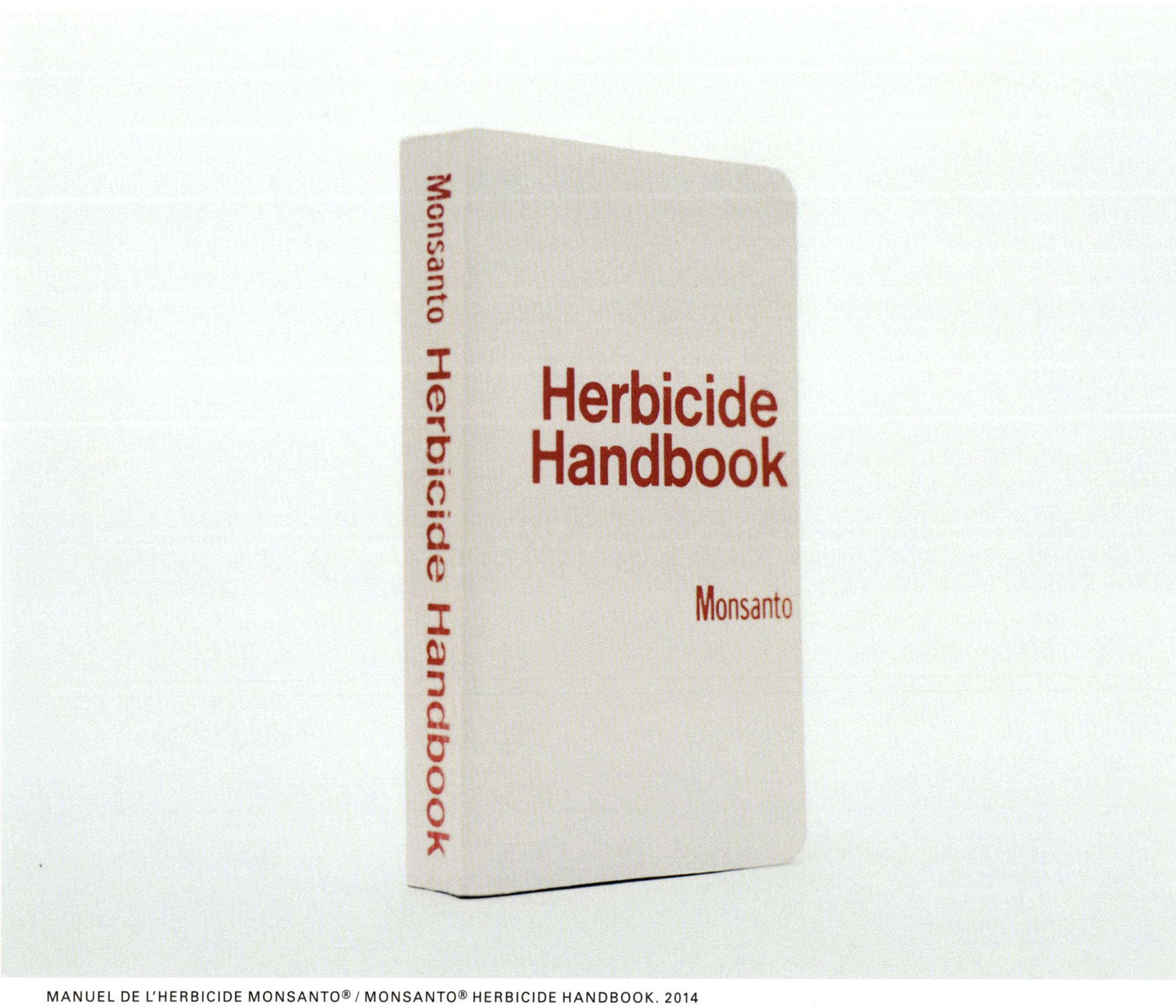

MANUEL DE L'HERBICIDE MONSANTO® / MONSANTO® HERBICIDE HANDBOOK. 2014

Without
Sans produits
chemicals,
chimiques,
many
des millions
more millions
de gens risquent
would
de connaître
go hungry.
la faim.

EXTRAIT D'UNE CAMPAGNE PUBLICITAIRE DE MONSANTO®, 1977.
EXCERPT FROM A 1977 MONSANTO® AD.

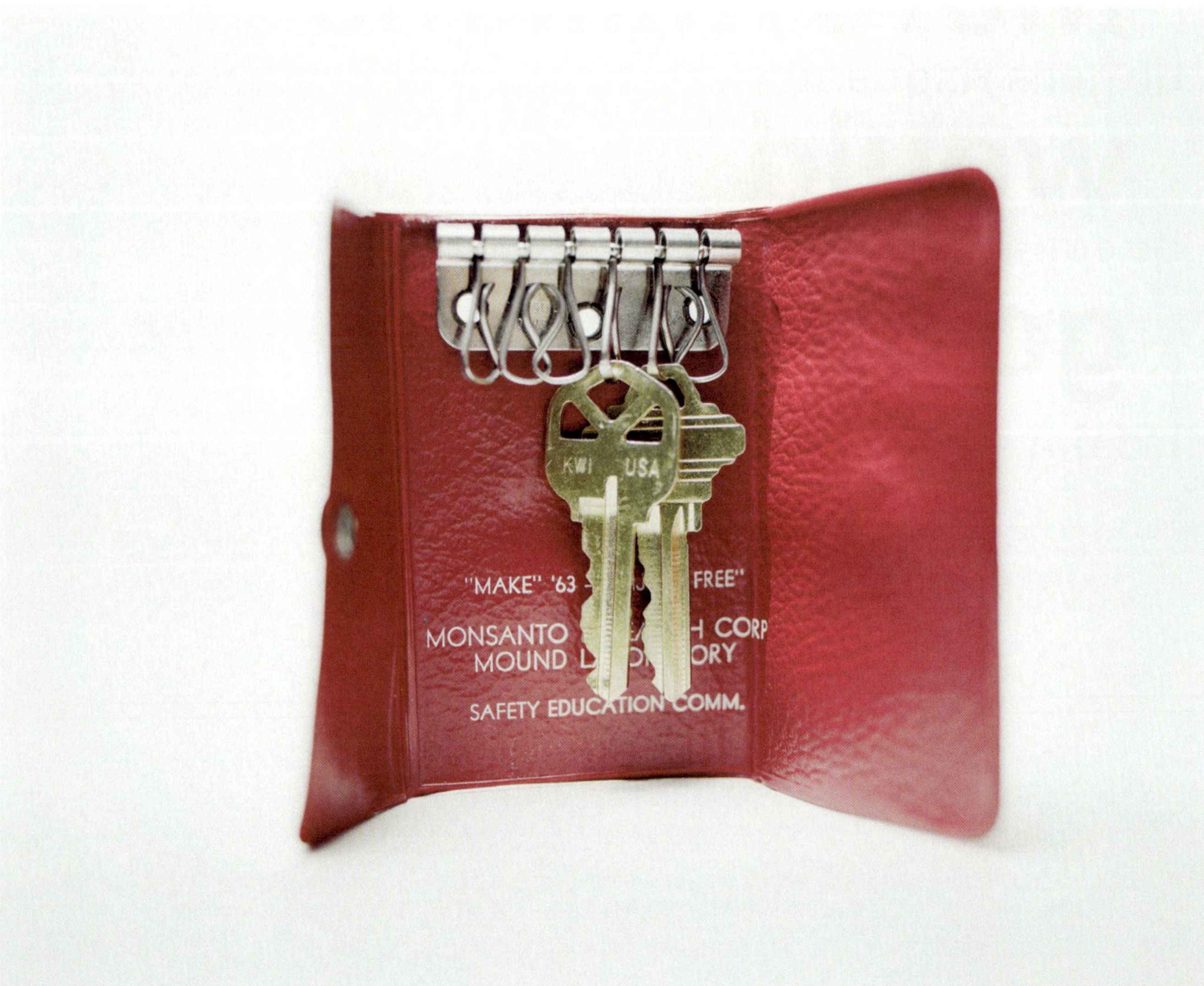

PORTE-CLÉS MONSANTO® / MONSANTO® KEY HOLDER. 2014

Without

Sans produits

chemicals,

chimiques,

life itself

la vie elle-même

would be

serait

impossible.

impossible.

EXTRAIT D'UNE CAMPAGNE PUBLICITAIRE DE MONSANTO®, 1977.

EXCERPT FROM A 1977 MONSANTO® AD.

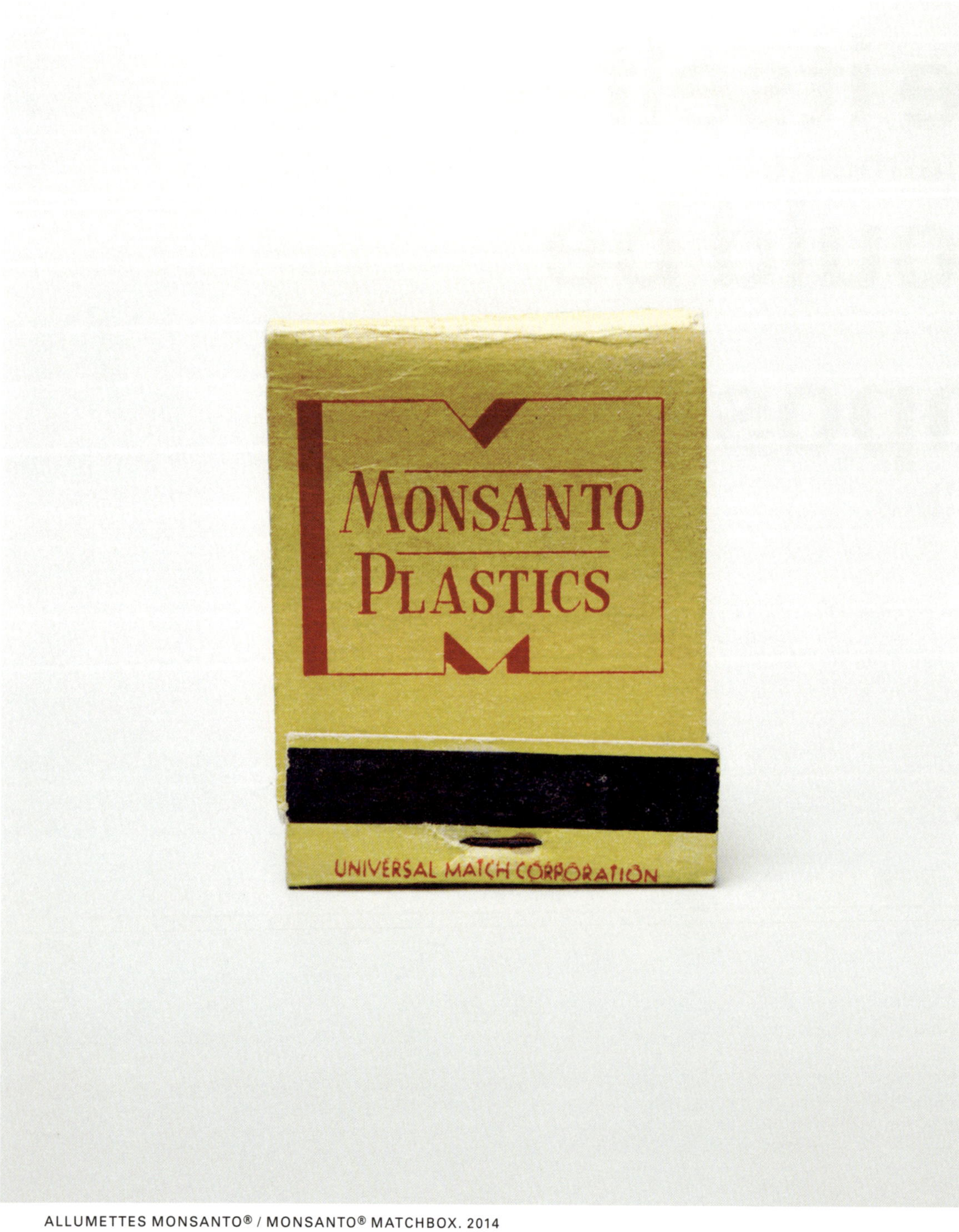

ALLUMETTES MONSANTO® / MONSANTO® MATCHBOX. 2014

Life is chemical.
La vie est chimique.
And with
Avec les produits chimiques,
chemicals,
les sociétés
companies like
comme
Monsanto®
Monsanto®
are working to
contribuent à
help improve
améliorer
the quality of life.
la qualité de vie.

EXTRAIT D'UNE CAMPAGNE PUBLICITAIRE DE MONSANTO®, 1977.
EXCERPT FROM A 1977 MONSANTO® AD.

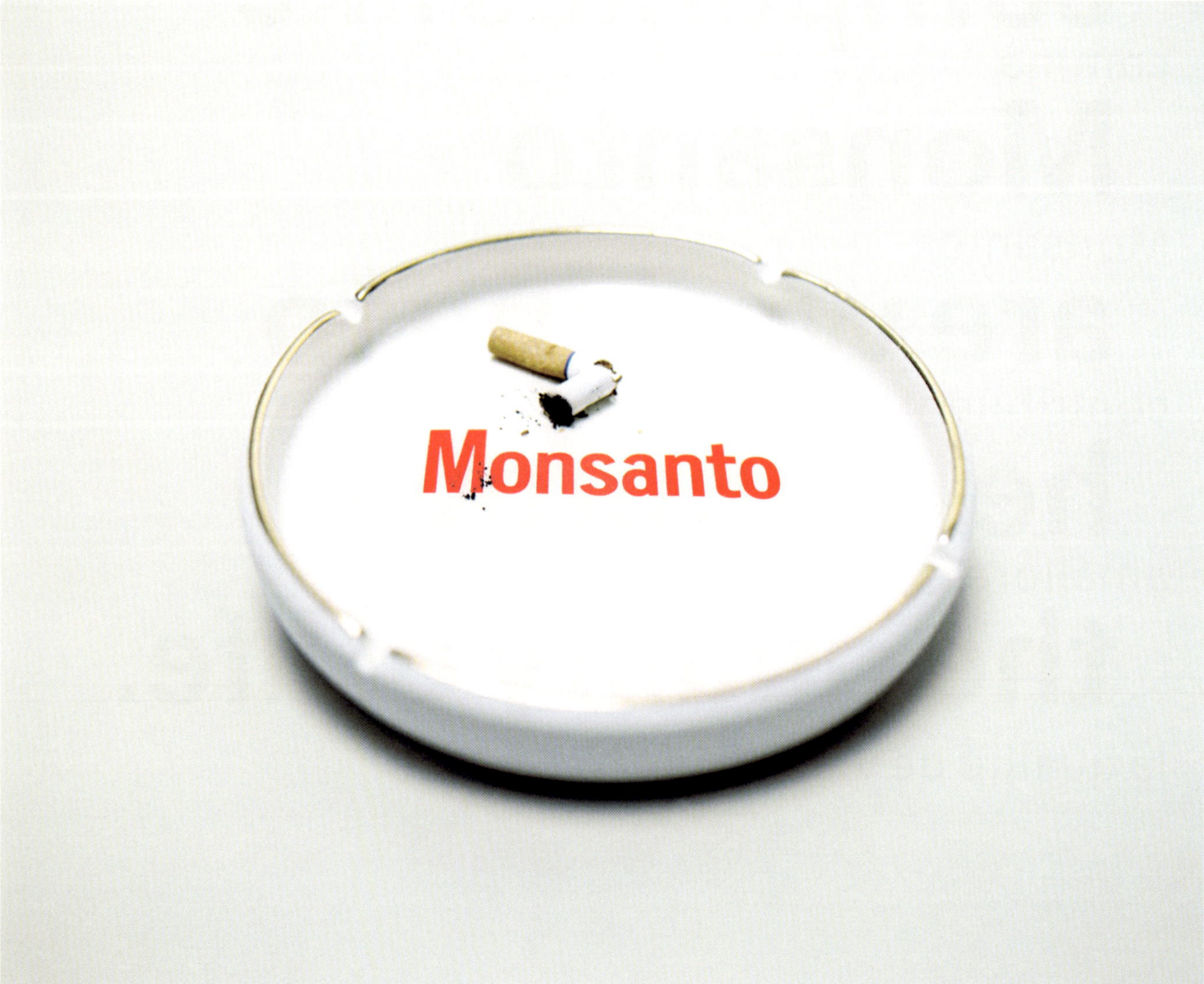

CENDRIER MONSANTO® / MONSANTO® ASHTRAY. 2014

Chemicals
Les produits chimiques
help you
vous aident à vivre
to live longer.
plus longtemps.

EXTRAIT D'UNE CAMPAGNE PUBLICITAIRE DE MONSANTO®, 1977.
EXCERPT FROM A 1977 MONSANTO® AD.

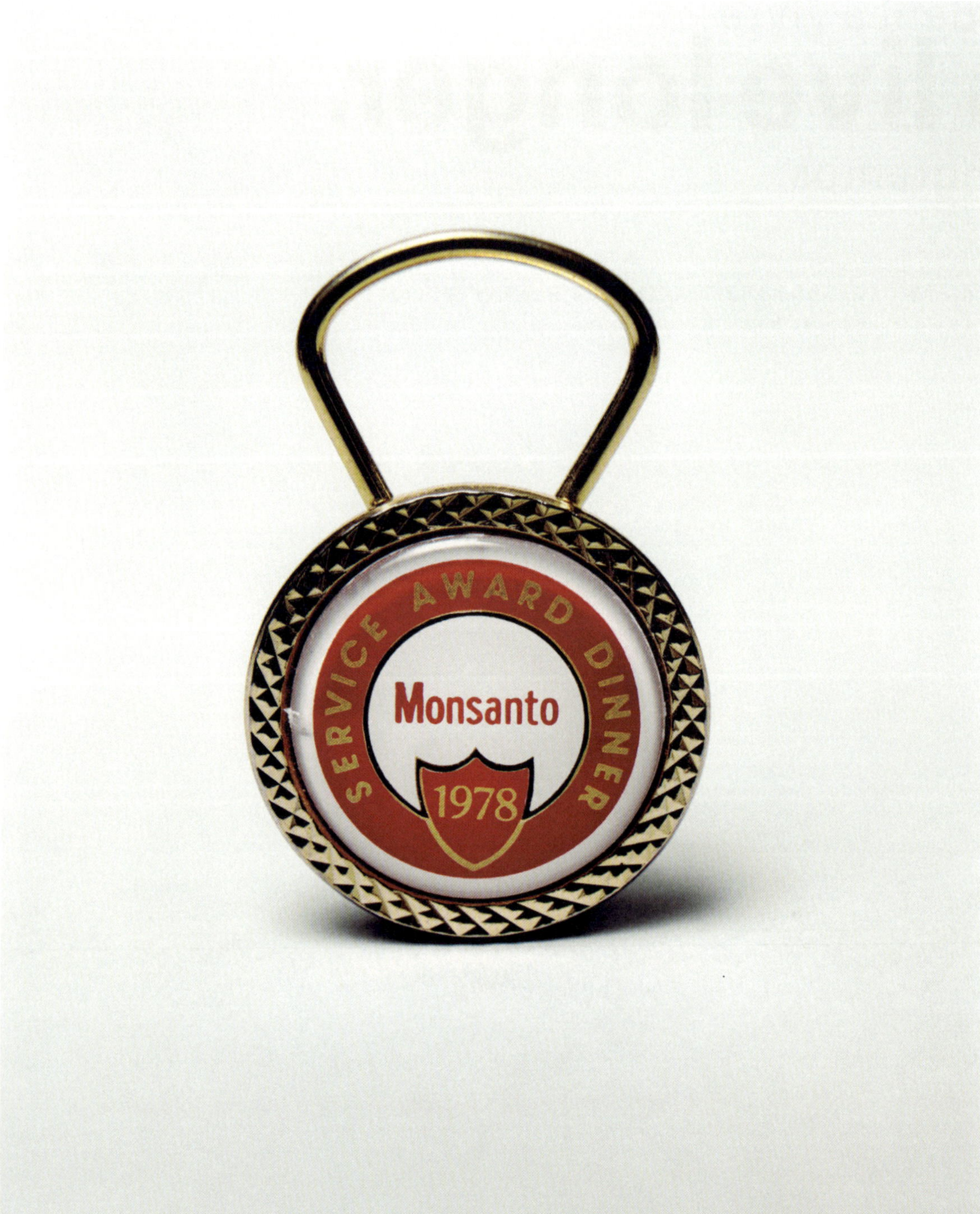

PORTE-CLÉS MONSANTO® / MONSANTO® KEY HOLDER. 2014

Chemicals

Les produits chimiques

help you

contribuent

eat better.

à une meilleure alimentation.

EXTRAIT D'UNE CAMPAGNE PUBLICITAIRE DE MONSANTO®, 1977.
EXCERPT FROM A 1977 MONSANTO® AD.

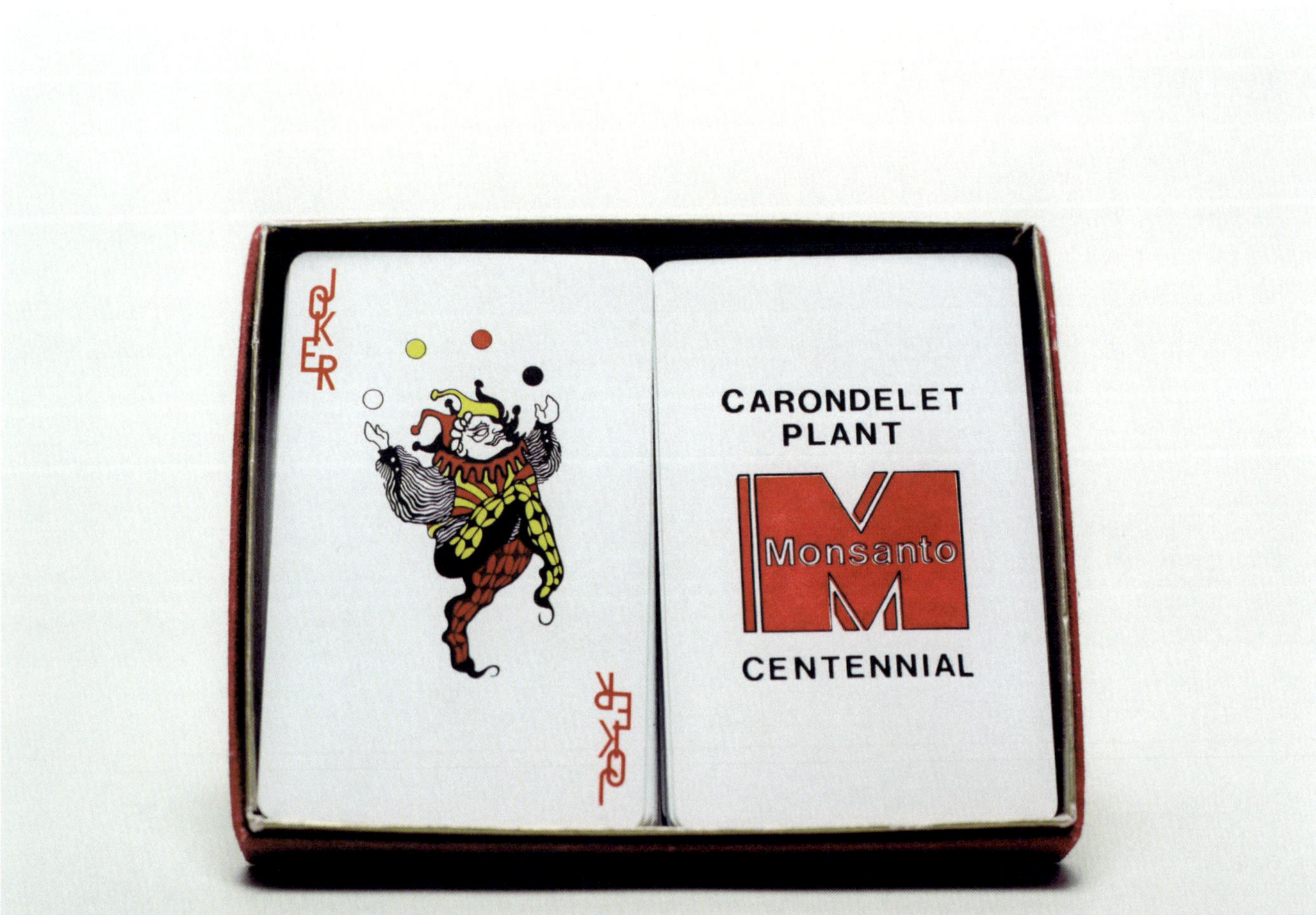

JEUX DE CARTES MONSANTO® / MONSANTO® PLAYING CARDS SET. 2014

There really
Il n'y a pas
is not much
vraiment de
difference
différence
between foods
entre
made by
les produits
Mother Nature
de Mère Nature
and those
et ceux fabriqués
made by man.
par l'homme.

EXTRAIT D'UNE CAMPAGNE PUBLICITAIRE DE MONSANTO®, 1980.
EXCERPT FROM A 1980 MONSANTO® AD.

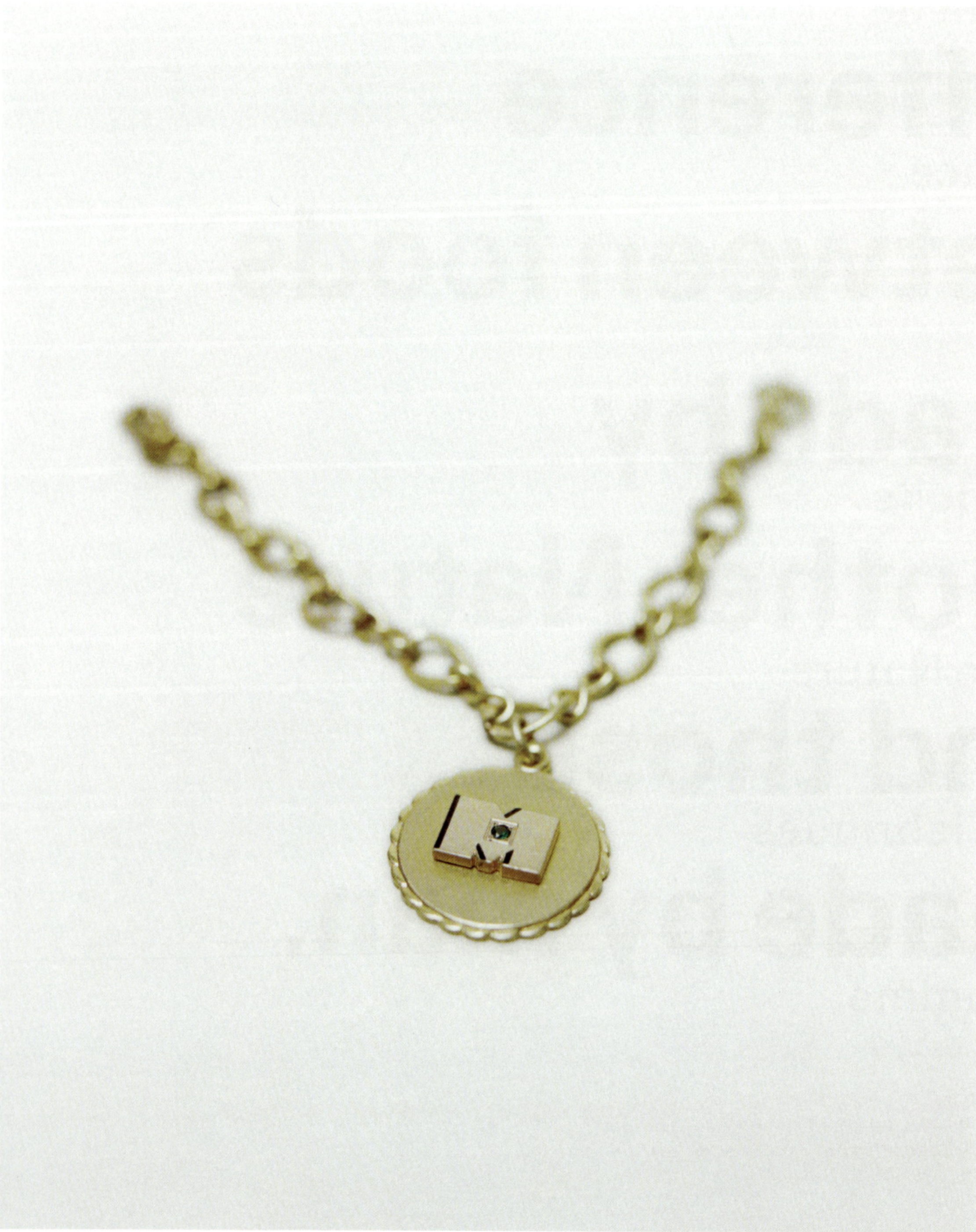

COLLIER MONSANTO® / MONSANTO® NECKLACE. 2014

All man–made
Tous les produits
foods are
artificiels subissent
tested for safety.
des tests de sécurité.
And they often
Et ils sont souvent
provide more
plus nutritifs
nutrition, at a
et moins coûteux
lower cost, than
que les
natural foods.
produits naturels.

EXTRAIT D'UNE CAMPAGNE PUBLICITAIRE DE MONSANTO®, 1980.
EXCERPT FROM A 1980 MONSANTO® AD.

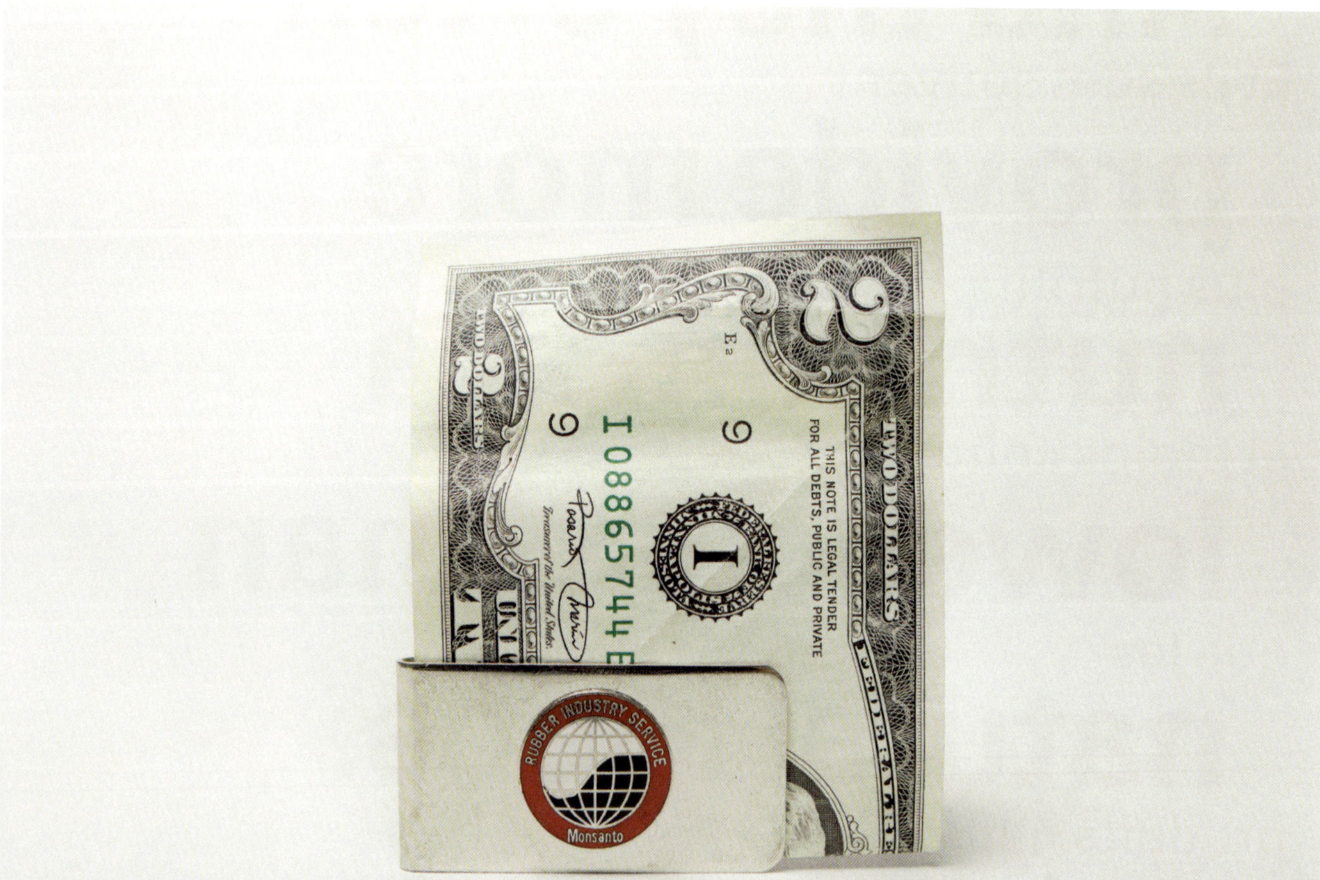

PINCE À BILLETS MONSANTO® / MONSANTO® BILLS HOLDER. 2014

The real
Le vrai défi
challenge is
repose dans
to use
la bonne
chemicals
utilisation
properly.
des produits chimiques.

EXTRAIT D'UNE CAMPAGNE PUBLICITAIRE DE MONSANTO®, 1977.
EXCERPT FROM A 1977 MONSANTO® AD.

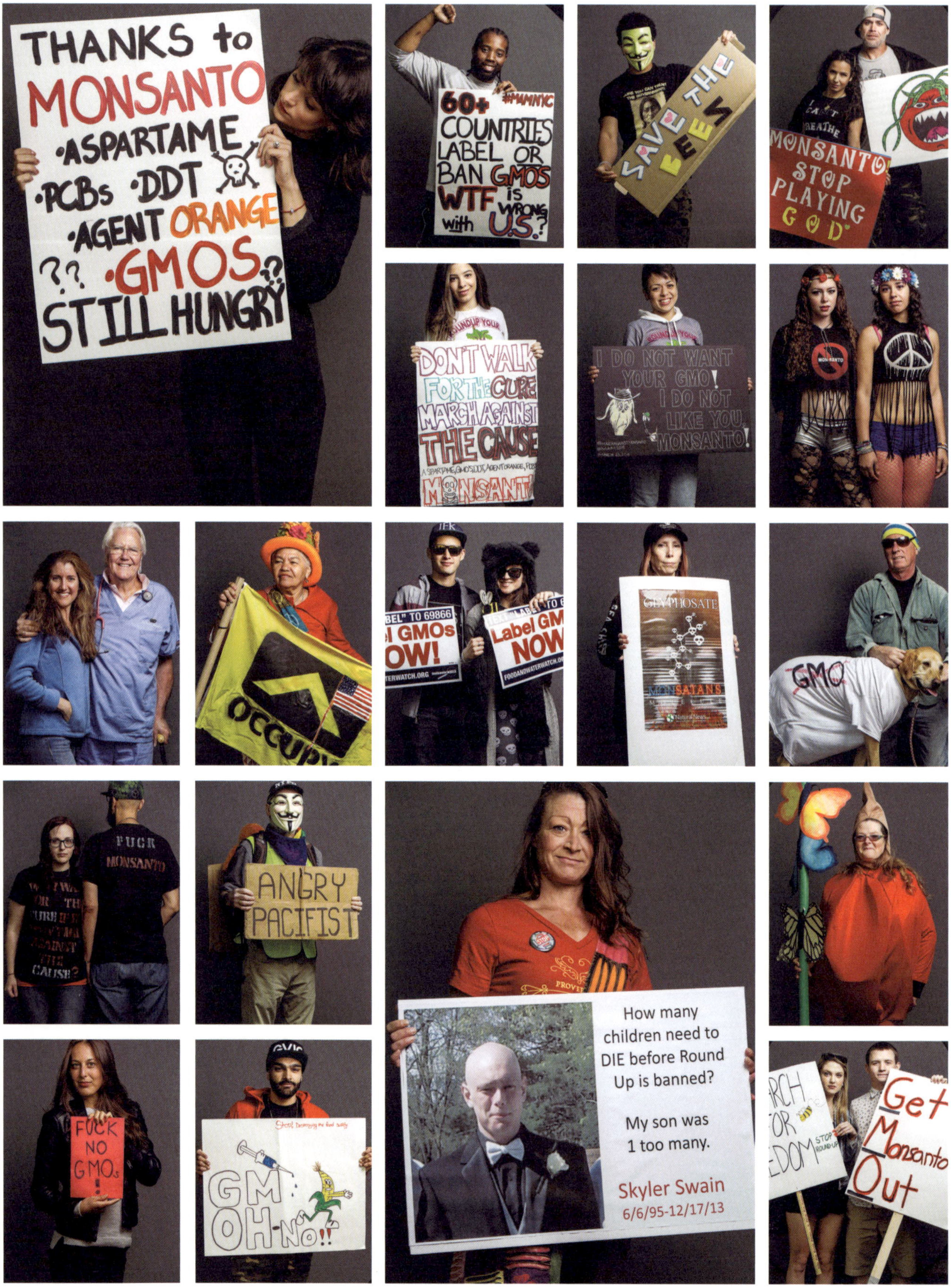
THANKS to MONSANTO
•ASPARTAME
•PCBs •DDT
•AGENT ORANGE
??•GMOS??
STILL HUNGRY
60+ #MAMNYC
COUNTRIES LABEL OR BAN GMOS WTF is WRONG with U.S.?
SAVE THE BEES
MONSANTO STOP PLAYING GOD
DON'T WALK FOR THE CURE MARCH AGAINST THE CAUSE
MONSANTO
I DO NOT WANT YOUR GMO! I DO NOT LIKE YOU MONSANTO!
Label GMOs NOW
GLYPHOSATE
MONSATANS
GMO
FUCK MONSANTO
ANGRY PACIFIST
How many children need to DIE before Round Up is banned?
My son was 1 too many.
Skyler Swain
6/6/95-12/17/13
FUCK NO GMOs
GM OH-NO!!
Get Monsanto Out

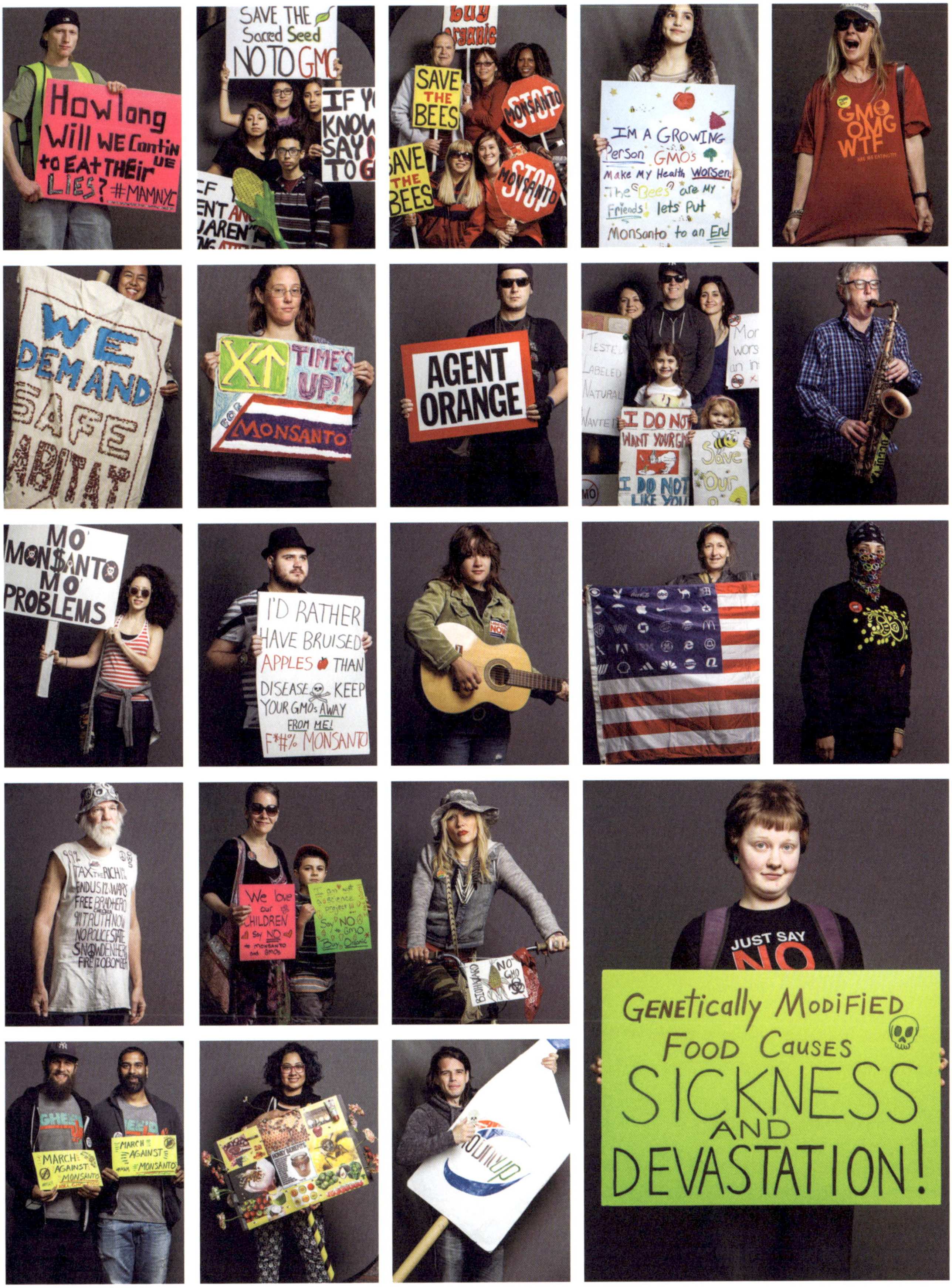

MARCHE MONDIALE CONTRE MONSANTO®. NEW YORK, ÉTATS-UNIS. MAI 2015
WORLDWIDE MARCH AGAINST MONSANTO, NEW YORK CITY, USA. MAY 2015

Postface par Jean-Claude Asselin, activiste, écologiste, citoyen du monde

Ayant fait fortune en temps de guerre, Monsanto® n'entend pas déposer les armes et mettra tout en œuvre pour faire fructifier son pactole en temps de paix, s'ingéniant à écouler ses produits nocifs sur les marchés coûte que coûte. Constat terrible, révélateur d'une économie sans scrupule qui s'enorgueillit de ses stratégies guerrières sous le couvert d'une image fabriquée de toutes pièces de bienfaiteur de l'humanité.

Il s'étonne « candidement » de la stigmatisation de l'entreprise auprès de l'opinion française. Nous l'invitons à regarder, pour son éclaircissement et sa gouverne, les photos prises par Mathieu sur les lieux de l'implantation de ses fabriques et sur ceux, comme au Viêtnam, où la population souffre encore aujourd'hui des séquelles de l'Agent orange. Ces photos témoignent et parlent un langage cru, véridique.

Ce n'est pas sans appréhension que je reçus l'annonce que me fit Mathieu de se lancer dans ce projet, connaissant la hargne avec laquelle Monsanto® attaque et poursuit ses détracteurs et, dans ce cas précis, ceux qui ont l'audace d'entamer sa belle image. Parce qu'il s'agit, en temps de guerre économique perpétuelle, de propagande dans un monde où les grands prédateurs ne lésinent pas sur les moyens octroyés à celle-ci. David contre Goliath ? Certainement. Les paysans et autres victimes qui se sont sentis lésés par les pratiques de Monsanto® et qui ont voulu se défendre le savent bien, à leur détriment. Rendons hommage à leur courage et à celui des particuliers, des associations, des ONG qui se sont opposés et s'opposent encore avec ténacité, à leurs risques et périls, aux prétentions du lobby « monsantesque ».

Entrez donc dans les coulisses du Monde idéal selon Monsanto® — l'envers du décor — et vérifiez de vos propres yeux le prix exorbitant qu'il nous fait payer, brandissant ses promesses mirifiques et nous persuadant, grâce à l'usage de ses produits, des progrès significatifs de l'humanité en marche vers un monde meilleur !

Comment avez-vous dit ? « Un marché de dupes » ?

Postface by Jean-Claude Asselin, activist, ecologist, citizen of the world

Having made a fortune in times of war, Monsanto® spurned the opportunity to lay down arms and allow this fortune to bear further fruit in times of peace. Instead, it chose to hawk its destructive products on the market at all costs. Its actions are demonstrative of a company that pridefully embodies a winner-take-all strategy, obscured behind its fabricated image of a benefactor to humanity.

The company is "candidly" astonished by the stigmatization it faces from the French public. We welcome it to observe, for insight and guidance, Mathieu's photographs of its production sites, where local populations continue to suffer, as Viet Nam continues to suffer the lingering effects of Agent Orange. These photographs bear witness to the raw truth.

It was not without apprehension that I received Mathieu's announcement to launch this project, knowing the acrimony with which Monsanto® attacks and pursues its detractors — particularly those who, as in this case, show the audacity to rattle its image. An image built on disinformation, in a time of perpetual economic war, in a world where predators are armed with unlimited means. David vs. Goliath? Certainly — as farmers and other victims who have been adversely affected by Monsanto®'s practices and tried to defend themselves know all too well. Let us honor their courage, and that of the individuals, associations and non-governmental organizations who tenaciously, at their own risk and peril, oppose the pretensions of the Monsanto® lobby.

Let us go behind the scenes of the ideal world according to Monsanto®. Let us see, with our own eyes, the exorbitant price of its grandiose promises, persuading us of mankind's progress toward a better world by virtue of the use of its products.

It is indeed a fool's bargain.

REMERCIEMENTS

REMERCIEMENTS PARTICULIERS À :
Ma mère, mon frère, ma sœur et Mario
Olga Yatskevich
Nathan Nguyen
Quinn Ryan
Jere Gettle
Quint Smith
Michael Saur
Rémi Coignet
Víctor Sira
Matthew Carson
Kike Arnal
Russet Lederman
Nicola Coppola
Delphine Bedel
Leo Sorel
Javier Aizpúrua

UN GRAND MERCI POUR LEUR AIDE ET LEUR SOUTIEN À :
BAKER CREEK HEIRLOOM SEEDS (pour le financement participatif de mon voyage au Viêtnam)
www.rareseeds.com
CHILDREN OF VIET NAM VETERANS HEALTH ALLIANCE
www.covvha.net
CENTER FOR FOOD SAFETY
www.centerforfoodsafety.org
TÛ DÛ OBSTETRICS HOSPITAL, HÔ CHÍ MINH CITY
www.tudu.com.
VIET NAM VETERANS OF AMERICA (Mokie Pratt Porter)
www.vva.org
WOOD PRAIRIE FARM
www.woodprairie.com

UN GRAND MERCI à Marie-Monique Robin dont la recherche sur Monsanto®
fut une source d'inspiration pour la création de ce livre.

Le chapitre V a été réalisé en collaboration
avec Sergio Valenzuela Escobedo, commissaire, et Ricardo Báez, designer.

Monsanto® : une enquête photographique

Conception graphique : Mathieu Asselin
Design et mise en page : Ricardo Báez
Textes et documentation : Frédérique Wallis Davy (c. I-IV), Michael Saur & Frédérique Wallis Davy (c. V)
Introduction : Jim Gerritsen
Postface : Jean-Claude Asselin
Traduction de l'anglais : Anatole Pons, pour les légendes et les textes des pages 5, 121 et 148
Traduction du français : Vanessa Rich
Photogravure : Ex Libris, Caracas

ISBN : 978-2-330-12407-6

Édition originale : Verlag Kettler, Dortmund, Allemagne, 2017

Ouvrage achevé d'imprimer sur les presses de Editoriale Bortolazzi Stei à Vérone
pour le compte des éditions Actes Sud, Le Méjan, place Nina-Berberova, 13200 Arles

Dépôt légal 1re édition : juin 2017
Dépôt légal 2e édition : octobre 2019

(Imprimé en Italie)

ACKNOWLEDGMENTS

SPECIAL THANKS TO:
My mother, siblings and Mario
Olga Yatskevich
Nathan Nguyen
Quinn Ryan
Jere Gettle
Quint Smith
Michael Saur
Rémi Coignet
Víctor Sira
Matthew Carson
Kike Arnal
Russet Lederman
Nicola Coppola
Delphine Bedel
Leo Sorel
Javier Aizpúrua

MANY THANKS FOR THEIR HELP AND SUPPORT TO:
BAKER CREEK HEIRLOOM SEEDS (for the crowdfunding to travel to Viet Nam)
www.rareseeds.com
CHILDREN OF VIET NAM VETERANS HEALTH ALLIANCE
www.covvha.net
CENTER FOR FOOD SAFETY
www.centerforfoodsafety.org
TỪ DŨ OBSTETRICS HOSPITAL HO CHI MINH CITY
www.tudu.com.vn
VIET NAM VETERANS OF AMERICA (Mokie Pratt Porter)
www.vva.org
WOOD PRAIRIE FARM
www.woodprairie.com

A BIG THANK YOU TO Marie-Monique Robin whose research on Monsanto®
was a source of inspiration in the creation of this book.

Chapter V was made through the collaboration
of curator Sergio Valenzuela Escobedo and designer Ricardo Báez.

Monsanto®: A Photographic Investigation

Concept & photography: Mathieu Asselin
Book design & layout: Ricardo Báez
Texts & documentation: Frédérique Wallis Davy (c. I-IV), Michael Saur & Frédérique Wallis Davy (c. V)
Introduction: Jim Gerritsen
Postface: Jean-Claude Asselin
Translation from English: Anatole Pons, for the captions and texts of pages 5, 121 and 148
Translation from French: Vanessa Rich
Prepress: Ex Libris, Caracas

ISBN: 978-2-330-12407-6

Original edition: Verlag Kettler, Dortmund, Germany, 2017

Printed by Editoriale Bortolazzi Stei in Verona
on behalf of Actes Sud, Le Méjan, place Nina-Berberova, 13200 Arles

Legal Deposit 1st Edition: June 2017
Legal Deposit 2nd Edition: October 2019

(Printed in Italy)